£25.00

A Bicentenary History
of
The Linnean Society of London

The Arms of the Linnean Society

Natural History : The Linnean Society
Issue Date — 19 January 1988

Reproduced by permission of Royal Mail Letters

A Bicentenary History
of
The Linnean Society of London

†Andrew Thomas Gage

and

William Thomas Stearn

Published for the Linnean Society of London

ACADEMIC PRESS

LONDON   SAN DIEGO   NEW YORK
BOSTON   SYDNEY   TOKYO   TORONTO

ACADEMIC PRESS LIMITED
24/28 Oval Road
London NW1 7DX

United States edition published by
ACADEMIC PRESS INC.
San Diego, CA 92101

© 1988 The Linnean Society of London

British Library Cataloguing in Publication Data

Gage, A. T.
 A bicentenary history of the Linnean
 Society of London.
 1. Linnean Society of London—History
 I. Title   II. Stearn, William T.
 508'.06'041   QH1

 ISBN 0-12-273150-6

Printed in Great Britain by Galliard (Printers) Ltd, Great Yarmouth, Norfolk

Preface

To commemorate the bicentenary of the founding of the Linnean Society of London in 1788, the Society's Council considered that a suitable publication would be a chronological record of activities from foundation onwards and asked me to undertake its preparation. Although there has undoubtedly been much sameness as regards the Society's mostly uneventful activities, that certainly does not apply to those who have taken part in them. Because the Linnean Society is the world's oldest active biological society and because for virtually 200 years it has provided common ground for both zoologists and botanists, both amateur and professional, no other society has gathered into its fellowship so many distinguished naturalists. Moreover, the numerous volumes of its publications constitute a vast repository of information still relevant to research, with much still remaining both interesting and readable, particularly but far from exclusively in taxonomic and biohistorical floristic and faunistic biology. Thus the preparation of a modern history would have been an enormous intimidating task but for the comprehensive *A History of the Linnean Society of London* by Andrew Thomas Gage (1871–1945) which the Society published in May 1938 as a volume of 178 pages.

Benjamin Daydon Jackson (1846–1927) had been engaged on a history of the Society at the time of his death but his manuscript had not reached a state suitable for publication. The Council accordingly encouraged Gage to produce a new history, which he completed by February 1937. The reader of his work cannot but be much impressed by the thoroughness with which he delved into the Society's extensive records and selected material for inclusion. He served the Society as Librarian and Assistant Secretary, i.e. the Society's executive officer, from the autumn of 1924 to October 1929 when ill health caused his retirement. An efficient administrator, he somehow made time without neglecting his duties to gather information from the Society's archives for his *History* during his last two years of service when he and Mrs Gage lived in the Society's flat at Burlington House. There, of course, he had everything conveniently at hand. Despite continued ill health, even after returning to his native Scotland, he worked for years on the *History*, much aided, as he gratefully acknowledged, by his friend and successor Spencer Savage (1886–1966). It must have been gratifying indeed for him to learn after publication in 1938 how much his labours were appreciated by Fellows of that Society, to which he had been elected a Fellow in 1901.

My task in preparing this bicentenary record has been primarily to extend Gage's account to cover the period 1936 to 1987 but I have found it necessary to edit his work by removing some material which seemed no longer relevant or interesting, occasionally adding to it and making textual emendations. His general arrangement and most of his text stand despite these alterations. The present account is thus to be considered a joint work, but for any deficiencies in it I, not Gage, must take the blame.

The Society has cause to be grateful that the gladly given voluntary work of the Fellows who have served as its officers, especially as Secretaries and Treasurers, and on its committees, together with the diligence of its small paid staff, have enabled it to contribute so much to the progress of natural history over the years, through its impressive series of publications, its meetings and symposia on a diversity of biological matters, the maintenance of its library, the conservation of the Linnaean and Smith collections. They have kept it going through periods of difficulty; they have contributed to its growth and utility. At the same time, the Royal Society of London, often a good friend when especially needed, is to be thanked for continuous support and generous help from the funds at its disposal for the furtherance of science.

On the whole the Society's life has seemed unexciting, almost at times lethargic, and has either been so respectable or so adept at the suppression of possible scandal – witness the unfortunate Marsham's handling of the Society's funds – that unfortunately the readers will not find records here of the personal infighting and jealousy which enliven the histories of the British Museum, the British Museum (Natural History) and the Botanical Society of the British Isles; in such discreetness it resembles the Royal Society, at times the clandestine scientific intrigue centre of London. Despite lack of sensation, however, much of interest will be found, one hopes, in the variety of characters who have contributed to the Linnean Society's maintenance and achievement for two centuries.

It seems appropriate here to outline Gage's career. He was born in Aberdeen, Scotland, and educated at the Grammar School in Old Aberdeen, King's College and Marischal College, where he qualified in medicine. He then became in 1894 assistant to the Aberdeen Professor of Botany, J. W. H. Trail. Sir George King, Superintendent of the Royal Botanic Gardens, Calcutta, and David Prain, Curator of the Herbarium, were both Aberdeen-trained Scots and friends of Trail. Hence, in 1897, Gage entered the Indian Medical Service, the intent being to transfer him, after a short period of medical service with an Indian regiment, to the Calcutta Botanic Garden. In 1898, on King's retirement, Prain became Superintendent and Gage succeeded him as Curator of the Herbarium. On Prain's appointment in 1905 as Director of the Royal Botanic Gardens, Kew, Gage succeeded him as Superintendent and in due course another Scot, William Wright Smith, became Curator of the Herbarium, thus preserving the Scottish association with the Calcutta Botanic Garden going back to Thomas Anderson, Roxburgh and Kyd. After leaving India, Gage joined the Linnean Society's staff. Spencer Savage, who worked under him, wrote that "the society was at once influenced by his kindly but decisive personality...from the start he set about bringing the Library into better order...Everything he undertook he did with the same characteristic thoroughness...As head of a staff, Colonel Gage was greatly liked and respected. His warm humanity and sense of humour, his philosophical outlook on life and his consideration for others, saved him from the least taint of that unfairness to subordinates which sometimes mars the work of an otherwise good administrator". In making so much of his *History* again available for the interest of a later generation of Fellows, the Linnean Society again acknowledges gratefully his valuable contribution to its affairs.

In preparing the present history my thanks go to Gina Douglas, the Society's Librarian, and other members of the Society's staff for much information requiring time-consuming search in the Society's records, and to my wife for much constructive criticism and for proof-reading. For typing my somewhat complicated manuscript I am indebted to Mrs Janet Aylward.

My own association with the Society began in 1934 when I was among the youngest of Fellows; thus I can recall from firsthand knowledge the ungrudging service given to the

Society's members over many years by the late Spencer Savage and his assistant and ultimate successor Theodore O'Grady. Presidents come and go every three years and the composition of Committees alters, but devoted servants like them maintain a valuable continuity in the Society's affairs for which one is grateful.

Gage's chronological record formed the major part of his work but he also provided special chapters, inevitably burdened with rather dull statistics, relating to publications, finance etc. To be relatively self-contained such chapters must necessarily repeat some information already provided in the general narrative. The reader who finds this repetition exasperating or boring will be well advised to skip these but their matter nevertheless comprises essential parts of the Society's history.

William T. Stearn
President, 1979–82

TO THE MEMORY OF

BENJAMIN DAYDON JACKSON
1846–1927

AND

SPENCER SAVAGE
1886–1966

DISTINGUISHED LINNAEAN SCHOLARS
AND
SECRETARIES OF THE LINNEAN SOCIETY

IN GRATITUDE FOR THEIR
DEDICATED SERVICE
TO THE SOCIETY
AND TO LEARNING

Contents

Chapter 1

Forerunners and foundation of the Linnean Society
1721 to 1788

The founding of the Linnean Society of London was in 1788 but the concepts underlying its foundation as a society for the promotion of natural history go much further back. Indeed, its antecedents, notably the founding of the Royal Society of London in the seventeenth century, strongly influenced its aims and development. That the acquisition and understanding of knowledge about the natural world are sources of intellectual pleasure, a worthy exercise of the mind, and thrive upon the sharing of information among people with like interest, became the view of many scattered over Europe in the sixteenth century. However, without co-operative activity, science can make little progress and may perish. Therein lay the motivation behind the rise of scientific academies and societies in Europe from the sixteenth century onwards.

As people became more and more aware of the intricacy and diversity of the natural world, they also became likewise conscious of their ability to investigate it and the satisfaction of so doing. "To the carrying it on," as Joseph Glanville wrote in 1668, "it was necessary there should be many Heads and many Hands and Those formed into an Assembly that might intercommunicate their Tryals and Observations that might joyntly work and joyntly consider." Carl Pantin in his Presidential Address to the Linnean Society in 1961 emphasized this in his remark that the "collection together of people with very varied sorts of learning is one of the most valuable features of learned societies of any kind and this is particularly true because they make known to many the work of those dynasties and schools which hand on a tradition of learning". The absence of such assemblies of "many Heads and many Hands" had been one of the major restraints upon the development of science in medieval Europe. The few learned and enquiring men interested then in the observation of nature were geographically isolated; they lacked means of knowing about their common interests and of pooling their knowledge as a mutual stimulus for continuing endeavour. A man such as Albertus Magnus of Regensburg (1193–1280) stood alone; his works never came into the hands of his lesser known contemporary Rufinus of Genoa, who had a like curiosity for plants. A cosmopolitan court, such as that of the scientifically minded Emperor Frederick II (1194–1240) *stupor mundi* at Palermo, where Latin, Greek and Arab civil servants, courtiers and translators and the "philosophers" Michael the Scot and Theodore, possibly a Jew, mingled their culture and scholarship, stands out because it was so exceptional. Medieval universities, conservative, scholastic and heresy-fearing, provided no such favourable environment for scientific enquiry. However, in sixteenth-century Italy there arose outside the universities several organized groups for the investigation of nature, notably the Accademia del Cimento in Florence and the Accademia dei Lincei in Rome, with the new art of printing at their service. Where the laborious medieval copying of manuscripts had engendered conservatism, printing emancipated. These Italian academies gave precedent for the founding of others during the seventeenth century, notably: the Societas Ereunetica (established at Rostock in 1622) and the Academia Naturae Curiosorum (now the Leopoldina) in Germany; the Académie des Sciences in France; and the Royal Society of London. They were concerned with the general advancement of science by experiment and observation, but the very width of their scope caused the founding in the eighteenth century of lesser societies with more specialized interests, among them the Linnean Society of London. The Society accordingly owes its origin to the zeal for investigation and communication characteristic of sixteenth-century Italian academic groups.

Seven scholarly men interested in natural history founded the Linnean Society of London in 1788. Its title commemorates the great Swedish naturalist Carl Linnaeus (1707–1778), ennobled in 1761 as Carl von Linné, whose collections and library had been acquired in 1784 by one of the Society's founders and its first president, James Edward Smith (1759–1828). In 1802, more for legal reasons than prestige purposes, it obtained a Royal Charter from King George III. The preamble begins: "Whereas several of our loving subjects are desirous of forming a Society for the cultivation of the science of Natural History in all its branches and more especially of the Natural History of Great Britain and Ireland and having subscribed considerable sums of money for that purpose have humbly besought us to grant unto them Our Royal Charter of Incorporation for the purposes aforesaid...."

The "cultivation of the science of natural history", with diligence and success, has always been the purpose of the Linnean Society. In the present context, the Society promotes all aspects of pure and applied biology, including genetics, ecology, anatomy, physiology, palynology, biochemistry, palaeontology and population studies concerned with the diversity, interrelationship and habits of organisms both living and extinct, as well as their taxonomy and naming which were the primary interests of the Society's eighteenth-century founders and members. The Society today looks back with admiration for their enthusiasm and enterprise, and this history provides a chronicle of major events arising from their pioneering efforts of the past two centuries.

Proud to be now the world's oldest surviving natural history society, the Linnean Society nevertheless had several predecessors in Britain. The second Charter of the Royal Society of London, granted in 1663, describes the purpose of that society to be "for promoting Natural Knowledge". Although the Royal Society, being an elitist and partly aristocratic body of limited membership, could neither claim nor maintain a monopoly of promoting natural knowledge, it none the less remained for the following 100 years the only important scientific society in London. During that time, however, the increase in knowledge of minerals, plants and animals among the general well-to-do public, especially among physicians, apothecaries and surgeons, made inevitable the formation of other less exclusive societies for the advancement of knowledge along lines, then as now, only sparsely within the Royal Society's coverage. That Olympian body in no way met the needs of botanists and entomologists for the sharing of information in convivial circumstances. Within the Royal Society, complained Walter Moyle in 1719, "mathematics have engrossed all". As J. E. Smith said in his Presidential Address in April 1788 to the newly formed Linnean Society, "it is altogether incompatible with the plan of the Royal Society, engaged as it is in all branches of philosophy, to enter into the minutiae of natural history", although the Royal Society had indeed earlier given much encouragement to the pioneer microscopists Grew, Hooke and Leeuwenhoek. Such investigations became in the eighteenth century the province of other societies.

Between 1689 and 1713 there existed in London a Temple Coffee House Botanic Club – a group of about 40 members who assembled for pleasant and profitable discussion, but had no formal organization. Apparently, the first formally organized body was the Botanical Society founded in London in 1721. Its chief institutor was seemingly its secretary, John Martyn (1694–1768). The president was Johann Jacob Dillen or Dillenius (1681–1747), brought to England from Darmstadt in 1721 by William Sherard as his botanical assistant. On Sherard's death in 1728, Dillenius became the first occupant of the Sherardian Chair of Botany at Oxford endowed by Sherard. Martyn was the son of a London merchant and was employed as a clerk in his father's "compting house". D. A. Allen's 1976 investigation of the lives of the 23 known members shows that, of all whose age can be established, only six were above 25 in the year of the Society's founding. Their subsequent careers show that they were "far above average in intellectual ability": a third became apothecaries; a third physicians; and most of the rest surgeons or surgeon apothecaries. One member, Philip Miller, was the celebrated Chelsea Physic Garden curator. The small group at first had informal meetings in the Rainbow Coffee House in Watling Street, but later met in a private house. They held their meetings every Saturday at six in the evening. Sir Hans Sloane was invited in 1725 to become its President. He was not an officer of the Royal Society in 1725 (he had been secretary from 1693 to 1712 and was to succeed Newton as President from 1727 to 1741), but his high standing therein may have influenced his refusal to become President of the Botanical Society just as, more than 40 years later, Sir Joseph Banks, when President of the Royal Society, considered it inadvisable to become a Fellow of the Linnean Society. However, he became its first Honorary Member and was a generous benefactor. The Botanical Society did not survive beyond 1726.

John Martyn went to Cambridge in 1727 to read lectures for the Professor of Botany, Richard Bradley, and succeeded him in 1733. John Martyn was in turn succeeded by his son Thomas Martyn (1736–1825) as titular Professor in 1762 and held the Chair until 1825. Thus, father and son covered a period of over 90 years as Cambridge professors. In 1763, Thomas Martyn at Cambridge and John Hope, the Professor of Botany at Edinburgh, began to use the classification and nomenclature of Linnaeus in their teaching of botany. These had already been known in Britain since at least 1754 and popularized by the works of Benjamin Stillingfleet and William Hudson. Thomas Martyn was one of the first two men elected by ballot as Fellows of the Linnean Society on 17 June 1788, the other being John Rotheram (1750–1804), the physician, who had been a pupil of Linnaeus and was with him when he died. Thomas Martyn was also one of the four Vice-Presidents of the Linnean Society appointed in 1796.

By 1740, another specialist society, the Aurelian Society for the study of insects, had come into existence in London, possibly through the enthusiasm of Joseph Dandridge (1664–1746), a very influential collector. It took its name from the term *aurelia*, of Latin origin, which, like the alternative term of Greek origin, *chrysalis*, referred to the golden pupa of some Lepidoptera. These entomologists met in the Swan Tavern, Cornhill, where their library, collections and records were housed. In March 1748, a fire rapidly swept across Cornhill; the members of the Aurelian Society were lucky to escape from the Tavern with their lives, but the burning of all their material so completely disheartened them that the Society never revived. A second Aurelian Society was formed in 1762 but only survived until 1766. Nevertheless, the entomologists again gathered together and in 1780 formed the Society of Entomologists of London, but again this Society lived for only a short period of two years.

The immediate forerunner and, in a sense, the begetter of the Linnean Society was the Society for Promoting Natural History, which came into existence "at Mr. Dean's the Corner House by the turnpike, Pimlico" on Monday, 21 October 1782. The founders were William Forsyth, the Gardener of the Apothecaries' Physic Garden at Chelsea; George and John Prince of Water Steet, Strand; Captain Francis Robson of Sloane Square, Chelsea, afterwards Lieutenant-Governor of St Helena; and Charles Harris of Statuary, Strand. The first page of its minutes is headed "For the Promotion of Natural History", but at the beginning of its Book of "Rules and Orders" it calls itself "The Society for Promoting Natural History". The latter title, which became permanent, is evidently based on that of the Royal Society, but with the significant difference of "Natural History", in the narrower sense that the words had acquired, instead of "Natural Knowledge". From December 1789 to 1796, except for a few months in 1792 when it met in the house of one of its members, George Spence, in Pall Mall, the Society had its own rooms at 19 Warwick Street between Golden Square and what is now Regent Street, the latter not then being in existence. The Linnean Society was founded in 1788 and, by 1796, the Society for Promoting Natural History was drifting into shallow water. It could no longer afford to have rooms of its own and reverted to its early tavern-haunting habits. From 1796 to 1800 it met in the York Coffee House in St James's Street.

The "Rules and Orders" of the Society for Promoting Natural History laid down that "the Society shall meet once every month on the Monday next following the Full Moon, at seven o'clock in the evening". The Anniversary Meeting was held on the first Monday after the Full Moon in October. The invocation of the Full Moon had no occult significance, but merely indicated the poor lighting and unsafeness of London streets in the early 1780s. The contemporary, more intellectually brilliant Lunar Society in Birmingham met at the Full Moon for the same reasons. Some idea of the London Society's activities during its last years at the York Coffee House may be inferred from the fact that the charges at those meetings were invariably 10s. 6d. for the rooms and £1 1s. for sundries. What the sundries were is not mentioned, but it is improbable that they consisted purely of ink. Earlier, on 19 February 1786, Sir Joseph Banks wrote to Marmaduke Tunstall that the Society for the Promotion of Natural History was not flourishing: "Lee (of the Vineyard Nursery) Hammersmith is a leading man and he, I hear, sometimes adjourns the meeting to the 'Black Bear' in Piccadilly, there they drink grog till they do not know Monandria from Cryptogamia."

In September 1783, James Edward Smith came to London to complete his medical studies. He was the eldest child of James Smith, a cultured and well-to-do cloth and silk merchant of Norwich, where James Edward was born on 2 December 1759. Owing to ill health he was educated at home until his twenty-second year, when, having by this time decided to study for the medical profession, he went to Edinburgh University which, in accordance with its indebtedness to Leiden, tolerantly admitted non-conformist students (Smith was a Unitarian) excluded from the universities of Oxford and Cambridge. Smith's Norfolk and Norwich upbringing is important. Among the weavers, tailors and apothecaries of the city, as well as among gentlemen in the county, there had long existed an interest in flowers which had led to their study. Smith himself in 1804 referred to them as "a school of botanists in Norwich among whom the writings and merits of Linnaeus were perhaps more early or at least more philosophically, studied and appreciated, than in any part of Britain". They included the apothecary Hugh Rose, who published in 1775 *The Elements of Botany, a Translation of the Philosophia Botanica and other Treatises of the celebrated Linnaeus.* He showed Smith the works of Linnaeus with "the whole system of animals and vegetables contained in three octavo volumes", much to Smith's astonishment. On 9 January 1778, strangely enough a day before the death of Linnaeus in Uppsala, Smith, then aged 18, acquired a copy of John Berkenhout's *Outlines of the Natural History of Great-Britain and Ireland*, of which Volume 2 (1770) provided a synopsis of British plants according to the Linnaean system. He studied it diligently and thus early became acquainted with the Linnaean system, its arrangement and principles. At Edinburgh Professor John Hope, a notable figure of the Scottish Enlightenment and a convinced exponent of Linnaean method, treated young Smith "with almost paternal tenderness". There he found congenial company and soon had a wide circle of social and scientific friends. His strong bent for natural history found scope in Edinburgh by founding, along with some friends, a Natural History Society of which he was the first President. One of these friends was Richard Anthony Markham, who later changed his surname to Salisbury and became Smith's bitter enemy.

On coming to London, Smith studied anatomy under the famous John Hunter and medicine under David Pitcairn of St Bartholomew's Hospital. John Hunter joined the Society for Promoting Natural History in December 1783, and Smith was proposed in the following month and admitted in February 1784. Smith's interest in natural history also brought him in touch with men of like mind outside the Society. The most prominent of those was Sir Joseph Banks, then, and for many years thereafter, President of the Royal Society, a man of wide scientific interests, of great wealth, and of much influence in scientific, social and political circles. He had sailed round the world with Captain Cook aboard the *Endeavour* from 1768 to 1771, amassing natural history specimens, drawings and observations, and his big private herbarium and library at Soho Square had become the botanical centre of London. Banks's friendship with the young medical student was to form an important link in the chain of events leading to the formation of the Linnean Society.

When Linnaeus died in 1778, Banks had offered £1200 for the Linnaean Herbarium but the younger Linnaeus, Carl von Linné (1741–83), had obtained possession of all his father's collections before Banks's offer arrived. Young Linné, who had succeeded to his father's professorial chair at Uppsala, died in November 1783, soon after Smith's arrival in London, and the Linnaean collections reverted to the widow of the elder Linnaeus. She and her daughters instructed Dr J. G. Acrel, a friend of the family, to sell the collections and he, remembering Banks's 1778 offer, gave Banks the option of buying all the collections and the Linnaean library for £1050, probably a higher sum than would have been obtained in Sweden. When Banks received Acrel's letter on 23 December 1783 Smith was his guest at breakfast. Banks handed the letter to Smith, with the statement that he did not intend to buy the collections and the advice that Smith should do so. Smith acted at once upon this advice, writing that very day to Acrel, and on the following day to his father at Norwich for approval of his intention and for the money to carry it out. As late as 12 January 1784, James Smith replied that "I am afraid it is out of our abilities to attain" and cautioned his son against the enthusiasm of a lover or the heat of an ambitious man. After several more persuasive letters to the elder Smith, the son gained his point, and negotiations continued with Acrel until, in October 1784, he became the possessor of the whole collection, library and manuscripts of Linnaeus at a total cost of £1,088 5s. od. Smith's original idea in obtaining the collections was, as stated in his first letter to his father on the subject, "to settle in London as a physician and read lectures in natural history". Smith intended to deposit them in some spare rooms in the British Museum. This plan came to nothing and he then hired rooms at 14 Paradise Row, now part of Royal Hospital Road, Chelsea, for their storage.

While all this was going on, Smith had been attending, with fair regularity, the meetings of the Society for Promoting Natural History at the Black Bear inn. The Society had started by having as many Presidents as members, each presiding in turns at the meetings. This soon gave place to a phase of four annual Presidents and, at the Anniversary Dinner on 25 October 1784, Smith was elected one of the four Presidents for 1784–85. The quadruplicate phase was succeeded by one of two rotational Presidents before the Society discovered that one President at a time was enough. Smith filled the chair at several meetings, and his experience of the working of the Society convinced him that it could not carry out the functions indicated by its name. His opinion had good grounds. The financial basis of the Society – the admission fee, intended to form a Library Fund, was then 10s. 6d. and the annual subscription 10s. – was not enough to enable it to form a library and issue publications as well as rent rooms. At meetings, the exhibition of specimens, minerals and fossils bulked largely. Probably the predominance of the latter and not any reflection on the character of the Society prompted Edmond Rack, Secretary of the Philosophic Society at Bath and an Honorary Member of the Society for Promoting Natural History, to address a paper, which he submitted to the latter Society in 1784, to "The President and Members of the Fossil Society in London". Smith was not alone in his low opinion of the Society. Of the fellow-members who shared his views, two in particular, Samuel Goodenough and Thomas Marsham, joined forces with Smith in discussing plans for the formation of a new Society moulded closer to their desire.

Samuel Goodenough (1743–1827) was the third son of the Reverend William Goodenough, Rector of Broughton Poggs, Oxfordshire, and was born at Kimpton, Hants. He was educated at Westminster and Christ Church, Oxford. In 1766, he returned to Westminster as undermaster for four years, when he inherited from his father the advowson of Broughton Poggs and received from his college the vicarage of Brize-Norton, also in Oxfordshire. In 1772, he returned to teaching and established a school at Ealing, with which he continued for 26 years, starting on the path that was to lead to the bishopric of Carlisle. A man of powerful physique and broad views, he did not hesitate to express his decided opinions. He was a classical scholar, whose advice Smith sought, a keen naturalist and a lover of music. He became the Linnean Society's first Treasurer. The large Australian genus *Goodenia* and the family *Goodeniaceae* (*Goodenoughiaceae*) commemorate him.

In March 1785, while still at Ealing, the Rev. Dr Samuel Goodenough, as he then was, had been elected a member of the Society for Promoting Natural History, at a meeting chaired by Smith. He was then 42 years of age and about 17 years older than Smith. Before his election, Goodenough had corresponded with Smith on natural history questions and their association in the Society began a close friendship that, despite the differences in age, upbringing and religious outlook, was to remain unbroken until the end of their days.

Thomas Marsham (d. 1819), of China Row, Chelsea, was about four or five years younger than Goodenough and was employed in the Exchequer Loan Office and, in later years, at the West India Docks. He was particularly interested in insects and was the author of *Entomologia Britannica* (1802), of which only one volume appeared, and of several entomological papers in the Linnean Society's *Transactions*. He seems to have been an amiable man but unlucky in his personal financial affairs, a defect that led him into debt during his last years and to borrow money from the Society, when its Treasurer, that he was unable to repay. At his death he owed the Society a large sum.

Goodenough, Smith and Marsham decided to form a new Society. They consulted Sir Joseph Banks and gained his approval of their plan. Even the constitution and name of the projected new Society were virtually settled, but circumstances connected with Smith's private affairs delayed fruition. Smith's student days were drawing to an end in 1785. He had been elected FRS in May of that year, four years before his friend Goodenough attained that honour, but he still had to obtain his MD degree. His first intention was to return to Edinburgh for that purpose; however, on second thoughts, he decided to go to Leiden University and, in June 1786, went to Holland. After taking his degree, with a "Disputatio de generatione", he made a prolonged tour through Holland, France, Italy and Switzerland before returning home. The tour was a great success. As owner of the Linnaean collections, he had become a figure of international note amongst naturalists. This and his Royal Society Fellowship would in themselves have assured him a respectful welcome but, in addition, Smith was a young man of pleasing personality and wide culture. During his tour he met most of the prominent naturalists of the countries he visited, and his letters to his parents and others give very interesting accounts of his experiences and shrewd comments on men and things.

During Smith's absence, Goodenough and Marsham continued their efforts in connection with the proposed new Society and the former especially kept Smith informed. On 3 July 1786 Goodenough wrote: "I am glad to hear that you had your talk out with Sir Joseph [Banks]. I wrote to Marsham last night and told him what you said. See how our minds move! Marsham was at that instant writing to me upon the same subject. He says he has had a conversation with Forsyth [one of the founders of the Society for Promoting Natural History] and that we may have him if we please. But Forsyth thinks that we might form a party in this Society [the Society for Promoting Natural History] which he says wants weeding very much. But Marsham adds 'he told me many things which serve to convince me that that is impossible'." Again on 25 September 1786 Goodenough wrote: "I think of our new Society with pleasure and long for your return on that account, as well as others . . . I am preparing a complete list of the Linnean Nomenclature, through all the classes from Mammalia to Lapides, which will be ready for the press by your return. I should have liked to have given it to the publick 'By a Fellow of the L.S.'." On 3 November 1786 he wrote: "Pray take one thing into consideration. Members and Wealth are so far real necessaries to a society, as it enables them to carry matters into effect – to purchase, reward, publish." On 11 March 1787 he wrote: "As to natural history, which I busy myself about every day, more or less, I am in the first place amusing myself with the idea of our New Society, which must take the place of our present gross body, the instant it starts. The present society goes on in the usual way, of having a fossil or a plant go round the table: nothing is or can be said upon it. It is referred to a committee to consider of it; the committee call it by some name, and send it back to the society. The society desire the committee to reconsider it. In the meantime nothing is done; indeed it does not appear to me that any of them can do anything. I have had a short conversation with Sir Joseph, who repeated to me what he said to you. Were he not President of the Royal Society, I am sure he would join us."

Smith returned to London in November 1787 and, in the following February, removed from 14 Paradise Row to 12 Great Marlborough Street, now off Regent Street. The formation of the Linnean Society speedily followed Smith's change of residence. On Tuesday, 26 February 1788, the following met at the Marlborough Coffee House in Great Marlborough Street: Smith, Goodenough, Marsham; Jonas Dryander, the Curator of Sir

(b)

(a)

Joseph Banks's library and collections; James Dickson, originally a gardener from Scotland and at this time a Covent Garden Nurseryman; John Beckwith, a medical man interested in entomology; and John Timothy Swainson, then Secretary of the Board of Customs in London and subsequently Collector of the Port of Liverpool.

These seven formed the first "Fellows' Meeting", to be distinguished from the first "General Meeting", of the "Linnaean Society", as it is spelled on the opening page of the Fellows' Minutes and the General Meetings Minutes. The spelling was altered to "Linnean" (which accords with the name "von Linné" adopted by Linnaeus after being ennobled) on the first occasion at which the name of the Society occurs in either set of minutes, which were written by Marsham. The name of Linnaeus is also spelled "Linneus" in both sets of the early minutes. In the first printed list of "Rules and Orders", which bears no date but could not have been later than 1795, as it directs enquiries to be made at 12 Great Marlborough Street where the Society was housed up to that year, the Society's name appears as "Linnean Society of London". The spelling was in fact not constant, for Smith on the title page of *A Sketch of a Tour on the Continent* (1797) and of *The English Flora* (1824) is described as "President of the Linnaean Society". It soon became accepted that the adjective "Linnean" referred only to the Society and "Linnaean" to Linnaeus himself, his works, classification and nomenclature.

At this first Fellows' Meeting the three primary founders of the Society were appointed its Officers: Smith as President, Goodenough as Treasurer and Marsham as Secretary. Rules and Orders were considered. At the second Fellows' Meeting, also held in the Marlborough Coffee House, on 18 March 1788, a list of those constituting the Society was drawn up, showing a division into four classes: Honorary Members, Foreign Members, Fellows and Associates. The Rules and Orders were adopted and ordered to be inscribed in a book for signature by Fellows only. The date, 18 March 1788, is given in the printed Rules and Orders, already mentioned, as the date on which the Society was instituted. So far, only Fellows, whose number had now gone up to 20,* had met and only formal business had been transacted, but on 8 April 1788 the first General Meeting took place in Smith's house, when Fellows, Associates and visitors were present to a total of 16. At this meeting Smith delivered the first Presidential Address, being the first part of his "Introductory discourse on the rise and progress of natural history", afterwards published in 1791 as the first paper in the Society's *Transactions*. Here Smith proclaimed that, as the minutiae of natural history were outside the scope of the Royal Society, apparently beneath its notice, "such an institution therefore as ours is absolutely necessary, to prevent all the pains and expenses of collectors, all the experience of cultivators, all the remarks of real observers being lost to the world". He emphasized the need for the Society's attention to the British fauna and flora.

There were no more Presidential Addresses until the Anniversary Meeting of 1854, when the then President, Professor Thomas Bell, gave one, and started a practice which, with rare intermissions, has ever since been observed. Smith ended his discourse at the next

* This number excludes the Rev. John Lightfoot, who is described in the Minutes of the second Fellows' Meeting as one of the Institutors of the Society, but who had died on 20 February 1788, thus before and not, as the Minutes have it, "a few days after" the first meeting.

Plate I   (a) Portrait of James Edward Smith as a young man, from the drawing by Mrs Anna Louisa Lane in the Society's collection.
(b) Portrait of Samuel Goodenough, Bishop of Carlisle, from the engraving by Henry Meyer after the painting by James Northcote RA.

We who have hereunto subscribed do hereby Promise, each for himself, that We will Endeavour to promote the Good of the *Linnaean Society* of London for the Cultivation of Natural History, and to pursue the Ends for which the same was instituted: That We will be present at the Meetings of the Society as often as conveniently we can, especially at the Anniversary Elections, and upon extraordinary Occasions; and that We will observe the Rules and Laws of the said Society. Provided that whensoever any of us shall signify to the President under his Hands that he desires to withdraw from this Society, he shall be free from his Obligation for the future.

Jas. Edwd. Smith

Samuel Goodenough

William Curtis.

Jon: Dryander

George Adams

James Dickson

John Beckwith

John Zier

Tho.s Marsham

John Tim Swainson

Jno Sims

John Rotheram

Tho.s Martyn

John Sibthorp

John Fairbairn
Thomas Hoy.

Edmd. Davall

John Lyon

Rd Salisbury

Robert Barclay

John Lord

General Meeting on 6 May with the following remarks, which are of special interest with reference to what afterwards happened to the Linnaean collections:

> A train of events, which I cannot help calling most fortunate, having brought into my hands every thing which Linnaeus possessed relating to natural history or medicine, his entire library, manuscripts, and the correspondence of his whole life, as well as all the acquisitions made by the younger Linnaeus in his tour through Europe, after his father's decease, but which his own premature death prevented him from communicating to the world; all these will be a never failing resource to us in every difficulty, as well as a fund of information not easily to be exhausted. For my own part I consider myself as a trustee of the public. I hold these treasures only for the purpose of making them useful to the world and natural history in general, and particularly to this society, of which I glory in having contributed to lay the foundation, and to the service of which I shall joyfully consecrate my labours, so long as it continues to answer the purposes for which it is designed.

These were good sentences and doubtless well pronounced and would have been better if well followed; but this, after a few years, they were not.

It will be noted that Smith refers to himself as having "contributed to lay the foundation" of the Linnean Society. Although he has usually been described as the sole founder, Smith made no such claim but always associated Goodenough and Marsham with himself as Goodenough always associated Marsham and himself with Smith; both Smith and Goodenough have left evidence supporting this. In a letter to his wife dated 24 and 25 May 1808 Smith gives an account of the Anniversary Dinner of the Society, held on 24 May, in which he states: "Then Lord Valentia got up and proposed my health, with a rather long speech about my merits in the Society and 'whatever it is or has been owing to me' etc., so that I was quite overcome with such compliments. It was drunk all standing! and followed by three great rounds of applause!! I returned my thanks and good wishes as well and concisely as I could and was again applauded. Then I gave the Bishop of Carlisle [Goodenough] and Mr. Marsham as being with me the 3 first projectors of the Society." In a letter to Goodenough dated 6 April 1808, in which reference is made to the Society, Smith writes: "I am really anxious to hear what was said or read at our Society yesterday – how proud am I to say our Society." In a letter to Smith from Goodenough, then on one of his episcopal visits to London and staying in Berners Street, dated 17 March 1809, there is the following passage: "Will you dine with me on Tuesday and I will go with you to the Linn. Society, and get Marsham to meet you. The sight of the three fathers of the Society marching in together, must be, as the French say, grand and magnificent."

The establishment of the Linnean Society, of course, affected the Society for Promoting Natural History, and in 1791 the latter made overtures for a union of the two. The Linnean Society rather curtly rejected the proposal on the ground that neither Society would benefit by such a union. The Society for Promoting Natural History then had quite a number of distinguished names on its List, including some who were also Fellows of both the Royal and the Linnean Societies, such as Smith and Goodenough themselves, its President, Viscount Lewisham, and Thomas Martyn, Professor of Botany at Cambridge. Despite a resolution passed in May 1790 to publish scientific papers the Society for Promoting Natural History printed none and gradually grew weaker. The Minute Books end with the hundred-and-ninety-seventh meeting, which was adjourned on 14 November 1800. Later meetings were held but the loose drafts of the proceedings were never transcribed into the Minute Book.

Plate II   Page of the Roll Book showing the first signatures, 1788.
Ivory gavel from the Society for Promoting Natural History.

The last meeting of the Society for Promoting Natural History was held on 30 May 1822 in the Linnean Society's rooms in Soho Square and was attended by Smith. It was resolved to transfer to the Linnean Society the funds, books and collections of the Society for Promoting Natural History, also its Presidential ivory gavel, which the President of the Linnean Society uses to this day. It was not until 1825 that the accumulated funds, amounting to £190 of $3\frac{1}{2}$ per cent Consols and £136 6s. 10d. of accumulated dividends in cash, of the defunct Society were transferred to the Linnean. In the preamble to the last resolution made by the dying Society occurs this testimony to the origin and work of the Linnean Society: "And it also appearing that the Linnean Society, which originally emanated from this Society and embracing its principal objects is now in full operation and activity ... it was duly moved seconded and carried unanimously that all the property of this Society ... be transferred to such Trustees as the Linnean Society shall appoint for the absolute use and benefit of that Society."

The Society for Promoting Natural History had had a life of meagre achievement, but it made a generous end.

SOME SOURCES OF FURTHER INFORMATION

ALLEN, D. A., 1966. Joseph Dandridge and the first Aurelian Society. *Entom. Record*, **78**: 89–94.

ALLEN, D. A., 1967. John Martyn's Botanical Society: a biographical analysis of the membership. *Proc. Bot. Soc. Brit. Isles*, **6**: 305–324.

ALLEN, D. A., 1976. *The Naturalist in Britain, a Social History*, London: Allen Lane, Penguin Books.

ALLEN, D. A., 1978. James Edward Smith and the Natural History Society of Edinburgh. *Journ. Soc. Bibl. Nat. Hist.*, **8**: 433–493.

BRISTOWE, W. S., 1967. The life and work of a great English naturalist, Joseph Dandridge (1664–1746). *Entom. Gazette*, **18**: 73–89.

GELDART, A. M., 1914. Sir James Edward Smith and some of his friends. *Trans. Norfolk & Norwich Nat. Hist. Soc.*, **9**(5): 645–692.

HASKINS, C. H., 1924. *Studies in the History of Mediaeval Science*, Cambridge, Mass.: Harvard University Press.

NEAVE, S. A. & GRIFFIN, F. J., 1933. *The History of the Entomological Society of London*. London: Entomological Society.

ORNSTEIN, M., 1928. *The Role of Scientific Societies in the Seventeenth Century*, Chicago: University of Chicago Press.

PORTER, R., 1988. The new taste for nature in the eighteenth century. *The Linnean*, **4**: 14–30.

STEARN, W. T., 1957. An introduction to the *Species Plantarum* and cognate botanical works of Carl Linnaeus. Prefixed to Ray Society facsimile of Linnaeus, *Species Plantarum*, Vol. 1, London: Ray Society.

STEARN, W. T., 1986. John Wilkins, John Ray and Carl Linnaeus. *Notes & Records of Royal Soc.*, **40**: 101–123.

STEARN, W. T., 1988. James Edward Smith (1759–1828), first President of the Linnean Society, *Biol. Journ. Linnean Soc.*, 96 (in ed.).

THOMAS, K., 1983. *Man and the Natural World. Changing Attitudes in England 1500–1800*, London: Allen Lane.

WALKER, M., 1985. Smith's acquisition of Linnaeus's library and herbarium. *The Linnean*, **1**(6): 17–19.

WALKER, M., 1988. *Sir James Edward Smith*, London: Linnean Society.

Chapter 2

From foundation to incorporation
1788 to 1802

The Society started with three Honorary Members, 20 Fellows, 39 Foreign Members and 11 Associates. The Honorary Members were Sir Joseph Banks, Louis Duc de Noailles (1713–93) and Petrus Camper (1722–89), the famous Dutch anatomist and naturalist. The Duc de Noailles had been an old friend of Linnaeus and hospitably received Smith when the latter visited Paris. He was then a man of 75, a Maréchal of France and persona grata at the court of Louis XVI. He died in time to escape the guillotine that claimed his widow. The selection of Petrus Camper was an unfortunate one, as that gentleman, not long elevated to the Council of State at The Hague, refused the honour in a letter in which he expressed disapproval of Linnaeus and of the linking of his name with the title of the Society, although he had been responsible in 1749 for publication of Volume I of Linnaeus's *Amoenitates Academicae*; he died in 1789. In consequence, the name of Camper does not appear in the first printed list of the Society. Camper's letter drew from Smith an interesting reply, wherein he gave the reasons for adopting the name "Linnean":

> The Linnean Society is a body of naturalists associated for the purpose of cultivating the Science, not to enlist themselves as the followers of any person whatever, any further than truth directs them. They have taken the name which you unfortunately dislike, but which I do not think they would readily change, unless it were generally disapproved, nor should I soon be brought to consent to such an alteration. We have always conceived this name peculiarly proper for us, who have among us the very Museum & Library of Linnaeus in the house where we meet, for you know, Sir, I purchased all his remains. We consider his works as a good foundation to work upon, we are best able to determine the different objects he described, to correct his errors & improve what he has left imperfect. On this ground we call ourselves the Linnean Society and I hope you will not think it an improper one.

The letters are printed in full in the Society's *Proceedings* for 1897–98, 55–57. Although Smith rightly claims the name "Linnean" as peculiarly proper for the London Society founded in March 1788, it had no exclusive rights outside London, and a number of other Linnean Societies came into being in different places. These included the Société Linnéene de Paris (December 1787) and others at Boston (USA), Bordeaux, Lyons, Caen, Stockholm, Amiens, Berlin, Brussels, Angers, Sydney, New York, Ashton-under-Lyne, Marseilles, Uppsala and Quebec. Some of those still exist, such as, to take two widely separated ones, the Société Linnéene de Lyon (founded 1822) and the Linnean Society of New South Wales (founded 1875).

The Foreign Members were selected mostly from the naturalists whom Smith had met on his continental tour. At first glance the infant Society would seem to have been overloaded with non-paying Foreign Members and Associates, but as yet there were no publications, and when these were started Foreign Members and Associates were entitled only to copies of such publications as contained papers by them.

There were two kinds of meetings: the General Meetings open to all members and to visitors, held on the first Tuesday of every month, and the Fellows' Meetings, open to Fellows only, held on the third Tuesday of every month. Both sets of meetings were held in the evening at six and, later on, at seven o'clock.

From the first General Meeting on 8 April 1788 until the autumn of 1795 both sets of meetings were held in Smith's house at No. 12 Great Marlborough Street. At the first meeting of the Fellows there, Dryander agreed to act as Honorary Librarian, and at the following Fellows' Meeting in May the Society arranged to pay an annual rent of £20 to Smith for the use of two rooms, one as a meeting room, the other as a library. In April 1789, the Society engaged Smith's servant, Francisco Borone, the "Milanese lad" whom Smith had brought to England with him in 1787, to attend on the Society at all times. This arrangement seems to have gone on until 1794, when Borone accompanied John Sibthorp to Greece, where he was accidentally killed in Athens by a fall from a window apparently while sleep-walking. "Truly good and amiable as well as intelligent," wrote Smith in 1795, "I think he had more acuteness in finding out specific differences of plants than anybody I ever knew." Smith dedicated the fragrant Australian genus *Boronia* to his memory. As Borone was paid only two to five guineas per annum he probably attended at meetings only.

Although the Linnaean collections were in the house, there is no evidence that the Society received any special privileges in consulting them. Even access to the Society's own library was restricted to the days and hours convenient to the President.

The Society at first held both a Fellows' Meeting and a General Meeting every month, and went on doing so for the first 16 months. By the thirteenth month, however, the Society had begun to feel the strain, and prudently instituted a recess from the July to the October meeting in 1789. There has been an annual recess ever since that year. The first 16 months are reckoned as the first of the 148 sessions held up to the year 1935–36. Thus, 1987–88 is the two hundredth session.

At the Fellows' Meetings usually only the administrative business of the Society was discussed; in short, they were the equivalent of the modern Council Meetings. At the General Meetings scientific papers were read fully. The audience was not let off with previously printed and distributed abstracts as in later, softer days; no lantern-slides or films lightened the rigour of the entertainment. As the meetings lasted only about an hour, a long paper would sometimes take more than one meeting to finish. Members had no refreshment either before or after meetings, and no discussion of papers during them, so the meetings were rather severe functions. To add to the dignity of the occasions, whoever occupied the Chair either wore or had on the table in front of him a three-cornered hat as was the custom with such learned bodies as the Royal Academy. In 1823 this hat, or one of the dynasty of hats, cost seven shillings for repairs.

At the Anniversary Meeting in 1898, Sir Joseph Hooker, when acknowledging the presentation to him of the special gold medal in recognition of his services to science, stated that he had been informed that A. B. Lambert, a Vice-President from 1796 until his death in 1842, was the last, when in the Chair, to wear the three-cornered hat. Lambert occupied the Chair for the last time on 18 April 1837, five years before Hooker's election. In September 1899, William Pamplin died at the age of 93. He had been elected an Associate in 1830, and thus belonged to the Society during seven years in which Lambert was often in the Chair.

In Pamplin's obituary notice (*Proceedings* 1899–1900: 80) it is stated that even in old age he had a vivid recollection of men and things at the Linnean Society: "A. B. Lambert as

Vice-President in the Chair, with the official cocked hat in front of him on the table, Robert Brown on his right, Richard Taylor the printer, as Under-Secretary, on his left...." Possibly by the end of Lambert's time the hat had become more a symbol than a covering, but there is no certainty of this or that Lambert was the last to wear it or have it in front of him, for in the Bye-Laws printed in 1848, 11 years after Lambert had ceased to occupy the Chair, it is laid down that the President "being in the Chair, may be covered, while speaking to or hearing particular Members, notwithstanding their being uncovered". In any case, whether on the head or on the table, the hat was clearly authoritative and honorific. This historic custom had a short-lived revival during the Presidency of W. T. Stearn, 1979–82.

At the General Meetings, Fellows, Associates and Foreign Members were admitted. The only ceremony about this was the signing by Fellows of the Book of the Obligation and Rules, but in 1791 Goodenough proposed the sentence of welcome which, slightly modified and extended, is still pronounced by the President while he gives the right hand of Fellowship to the elected one: "By the Authority and in the Name of the Linnean Society of London, I admit you a Fellow thereof."

There is a corresponding formula for the ejection of not only Fellows but any member of the Society. This extreme but entirely verbal procedure (except that the physical antithesis to the handshake of welcome is symbolized by the erasure of the offender's name from the Register) used to be employed in bygone years not infrequently in cases of pertinacious refusal to pay dues. At one General Meeting in 1843 the Society was purged of no fewer than 11 Fellows by this process. Latterly, ejection has been a rare occurrence, being employed only in cases of defamation or dishonour of the Society, or of contemptuous or contumacious disregard of its Statutes or Orders.

Before scientific societies came into existence in the seventeenth century the more or less isolated men of science could communicate their ideas or discoveries to each other only by correspondence, a slow and restricted method of spreading knowledge, or by publishing books at their own expense or by subscription. The instruments, collections and literature required for their investigations were difficult and expensive to obtain. The societies had therefore to serve as a means of direct intercourse between those interested in the same part of science, and had to endeavour to provide instruments or collections and books for their members and arrange for publication of the investigations made or communicated by their members. When the Linnean Society was founded, although a good beginning had been made in the forming of collections and libraries here and there, neither the Universities nor the State had realized the importance of scientific libraries, laboratories and museums. The Linnean Society from the first was aware of its obligations in those respects and set about fulfilling them to the best of its resources. In 1789 it appointed a committee to select papers for publication. A museum was begun with donations of botanical and zoological specimens that continued to flow in for many years. A library was started, also largely with donations, chief among the early donors being Banks and Dryander; and early in 1790 the first bookcase was ordered. In that year the Society also had the first volume of the *Transactions* ready for the press, with Banks paying the cost of the plates.

Year after year, the three founders of the Society, Smith, Goodenough and Marsham, were re-elected to their respective offices, and there is no doubt that all three would have continued *ad vitam aut culpam* or as long as they were willing to serve. Dryander also continued to be Honorary Librarian until 1796, when he gave way to Alexander McLeay. In 1798 Goodenough was appointed Canon at Windsor; but since the journey from

Windsor to London in those days took too much time to allow of his attending to the duties of treasurer he resigned office. Marsham then became Treasurer and was re-elected annually until 1816, when financial irregularities caused his resignation. The Secretaryship, made vacant in 1798 by Marsham's transfer to the Treasurership, was filled by Alexander McLeay, who continued to be re-elected until his departure for Australia in 1825.

Alexander McLeay (1767–1848) was the first of a distinguished family that continued in Fellowship of the Society for nearly a century and left to another Linnean Society, that of New South Wales, an enduring and valuable heritage. He was the son of a leading townsman of Wick in Caithness. He began in commerce but soon entered Government service. In 1795 he was Chief Clerk in the Prisoners of War Department, and in 1797 held a similar post in the Transport Board of which he became Secretary in 1806. On the abolition of the Board in 1819 he retired on pension. Towards the end of 1824 he was appointed Colonial Secretary to the Government of New South Wales and left for Australia in 1825. He held this office until 1837, when he retired, but continued to reside in Sydney. In 1843, when the Legislative Council of New South Wales was established, he was chosen as its first Speaker, and retained this office until his final retirement in 1846. He died in Sydney in 1848, his end being hastened by a carriage accident.

While in Britain, Alexander McLeay had a great reputation as an entomologist and is said to have possessed the finest private collection of insects in the country. This collection went with him to Australia. Within a few years of his arrival at Sydney he received a grant of about 50 acres at Elizabeth Bay, then near but now part of Sydney, and purchased about 15 000 acres at Brownlow Hill, about 40 miles out of Sydney. Those acquisitions developed the botanical and horticultural sides of McLeay's interests, and he enriched his garden at Elizabeth Bay with plants from all over the world. On part of this famous garden the Hall of the Linnean Society of New South Wales stood from 1885 to 1924. McLeay was elected FLS in 1794 and FRS in 1809. A man of great ability, and of a personality that made him many friends, he was on especially good terms with the three founders of the Society. One friend, Robert Brown, dedicated the genus *Macleaya* (Papaveraceae) to him as "a general naturalist, a profound entomologist, and a practical botanist". In the collection of his correspondence presented to the Society by his third son, Sir George MacLeay, we find him asking and receiving advice from Goodenough regarding the sending of his eldest son, William Sharp MacLeay (1792–1865), who became a distinguished Australian entomologist, to Goodenough's old school, Westminster.

Mindful of Goodenough's remarks regarding the need for numbers and wealth, the Society grew in numbers, but it had not yet succeeded in attaining the second of his requisites, possibly because it has never set itself in earnest to attempt it. The List of the Society for 1794 shows 97 Fellows and 21 Associates. In 1794 the majority of the Fellows consisted of men for whom science was a hobby or minor occupation. They were mostly men of independent means or those whose vocations were in one or other of the three then learned professions, in business or in commerce. Now the List is thickly studded with the names of both men and women professionally employed as scientists.

Although Smith was titular head of the Society, Goodenough exercised great if not predominating influence in its guidance. He was much older than Smith, who often consulted him and almost always acted on his advice. Goodenough also served as Smith's mentor in the preparation of the latter's scientific works. Smith was not strong in the classics, for he had begun to study Latin only when at Edinburgh, at the instigation of

John Hope. He frequently wrote to Goodenough regarding the proper words and expressions to use, as well as consulting him on his scientific work generally.

In 1795, the date of the Anniversary Meeting of the Society was changed from the third Tuesday in April to 24 May, which was taken to be the birthday of Linnaeus according to the New Style Calendar. This date is, as a matter of fact, a day out, the correct date being 23 May, as B. D. Jackson pointed out in his article on Linnaeus in the *Encyclopaedia Britannica* (9th edn, 1882). Conservatism and the terms of the Society's Charter have prevailed, however, and the Society still holds its Anniversary ordinarily on 24 May. The error, due to a misunderstanding of the number of days dropped by Sweden in the change from the Old to the New Style Calendar, was not confined to the London Society, for the now defunct Société Linnéene de Paris used to hold its Fête Champêtre also on 24 May.

In 1795, Smith moved from Great Marlborough Street to Hammersmith, taking the Linnaean Collections with him, and thus began to make meaningless the brave words about them in his introductory discourse and in his letter to Petrus Camper. This change of residence also made the Society search for another house. The Westminster Library Society or "Westminster Subscription Library", as it is also called in the Society's Minute Book, was looking for quarters at the same time, and the two Societies jointly leased No. 10 Panton Square from September 1795, at a yearly rent of £90, the Westminster Library taking the ground floor and the Linnean Society the first floor. Panton Square, or Yard, as it was first called, derived its name from its builder, Colonel Thomas Panton, the successful proprietor of a gambling hall, which had flourished in the previous century.

Hitherto the Society had conducted its affairs without a paid staff, but its increasing membership, library and collections, and the new requirements of its habitation, led to the engagement of Benjamin Price, the Secretary to the Westminster Library, to act as Clerk to the Society at 20 guineas (according to the Cash Book entries, not £20 as the Minutes state) per annum. He had also to reside in the house, so that he probably acted as housekeeper and librarian as well. These developments led, of course, to an increase in the Society's expenditure. Its income had already begun to suffer from forgetful Fellows at home, but it was determined not to run any risks of this sort with Fellows resident abroad, and it laid down that such Fellows should within two months of election pay their full life fee in addition to the admission fee. This seems at first sight rather severe but was rational and defensible in those days of slow communications and lack of agencies for ensuring payment of annual contributions. Nevertheless, it caused protest. More recently, the Society has suffered much financial loss from overseas Fellows through some countries being unable to send money abroad because of currency restrictions.

As soon as Smith moved to Hammersmith, his attendance at the Society's meetings began to wane and the Society itself seemed in danger of going the way of its predecessor. Both Goodenough and Marsham have left records of their feelings, and Marsham unburdened himself on the subject in a letter to Smith, dated with particularity "Upper Berkeley Street, Thursday Evg, ½ past 11, Sept. 22, 1796", from which the following is an extract:

> Dr. Townson's letter is only one of the many unpleasant things I have to encounter as Secretary of the Linnean Society, for of late they have been so many and disagreeable, that my Zeal is much abated and I told Dr. Goodenough, when I had pleasure of seeing him a few days since in Town, that in future I never meant to put off any engagement to attend the Society's Meetings, for that after giving up every private engagement for 8 years, I had become completely tired of attending there by myself, for of the Seven Officers (President, 4 Vice-Presidents, Treasurer, and Secretary) now belonging to the Society I was in general the only one that attended – and frequently had not Members enough to make a Society, which was the case at the very last

Meeting, neither President, Vice-President or Treasurer and but two members beside myself, so that the Elections that ought to have taken place on that Day were postponed for three Months; the Members are near £100 in arrear, and when I apply you see I give offence – The Rules are not kept to, the Museum in a state of confusion, No one knows what is in it – The Volume of Transactions, two years in the press when two Months ought to finish it – In short the whole System is so completely relaxed that as a Society it is not worth attention – It is become a perfect lounge once a Month for a few persons and I am now so fully persuaded that it will grow worse and worse on your quitting London, that I am determined not to witness its disgrace, for all my ideas of making it what I had set my mind upon, are totally vanished; I would have exerted myself for its support, but I have not abilities to do it by myself.

The extract throws a light, probably coloured by Marsham's pessimistic mood of the moment, both on the Society and on Marsham. Robert Townson, a surgeon elected a Fellow in 1794, who had refused to pay his Admission Fee, clearly belonged to the type of Society member which has always been a trouble to Treasurers and Secretaries: the member who signs a solemn obligation makes no effort to fulfil it and waxes indignant when reminded of it. Fortunately, Marsham's vexation passed and the Society survived Smith's desertion.

Early in 1796 Smith married Pleasance Reeve, a Lowestoft lady, and later in the year left Hammersmith to reside in his native Norwich, despite all the arguments and protests with which Goodenough plied him. Smith's reasons for returning to Norwich are given in a letter to his friend Davall in Switzerland: "We are going to live at Norwich! The reasons are too long to particularize, they are family comfort, leisure and command of my time chiefly." Before he left Hammersmith, Smith sold by auction the minerals of the Linnaean Collections, but took to Norwich the botanical and zoological specimens and the library and manuscripts of Linnaeus. The letter to Petrus Camper, already quoted, makes it practically certain that Smith's possession of these collections occasioned the name of the Society and that his first intention was to make them available to it. With his removal to Hammersmith, and still more with his departure to Norwich, the Society's name ceased to be "peculiarly proper" for the following 33 years. Then, the year after Smith's death, the Society acquired the collections and resumed the peculiar propriety of its name. Smith's departure of course caused a stir in the Society, and the question of the future of the presidency was informally discussed. According to the evidence in Goodenough's letters to Smith, the difficulty was to find a successor to Smith if he should resign. Smith had sounded Dryander as a possible successor, but Dryander declined to become President, although prepared to become "a fixed Vice-President". Smith, doubtless in anticipation of his removal to Norwich, had appointed at the Anniversary Meeting in 1796, for the first time in the history of the Society, four Vice-Presidents, of whom Dryander was one; the other three being A. B. Lambert, Thomas Martyn and George Shaw.

Goodenough urged that Dryander should be "constant Vice-President" and, as usual, had his way. Smith did not resign and never afterwards offered to do so, and the Society, in the absence until many years afterwards of any limitation of the tenure of the Presidency, continued to elect him year after year, just as it did the other two officers. Smith intended to spend three months every year in London, but actually seldom spent more than two months, so that the ordinary work of the Society was carried on by the senior Vice-President, the Treasurer and the Secretary. Dryander, until his death in 1810, usually presided at the meetings in Smith's absence.

In 1800, the future constitution of the Society came under consideration. The alternative proposals were to execute a Deed of Trust, with the three Officers as Trustees, or to obtain a Charter. There was a good deal of opposition to the latter proposal, but

McLeay's argument that payment of the Annual Contributions of Fellows could not be enforced without a Charter gained the day. The Charter was granted on 26 March 1802. It cost £460 5s. 6d., the Fellows subscribing over £422 towards it. In connection with the raising of this subscription McLeay, in a letter to Smith urging the latter to make his friends subscribe, writes: "I think there remains but little doubt of our being able to make up the sum wanted, although I understand there are many perverse souls among us who will not give a farthing." Amongst those "perverse souls" was Erasmus Darwin, who bluntly stated that he was in no way interested in the Society. Two legal Fellows, William Mathews, Barrister of Middle Temple, and Stephen Claudius Hunter, with Henry Kebbit, partner of the latter, gave their professional assistance in drawing up and obtaining the Charter.

With the granting of the Charter the Society as theretofore existing was by legal fiction held to have been dissolved and a new Society formed. Whereas the old Society had styled itself successively "Linnaean Society", the "Linnean Society" and the "Linnean Society of London", the new Society was named in the Charter "The Linnean Society of London", the definite article being an integral part of the title. Fifteen names are mentioned in the Charter as those of the first Fellows; of these, only four, Smith, Goodenough, Marsham and Dryander, are the names of original Fellows of 1788.

The first Fellow mentioned in the Charter is the Earl of Dartmouth, who, as Viscount Lewisham, had been elected FLS in 1790, when he was President of the Society for Promoting Natural History, of which he had been a member since 1789.

The same 15 Fellows were appointed in the Charter as the first Council; Smith, Marsham and McLeay were appointed respectively first president, first treasurer and first secretary. As, to begin with, the same 15 had to act as the whole incorporated Society and as the Council, there was a somewhat confusing succession of meetings of them in their alternating capacities. They first met as Fellows on 11 May 1802 and, as directed in the Charter, appointed to the new Society so many Honorary Members, Fellows, Foreign Members and Associates who were on the List of the old Society as they could get through in the time. On 17 May they held two meetings, one as Fellows, when they got through another batch of appointments, the other as the first meeting of the new Council, when they started to draw up Bye-Laws. On 21 May they again held two meetings in the same alternating capacities and with the same work; on 22 May they contented themselves with one meeting, as a Council; on 24 May they held three meetings, two as Fellows and one as Council, at which they finished respectively the appointments of the other Fellows and the Bye-Laws.

Altogether, they appointed 228 Fellows whose names were on the roll of the old Society. In addition, they appointed on 11 May three new Fellows: Sir Thomas Gage Bt, of Hengrave Hall, Suffolk, who is commemorated in the Liliaceous genus *Gagea*; Edward Rudge, who bequeathed a legacy for a Linnean Gold Medal in 1846 on terms found unacceptable; and Samuel Statham. The certificates of recommendation of those three had been presented in March and April 1802. They are the only three Fellows, in addition to the original 20 admitted without election up to 19 August 1788, appointed without a previous election, and they are the first of the post-Charter Fellows.

On 24 May the first General Meeting of the incorporated Society was held, with a large attendance. After that meeting, the fourth which they, or some of them at least, had attended that day, the 15 ceased to be the whole body of the Society. At this first General Meeting the Charter was read and the new Bye-Laws presented. The latter were finally passed at the fourth General Meeting on 6 July 1802. With the grant of the Charter the

Society modified its procedure considerably. The meetings of Fellows only, which in the old Society had alternated with the General Meetings, ceased, the Fellows as an administrative body being replaced by the Council. Succeeding Councils were elected annually as at present from amongst and by the Fellows only, one-third of each successive Council then being "amoved", as the Charter has it, every year. The Council, however, did not keep up the old practice of Fellows meeting every month. In fact, the first 15, presumably exhausted by their surfeit of meetings in May 1802, appear to have parted in the vein of the melancholy Jaques, "God be wi' you, let's meet as little as we can", for they did not meet again until 27 November of that year; and for many years thereafter the Council met only at irregular and infrequent intervals.

Up to the granting of the Charter the Society had held 13 complete sessions and was well into the fourteenth. Altogether, there were held under the old regime 145 Fellows' Meetings, the last being on 20 April 1802, and 144 General Meetings, the last on 4 May 1802. The attendance of Fellows and other members of the Society and visitors at the General Meetings varied from seven to 40, the average being 18. As the old Society was held to have been dissolved, the original Fellows' Meetings and General Meetings Minutes Books, bound in green vellum and brass-clasped, were closed. Up to 1795 both sets of Minutes were inscribed in Marsham's beautifully clear hand, but in that year Benjamin Price, already mentioned, took over the work. Price may have been an excellent Secretary to the Westminster Library, but to the Linnean Society he was a scrawly scribe and not always careful of what he wrote. The similarly bound book containing the original Rules and Orders for the Society as a whole, the Bye-Laws relating only to the Fellows and the signatures of Fellows admitted up to 20 April 1802 was also closed. It had been signed by 183 Fellows, beginning with Smith and ending with Richard Simmons. In its place a much larger volume was opened, which continues in use to this day. On the recto of every ordinary folio of this book is written the following Obligation:

> We who have here unto subscribed, do hereby promise, each for himself, that we will endeavour to promote the Good of the Linnean Society of London: and to pursue the Ends for which the same was instituted: That we will be present at the Meetings of the Society, as often as conveniently we can, especially at the Anniversary Elections, and upon extraordinary Occasions; and that we will observe the Statutes, Bye-Laws and Orders of the said Society. Provided that, whensoever any of us shall signify to the President, under his Hand, that he desire to withdraw from the Society, he shall be free from this Obligation for the future.

This volume contains the signatures of the first 15 Fellows of the incorporated Society, those of as many of the Fellows of the old Society as could be obtained again to sign it, also those of all Fellows admitted since 1802. The book is a record of admission only, as not all Fellows elected, especially those residing abroad, can arrange to present themselves for admission.

Interspersed with the ordinary folios of this book are illuminated vellum leaves bearing the signatures of the Society's Royal Patrons from George IV onwards and of Royal Honorary Members. The decoration of these leaves varies from the elaborate multicoloured floral wreath encircling Queen Victoria's name to the severely simple treatment of the folio prepared under the supervision of the College of Arms for the signature of Queen Mary. The vellum leaf (1932), which holds the signature of Hirohito the Emperor of Japan, had its symbolic illumination designed and painted in Japan, and is the most elegant of the series. The design, as described in the *Proceedings* for 1932–33: 56, represents "the entwined branches of *Chrysanthemum* and *Paulownia*, the emblems of the Japanese Imperial Family, crowned with the Imperial crest between two phoenixes. The ribbon is of Wungen-Nishiki, or literally halo-brocade, for in the pattern stripes are graduated like a halo round the sun. Wungen-Nikishi has been used as a border of the mat for the Throne from ancient times. No subject in Japan has ever been allowed to sit on a Wungen-bordered mat. The particular ribbon, for this reason, seems full of meaning to be put under the Imperial autograph in the design." The Emperor, a distinguished biologist, and the Empress visited the Society in 1971 and their son, Akihito, the Crown Prince of Japan, was formally admitted as a Foreign Member in 1980 in appreciation of his ichthyological research and was appointed an Honorary Fellow in 1986.

Chapter 3

From incorporation to purchase of the Linnaean Collections 1802 to 1829

The 15 Fellows appointed by George III appointed in turn 231 other Fellows, four Honorary Members (Sir Joseph Banks, the Marquis of Blandford, the Duke of Portland and the Bishop of Winchester), 38 Associates and 82 Foreign Members, making a total of 370 members. On 24 May 1802 the 15 ordered in Council the purchase of an iron chest with three locks, the different keys of which were held respectively by the acting President, Treasurer and Secretary. This still enshrines the Charter and other valuables.

In November 1802, the Society applied to the College of Arms for a grant of Arms, Crest and Supporters, with the motto "Naturae discere mores" (to learn the ways of Nature) neatly summarizing the Society's aim. The Arms, which were granted in December, were based upon those which Linnaeus had suggested for himself in 1761 and ultimately obtained approval: "My little *Linnaea* in the helmet, but three fields in the shield, black, green and red, the three kingdoms of Nature, and upon it an egg cut in two or a half-egg to denote Nature which is continued and perpetuated in the egg." So wrote Linnaeus. In the Society's Arms, the helm was replaced by a Mount; a Lion and an Eagle support the shield with the Mount above it. The Society lost no time in having its Arms engraved on a new steel seal at a cost of over £38 to replace the less heraldic but more artistic seal in use up to 1802. The original seal vanished, when or where is unknown, but was restored to the Society in peculiar circumstances more than a century after its use had ceased.

In May 1919, the seal returned to the Society through the courtesy of John Slade of Worthing, who had found it amongst the effects of an uneducated old man of over 90. The seal, still clear and sharp, shows an Adamic figure in the foreground, standing on terra firma, with a rod in his right hand and a sprig of *Linnaea borealis* in his left. A lion stands on his right. Two plants spring out of the earth, an insect and a large shell lie on it and a snake wriggles past behind his heels. In the background of sky and sea there is an aquiline fowl volant in the first and a spouting cetacean with head and tail emergent from the second. Behind the cetacean arises an irregular pyramid of what look like basaltic columns. Surrounding the upper half of the seal is the legend "Sigillum Societatis Linneanae Londin". The design of the seal seems to have been drawn from several sources. The reverse of this medal shows a clothed Cybele holding a key, with a lion by her side and plants springing out of the ground.

The conjoint occupation with the Westminster Library of No. 10 Panton Square began to prove inconvenient because of the growth of the Society's museum. After a vain attempt to buy a house in Dean Street, Soho, a nine-year lease of No. 9 Gerrard Street,

(a)

(b)

(c)

(d)

also in Soho, was purchased for £300, with a yearly rent of £105. At the time the Society leased it, the house was a private residence, but had not always been so. In the previous century it had been the Turk's Head tavern and was the first meeting place of the Literary Club founded by Sir Joshua Reynolds in 1764. The Club, which numbered amongst its members Samuel Johnson, Goldsmith, Burke, Garrick and other literary and social notables, used to meet in the Turk's Head one evening a week. After the tavern became a private house, the Club continued to meet in other taverns, one of them being the Thatched House in St James's Street where, later in the following century, the Linnean Club used to dine and where the Society held its Anniversary Dinner for several years in succession. After spending about £300 on repairs, the Society occupied the house in the autumn of 1805, and soon thereafter created a new threefold post of Clerk, Librarian and Housekeeper, at £100 per annum, with free quarters in the house, in which residence was compulsory. There were three candidates for the post: Benjamin Price; the Rev. Patrick Keith, FLS (1769–1840); and Robert Brown, ALS (1773–1858). The statement in the Minutes of the General Meeting of 17 December 1805, attributed to the Vice-President (Dryander) in the Chair, that Brown was the only candidate is incorrect, but the Council may have submitted only Brown's name to the meeting. Brown had not long returned from Australia, having been naturalist on Flinders's voyage. Price failed to convince the Council that he could continue to serve two masters now in widely separated houses, and Keith could not stand up against Brown. So the last was elected in December 1805, and the most distinguished paid officer who has ever been in the service of the Society began his duties. These were not excessive and thus allowed Brown time to prepare his important *Prodromus Novae Hollandiae* (1810). He had to attend in the Museum and Library on two days a week from noon to four o'clock, although no books were lent. Goodenough later complained to Smith of the small amount of service rendered and expressed the desirability of better facilities for consulting the Library.

The financial drain of the rent of the house was lessened by allowing the Horticultural Society of London (later the Royal Horticultural Society), which had been founded in 1804, to use the Linnean Society's meeting room for £25 a year and by letting the house vaults for £20 per annum.

In 1809, the Society celebrated the Jubilee of George III by expending ten shillings and sixpence on the poor and five shillings on candles for illumination. Presumably there were few poor, or at least in the Council's opinion few of the deserving sort, in the neighbourhood of Gerrard Street, and probably five shillings were enough for brightening the Society's windows.

In 1810, Jonas Dryander died and Brown succeeded him as Curator and Librarian to Sir Joseph Banks, but continued to hold his triple post in the Society. Dryander, who was a native of Sweden but had never been a student of Linnaeus, had been a Vice-President of the Society since 1796. He was also Librarian of the Royal Society and, in addition to being an excellent botanist, was the best natural history bibliographer of his generation, as his *Catalogus Bibliothecae historico-naturalis Josephi Banks* (5 vols, 1798–1800) demonstrates.

So far the Society had been able to function with only one Secretary but now it was

Plate III   Early homes of the Linnean Society: (a) No. 12 Great Marlborough Street, photograph taken in 1932. (b) Panton Square, from the watercolour by T. H. Sheperd in the Crace Collection. (c) No. 9 Gerrard Street, Soho, photograph taken in 1932. (d) No. 32 Soho Square, photograph taken in 1932.

found necessary to establish the additional honorary office of Under-Secretary, and in 1810 Richard Taylor, who had been elected a Fellow in 1807, was appointed.

Richard Taylor (1781–1858) belonged to an intellectually distinguished Norwich family. He was a son of John Taylor (1750–1826), a wool comber at Norwich; his parents were Unitarians, like James Edward Smith, and formed part of the liberal and literary circle of Norwich. After his education at a day school in Norwich, where he was grounded in the classics and also learned some chemistry and other scientific subjects, young Taylor was apprenticed on Smith's recommendation to a printer in Chancery Lane, London. During his apprenticeship Taylor not only continued to read the classics but also became a student of medieval Latin and Italian writers and a proficient scholar in French, Flemish and Anglo-Saxon. After his apprenticeship, in 1803 he started with his father a printing business in Blackhouse Court, Fleet Street, whence he removed first to Shoe Lane and then to Red Lion Court. He soon became the printer for the Linnean, the Royal and many other Societies, printing Smith's *Exotic Botany* (1804–08), Linnaeus's *Lachesis Lapponica* (1811) and Sibthorp and Smith's *Flora Graeca* (10 vols. 1806–40), typographically and aesthetically among the most beautiful and costly British books. Beautiful editions of the classics also issued from his press. His scientific interests ranged widely, for he was a member of the Society of Antiquaries and of the Astronomical and Philological Societies, and supported from its beginning the British Association for the Advancement of Science. He was co-editor of the *Philosophical Magazine*, and in 1838 he founded the *Annals of Natural History*, with which was united in 1841 Loudon and Charlesworth's *Magazine of Natural History*. His own literary work was in biblical and philological research. He was active in the foundation of the City of London School and of the Corporation Library, and helped in the establishment of London University (later University College) and hence of the University of London. His personal qualities gained him the friendship and esteem of the large circle of eminent men with whom both his business and his outside interests brought him into contact. In 1852, the firm became Taylor and Francis when William Francis (1817–1904), his illegitimate and only son, who entered the business as an apprentice in 1834, became a partner. Francis, who in time became a PhD of Giessen University, was almost as remarkable a man as his father in the extent of his literary and scientific interests, and was a Fellow of the Society for 60 years until his death in 1904. *The Lamp of Learning, Taylor and Francis and the Development of Science Publishing* (1985) by W. H. Brock and A. J. Meadows provides a detailed account of them both and their association with the Linnean Society as the Society's printers.

In 1812 the Prince Regent became first Patron of the Society, and thus instituted an honour that succeeding Sovereigns have graciously continued ever since. Having petitioned for a knighthood, Smith attended the Prince Regent's Levee on 28 July 1812 to present a copy of the *Transactions*, and was thereupon knighted as "Institutor and President of the Society".

In 1814, the Horticultural Society was allowed to keep its library in the Linnean Society's Council Room. In 1817, that Society asked for the daily use for five hours of the Linnean Council Room and for the use of another room for fruit storage, but this request was not granted. Two years later, in May 1819, the Horticultural Society, to the relief of the Linnean Society, acquired premises of its own in what is now Lower Regent Street.

In 1816, Marsham resigned the treasurership, which he had held since 1798, in unfortunate circumstances, associated with mismanagement and loss of Society money entrusted to him. His investment of Government money to provide a dowry for a daughter having been unsuccessful, he had used the Society's money to pay off his debts and was never able to return it. Despite this, McLeay recalled that in the critical years of the previous century Marsham had done more than anyone else to keep the Society in being. His friend of former days, since becoming Bishop of Carlisle, comments severely in his letters to Smith on Marsham's dereliction of duty as treasurer, but Smith was less harsh in his judgement. From the poignant letters that Marsham wrote to his colleague McLeay and from other correspondence one can picture his pitiable condition until his death in 1819. Of the three founders of the Society, Smith was knighted, Goodenough became a bishop and Marsham died "sick in the world's regard, wretched and low".

In April 1822 occurred an incident which reflects no credit on the Society – the disgraceful blackballing of John Edward Gray (1800–75). His father, Samuel Frederick Gray (1766–1828), a druggist and botanical lecturer, published in 1821 *A Natural Arrangement of British Plants* which had a strong anti-Linnaean flavour, rejecting Linnaean names and classification and referring to "the prurient mind of Linnaeus". Much of this was the work of J. E. Gray but the highly unpopular, and somewhat devious, Richard Anthony Salisbury (1761–1829), a friend of the Grays and an opponent of Smith, was suspected of having a hand in it. Salisbury and Smith had originally been close friends, but Smith was shocked by Salisbury's conduct in declaring himself bankrupt to avoid payment to his wife's family and in offering to introduce Smith's young protegé to a girl who may have been a prostitute. Although the introduction on p. 32 refers to "Sowerby and Smith, English Botany", on p. xi the same work is simply mentioned as "Sowerby's English Botany" without mention of Smith. When J. E. Gray, sponsored by Salisbury, applied in 1822 for election to the Society, he was therefore rejected by ballot on the pretext that he had thereby insulted Smith. It seems a trivial reason but a sentence in McLeay's letter to Smith on 4 May 1822 puts it beyond doubt: "the Society had almost unanimously blackballed a man because he had not treated their President with the respect he so highly deserved". Behind this shabby act lay animosity against S. F. Gray and Salisbury on personal grounds and resistance by die-hard adherents of the Linnaean system to increasing attacks upon it on scientific grounds. This cruel blow to an ambitious, strong-willed, brilliant, industrious and sensitive young man fortunately only strengthened his determination to prove his worth in science and the futility of those misguided opponents. William Carruthers, President of the Society from 1886 to 1890, wrote in 1865 that it "filled one with shame that party feeling and personal ill-will could have influenced men of science in England to such an extent" as regards their deliberate neglect of *A Natural Arrangement*. In 1857, long after Smith and his touchy friends had passed away, Gray, then Keeper of the Zoological Department of the British Museum and one of the world's best-known zoologists, condescended to be elected a Fellow of the Linnean Society.

With Marsham's resignation, Smith remained the only one of the original officers still in office. Since 1798 Goodenough had been less and less able to take an active part in the management of the Society; in 1802 he had been transferred from Windsor to Rochester as Dean and in 1807 made Bishop of Carlisle. Even from Carlisle he used to drive to London, often in his own carriage, to attend the Sessions of the House of Lords, and when in London he usually presided at any meeting of the Council or Society that then took place. He was wont to complain to Smith of the inconvenient hour, nine o'clock in the evening, at which the Council often met. A sermon preached by him in 1809 before the House of Lords gave rise to John Wolcot's libellous epigram on the Peerage:

> 'Tis well enough that Goodenough
> Before the Lords should preach
> But, sure enough, full bad enough
> Are those he has to teach.

(a)

(b)

(c)

(d)

Marsham's successor as Treasurer was Edward Forster (1765–1849), a partner in the banking house of Lubbock, Forster and Company, elected a Fellow in 1800. He was born in Essex and spent his whole life there when not travelling. A keen and competent botanist, he discovered in Wales a new species of stonecrop, which Smith named *Sedum forsterianum*, and in Essex a new species of woodrush, *Luzula forsteri* (Smith) DC, which Smith named *Juncus forsteri*.

In 1820, Sir Joseph Banks died and left Brown a life interest in his large house at No. 32 Soho Square, which extended back to Dean Street, together with his library and collections. This led to a change in Brown's position. He shed the functions of clerk and housekeeper to the Linnean Society but, being a canny lowland Scot, retained the librarian part of his post, together with the salary attached to the threefold duties! However, this arrangement lasted only a short time.

The Society was finding No. 9 Gerrard Street inconvenient and made an arrangement with Brown whereby the Society took a sublease of the Soho Square half of Banks's, now Brown's, house at an annual rent of £140, while Brown retained the Dean Street half, which contained the Banksian Collections. Although the 30-year lease was not drawn up until August 1822, the Society apparently met for the first time in No. 32 Soho Square on 24 May 1821. In May 1822, Brown resigned the librarianship and David Don was elected the following November to succeed him, with the clerkship again appended.

David Don (1800–41) was the son of a botanically-minded Scottish nurseryman, George Don the Elder (1764–1814), of Forfarshire, and brother of George Don the Younger (1798–1856), likewise a gardener botanist. His father was for some time on the staff of the Edinburgh Botanic Garden and, during that period, David Don attended some university classes. On his father's return to Forfar, David went with him and there received his early botanical training. After a second period in Edinburgh, in the employment of Messrs Dickson, nurserymen, Don came to London in 1819. Soon thereafter he became librarian and herbarium-keeper to A. B. Lambert. He published a monograph of the genus *Saxifraga* in the Society's *Transactions* 13: 341–452 (1822) and a *Prodomus Florae Nepalensis* (1825), an important work despite being written in what his contemporary, John Lindley, described as "so strange a language, some new kind of Latin, without the incumbrance of previous education", as well as 52 papers in scientific periodicals, 16 of them in the Society's *Transactions*. His reputation as a botanist led to his election as an Associate of the Society in 1823. In 1836, he succeeded C. S. Burnett as Professor of Botany at King's College, London, an office he continued to hold along with the Society's librarianship until his untimely death from cancer. He never actually became a Fellow of the Society, since in those days it was not permissible for a paid officer of the Society.

Don had to reside in the Society's premises and, as his elder brother George lived with him for some years after returning in 1823 from his travels in Africa and South America on behalf of the Horticultural Society, there were three Forfarshire botanists, Brown and the two Dons, occupying quarters in the same house.

In the first years of his service with the Society, Don was not on the happiest terms with

Plate IV (a) James Dickson, from the watercolour by Wageman, 1822. (b) Richard Taylor, from the lithograph by J. H. Maguire, in the "Ipswich" series published in 1852. (c) Jonas Dryander, from the soft ground etching by Wm. Daniell after the drawing by Geo. Dance made in 1796. (d) Edward Forster, from the painting by Eddis in the Society's collection.

his fellow countryman Alexander McLeay (1767–1848), the Society's Secretary from 1798 to 1825. The latter, in a letter dated 5 January 1825 informing Smith of his appointment to the Colonial Secretaryship of New South Wales, makes the following severe comment on Don: "Whoever may be the Secretary [of the Society] I shall feel it my duty to recommend the removal of Mr. Don, whose Pride and Self Conceit are really intolerable. I had determined to act no longer with him and I consider that I should be dealing unjustly by my successor unless I recommend that some Person should be appointed as Clerk who is likely to attend punctually to the orders he receives." This testimony did not bring about Don's dismissal, but it may have indirectly led to improvement in his demeanour. His obituary notice at least is appreciative enough.

For about the first 40 years of its existence the Society was the main channel for the communication and publication of biological investigations, apart from those more particularly concerned with anatomy and physiology; had the Society possessed sufficient funds it might have retained that position. With its very limited resources, however, the Society could not cope with the increasing flood of investigations, and this made the rise of new societies inevitable. The first signs appeared within the Society itself. Although, hitherto, there had been similar numbers of many zoological and botanical papers published in the Society's *Transactions*, and although the botanical papers read at the General Meetings were not greatly in excess of the zoological ones, botany seemed to claim more than its fair share of time at meetings, considering the vastly greater field of zoology.

After the dissolution in 1782 of the short-lived Society of Entomologists of London, there existed no Society devoted specially to zoology or any of its branches until 1801, when Adrian Hardy Haworth (1768–1833), who had been a Linnean Fellow since 1798, set up a third Aurelian Society. This Society broke up in 1806, but immediately its members formed the Entomological Society, later styled the Entomological Society of London, which seemed more or less awake up to 1812 and more somnolent from 1812 to 1822, in which year some of its members created another Society, the Entomological Society of Great Britain. Not content with this, some of those same people in that same year considered, confusingly, forming still another Entomological Society.

The leading entomologist in England at that time was the Rev. William Kirby (1759–1850), Rector of Barham in Suffolk, who had been elected ALS in 1791 and FLS in 1815. The promoters of the proposed new society greatly desired Kirby's support, and one of them, Nicholas Aylward Vigors, corresponded with Kirby on the subject. Vigors (1787–1840), a native of County Carlow, had been a student at Trinity College, Oxford, and an officer in the Grenadier Guards. He later became MP for Carlow. He had been elected FLS in 1819 and was specially interested in insects and birds. One letter from Vigors to Kirby, dated 1 October 1822, is printed in John Freeman's *Life of the Rev. William Kirby* (1852). From this letter it is evident that Kirby was against forming a new society, but had suggested the formation of "separate committees in the Linnean Society to attend to the separate branches of Natural History and the publication of a Naturalists Journal, which would include all that intelligence which does not accord with the general plan of the Linnean Transactions". Vigors expresses his approval of this suggestion as "not only most desirable of itself, but particularly so as it would supersede the necessity of forming contemporary societies which might interfere with the interests of the parent one". Vigors offers to help in furthering Kirby's plan, but hopes that, if it should fail, Kirby would join in forming the new Entomological Society. Vigors also states that the final settlement of the proposed new society would take place before 29 November, Ray's birthday. The settlement did take place before 29 November, for on Wednesday, 27 November 1822, seven Fellows of the Linnean Society, "desirous of promoting the study of Zoology", met in the Society's rooms. They were the Rev. W. Kirby (in the Chair); W. S. MacLeay, the eldest son of Alexander McLeay, the Secretary; N. A. Vigors, G. Milne, J. F. Stephens, A. H. Haworth and J. Hatchett, all entomologists. There were also two "Visitors", E. T. Bennett and J. E. Gray, who were not Linnean Fellows.

The meeting on 27 November 1822, obviously influenced by Kirby, resolved not to form a new Entomological Society but to found a Zoological Club and it appointed a committee to draw up regulations. The next meeting was held on 8 April 1823, with Alexander McLeay in the Chair, to hear the committee's report. This meeting was adjourned until 23 May 1823, when 17 Fellows were present, with Kirby in the Chair. Now the Bye-Laws were approved and the Club came into being.

Only Fellows and Associates of the Linnean Society were eligible for membership, and only so long as they were members of the Society. So J. E. Gray, Secretary of the Entomological Society of London, again suffered humiliating exclusion. The admission fee was £2 2s. and the Anniversary Day was 29 November. The Bye-Laws of the Society applied to the Club in all cases not covered by the Club Bye-Laws, and no alteration or additions to the latter were valid without the approval of the Linnean Council.

In June 1823, the Council directed that the name of the Club should be "The Zoological Club of the Linnean Society of London". The Club met at 8 pm on the second and fourth Tuesdays of every month throughout the year, except on the fourth Tuesday in December. Papers were presented to the Society for another reading at a General Meeting. No paper read at the Club could be published unless it had first been submitted to the Society. The proceedings of the Club were less formal than those of the Society with discussion of papers being a feature of the meetings. Possibly it was his experience as a member of the Club that emboldened Thomas Bell (1792–1880), when he became President of the Society more than 30 years later, to introduce discussion of papers at the Society's meetings.

The restrictions laid upon the Club by the Linnean Council would not have mattered so much if the Society had adopted Kirby's suggestion to start a journal, but apparently this was never even considered. Not until Thomas Bell became President in 1853 were steps taken to realize Kirby's idea. As it was, the Club had only the Society's *Transactions* as a vehicle of publication, and a very slow one in those days. This fettered the Club from the start. If one did not know of the financial difficulties into which the Society was to plunge within a few years, it would be easy to criticize the attitude of the Society towards the Club, but as events turned out this did not matter much. The Society's failure to start a journal was overcome to some extent by the establishment in 1824 of *The Zoological Journal*, an independent publication conducted by Bell, Children, James de Carle Sowerby and G. B. Sowerby, all Linnean Fellows and members of the Club.

Evidently, other members of the Society viewed with suspicion the formation of a club by the zoologists. Kirby, in a letter of 11 November 1824 to W. S. Macleay, wrote: "I am sorry to find from V's [N. A. Vigors] letter that a strong feeling inimical to the Club still exists. I had hopes that by this time it would have softened down a little." The basis for this feeling towards the Club cannot now be certainly determined, but possibly it expressed the then proprietary attitude of the Society, or at least of the Council, to botanical and zoological investigations, an attitude made clear enough soon afterwards.

In 1823–24, the Asiatic Society of Great Britain and Ireland was applying for a Charter. The Linnean Society opposed the grant of a Charter unless the Asiatic Society

(a)

(b)

(c)

(d)

expressly excluded Natural History from its purview. It based its opposition on the ground that the Linnean Society had been incorporated "for the Cultivation of Natural History in all its branches". This exclusively proprietary view of the Linnean Society's relation to biological studies found, of course, no favour in the sight of the law officers of the Crown.

In 1824, the Council attempted to get the President appointed one of the *ex-officio* Trustees of the British Museum, but the application was too late.

In 1825, Alexander McLeay resigned as Secretary on his departure to New South Wales as Colonial Secretary. The selection of a Fellow to succeed McLeay caused some difficulty. Robert Brown, who from an Associate had become a Fellow in 1822, was suggested, but Goodenough, then 82, opposed him for several reasons, which were too varied all to be sound. In his letter of 10 January 1825 to Smith, the Bishop adduces two reasons: "Mr. Brown, I am told, has an invincible objection to reading aloud in public. so that I sh. think he would not think of it . . ." and "I have invincible objection to letting the Linn. Society be thrown into the lap of the Horticultural. – This must be the case if Brown is chosen". Notwithstanding Goodenough's objections, Smith offered the post to Brown, who declined it for the pertinent reasons that he had not the habits of a man of business and was unwilling to give up the time which the Secretaryship would take from his scientific work. So, for about the last time, the Bishop had his way and Brown's name was not put forward.

The new Secretary was James Ebenezer Bicheno (1785–1851), a native of Newbury in Berkshire, where his father was a Baptist Minister. Although by profession a lawyer, Bicheno practised only for a few years. In 1829 he toured Ireland, studying its economic conditions, and in 1830 published a book called *Ireland and its Economy*. In 1832 he left London for Glamorganshire, where he had become a partner in some ironworks. When they failed he had to look for employment. As a result of his Irish studies he was appointed in 1836 one of the Commissioners to investigate the question of introducing Poor Laws into Ireland. In 1842, he became Colonial Secretary of Van Diemen's Land (Tasmania), where he died at Hobart in 1851. Botany was his chief interest – he published in 1818 in the Society's *Transactions* a revision of the British species of *Juncus* – but he also belonged to the Zoological Club. It is remarkable that two successive Secretaries of the Society should have gone to the Antipodes as Colonial Secretaries.

In 1825, the inevitable tendency of zoology to cease to be entirely under the wing of the Linnean Society advanced a further stage: in March a proposal appeared for establishing a Zoological Society. In the circular, dated 1 March, setting forth the proposal, out of the 22 names of the formative committee 14 were Linnean Fellows and four on the Linnean Council. At first it would seem inexplicable that the very men who were on the Council of the Linnean in 1823–24, when it opposed the grant of a Charter to the Asiatic Society, should now take a leading part in the formation, and afterwards in the direction, of a new Society that was to seize from the Linnean Society a far greater part of the domain which it had claimed as exclusively its own than the Asiatic Society was ever likely to do. Perhaps they never envisaged such a development.

Sir Thomas Stamford Raffles (1781–1826) was elected FLS in February 1825, when he was described as "late Governor of Fort Marlborough in Sumatra". A keen naturalist as

Plate V (a) Alexander McLeay, from the painting by Sir Thos. Lawrence P.R.A. in the Society's collection. (b) James Bicheno, from the painting by Eddis in the Society's collection. (c) Francis Boott, from a photograph in a series "Literary and Scientific Portrait Club", begun in 1854. (d) Robert Brown, from the painting by H. W. Pickersgill in the Society's collection.

well as far-sighted colonial administrator, even if not a member of the Zoological Club, he certainly attended some of its meetings in that year. When he first put forward the proposal to found a Zoological Society his idea was – as he expressed in a letter, dated 9 March 1825, to his cousin the Rev. Dr Thomas Raffles – that it should be "a Society for the introduction of living animals, bearing the same relation to Zoology as a science that the Horticultural Society does to Botany". In the resolution passed at the first General Meeting of the Zoological Society in April 1826 the objects of the Society were declared to be: "The formation of a collection of living animals; a museum of preserved animals, with a collection of comparative anatomy; and a library connected with the subject." There is no mention of any intention to publish scientific papers. A Society with only these declared aims would, of course, readily gain the support of Fellows of the Linnean Society, just as the Horticultural Society did when it was established in 1804. In 1827, a year after its foundation, two-thirds of the Council of the Zoological Society were Fellows of the Linnean Society, and four, including Joseph Sabine and N. A. Vigors, respectively Treasurer and Secretary of the Zoological Society, were also on the Council of the Linnean; one of them, J. E. Bicheno, was actually Secretary of the Linnean. The following two years were to bring forth events very materially affecting the future of both the Linnean and Zoological Societies.

In 1827, a proposal was discussed to join with the Astronomical and Geological Societies in asking the Government to provide accommodation, but the matter was not followed up. In the same year Goodenough, the Bishop of Carlisle, the Nestor of the Society, died at Worthing in his eighty-fourth year and was buried in the north cloister of Westminster Abbey. Although advancing years and his duties at Carlisle had latterly removed him from direct touch with the Society, the younger generation that had been for some years controlling, not too efficiently from a business point of view, the Society's affairs regarded the venerable Bishop with wholesome respect. The name did not vanish from the Society's list with the Bishop's death, for in 1826 his son, the Rev. Edmund Goodenough, then headmaster of his father's old school, Westminster, had been elected a Fellow. Moreover, a descendant, Frederick Roger Goodenough, elected in 1964, served the Society as Treasurer from 1970 to 1975. The Society's Goodenough Fund commemorates him.

With the death of the Bishop, the President, James Smith, alone remained of the little band that had first met in February 1788, but he survived his friend of many years only a few months, dying on 17 March 1828, in his sixty-ninth year. He had been President for 40 years, a period rivalling that for which his other friend, Sir Joseph Banks, had held the Presidency of the Royal Society. The Council Minutes do not even report Smith's death, but merely mention the proposal to nominate Lord Stanley for election as his successor in May. The General Meeting held on the day after Smith's death was adjourned with the resolution: "That in consequence of the death of the respected and valued President of the Society the meeting do adjourn to Tuesday the 1st April." On the latter date, however, Lord Stanley, the Vice-President in the Chair, paid fitting tribute to the memory of the late President.

Smith's contribution to botany, notably his purchase, preservation and study of the Linnaean collections, and through his *English Flora* (1824–28), the text of *English Botany* (1790–1814) with illustrations by James Sowerby, Vols 1–6 (1806–27) of Sibthorp and Smith's *Flora Graeca* and numerous botanical articles in *Rees' Cyclopaedia*, Vols 10–39 (1808–20), was very great, even though his adherence to Linnaeus's artificial botanical classification made him vulnerable to scathing attacks by younger botanists, notably John

Lindley. However, over many years his presidential activity for the Linnean Society had been minimal.

In April 1828, the records of the Society mention for the first time the Library and Collections of Linnaeus in connection with the offer made by Smith's executors to sell them to the Society together with Smith's own collections for £5000, with conditions attached as laid down in his Will:

> I, James Edward Smith, Knight, now residing in the parish of Saint Stephen Norwich . . . leave all my collections of Natural History consisting of shells insects animal productions or other things in bottles fossils and dried plants with all the cabinets boxes or papers thereunto belonging as well as all my drawings prints manuscripts and books relating to Botany or other branches of Natural Science including not only everything that ever belonged to the great Linnaeus whether relating to Botany Zoology or any other subject all his books being marked by me in their title pages but likewise everything whether books prints or natural productions that I have added or may add thereto relating to the same subjects (except only what I may hereafter under my own handwriting order to be otherwise disposed of as well as all letters addressed to me or by me to anyone) in trust to my Executors to be disposed of all together as complete as I shall leave them at my death in one lot by sale to some publick or corporate body in this Kingdom or elsewhere in such a manner & on such conditions that the whole of these collections with the books manuscripts and other things (letters to or from me as above only excepted) shall be forever kept together without any separate sale or dispersion in future . . .

After much discussion, the Council decided to attempt to acquire the collections, but as the Society had only £190 of invested capital, which had been bequeathed by the Society for Promoting Natural History, and about £550 in cash, the Council had the tough problem of raising much more money, which it tackled along three lines. Application was made to the Treasury for a grant of £1000 in aid of the purchase; Smith's executors were held in play with a view to obtaining a reduction in the price; and a subscription list was opened in the Society. The attack along the first line, of course, failed, but the others were so successful that Smith's executors agreed in February 1829 to accept 3000 guineas, and in 1828–29 over £1260, later increased to over £1500, was subscribed by the Society's members. The difference between the price and the amount subscribed was bridged by using £500 of the cash balance of £550, and by raising between 1829 and 1831 an internal loan of £1000 in 5 per cent bonds, of which £400 were subscribed by one Fellow, William Horton Lloyd, and the remainder by six other Fellows. With an eye to the future, the admission fee was raised to £6, the annual contribution to £3 and the composition fee to £30.

Although the Society received the Linnaean and Smithian collections in 1829, payment for them was not completed until 1835, after another £500 had been raised by a second issue of bonds from 1834 to 1837. The embarrassment caused by the deflection of almost the entire cash balance of the Society in 1829 was increased in the session of 1830–31 by an abnormal expenditure on publications, and for many years thereafter the Society had to live financially from hand to mouth.

A tradition, which, without any satisfactory evidence for its accuracy, has been transformed into a statement of fact, is that the Society continued annually to elect Smith as President in the expectation or belief that, in return for forebearance regarding his absenteeism, he would bequeath the Linnaean Collections to the Society. The only evidence discovered to support this claim is a statement recorded by B. D. Jackson that Bentham had informed him (at least 40 years after Smith's death) that the Society had so acted. Bentham did not become a Fellow until after Smith's death, so his knowledge of the attitude of the Society can scarcely be said to be authoritative, however intimate he may have been with some of the Fellows prior to his election during the 32 years between Smith's return to and death at Norwich. It is quite credible that in or before 1828 some of the older Fellows may have expressed to young Bentham their hopeful expectation that Smith would bequeath the collections, but it is incredible that Smith could have given grounds for such belief during at least the last four years of his life, for his will is dated 25 June 1824. Obviously he had to make adequate provision for his wife even without anticipating that she would outlive him by 48 years: Lady Smith died in her home town, Lowestoft, in 1877, aged 103.

There is no need to attribute to the Society any motive for its perennial election of Smith as President other than the fact that he was a very distinguished and highly esteemed man, whose works were considered an honour to the Society which he had been instrumental in founding. The Society went on electing him President, just as it did his two co-founders as Treasurer and Secretary, so long as they were willing to serve. The Society probably did not trouble itself overmuch regarding Smith's absenteeism. This absenteeism, which had begun when Smith went to live at Hammersmith, became much more pronounced after his departure to Norwich. From the session of 1797–98 to the session of 1826–27, the last complete one before his death, Smith was present at only 97 General Meetings out of 434 held. Only in one session during all those years did he attend more than five times. In two sessions he was absent from all meetings, and in six sessions he attended only two. This was bad enough, but it was even worse in that it inured the Society to a figurehead President and made a precedent for Smith's successors during the 21 years after his death. His immediate successor, Lord Stanley, attended only 10 General Meetings out of 90 held during his Presidency, the Duke of Somerset only 12 out of 50 and the Bishop of Norwich only 56 out of 179 General Meetings.

The Society possesses a marble bust by Francis L. Chantrey of Smith as he was at about the age of 65, and a bust of Sir Joseph Banks, also by Chantrey. The Society has also a large portrait in oils of Smith as a considerably younger man, but when and how it came into the Society's possession is unknown. The canvas was found lying neglected in a recess in 1882 by Murie, then Librarian, and the Council ordered it to be framed. It is the portrait painted by John Rising (1756–1815) about 1795, referred to in two letters from Marsham to Smith. In the first, dated 5 February 1796, Marsham writes: "I accidentally heard a few days since that there was a Picture of you existing which the Artist was desirous to have a Print from and I likewise understood that he had proposed to offer the Picture to the Linnean Society, provided the Members would subscribe for the Print. I went immediately to see the Picture and gave in my name and Dr. Goodenough's by way of beginning and also invited Mr. Rising to the Meeting on Tuesday last when I believe he picked up several more." The second letter, dated 29 January 1797, has the following: "The Meeting in the evening [a Fellows' Meeting on 17 January 1797] was much better attended than any private one I have even seen ... After most of the Members were gone Mr. Rising brought your Picture which was admired by all who remained, all of whom gave their names as subscribers to the print to be done in Stroke by Sharp [probably William Sharp (1749–1824) a celebrated line-engraver] in the manner of John Hunter's – I hope the Man will succeed and that we may at least have the pleasure of looking at your resemblance when you are absent."

Nineteen volumes of Smith's scientific correspondence, mostly letters to him, were presented to the Society by Lady Smith in 1857, on condition that they should not be removed from the Society's rooms and that, if the Society should cease to exist or be merged in any other Society, they should be placed in the British Museum along with the

Banksian Library there. The Society published in 1934, as Part 1 of the *Catalogue of Manuscripts*, a list of them compiled by Warren R. Dawson. Extracts from part of this correspondence were printed by Pleasance Smith in her *Memoir and Correspondence of the late Sir James Edward Smith* (2 vols, 1832). Henry Stevenson of Norwich presented the Society with a portrait in oil of Lady Smith (1773–1877) from a photograph taken in 1872, when she was in her hundredth year.

With the passing of the first President there began a period of 21 years during which the three successive Presidents were more socially than scientifically exalted, but nevertheless interested in the objects of the Society.

At the Anniversary Meeting on 24 May 1828, Edward Smith Stanley (1775–1851), then known by the courtesy title of Lord Stanley, was elected the second President. He was the eldest son of the twelfth Earl of Derby and became thirteenth Earl in 1834. Primarily interested in zoology, he was from 1831 until his death in 1851 President of the Zoological Society of London and himself had a well-stocked menagerie on his estate at Knowsley near Liverpool. A finely illustrated folio work entitled *Gleanings from the Menagerie and Aviary at Knowsley Hall* with plates by Edward Lear was issued for private distribution in two parts in 1846 and 1850: during his stays at Knowsley between 1832 and 1836, Lear executed over 100 drawings for Lord Derby and entertained his grandchildren with nonsense verse. The Stanley Crane commemorates him in ornithology. His politically celebrated son, the fourteenth Earl (1799–1869), was Prime Minister three times during the 1850s and 1860s.

Chapter 4

From purchase of the Linnaean Collections to July 1858
1829 to 1858

While the possession of the Linnaean Collections restored to the Society "the peculiar propriety" of its name and added to its prestige, their acquisition directly impoverished it financially for a generation and indirectly speeded the loss of a considerable part of its scientific domain. The taxonomists consulting these collections nowadays have mostly no concept whatever of the burden the Society carried for so long in order to preserve and make them available for scientific use.

During 1828 and 1829, while the negotiations and efforts to raise money for the purchase of the collections were in progress, the Zoological Club still existed but was as shackled as when it started. In 1829, when the Society hung a financial millstone round its neck, its zoologists, whether members of the Zoological Club or not, could not fail to see that the prospect of the Society being able to help zoological research to the increasing extent desirable was now very remote. The Zoological Club itself had by 1829 got into difficulties. Towards the end of 1828 its membership numbered only 43, and the attendance at its meetings was diminishing. The Club was also running into debt, which by May 1829 exceeded £45. A special subscription had to be raised to clear this off, and an annual subscription of 10s. 6d. instituted, but all was in vain. On 24 November 1829 the Committee of the Club resolved: "That it be submitted to the Club to determine whether in consequence of the diminished attendance of the Members the Meetings shall be discontinued after the 29th Instant." At its Anniversary Meeting on 29 November 1829, the Club resolved to discontinue meetings, and to ask the Linnean Society to accept and preserve the books of the Club. In all this there is not a word about the Zoological Society, but there can be no doubt that certain members of the Club, who were also helping to manage the affairs of the Zoological Society, knew of impending developments in that society, and could therefore look with equanimity upon the dissolution of a club that had ceased to be attractive, was hard up for money and doomed to be ineffective. The Zoological Society had become in April 1829 a chartered body as "The Zoological Society of London". Bicheno, then Secretary of the Linnean, took part in the business of obtaining the Charter, together with Joseph Sabine and N. A. Vigors, named in the Charter as first Treasurer and Secretary respectively, being also Fellows of the Linnean Society, and all three members of the Zoological Club. The Zoological Society, while still adhering to its originally formulated scope, was rapidly gaining members and money; its gardens and collections of living animals gave it a much wider appeal than did a purely scientific society like the Linnean. In the circumstances, the best the zoologists could do in the interest of their science was to employ the means available in the Zoological Society.

In July 1830 the Zoological Society appointed a Committee of Science and Correspondence, and on 9 November held its first regular scientific meeting, at which Vigors and Richard Owen were the speakers. In that same year the Zoological Society started to issue its *Proceedings*.

Three years later, on 3 May 1833, some of the entomologists, whom Kirby had persuaded in 1822 to forego establishment of a new Entomological Society and form instead the Zoological Club, once more assembled, this time under the chairmanship of Vigors, who had now become an MP. At this meeting, in the rooms of J. G. Children in the British Museum, they resolved to form a new Entomological Society to be called the "Entomological Society of London", the name of the society that had faded out of active existence in 1822. At the first General Meeting, on 22 May, Kirby was elected Honorary Life President. The society, unlike its predecessors, has not merely endured but has grown in size and influence, and since 1933, its Centenary year, has been designated the Royal Entomological Society of London. Its establishment made little difference at the time to the Linnean Society, for many members were also Fellows of the Linnean, and the latter had in any case little enough left of its meagre financial resources.

Thomas Bell, in his Presidential Address to the Linnean Society on 25 May 1857, made the loose statement that the Zoological Club was transferred to the Zoological Society and formed its scientific department. Bentham, Bell's successor as President of the Linnean, in his Presidential Address on 24 May 1865 added confusion to Bell's imprecision in his remarks that "The Zoological, or, as it soon became, the Entomological Club of the Linnean Society, was first separated from us as a distinct Zoological Society with a view chiefly to establish and maintain a collection of living animals which could not come within our proper attributes; and had we been active we might have retained our connexion so as to secure the scientific business, in correspondence with but apart from the more special objects of the new establishment".

The facts are that the Zoological Club never became the Entomological Club of the Linnean Society, for there never has been such an Entomological Club. Bentham had evidently confused the Zoological Club with the Entomological Club, an entirely independent body, founded in 1826. The Zoological Club did not become the Zoological Society, which was founded three years before the Club was dissolved, nor did the Club become the scientific department of the Zoological Society. The Club, as such, was an integral part of the Linnean Society and could not be transferred to or transformed into any other society; on its dissolution its books and papers remained, and still remain, with the Linnean Society. The most that can be said is that certain men, who were Fellows of the Linnean Society, had been members of the Zoological Club of that Society and were also Fellows of the Zoological Society, helped in their last-named capacity to start the purely scientific activities of the Zoological Society.

In his Presidential Address to the Linnean Society in 1858, Bell refers to the almost suicidal act of the zoological body of the Linnean Society in organizing the scientific element of the Zoological Society. From the limited Linnean Society point of view, the action of those zoologists who were Fellows of both the Linnean Society and the Zoological Society was unfilial towards the older Society. They were faced, however, with the choice of the Society or their science, and they took the broader view that societies existed for science, not science for societies; therefore, in helping as Fellows of the Zoological Society to establish its scientific side they helped to develop their science far more than the Linnean Society in its then burdened circumstances could hope to do. Fortunately, the separation of zoology from the Linnean Society was not complete, and the Linnean is still a meeting place and its journals still form a medium of publication for both botanists and zoologists.

The remarks of Bell, Bentham and other critics after them on the inactivity of the Linnean Society at this time are not entirely to the point, for the Society could not give what it did not have and could not get. The practical moral of all this is that, in the advancement of science and of scientific societies, no less than in other mundane affairs, money counts. The zoologists knew this, and went where it could be found.

In 1829, the scientific severity of the General Meetings began to be softened by the practice of recuperating members and visitors after the meetings with tea and cake. Owing to the change of the hour of meeting from 7 o'clock to 5 o'clock, which took place in 1914, members and visitors are now fortified before entering the Meeting Room. In the present home of the Society tea at first used to be served in the East Library. It was then shifted downstairs to the small ante-rooms off the Meeting Room, and members continued to endure rather than enjoy their refreshment in these cramped quarters until 1927, when they moved upstairs again to the West Library, not without withering comments from old Dr Jackson on their inability to keep crumbs in their proper place. From 1930 tea was dispensed, as it was in the beginning, in the East Library, which was also the Council Room up to that year. More recently the West Library or Reading Room has been used for refreshments.

Before 1829, the only opportunity open to the rank and file of the Society for convivial gathering had been Anniversary Dinners, held after every Anniversary Meeting. The dinners were held without a break for 75 years, from 1789 to 1863. Up to 1794 they were held in April, and from 1795 onwards on or about 24 May. The first one was held in Old Slaughters Coffee House in St Martin's Lane. From 1790 to 1800 they took place in the Crown and Anchor Tavern in the Strand, and from 1801 to 1857 (except for 1802) in the Freemasons' Tavern, Great Queen's Street, Lincoln's Inn Fields. In 1802, 1862 and 1863 the Society dined in Willis's Rooms, King Street, St James's Square. From 1858 to 1861 the dinners were held in the Thatched House Tavern, the site of which is now partly occupied by the Conservative Club, St James's Street. Before the Society's incorporation, the dinner hour was 4 or 4.30 pm. After 1802 the hour was 5 or 5.30 pm. Up to 1802 the dinner tickets were 5s.; thereafter the price began to soar: 14s. in 1803, from 1804 to 1822 one shilling more and from 1823 onwards £1. In 1803 Goodenough complained to Smith of the exorbitant cost of the tickets. In 1848 and 1849 the Council invited all such members of the Entomological, Botanical (there existed then a Botanical Society of London of which the rejected J. E. Gray was President) and Microscopical Societies as might be disposed to attend the dinner, but later years record no repetition of this friendly gesture.

In 1862 and 1863, when the dinners were held in Willis's Rooms, not the Freemasons' Tavern as incorrectly stated both for this and previous years in B. D. Jackson's *George Bentham* (1906), the attendance was so poor that then President Bentham at the General Meeting of 5 May 1864 stated that the circulars hitherto sent out would not be issued, but if 25 members would declare their intention of dining before the next Council Meeting arrangements would be made. It is sad to relate that not even that small number appears then to have leavened the Society, for there were no more dinners after 1863 for many years, except in 1866. In that year the Botanical Congress met in London, and a special effort was made to hold a dinner, to which the principal foreign members of the Congress were invited as guests, a subscription being raised for that purpose.

A less generally known aspect of the social life of the Society is the Linnean Club. The dining club was founded in December 1811 by William George Maton (1774–1835), who, in his letter to Smith of 16 December 1811, explains his "project of forming from the more zealous and respectable members of our Society a Linnean Club . . . My views are that the Club should consist of about 15 or 20 members, who should meet once a month, on one of the days of the Society's meeting, to a frugal dinner, at some respectable tavern as near as may be to the Society's house . . . The Bishop of Carlisle says that there is a very comfortable tavern not farther off from the Society's house than Dean Street."

Although the Bishop approved of the Club he declined to become a member on the ground that, although there would be no harm in him dining in a tavern, it would not look well for the Bishop's carriage to be seen waiting outside the door! This club has continued unbroken since its foundation and its membership has always been restricted to a limited number of Fellows only. Its dinners were held up to the 1914–18 War before the ordinary meetings of the Society, and since the war after them. The President of the Society is *ex-officio* President of the Club. Although not an official body, the Linnean Club serves the Society by entertaining distinguished visitors and lecturers at meetings.

Several years after the Linnean Club had been founded some of its members, either displeased with the then scene of its "frugal dinner" or dissatisfied with its frugal character, seceded and founded a Linnean Society Club. The leading lights in this club were A. B. Lambert and H. T. Colebrooke. So much disharmony was caused through these two endeavouring to seduce the faithful of the original club that Alexander McLeay in consequence expressed his desire in a letter to Smith, dated 3 April 1820, to resign the Secretaryship of the Society. According to B. D. Jackson, in his *George Bentham*, the members of the Linnean Club were known as the "Bees" and those of the Linnean Society Club as the "Drones". The "Bees" still have their evenings of nectar and ambrosia, but the "Drones" vanished long ago, and were so utterly forgotten that when Frank Crisp was Treasurer of the Linnean Club he actually had its name printed as "Linnean Society Club".

The increase of work caused by the ever-growing Library and Museum led in 1830 to the creation of a second paid post, that of assistant in the Library and Museum, to which Richard Kippist (1812–82) was appointed at 7s. 6d. per week. He served the Society for the following 50 years.

In 1832, the Society made its first attempt to obtain accommodation from the Government in Somerset House, an attempt repeated in 1836 but to no effect. Also in 1832, the Society Secretary, J. E. Bicheno, left for Tasmania to take up his post of Colonial Secretary, and on 24 May 1832 Francis Boott (1792–1863) was elected in his place. Boott, the son of an English father and a Scottish mother, was born in Boston, Mass., USA, and, after an early education at Harvard University, came to England in his seventeenth year. He became acquainted with Banks, Brown, W. J. Hooker, J. E. Smith and other eminent men, and elected a Fellow of the Society in 1819. During 1818–20 he formed a herbarium of Massachusetts plants, which he later gave to Kew. After returning to Britain in 1820, he studied medicine at Edinburgh University, and finally settled in London in 1825, practising as a physician for some years. Inheritance of a competency enabled him to give up medical practice and devote his time to literary studies and the investigation of the genus *Carex*, which later resulted in his magnificent *Illustrations of the Genus Carex* (1858–67). He was a tall fragile-looking man, with a silvery voice and great tact and kindliness of manner. While in practice he had discarded the then professional black attire, and wore a blue coat with gilt buttons and a buff waistcoat, a costume that he continued to wear to the last. His portrait, a copy of the original by Gambardella, was presented to the Society by his widow. Later he became one of the three Fellows, Thomas Marsham and Frederick Currey being the others, in the history of the Society who have held the posts both of Secretary and Treasurer.

In 1834, Lord Stanley succeeded his father as Earl of Derby, and resigned the Presidency of the Society. He was succeeded by Edward Adolphus Seymour (1775–1855), eleventh Duke of Somerset. The third President was an amiable and accomplished nobleman with a wide interest in literature and science generally, but especially mathematics. He had been elected a Fellow in 1820 and was also a Fellow of the Royal Society and of the Society of Antiquaries. He was for some years President of the Royal Institution and took part in the formation of the Zoological Society. He held office for only three years, resigning in November 1837.

The Society had lost part of its zoological domain, and a similar loss in its botanical province threatened it. On 29 November 1836, the anniversary of John Ray's birthday, the Botanical Society of London was formed. One of its promoters and its President was that same enterprising John Edward Gray already mentioned as having been so unjustly blackballed. In 1836, he was an assistant in the Natural History Department of the British Museum, and in 1840 became Keeper of Zoology. This society did not become a serious rival to the Linnean, although it seems to have struggled on until 1857. One of its original objects was the establishment of a botanic garden, but in this it was forestalled by the institution in 1839 of the Royal Botanic Society with its garden in Regent's Park. Moreover, in 1841, the Royal Gardens at Kew were made a public botanic garden. The Botanical Society of London started to issue *Proceedings* in 1839, but only one part appears ever to have been published. It also published the first three editions of the *London Catalogue of British Plants* (1844 *et seq.*) edited by Hewett Cottrell Watson. A Minute Book of this Society, covering the period 1844–51, was presented to the Linnean Society by the Director of the Royal Botanic Gardens, Kew, in 1888.

On 2 December 1837, Edward Stanley, who had not long before been appointed Bishop of Norwich, was elected the fourth President. Edward Stanley (1779–1849) was the younger son of Sir John Thomas Stanley, Bt, of Alderley Park in Cheshire. He desired a naval career, but family influence made him accept a less exciting life, and after he had obtained his MA degree in 1805 at Cambridge, where he was a member of St John's College, his father presented him with the living of Alderley. There he lived as Rector for 32 years, until he became Bishop of Norwich. He was elected FLS in 1828 and belonged to various other societies. A man of wide culture and extensive interests, keenly interested in education, he engaged strongly in church reform. While at Alderley, natural history became one of his pursuits, particularly the habits of birds. His *Familiar History of Birds* appeared in 1835, with a second edition in 1847. He died in 1849 at Brahan Castle, near Strathpeffer, whence his body was removed for burial in Norwich Cathedral. His sons were likewise distinguished, one being the celebrated Dean Stanley and the other Captain Owen Stanley, who commanded HMS *Rattlesnake* on which T. H. Huxley was Assistant Surgeon in 1847. The Society possesses a portrait of him by J. H. Maguire, presented in 1850. His election as President was unusual in that it was not unanimous, for Aylmer Bourke Lambert (1761–1842) received three votes against 33 for the Bishop. Lambert had been a Vice-President since 1796, but by this time was 77 years old. He probably had no aspirations to the office, and probably knew nothing about the action of his three sympathizers, who scored out the Bishop's name in their voting papers and inserted Lambert's instead.

The Society had celebrated the Jubilee of George III, but the Society's own Jubilee

(a)

(b)

(c)

(d)

year, 1838, passed without the poor or the candlemakers being a penny the better. In that year, however, the Society had added its own petition to those of others wishing the Government to convert the Royal Gardens at Kew into a public botanic garden.

So far the only information given to members regarding the business and meetings of the Society was restricted to extracts from the Minutes of the General and Council Meetings, printed as appendices to the volumes of the *Transactions*, but in December 1838 the Council ordered the Secretary "to prepare and publish from time to time an abstract of the Proceedings of the Society". This innovation led later on to a regular issue of the *Proceedings*, which are dealt with in a later chapter.

In 1839, an item of historical interest was the announcement to the Society at the General Meeting of 18 June that Louisa von Linné, the third and last surviving daughter of Linnaeus, had died at Uppsala on 21 March of that year, aged 90 years. Unmarried, she was the last of Linnaeus's descendants to bear the family name Linné. At the Anniversary Meeting on 25 May 1840 John Joseph Bennet succeeded Boott as Secretary on the latter's resignation.

J. J. Bennett (1801–75) was born at Tottenham, Middlesex. After schooldays at Enfield, where he had Keats for a school-fellow, he studied medicine at Middlesex Hospital. On qualifying, he settled along with his elder brother in London, but could not have practised very long for, being interested in botany, he became associated with Robert Brown in 1827. In that year, the Banksian Herbarium and Library which Sir Joseph Banks had bequeathed in 1820 to Brown for life, along with the house in Soho Square and Dean Street, were transferred to the British Museum. Brown became the official Keeper of the Banksian Collections, and later of all the Botanical Collections, and Bennett was appointed his assistant, a position he occupied for the following 31 years until Brown's death. Bennett held this post and then became Keeper until his retirement in 1870, whereafter he lived in Sussex. He was elected FLS in 1828 and FRS in 1841. He was a quiet retiring man, apparently rather too much under the conservative influence of Brown to give the Society a much-needed stirring up. This did come during his 20 years of office, but chiefly by hands other than his. His chief botanical work is, in collaboration with Brown, *Plantae Javanicae rariores* (1838–52). The Society has a portrait of him at the age of about 62, painted by Eddis.

In 1840, Prince Albert, the Prince Consort, became an Honorary Member of the Society.

The General Meeting of 7 December 1841 was held in gloomy circumstances, for David Don, the librarian, was known to be in a room above at the point of death. He died the following day. The appointment of Clerk, Librarian and Housekeeper was in those days not at the disposal of the Council but in the hands of the Fellows. There were two candidates for the post, and this caused vastly more excitement than has ever been exhibited over the election of any Honorary Officer. One candidate was Richard Kippist (1812–82), already mentioned as having been appointed library assistant in 1830. The other was Charles Morgan Lemann, MD, FRCP (1806–52). The son of a well-known biscuit maker, he had been educated partly in England and partly in Switzerland, where he was a pupil of Pestalozzi. Later he entered Trinity College, Cambridge, where he took his MD

Plate VI   (a) George Bentham, as a young man, from a watercolour by C. Leblanc in the Society's collection. (b) Edward Stanley, Bishop of Norwich, from the engraving by W. H. Mote, 1850. (c) Joseph Hooker, from the lithograph by T. H. Maguire in the "Ipswich" series, published in 1852. (d) Thomas Bell, from a photograph in a series "Literary and Scientific Portrait Club" begun in 1854.

degree, studying also in London, Paris and Edinburgh. Under no financial compulsion to practise his profession, and being a keen botanist and a frequent visitor to southern Europe, the Canaries and Madeira, he formed an extensive herbarium, which he bequeathed to Cambridge University. He was an unassuming man, much liked by those who knew him, and in general culture much superior to Kippist. At this time he was about 35 years of age and had been a Fellow since 1831. Supporters of the rival candidates did much canvassing amongst the Fellows. Bentham heartily supported Lemann – he named the genus *Carlemannia* in his honour – and a letter signed by Bentham, Lindley, Boott, Royle, R. E. Grant, Loddiges and J. S. Henslow, the teacher of Darwin, was presented to the Council, urging it to recommend Lemann. The Council replied that it had no authority to recommend anyone. On the other hand, there was a strong feeling among the Fellows in or about London in Kippist's favour. On 15 February 1842 the ballot took place, and Kippist won by 87 votes against 69 for Lemann. The figures show that the Meeting Room on that evening must have been crammed almost to the point of suffocation. Kippist proved a faithful servant of the Society and contributed botanical papers to its publications. He was elected an Associate in April 1842.

In November 1845, the Council applied to the Government for accommodation in the rooms then occupied in Somerset House by the University of London, should those rooms become vacant. The application was rejected, first because the University of London, far from wishing to quit their rooms, wanted more; secondly, because the Geographical Society had submitted a prior claim, which had considerable weight on the grounds that the Geographical Society had not only suggested expeditions, but had in many cases contributed towards them. The latter reason threw light upon the mentality of the Government Department concerned. At the time, the financial condition of the Society was deplorable, but in any case its statutes did not allow it to contribute towards the cost of expeditions. So the remarks regarding the Geographical Society were as irrelevant as they were unconsciously ironical.

In 1846, a proposal for the institution of a Linnean Gold Medal came before the Council. Edward Rudge (1763–1846), already mentioned as having been appointed a Fellow in 1802, was a man of independent means, both a botanist and an antiquary. To botanists he is known primarily as the author of the folio volume of *Plantarum Guianae rariorum Icones et Descriptiones* (1805–6). He bequeathed £200 to the Society for investment in 3 per cent Consolidated Bank Annuities, the dividend to be used in purchasing a gold medal to be called The Linnean Medal, for award to the Fellow writing the best communication in each volume of the *Transactions* in any of the four departments of Natural History. The medal was to have on one side the profile bust of Linnaeus in full dress, with name and dates of birth and death, and on the other the name of the Fellow encircled by a wreath of *Linnaea borealis*. The Society disclaimed the bequest for the following cogent reasons: the medal would offer no inducement to some of those who had contributed to the *Transactions*, and might deter them from submitting future contributions to such an ordeal; it would probably not stimulate the production of more valuable essays from any other class of the Society; dissatisfaction would probably arise in the minds of some Fellows who, after contributing to more than one volume of the *Transactions*, should fail to be awarded the medal; there was no discretionary power of withholding the medal, which had to be awarded to the best paper in every volume, and so to papers of very unequal value, thereby lowering the character of the medal and affecting the scientific reputation of the Society; dissatisfaction was likely to arise in deciding upon the comparative merits of papers in Botany and Zoology; and there was the not improbable likelihood of the award of the medal by the Council to one of its own body in strict conformity with the conditions of the bequest. Thus the Society wisely avoided potentially embarrassing situations.

In 1847, the Society again applied to the Government for accommodation, this time in the broad terms of "in some public building", but the latitude of the request did not affect the customary refusal.

In February 1849, Edward Forster (1975–1849), who had been Treasurer for almost 33 years, the longest period of any Treasurer, died in his eighty-fourth year and, on 24 May, William Yarrell succeeded him. William Yarrell (1784–1856) was the son of one of the partners in a newspaper agency in Duke Street, off Piccadilly and opposite the present home of the Society. After a schooling at Ealing he became a clerk in the banking firm of Herries, Farquhar and Co., who were the Society's bankers, and in a sense still are, for they were amalgamated with Lloyds Bank, the Society's present bankers, in 1893. Yarrell soon left the bank to join his cousin in the newspaper agency that had belonged to their fathers. The business was transferred to the corner of Bury Street and Little Ryder Street, and in this locality he spent the rest of his life. Outside his business, Yarrell was a keen fisherman and excellent shot. At first chemistry and zoology divided his scientific interests, but the latter soon became his favourite pursuit. Birds and fish were his chief study. He was the author of a long series of papers in the Linnean *Transactions* and other publications. He also wrote *A History of British Fishes* (1836) and *A History of British Birds* (1843), which were so popular as to earn him over £4000. A robust, straightforward, unpretentious man of simple character and even temper, his qualities made him highly appreciated. He was elected FLS in 1825. He was one of the original members of the Zoological Society, and its Secretary from 1836 to 1838. In the index to the Centenary History of that Society he appears by a slip as the Rev. William Yarrell. He was also one of the founders of the Entomological Society of London in 1833, and its Treasurer from 1834 to 1852. His portrait by Mrs Carpenter is in the Society's collection. The monument to Yarrell in St James's Church, Piccadilly, is fittingly decorated with two swans, for he distinguished and named Bewick's Swan, *Cygnus columbianus bewickii* (Yarrell).

In July 1849, the Council resolved to apply to the Government for the house in Craig's Court, off Whitehall, about to be vacated by the Museum of Economic Geology, but either the resolution was not carried out or it had no effect, for in December another resolution was passed to confer with the Royal Geographical Society on the subject of a joint application to the Government for accommodation for the two Societies. The Council had clearly not much hope of speedy help from Government, for at the same time it discussed the renewal of the lease of No. 32 Soho Square.

The President, the Bishop of Norwich, died on 6 September 1849 and with him the succession of more or less figurehead Presidents came to an end. Apart from the special case of the first President, his successors had multitudinous calls on their time, and they could not be regularly present at either Council or General Meetings. At the Council Meetings during the times of Lord Stanley and the Duke of Somerset the Chair was most frequently taken by A. B. Lambert and in the Bishop's time by Robert Brown.

On 4 December 1849 Robert Brown (1773–1858), now aged 76, was elected the fifth President. The second son of the Rev. James Brown, Episcopalian Minister at Montrose, he inherited his father's intellectual honesty and sturdiness of character. After attending a local grammar school he entered Marischal College, Aberdeen, in 1787, where he studied for two years. He then went with his father to Edinburgh, where he continued his medical training. While there he was a member of the Natural History Society, though whether this was the one of which J. E. Smith was first President, while a medical student in Edinburgh, is uncertain. To this Society Brown, at the age of 18, read his first botanical paper. In 1795, he was commissioned as Ensign and Assistant-Surgeon to the Fifeshire Fencibles, and went with his regiment to the north of Ireland. His medical duties being light, he devoted his time to learning the German language and studying plants. In 1797, he was sent across to England on recruiting duty. This service allowed him to spend some time in 1798 and 1799 in London, where he was introduced to Sir Joseph Banks, ever an astute judge of men, and the zeal, knowledge and talent of this obscure young Scot much impressed that great influential patron of science. In 1798 he was elected ALS. In 1799, he returned to his regiment in Ireland but an offer from Banks of the post of naturalist with the expedition of Matthew Flinders to survey the coast of Australia (then thought to consist possibly of two islands, New Holland and New South Wales) led Brown to leave Ireland and military service for good in December 1800. Flinders's ship *Investigator* left England in July 1801. Brown and the artist Ferdinand Bauer returned in October 1805 with a harvest of specimens of nearly 4000 species of plants as well as zoological material and Bauer's superb drawings. In 1806, Brown became the Linnean Society's "Clerk, Librarian and Housekeeper", but this post did not impede his scientific work. In January 1809, he read a very important paper, "On the Proteaceae of Jussieu", a difficult family of plants he had studied in life both at the Cape of Good Hope and in Australia. R. A. Salisbury was present at the meeting. In August 1809 the issue of a book on Proteaceae by a gardener, Joseph Knight, much of it undoubtedly contributed by Salisbury, deprived Brown of priority of publication. The *Transactions*, Vol. 10, containing Brown's paper did not appear until February 1810. Resentment at Salisbury's sharp practice, "Salisbury's surreptitious anticipation of Brown's paper on the New Holland plants, under the name and disguise of Mr. Hibbert's gardener", as Goodenough described it in a letter to Smith in December 1809, led many Fellows of the Society to ostracize him. Unfortunately, as mentioned earlier, it contributed to the rejection of J. E. Gray in 1822. Brown, on the contrary, grew in esteem as the publication of a series of papers, together with his *Prodromus Florae Novae Hollandiae* (1910), notable for profound original observations, made him known as the most illustrious botanist of his time. Banks bequeathed to him a life interest in the Banksian library and collections (ultimately destined for the British Museum) of which he had become curator in 1810, on the death of Dryander, without relinquishing his Linnean post. Banks's bequest to Brown in 1820 also included the lease of his house in Soho Square, which became for some years the home of the Society. Brown soon thereafter resigned the post of Librarian to the Society and was elected FLS in December 1822. He continued to take an active part in the Society's affairs; he was indeed never so happy as when in the congenial company the Society provided. His presidency extended from 4 December 1849 to 24 May 1853; he died on 10 June 1858.

In 1850, the Council agreed to renew from the Trustees for the Glossop Estate the lease of the premises in Soho Square and Dean Street, in short the whole block, from Michaelmas 1851, on the expiry of the lease which Brown had inherited from Sir Joseph Banks, for seven, 14 or 21 years at a rent of £200 and also to pay all taxes. Brown still occupied the Dean Street part of the building and this the Society sub-leased to Brown at £80 rent, also allowing him the use of five rooms in the Soho Square part.

So far the Society had played a lone hand in its attempts to gain the help of the Government, but henceforth it had support from an influential ally. In 1852, certain Fellows of the Royal Society submitted to its President, the Earl of Ross, a memorandum urging the propriety of asking the Government to accommodate the five chartered scientific Societies, the Royal, Linnean, Geological, Astronomical and Chemical, under one roof, leaving to each society the conduct of its own affairs, and each society's library remaining distinct. The Council of the Royal Society discussed this proposal at a meeting which the Presidents of the four other societies also attended. It was resolved that those Presidents should ascertain the views of their respective Societies. Meanwhile it had been rumoured that the Government had purchased land at Kensington Gore on which to build a house for the scientific Societies. They considered this site to be very unsuitable, but nothing more was heard of it, and for two years nothing more was done.

In 1853, Brown resigned office, and Thomas Bell, then Professor of Zoology at King's College, London, was elected the sixth President. Brown, living in the Society's house, could not fail to be more attentive to his strictly official duties than his predecessors, but he was too old, being 80 at the time of his resignation, to infuse some much more needed life into the Society, and in Bentham's words he "rather fell asleep". His successor, on the other hand, was one of the most stimulating Presidents the Society has ever had. Thomas Bell (1792–1880) was the only son of Thomas Bell, surgeon, and was born at Poole, Dorset. After medical training at Guy's and St Thomas's Hospitals he qualified as MRCS (Royal College of Surgeons) in 1815, and was elected FLS in the same year. In 1817 he became dental surgeon at Guy's Hospital, a post he held for 44 years. For many years he was the only surgeon who brought scientific surgery to bear upon dental disease. He was early interested in natural history, more particularly zoology, and for some years was lecturer on comparative anatomy at Guy's Hospital. In 1836 he became Professor of Zoology at King's College, London. One of the early members of the Zoological Club, after its dissolution in 1829, he became a member of the original Committee of Science and Correspondence of the Zoological Society of London, which in 1830 started the purely scientific activities of that Society; and for 11 years he served as a Vice-President. This did not in the least embarrass him when, as President of the Linnean, he referred in the course of several Presidential Addresses on the setting up and continuance of the scientific activities of the Zoological Society and on the apathy of the Linnean Society in making no attempt to retain those activities. He was President of the Ray Society from its foundation in 1843 for 16 years, and one of the Secretaries of the Royal Society (to which he had been elected in 1828) from 1848 to 1853. His special zoological interests were concerned with chelonia, crustacea and reptilia, but he also wrote *A History of British Quadrupeds* (1837). He was an excellent administrator and had very attractive personal qualities. According to the *Dictionary of National Biography*, "he was more at home in his study than in the field, and he made few original contributions of special value to zoology". When about 70 he retired from practice to live in Gilbert White's old house, "The Wakes" at Selborne, which he occupied until his death in 1880, producing in 1877 the standard edition of White's *Natural History of Selbourne*. He was very keen to resuscitate the Society, but his good nature caused him considerable difficulty in dealing with the resistant Brown, who combated every new proposal. Fortunately, Bell had Bentham and J. D. Hooker to stiffen his resolution, and reforms were accomplished. The Society possesses his portrait by H. W. Pickersgill, RA, presented by the Linnean Club in 1862. During his presidency, in 1856, the Society began publication of the octavo *Journal of Proceedings*, a more convenient medium for scientific papers than the quarto *Transactions*.

In 1854, the Government purchased Burlington House in Piccadilly from the Cavendish family for accommodating the scientific societies. The architect of the first Burlington House, built in 1665, was Sir John Denham, the Surveyor of Royal Palaces, and also a poet. If not expressly built for him, it was certainly soon after erection occupied by Richard Boyle (1612–97), second Earl of Cork. He was for a time Lord-Lieutenant of the West Riding of Yorkshire, and when he was created the first Earl of Burlington in England he took his title from the borough of Bridlington or Burlington in the East Riding, hence the name of the house. One of his younger brothers was Robert Boyle (1629–91), the famous natural philosopher and a member of the first Council of the Royal Society on its incorporation. The original Burlington House consisted of a central block with two wings extending southwards at right angles to it. A print dated about 1700 in the Linnean Society's Library shows a perspective view of it.

In the following century, the third and last Earl of this creation, Richard Boyle III (1695–1753) (the title was revived in the nineteenth century for the Cavendish family), a very accomplished nobleman, skilled in architecture, the friend of Pope, Swift, Gay and Handel, considerably altered the house. He built a new front, the lower part of which still forms the lower half of the façade of the Royal Academy of Arts, and also erected a semicircular colonnade to sweep across the front of the extensive courtyard facing Piccadilly. The house and grounds occupied a rectangular area of about eight acres, the long axis of the parallelogram running northwards from Piccadilly, with an extensive garden behind or to the north of the house and a high brick wall enclosing the whole site.

The third Earl's daughter and only child became the wife of the Marquess of Hartington and, on her father's death in 1753, Burlington House came into the possession of the Cavendish family. According to a writer in *The Building News* of 29 July 1866, Lord George Cavendish purchased the house from his nephew, the Duke of Devonshire, in 1815 for £75 000, and in 1818 he cut off a strip along the western boundary for the erection of Burlington Arcade. This covered shopway was built, according to a writer in the *Gentleman's Magazine*, "for the gratification of the publick and to give employment to industrious females", but what gave birth to the idea, according to the same writer, was the annoyance caused by "the inhabitants of a neighbouring street throwing oyster shells etc. over the walls". Later, the making of the street called Burlington Gardens cut off another strip along the northern boundary. In 1854, when the Government purchased the house and grounds for £140 000 – the figure stated by a writer in *Chambers Journal* for 1857 – they were still hidden on all sides by brick walls, three prison-like gates piercing the Piccadilly wall. The garden behind the house then consisted of broad grass plots in the centre, surrounded on three sides by a terrace bordered by a double row of elms. The Museum of Mankind now occupies this area.

In November 1854, the Linnean Council laid claims for accommodation of the Society before Lord Aberdeen, then Prime Minister and a Fellow of the Society. Lord Aberdeen assured the Society's representatives of his concurrence in its object and he acknowledged the justice of its claims. In the following year a deputation, evidently representing the five societies, submitted their case to Lord Palmerston, who had succeeded Lord Aberdeen as Prime Minister. He also politely concurred with the general principle of the deputation's argument, but gave no definite pledge. Still, the outlook began to be more hopeful.

The Linnean Society, however, had to reckon with the Treasury, which, with its characteristic narrowness from which the British Museum also suffered, at first refused to recognize the claims for accommodation in Burlington House of any society other than those already lodged in Somerset House. All the Treasury then wanted were the rooms in that house occupied by the Royal, Geological, Astronomical and the Antiquaries Societies. Meanwhile, according to Bell in his Presidential Address to the Linnean Society in 1856, the Royal Society, on whose help the other scientific Societies depended, failed to press their claims with sufficient energy. The University of London, which was being squeezed out of Somerset House to make room for the Registrar-General, stepped in and secured the eastern wing of Burlington House. This left room for only three of the five scientific Societies concerned. Whether Bell's reflection on the inactivity of the Royal Society was well-founded or otherwise, that Society soon thereafter made a strong representation to Government on behalf of all five societies. This resulted in representatives of the four societies in Somerset House being summoned to meet the Secretary of the Treasury, who, to their astonishment, informed them that the Government did not wish to turn any of the societies out of Somerset House, and they could still remain there if they preferred to do so. Accordingly the Society of Antiquaries, the Geological and the Astronomical Societies elected to remain in Somerset House, while the Royal Society chose to remove to Burlington House. This left only the Linnean and Chemical Societies to be accommodated. The Royal Society, having first ascertained that the other two societies would be glad to accept rooms with the Royal in Burlington House, then submitted proposals for the accommodation of the three societies, and this time the Treasury capitulated. The terms of accommodation were laid down in the Treasury's letter of 22 May 1856 addressed to the President of the Royal Society. The accommodation was described as temporary, and it was laid down that a common library was to be formed for the use of the three societies, men of letters and science being admissible to consult the library on orders given by Fellows of the three societies. The societies were to be allowed the use of a hall to be constructed in the west wing of Burlington House, when it was not required by the University of London. The portraits in the possession of the Royal Society were to be hung in this hall, and open to public inspection.

The President of the Royal Society sent the Treasury letter to Bell in time for him to read it at the Anniversary Meeting of the Linnean on 24 May, and one can imagine how pleased the assembled members were at the news. Bell was able to explain that by "temporary" was meant that the accommodation now granted was merely until ample room was provided in the new buildings contemplated, and that the ownership and custody of the respective societies' libraries would not be altered, and the loan of books would be confined to members of the society that owned them.

In June 1856, a subscription was opened within the Society to meet the cost – estimated at £800 – of removal from Soho Square, fitting up the new quarters, and repairing the old ones before the expiration in 1858 of the first seven years of the lease of 32 Soho Square. Over £1100 was subscribed.

On 21 July 1856, the Council met for the first time in Burlington House to inspect the rooms allocated to the Society, but does not appear to have met there again until 17 February 1857, when it decided the uses of the different rooms.

The Society's new rooms were in the central block of Burlington House, the entrance hall being common to the three societies, as well as the old servants' hall which served as a kitchen for all three. The rooms exclusively Linnean were: in the basement, the old wine cellar; on the ground floor, two front rooms to the east of the entrance hall, the one next to the hall holding the Society's principal botanical collections and called the Herbarium Room, the other the Council Room, which was also used as the council room of the Chemical Society, to which it had originally been allocated; on the first floor, two rooms, the Meeting Room, which has since been displaced by the stairway leading to the Diploma Gallery of the Royal Academy and the Library, the latter being the old great ballroom; on the second floor, eight rooms, of which three were occupied by the Librarian and three by the Porter, one, the northwest attic, contained miscellaneous collections and

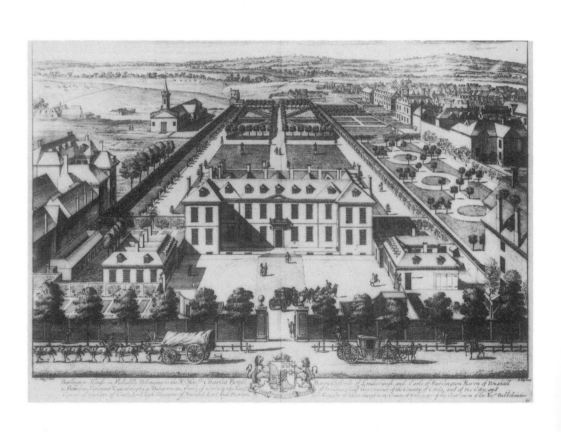

was known as the Upper Museum, and one, the southeast attic, held part of the stock of *Transactions* and was called the Transaction Room. Above those eight rooms were extensive dry lofts, used as store rooms. The Linnaean Library and Collections were placed at the north end of the great ballroom or General Library in new mahogany cases. The Council Room held 30 cases of Australian birds and quadrupeds.

The library and museum in Soho Square were closed on 1 April 1857, and by May part of them had been transferred to Burlington House. The first General Meeting in Burlington House was the Anniversary Meeting on Monday, 25 May 1857, not on Tuesday, 2 June, as incorrectly stated by Bentham at the General Meeting of 6 November 1873.

The Society still had the Soho Square house on its hands, but in July an agreement was made with the Glossop Trustees (from whom, not from Brown, as stated in Jackson's *George Bentham*, the Society had leased the property in 1851) whereby the Society gave up possession in August 1857, the Society being liable for the rent up to the expiry of the lease in 1858, but the Trustees allowing the Society any rent that they might obtain during that period. Brown, who was the sub-lessee of the Society for 17 Dean Street, acquiesced in the arrangement, subject to conditions agreed upon between himself and the Trustees for his continuing to occupy part of the premises. The Society had to pay £300 for dilapidations.

During those three years of suspense and transition Bell, ably supported by such men as Bentham and J. D. Hooker, was energetically rejuvenating the Society and striving to strengthen and extend its influence. At his first Anniversary Meeting as President in 1854 he introduced the practice of giving a Presidential Address, the first since Smith's Introductory Address delivered at the first General Meeting on 8 April 1788. Bell's Addresses, which are printed in the Society's *Proceedings*, are very interesting and informative, both as to the state of the Society and the development of botanical and zoological research during the years (1853–61) of his Presidency. He also started the discussion of papers read at the General Meetings. This was not done without some shaking of elderly heads or, as Bell himself expressed it in his Presidential Address in 1860, when he recalled the good produced by this innovation, "there were some of our most distinguished members whose intense conservatism led them to anticipate the ruin of the Society or that its meeting-room would become the arena of almost gladiatorial combats of rival intellects".

In 1854, the financial condition of the Society came under review; in 1856, the *Journal* of the Society was started, also not without opposition; in 1856, the Linnaean Library and Collections were examined and their much-needed better preservation secured. These activities are merely mentioned here, as they are discussed in later chapters.

Charles Robert Darwin (1809–82), who had been proposed as a Fellow on 20 December 1853, was elected on 7 March 1854 and admitted on 2 May 1854, the most illustrious member on the roll of the Society. Bell, in his first Presidential Address, spoke more prophetically then he knew, when he congratulated the Society on the accession to its list of one honoured name of whom the Society might well be proud.

William Yarrell, the Treasurer, died on 1 September 1856, and was succeeded on 4 November by Francis Boott, who had been Secretary from 1832 to 1840. Hitherto there had been only one Secretary, assisted by an Under-Secretary, but it was now recognized that two Secretaries, one for Botany and one for Zoology, were necessary, and that the simplest plan was to abolish the Under-Secretaryship and replace it by a Secretaryship.

Plate VII   Burlington House in the 17th Century.

(b)

(a)

This could not be done immediately, as an alteration in the Bye-Laws to authorize the change had first to be considered and confirmed by the Fellows, and Richard Taylor was still Under-Secretary. Taylor, who had held office since 1810, was then 75 and in feeble health. He resigned in 1857, but the Bye-Laws still stood in the way, so George Busk (1807–86), a distinguished surgeon, was elected to succeed him, with the designation "Under- (Zoological) Secretary" to indicate that, although still nominally Under-Secretary until the Bye-Laws were altered, he was to perform the duties of a Zoological Secretary, J. J. Bennett, the Secretary, being a botanist.

The day of the first General Meeting of the Society, 8 April 1788, was a Tuesday, and since then the ordinary meetings had been held on that day of the week. With the three societies now in the same house it was considered desirable that the members of all three should have the opportunity of taking tea and talking together after their respective meetings. To enable this, the Royal Society proposed early in 1857 that the Linnean should change its meeting days to the first and third Thursdays of every month, these being two of the days on which the Royal met. The President of the Royal Society agreed to arrange that papers likely to be of interest to those who were Fellows of both societies should not be read at the Royal Society on meeting days of the Linnean. This proposal was accepted by the Linnean to come into force at the beginning of the session of 1857–58. The first ordinary meeting on a Thursday took place on 5 November 1857, and the ordinary meetings have continued to be held on a Thursday ever since, except one held on Tuesday, 4 December 1877, and another on Tuesday, 4 June 1878, although the original reason for the change has ceased to operate long ago. The Royal Society arranged for the refreshments, the Linnean paying its share of the expenses in a lump sum every session.

In August 1857, the American Association for the Advancement of Science held its first meeting on British soil at Montreal. The Association invited the Linnean Society to be represented at the gathering, and backed up its invitation by placing at the disposal of the Society one of two free passages to America offered by the Cunard Company. Berthold Carl Seemann (1825–71) represented the Society, travelling to New York in the *Persia*, an iron paddle-steamer, built in 1856, and then the fastest vessel afloat. The voyage took 11 days. There is an interesting account of Seemann's trip, which lasted 59 days, in the Society's *Proceedings* for 1857–58. This account notes that the Linnean and the Geological societies were the only two of the scientific bodies in Europe invited to the meeting that had actually sent representatives.

Robert Brown died on 10 June 1858 and, as a tribute of respect to the great botanist and former President, the meeting of 17 June, which ordinarily would have been the last meeting of the session of 1857–58, was adjourned after formal business, without any papers being read. As Brown was a member of Council at the time of his death, a new member had to be elected within three months, and rather than call a special meeting of the Society during the September recess, when the attendance was likely to be very small, the Council decided to prolong the session of 1857–58 by an extra meeting on Thursday, 1 July, making the very unusual number of 16 meetings for the session. At this meeting the papers that had been postponed on 17 June were to be read, as well as a new Councillor elected. Historically, this delayed meeting proved to be the most epoch-making meeting of the nineteenth century, for here Darwin and Wallace made known to the scientific

Plate VIII   (a) Charles Darwin, from the lithograph by T. H. Maguire in the "Ipswich" series, published in 1852. (b) Alfred Russell Wallace, from the photograph in the Society's collection, dated 1895.

world their theory of evolution by means of natural selection. Neither, however, was present: Darwin was unwell and grief-stricken by the death of a child; Wallace was far away in the Moluccas.

On 18 June 1858, Darwin received at Down, Kent, a letter with an enclosure written at Ternate in February 1858 by Alfred Russel Wallace (1823–1913). The enclosure was a short essay, "On the Tendency of Varieties to depart indefinitely from the Original Type", in which Wallace expounded essentially the same hypothesis on the origin of species that Darwin had sketched as early as 1842 and, on the advice of Sir Charles Lyell, the celebrated geologist, had begun to expand in 1856. In accordance with Wallace's request, Darwin sent the essay to Lyell. He also informed J. D. Hooker of what had happened. As both Hooker and Lyell had been acquainted since 1844 with Darwin's views, and the former had actually read his manuscript in that year, they together persuaded Darwin to forsake his original unselfish intention of arranging for the publication of Wallace's essay without publishing his own long-withheld manuscript. It was, however, almost the end of June before Darwin consented to leave the matter in the hands of Hooker and Lyell and permitted them to communicate his own and Wallace's papers to the Linnean Society at the same time. To avoid delay, Hooker and Lyell determined to present the papers at the extra meeting of the session, and they were just in time to do so. Their joint letter to J. J. Bennett, the Secretary, together with the papers, was sent out on 30 June. The papers were entitled as follows:

(I)   Extracts from the second chapter headed "On the Variation of Organic Beings in a State of Nature; on the Natural Means of Selection; on the Comparison of Domestic Races and true Species" of the first part of a MS. work on Species by Mr. Darwin, which was sketched in 1839 (the correct date was 1842) and copied in 1844.

(II) Abstract of a letter from C. Darwin Esq. to Prof. Asa Gray, Boston, U.S. dated Down, September 5th 1857.

(III) "On the Tendency of Varieties to depart indefinitely from the Original Type", by Alfred Russel Wallace.

In those days members did not receive in advance the agenda of the meetings and the titles of papers to be read, but even if that had been the custom there would have been no time to inform them about the Darwin–Wallace papers, as they were sent to the Secretary only the day before the meeting. Hooker stated at the Jubilee celebration of the event held on 1 July 1908 that "no fourth individual [beyond Darwin, Lyell and himself] had any cognisance of our proceedings". They must therefore have come as a surprise item to almost all the members who attended the meeting. Although fewer than 30 Fellows, and only one Associate and two visitors, are named in the Minutes as being present, there were almost certainly more, for the names do not include any of the officers except the President, and after the names occur the words "etc., etc.". By 1858 the old practice of having papers read by a specially nominated Fellow, known as the "Reader", had ceased and they were read by the Secretary. After the formal business of recording gifts to the Library, electing Bentham as a Councillor and nominating him as a Vice-President in place of Brown, and after the passing of a resolution recording the meeting's appreciation of Brown's great services, the papers were read, the Darwin–Wallace papers coming first, followed by five of the six papers that had been postponed from the meeting of 17 June dealing with the organization of *Phoronis hippocrepis*, observations on *Ammocaetus*, a new genus of *Cucurbitales*, a new genus named *Hanburia*, the *Nueva Quinologia* of Pavon and the vegetation of Angola. The sixth paper was Bentham's, mentioned below.

As already mentioned, Darwin could not attend the meeting, as he was not only ill himself but an infant son had very recently died of scarlet fever and a daughter was ill with diphtheria. Hooker gives the following account of the meeting, written 28 years later, in his letter of 22 October 1886 to Francis Darwin (*Life and letters of Sir J. D. Hooker* by L. Huxley, 2: 300):

> I was present with Lyell at the meeting. We both I think said something impressing the necessity of profound attention (on the part of Naturalists) to papers and their bearing on the future of Nat. Hist. etc., etc., etc., but there was no semblance of discussion. The interest excited was intense, but the subject too novel and too ominous for the old School to enter the lists before armouring. It was talked over after the meeting, "with bated breath". Lyell's approval, and perhaps in a small way mine, as his Lieutenant in the affair, rather overawed those Fellows who would otherwise have flown out against doctrine, and this because we had the vantage ground of being familiar with the authors and their themes. Bell the President, in the Chair, was, though a personal friend of your father's, hostile to the end of his life. Busk, who was present as Secretary [Busk was actually Under- (Zoological) Secretary], said nothing, nor did Bennett, the Bot. Sec. [Bennett was sole Secretary]. Bentham was also there, and silent. I do not remember Huxley being present, you might ask him. [He was not; indeed he was first elected in December 1858.]

In the above statement Hooker, made with hindsight of the importance of the occasion, mentions one possible reason for the lack of discussion, but others can be suggested. Beyond Bell and Bentham few, if any, eminent naturalists of the old school were present. With five, originally six, papers to follow the Darwin–Wallace ones there would have been very little time for adequate discussion. Bell neither made nor called for remarks, and Bentham has indicated that Bell would not have allowed anyone else to initiate a discussion of the startling hypothesis so unexpectedly presented and thereby prolong an already long meeting.

Bentham, in his Presidential Address in 1862, remarked: "I do not refer to those speculations on the origin of species, which have excited so much controversy: for the discussion of that question, when considered only with reference to the comparative plausibility of opposite hypotheses, is beyond the province of our Society. Attempts to bring it forward at our meetings were very judiciously checked by my predecessor [Bell] in this Chair, and I should certainly be sorry to see our time taken up by theoretical arguments not accompanied by the disclosure of new facts of observations."

With Bell's attitude thus seemingly pontifical, it was perhaps just as well that Hooker and Lyell were delayed until the eleventh hour in sending in those fearful papers.

The hearing of the papers so perturbed Bentham at the meeting that, as related in his letter of 30 May 1882 to Francis Darwin (*Life and Letters of Charles Darwin*, 2: 293), he withdrew forthwith unread a paper which he had prepared in connection with his work on the British flora, supporting the idea of fixity of species.

Bell had apparently little or no idea that he was presiding over the start of a revolution in ideas of life in general, and of human life in particular, for in his Presidential Address in May 1859, when reviewing the period from May 1858, he made the following remarks, which now read strangely:

> The year which has passed . . . has not, indeed, been marked by any of those striking discoveries which at once revolutionize, so to speak, the department of science on which they bear; it is only at remote intervals that we can reasonably expect any sudden and brilliant innovation which shall produce a marked and permanent impress on the character of any branch of knowledge, or confer a lasting and important service on mankind. A Bacon or a Newton, an Oersted or a Wheatstone, a Davy or a Daguerre, is an occasional phenomenon, whose existence and career seem to be specially appointed by Providence, for the purpose of effecting some great important change in the conditions or pursuits of man.

These unappreciative remarks have so often been quoted against Bell and are almost the only ones of his which ever are quoted that it is only fair to recall his forgotten but valuable services to the Linnean and other learned societies, to British zoology and dental surgery, and his competence as a naturalist. Indeed, the communications of Darwin and Wallace printed in the Linnean Society's *Journal of Proceedings*, 3: 45–62 (20 August 1858), within two months of being submitted would not have been made so rapidly available to the public but for the far-sighted action of Bell in promoting the founding of the journal.

The small gathering at the Linnean Society on 1 July 1858, which had felt the first brief blast of the coming storm, must have dispersed, after the most momentous meeting in the life of this or any other society, all probably tired, some bored and others with thoughts perplexed and feelings deeply stirred if they realized its far-reaching significance. The orthodox might well have thought, as expressed in the words of Salisbury to King John, that

> In this the antique and well noted face
> Of plain old form is much disfigured.
> (*King John*, iv.2.21)

Nevertheless, as stated by J. W. T. Moody in *Journ. Soc. Bibl. Nat. Hist.*, 5: 475 (1971):

> it would appear, however, that the sheer volume of contributions practically buried the Darwin–Wallace papers. The fellows were not so much stunned by new ideas as they were overwhelmed by the amount of information loaded upon them at the meeting. Much of the Darwin–Wallace concept of natural selection went over their heads. This was in large measure the result of insufficient time to concentrate attention and discussion upon the Darwin–Wallace papers. The actual event seems to be second only to the presentation of Mendel's discovery of the laws of genetics as an historical "non-event". In both instances only later publication made evident the significance of these momentous occasions.

This meeting took place in the Society's old rooms within the building now entirely occupied by the Royal Academy. The Society did not move into its present accommodation until 1874, i.e. 16 years later.

Chapter 5

From 1858 to the Centenary
1858 to 1888

After the historic meeting on 1 July 1858, Darwin began to write what he called an "Abstract" of his hypothesis, with the intention of presenting it to the Society as a paper or series of papers, but towards the end of the year he concluded that the "Abstract" would have to be issued as a book independently of the Society. John Murray published it in 1859 with the title *On the Origin of Species by Means of Natural Selection, or the Preservation of Favoured Races in the Struggle for Life*. When one considers the storm of "misrepresentation, ridicule and denunciation", to quote T. H. Huxley's words, which the book aroused, it was probably well for the peace of the Society that Darwin did not carry out his original intention. In the Society's obituary notice of Darwin (*Proc.* 1880–82: 61) it is stated that "The Origin of the Species, when published in the following year, led to memorable debate. Several Fellows withdrew from the Linnean Society because the President refused to take steps to eject the author". The "memorable debate" probably refers to the one held at the Oxford meeting of the British Association in 1860 (for no debate was permitted in the Society) at which Huxley and Hooker dealt so devastatingly with what Huxley described as "the round-mouthed oily special pleading" of the Bishop of Oxford's attack on Darwin's *Origin of Species*.

In July 1858, the Society appointed a committee to revise the Bye-Laws as the first step towards the creation of the additional Secretaryship. After an incubation of over two years, the revision was completed and then confirmed by the Fellows in February 1861. Meanwhile, in 1860 J. J. Bennett resigned the sole Secretaryship, which he had held since 1840, and was succeeded by George Busk, who had been Under- (Zoological) Secretary since 1857. Busk was replaced in the Under-Secretaryship by Frederick Currey, thereupon designated Under- (Botanical) Secretary. So in the one case a zoologist succeeded a botanist, and in the other a botanist succeeded a zoologist. At the Anniversary Meeting in 1861 both Bell, the President, and Boott, the Treasurer, resigned; the two Secretaryships came into being and the Under-Secretaryship disappeared. George Bentham (1800–84) was elected seventh President, William Wilson Saunders sixth Treasurer, George Busk first Zoological Secretary and Frederick Currey first Botanical Secretary.

Bell had been President for eight eventful years. The reform of the Society's internal activities carried out during this period has already been mentioned, but Bell also much concerned himself with proposals for extending the Society's influence beyond its own members. Thus he suggested that the utility of natural history collections in local museums might be extended outside their local bounds by the Society publishing notes regarding their new acquisitions, observations by naturalists attached to such museums, and suitable papers read before such local societies as had no publications of their own.

What he considered the relative deficiency of zoological papers presented to the Society in his time troubled Bell, and he dealt with this subject in more than one Presidential Address. In 1858 he attributed the deficiency chiefly to the existence of what he called "minor societies", by which he meant more particularly the Entomological, the Microscopical and the Zoological Societies. He argued that the separate working of each of those bodies was at an expense that would be greatly lessened if their powers were concentrated "in one great machine ... In Botanical Science this distribution of the means of recording discovery has not been thought necessary, and it would certainly appear strange if we hear of the formation of a Ranunculaceous Society as distinguished from Liliaceous, or even a Cryptogamic as independent of and antagonistic to a Phanerogamic Society".

Bell suggested as a possible remedy for the conditions which distressed him as President of the Linnean that the three societies mentioned above should communicate to the Linnean such papers as might appear particularly suitable for publication by it. In order to attract erring members of those three "minor societies" to the Linnean fold he mentioned two proposals that had been made, but he considered neither very desirable nor practicable:

(1)   that members of any of the three Societies, who had been so for a definitive number of years, if elected Fellows of the Linnean should have their entrance fees remitted or reduced;

(2)   that a new body of Associates should be formed, paying a reduced annual contribution and having limited privileges.

It will be seen later what happened when the Entomological Society applied for affiliation with the Linnean on the lines of the second proposal. Since Bell's time "minor societies" have increased instead of diminishing in number. A "Cryptogamic Society" that appeared so strange to Bell would now in face of existing special societies, such as the British bryological, lichenological, mycological, phycological and pteridological societies, seem over-ambitiously comprehensive.

George Bentham (1800–84) was the second son of Samuel Bentham (1757–1831), a naval architect and brother of Jeremy Bentham, who, after 16 years in the Russian service, had returned to England about 1796 and been appointed Inspector-General of Naval Works. From 1805 to 1807 Samuel Bentham was again in Russia with his family, this time to build ships in Russian dockyards for the British Navy. From 1807 to 1814 the Benthams lived in Hampstead, where the children were educated at home. From 1814 to 1826 they all lived in France, and while there George became interested in botany, teaching himself with the aid of De Candolle's *Flore Française* (1805–25) and his other works. On the return of the family to England in 1826 George became acquainted with most of Britain's leading botanists, but for the following six years he was occupied mostly in the study of law and in assisting his uncle, Jeremy Bentham (1748–1832), the celebrated jurist and philosopher. After the death of his uncle in 1832, Bentham was left with independent means and was free to return to botany, to which he dedicated the remainder of his long life. He accomplished a vast amount of work, including the monumental *Genera Plantarum* (1862–83), the writing of which, in collaboration with J. D. Hooker, occupied him for 25 years. In addition to being a botanist and a logician – his *Outlines of a New System of Logic* (1827) was published when he was only 27 – Bentham was an excellent linguist and a musician. His reserved manner hid from many his generous nature. He was elected FLS in 1828, not 1826 as stated in the obituary notice in the

Society's *Proceedings*. His portrait, painted by Lowes Dickinson in 1870, hangs in the Society's Meeting Room. It was originally head and bust, but was enlarged in 1890 to half length at the desire and cost of his friend J. D. Hooker.

William Wilson Saunders (1809–79) was a man of ample means, an underwriter at Lloyd's who, after a short period of service in the Engineers, had settled in Reigate where he established a private museum and well-stocked garden. An early member of the Entomological Society, he was twice its President. He contributed many papers to that Society's *Transactions* and offered prizes to stimulate research in economic entomology. He accumulated a fine collection of living plants and started two short-lived botanical publications, the *Refugium botanicum* (1869–73) and *Mycological Illustrations* (1871–72). Unfortunately, being almost ruined by a financial crisis in 1872 through the loss at sea of over-insured unseaworthy ships, he had to sell his collections, terminate the periodicals and retire from business. He was elected FLS in 1833 and FRS in 1853.

George Busk (1807–86) was the son of Robert Busk of St Petersburg. He spent many years in the naval medical service, from which he retired in 1856 and thereafter gave himself to zoological, palaeontological and anthropological researches, in all of which he gained great distinction and recognition. He was elected FLS in 1846. His daughter was a portrait painter (see p. 193).

Frederick Currey (1819–81) was the son of Benjamin Currey, Clerk of the Parliaments. After education at Eton and Trinity College, Cambridge, he entered the legal profession. Botany, particularly the study of fungi, was his relaxation. His most important work was a translation, with additions of his own, of Hofmeister's account of the higher Cryptogamia, published by the Ray Society in 1862. He was elected FLS in 1856. Botanical Secretary until 1880, he then became Treasurer for the last year of his life.

In March 1802, the Council adopted a resolution, submitted by J. D. Hooker, regarding future Associates, which included rather severe conditions. Thus every Associate residing within ten miles of London was expected to attend at least three General Meetings during every session. Those beyond ten miles and not attending three meetings were expected to make at least one scientific communication during each session. Any Associate who did not during three years fulfil these conditions, except for satisfactory reasons, was to be considered as having withdrawn from Associateship. As there was no provision for the surveillance of Associates, and as the Society's staff was busy enough without the additional and invidious duty of keeping a dossier of each Associate, the resolution remained merely on record.

In the printed lists of members of the Society the addresses of Fellows and Associates were given in English, but those of Foreign Members were disguised in Latinized form. Probably this was supposed to lend a dignified air to the Foreign Members, but its absurdity for ordinary purposes was then realized and from 1864 their addresses have been in modern form (see p. 201).

Following a report by S. Ward, printed in *Journal Bot.*, 8: 135–139 (1864), in 1864 the Society presented a memorial to the Governor of Mauritius and the Seychelles for the preservation of the Coco-de-Mer (*Lodoicea maldavica*) against wanton destruction which was then threatening its extinction. This remarkable endemic Seychelles palm produces the world's largest seed of such a form that Commerson named it *callipyge*.

In 1865, the Royal Geographical Society sought the advice of the Linnean Society regarding the biological investigations that might be undertaken by the expedition then proposed to explore the North Polar regions. The Linnean Council expressed its views in a long minute, but ten years passed before the *Alert* and the *Discovery* set out for the Arctic.

In 1866, there was a prospect of realizing the co-operation between the Linnean and the Zoological, Entomological and Microscopical Societies, that for which Bell had hoped. According to Scherren, *The Zoological Society of London*, 144 (1905), the Council of the Zoological Society had "long entertained the view that it would be well if the scientific meetings could be held in more immediate connection with those of cognate bodies and especially of the Linnean Society". So with the permission of the Linnean, and the approval of the Royal, the Zoological Society held its scientific meetings in the Linnean rooms during the 1866–67 session. This arrangement could have continued during 1867–68, but after 1866–67 the Zoological Society returned to its own rooms in Hanover Square. The Entomological Society also was allowed to hold its meetings in the Linnean rooms, and continued to do so until 1874–75, when it sought affiliation with the Linnean. The request in 1867 of the Royal Microscopical Society for the use of the Linnean rooms had to be refused, for the Linnean's staff was not large enough to cope with more than a few meetings of other societies.

When the Society was accommodated in Burlington House it understood that its occupation there along with the Royal and Chemical Societies was only until other rooms could be provided. As early as 1858, the Office of Works informed the Royal and Linnean Societies that they need not trouble to sow the lawn behind Burlington House, as a building for the Patent Law Commission was to be erected there. In October 1866, the Society was informed that the Government intended to appropriate the central block of Burlington House for the Royal Academy, and to erect new buildings completely enclosing the quadrangle in front of the house for the learned Societies. The Linnean Society appointed a committee to discuss with the architects, Messrs Banks and Barry, the extent of accommodation desired. By 1867 a great building, intended for the University of London this time but now occupied by the Museum of Mankind, was being erected on the northern half of the garden behind Burlington House to face Burlington Gardens Street, while the southern half was being excavated for the additions to the central block of Burlington House to accommodate the Royal Academy, then still in Trafalgar Square. In 1868, the old wings of Burlington House were demolished, and during the next few years the building of the new wings and of the new front block went on. When, in 1872, the upper storey to the central block of Burlington House was begun, the three societies were still in occupation, but disturbance to them was lessened as much as possible by the stones being all prepared beforehand in the contractors' works. In addition to the upper storey to the central block, the Royal Academy wanted an arcade in front of its main entrance, and in consequence had to provide gas-jets for the Herbarium Room of the Society to compensate for the loss of daylight. The niches along the front of the upper storey of the Royal Academy are filled with statues of famous painters and sculptors. The corresponding niches on the building facing Burlington Gardens Street contain statues of celebrated philosophers and men of science. One of the latter is Linnaeus, his sculptor, P. MacDowell, RA, having been guided by an engraved portrait and a medallion lent by the Society.

For four years the three societies worked amid the turmoil of building on all sides, but by 1873 the new wings and front block were nearing completion. Henceforth, the three societies that for 16 years had entered by the same door in the central block were to have

Plate IX   Interior of the Society's apartments at Burlington House. (a) Meeting room: General Meeting in progress, Professor I. Manton in the chair. (b) Hallway. (c) Strong Room housing Linnaean Collections. (d) Part of the Library.

(a)

(b)

(c)

(d)

only the quadrangle in common, and the other three societies – the Antiquaries, the Geological and the Royal Astronomical – that had preferred in 1857 to remain in Somerset House now had rooms in the new building. During the recess of 1873 superfluous bookcases and other fittings were sold, the Royal Academy buying about £130's worth. The bulk of the Museum collections had been sold or given away in 1863 (see Chapter 10), so that the shifting of the library was the heaviest task and one to which Bentham himself gave special attention. The Council met for the first time in the new quarters on 30 October 1873, and the first General Meeting of the Society was held on Thursday, 6 November 1873, the first meeting of the eighty-sixth session. At this meeting Bentham gave a short address appreciative of the new conditions in which the Society found itself. He expressed regret at "the cessation of that close juxtaposition and intimate intercourse with the Royal Society which was so agreeable to us". A unanimous vote of thanks to the Government was also passed.

The Society has occupied the rooms allotted in 1873 up to the present time. The accommodation comprises the whole of the western half of the Piccadilly frontage and the rooms above the great central archway leading from Piccadilly into the quadrangle. The entrance to the Society's rooms is on the west side of the archway. Opposite the hall entrance is the door of the almost square Meeting Room, about 34 by 33 feet, with three windows facing Piccadilly. The portrait of Darwin by T. H. Huxley's son-in-law, the Hon. John Collier, occupies the central position to the right. Darwin's own feelings on the subject of this portrait are expressed in a letter, dated 27 May 1881, to Romanes, then Zoological Secretary:

> It tires me a good deal to sit to anyone, but I should be the most ungrateful and ungracious dog not to agree cordially, supposing that enough is subscribed, about which I have always felt very bashful. If I am to sit, it would be a pity not to sit to a good artist, and from all that I have heard I believe Mr. Collier is a very good one. I have seen a photograph of his picture of Hooker and it seemed very good. I shd. most particularly desire to sit to Huxley's son-in-law, if, as you say, he would like to paint me. Let me earnestly beg one thing of you, viz. that you will not permit any touting for subscriptions. I always understood that my agreement to sit was contingent on the subscriptions sufficing.

The other walls are covered with the portraits of distinguished members of the Society (see Chapter 13). The carved oak table on the platform was presented by Frank Crisp in 1890, and the clock above the door by the same Fellow in 1896. The Presidential Chair, emblazoned with the Society's Arms, was presented by Reginald Cory in 1925. At meetings the President in the Chair has the Treasurer and one Secretary on the left and the other Secretary on the right. The original position of the Presidential platform was along the north wall, with the members' benches facing it.

From the entrance hall a broad stone staircase leads to the first-floor landing. To the right of the landing is the main West Library Reading Room, a large and lofty room, about 47 feet long, 33 feet broad and 34 feet high. Two rows of four windows each look out on Piccadilly. Two galleries surround the north, south and east sides, the lower balustraded one supported on massive piers projecting inwards for about 7 feet from the north and about 5 feet from the south wall, the upper one resting on brackets. In the alcoves between the piers were tables for the use of members. From the inner ends of the piers arise columns which help to support the glass-panelled roof. High up on the west wall hangs the portrait of Sir Joseph Banks; below it hangs a portrait of Daniel Solander (1733–82), the Swedish friend and later librarian of Sir Joseph Banks, a distinguished naturalist and the first Swede to circumnavigate the world, having likewise sailed with Captain Cook.

To the left of the first-floor landing is a less imposing but fairly large room, now the East Library or Annexe, about 33 feet long, 28 feet broad and 16 feet high, with three windows facing Piccadilly and one the quadrangle. Along the walls are bookshelves. In this room secretarial work of the Society was formerly performed. From 1873 until the end of the 1929–30 session the Council and Committees held their meetings in this room, when it was known as the "Council Room". These meetings were held on the days of the Society's General Meetings, when many members of the Society came to the rooms, not merely to attend the General Meeting but to consult books and periodicals. As access by ordinary members to the Council Room was impossible while the Council or a committee was sitting, and as some of the bound and all current issues of periodicals were kept in the Council Room, murmurs of discontent were heard at times amongst the members assembled in the main library on the afternoon of a General Meeting day. This unsatisfactory arrangement was remedied in 1930 when the Council and committees began to meet on the second floor, necessitating a wearisome climb for the elderly, despite ropes along the stairway provided by the Royal Navy, now replaced by a rail.

From the first floor, the staircase continues more narrowly to a set of rooms which, with the exception of one retained by the Post Office until 1904, used to be the quarters of the Librarian or Assistant-Secretary when he had to, or was permitted to, live on the Society's premises. The rooms were occupied by the Librarian from 1873 to 1897, by the Assistant-Secretary from 1897 to 1902, and by the officer enjoying both designations from 1927 to 1929.

The Society had scarcely entered the new rooms when the Office of Works demanded that the Society should insure them for £12 000. As no charge for insurance of its old rooms in the central block had been imposed on the Society, Bentham successfully remonstrated with the Office of Works against this request.

In 1869, Busk resigned the zoological secretaryship and was succeeded by Henry Tibbats Stainton (1822–92), a London businessman and a keen entomologist, who had been elected FLS in 1859. He was a prominent Fellow of the Entomological Society, wrote much on entomological subjects and helped to found the Zoological Record Association, which issued the *Zoological Record* from 1871 until the Zoological Society took it over in 1886. The obituary notice of Stainton in the Linnean *Proceedings* describes him as "a genial and generous friend and a painstaking industrious worker".

As nothing had come of the North Polar expedition proposed in 1865, the Royal Geographical Society in 1872 again invoked the aid of the Linnean Society in urging the Government to organize one, and the two societies conferred on the subject. The expedition under Captain G. S. Nares, R.N, at last set off in 1875.

In May 1873, at the last Anniversary Meeting held in the central block of Burlington House, W. W. Saunders, who had been Treasurer since 1861, resigned, two years before the passing of Samuel Plimsoll's Merchant Shipping Act which, if passed earlier, would have saved him from ruin. He retired to Worthing. His successor, Daniel Hanbury (1825–75), was a son of Daniel Bell Hanbury, a partner in the pharmaceutical firm of Allen, Hanbury & Barry. Daniel Hanbury entered his father's firm in 1841 and thereafter devoted himself to scientific and historical research in pharmacy, more especially on drugs of vegetable origin. His most important work was the *Pharmacographia* (1874), written in collaboration with Friedrich A. Flückiger. He also took an important part in the preparation of the *Pharmacopoeia of India*. He had been elected FLS in 1855 and retained the treasurership for only two years before his death.

Between the last meeting of the Society in the central block and the first meeting in the new quarters the last living link with the old days of the Society in the eighteenth century

(a)

(b)

(c)

(d)

was snapped by the death, on 29 June 1873, of Thomas Garnier, Dean of Winchester, in his ninety-eighth year. He had been elected a Fellow on 16 October 1798 and had been a Fellow for almost 75 years. He had paid the original annual contribution of a guinea for 60 years and then compounded!

The Society entered into possession of its new home apparently under the happiest auspices, with Bentham as President, Hanbury as Treasurer, and Currey and Stainton as Secretaries. Unfortunately, the first session turned out to be the most troubled one so far in the life of the Society. The immediate cause of the problem was an honest difference of opinion over certain proposed alterations in the Bye-Laws.

The predisposing cause for many years was the inability of the Society's staff to cope with the heavy demands upon it. This had become apparent as far back as 1842, when Lemann and Kippist were candidates for the Librarianship made vacant by the death of David Don in 1841. On that occasion Jonathan Pereira (1804–53), the well-known pharmacologist, in a letter to N. B. Ward (1791–1868), the physician who invented the Wardian case, expressed his inclination to vote for Kippist, but pointed out that the Librarian should be a man "of classical learning" – which Kippist was not and Lemann was – in order that the Society's *Transactions* should be properly edited, a duty that fell to the Librarian although nominally a function of the Secretary. Pereira also expressed the opinion that, in order to permit of both library and museum being open daily and properly used, two full-time officers were necessary. He suggested that both Lemann and Kippist should be appointed to the staff and prophesied that unless some such arrangement were made the Society would suffer.

Pereira was right, but the Society was half strangled with debt. From 1842 to 1876 Kippist remained the sole full-time paid staff, but he received a modicum of assistance. From 1842 to 1853 Henry Sowerby attended thrice a week during the session and twice a week during the recess, at an annual salary of £30. From 1853 to 1876 Kippist was helped only by the Society's porter, who was also messenger, collector and housekeeper. In 1873 this assistant was a youth, James West, who had succeeded in 1872 his deceased uncle, Thomas West, in the capacities mentioned.

This hopeless state of affairs persisted even after the Society had got rid in 1863 of most of the heterogeneous collections which it called a "Museum". So in 1864 the Council began the practice of placing £100 at the disposal of the Secretaries towards the expense of editing the Society's publications. Up to 1874 no names are mentioned in the Society's accounts or records, but undoubtedly the Secretaries paid a Fellow or Fellows to do the editorial work. Strictly this was against the spirit, if not the letter, of the then existing Bye-Law which prohibited any Fellow holding an office to which salaries or emoluments were annexed. At the Council meeting in July 1873, Bentham went a step further in proposing that the Secretaries should be authorized to procure assistance in editing the publications and reporting proceedings at a salary not exceeding £80 per annum. Then trouble began.

On the Council were J. D. Hooker, the Director of the Royal Botanic Gardens, Kew, and Henry Trimen (1843–96), then Assistant in the Botanical Department of the British Museum but later Director of the Botanic Gardens, Peradeniya, Ceylon (now Sri Lanka). Bentham was then 73 and had been President for 12 years. Hooker was then 56 and had been on the Council and a Vice-President also for 12 years. Trimen was a young man of 30 and had just been elected to the Council in May 1873. Both the elder men, accustomed to getting their own way in the Society's affairs, must have been shocked and annoyed when this young fellow Trimen strongly opposed Bentham's proposal. Moreover, animosity coloured the official relations between Kew and the British Museum's Botany Department. Bentham's idea was to engage a Fellow of the Society to do the editorial work, but Trimen pointed out that this would break the Bye-Law.

The day after the Council meeting Bentham wrote to Trimen strongly expressing the opinion "that the engaging someone to report our Proceedings and assist in editing is no more appointing anyone to an office in the Society than engaging a printer or an engraver to do the Society's work. Still I think that the clause in the Bye-Laws which you referred to had better be repealed and that one or two other alterations might be made with advantage, but I find that for such alterations the Council must have been specially summoned, which I will take care to have done in due course". For the author of a book on logic this was not a very logical statement to make, for the Society did not engage printers or engravers at a limited salary per annum, and if the proposal did not conflict with the particular Bye-Law cited by Trimen there was no need for it to be repealed.

Trimen, in his reply to Bentham, stated that he found it "difficult to see what prevents our Secretaries from doing the work for which they were appointed: a little more energy on their part and on that of the Librarian would do away with the necessity for this, to my mind, very undesirable increment to our official staff and our expenses". In this Trimen displayed more zeal for the Society's purse than knowledge of its business. A record of a correspondence between Trimen and William Turner Thiselton Dyer (1843–1928) throws a sidelight on an aspect of the trouble not revealed in the Society's *Proceedings*. Thiselton Dyer was then a man of about 30. Professor of Botany to the Royal Horticultural Society, he had been a class-fellow and was a friend of Trimen; indeed, they published together, in 1869, a *Flora of Middlesex*. He was also on friendly terms with J. D. Hooker, assisting him unofficially in botanical work and marrying Hooker's eldest daughter, Harriet Ann. Bentham, in accordance with the resolution passed at the Council meeting in July 1873, asked Thiselton Dyer to undertake the salaried editorial work and the latter at first had been willing to do so, but on finding that there was a difference of opinion as to the propriety of the appointment and "that the Botanical Department [i.e. of the British Museum] was likely to be in opposition" had refused to have anything to do with it. In his place Bentham and the Secretaries engaged Alfred William Bennett (1833–1902), who had been a bookseller and publisher and was then Lecturer on Botany at St Thomas's Hospital. Thiselton Dyer's reference to the probable attitude of the botanical staff of the British Museum reveals a secret background. During the previous quarter of a century the scope of the work of Kew and the Botanical Department of the British Museum had been the subject of several investigations, and in 1873 the latest of these, held by the Devonshire Commission of 1871–75 on Scientific Instruction and the Advancement of Science, had not long been concluded and had left matters much as they had always been. The Botanical Department nevertheless remained highly suspicious of the imperialist designs of Kew and on guard against annexation by Kew. Hostility between them lasted until David Prain (1857–1944) from Calcutta became Director of Kew in 1905 and this antagonism unfortunately intruded into the Society's affairs. Early in the new session, at the Council Meeting on 13 November 1873, Bentham gave notice of a motion for those alterations in the Bye-Laws that he had already mentioned in his letter to Trimen. The motion was made at the Council Meeting of 4 December 1873 and passed for submission to the vote of the Fellows. Here the printed *Proceedings* are incorrect. They state (*Proc.* 1873–74: vi) that at the General Meeting of 6 November 1873 "the President read from the Chair certain alterations in the Bye-Laws, which in accordance with the Charter must be read at three consecutive meetings and then balloted by the Fellows". There is no mention of this in the Minutes of the General Meeting of 6 November, for the good reason that even the notice of motion was not given to the Council until 13 November. The statement should have appeared under the report of the General Meeting of 4 December 1873. The explanation is that Bennett was grossly careless in his reporting and the Secretaries remiss in supervision. Both Thiselton Dyer and Trimen, although holding opposite opinions regarding Bentham's proposals, were united in hearty disapproval of Bennett's editorial work.

The two most important changes in the Bye-Laws proposed by Bentham were the repeal of that whereby no Fellow was eligible for a paid post in the Society so long as he was a Fellow, and the removal of the election of the Librarian from the hands of the Fellows to the Council. They were both sound proposals, for the character of a paid officer's services to the Society depends, *ceteris paribus*, upon the character of the paid officer and not upon whether he is or is not a Fellow. Also, the Council is in a much better position to weigh the merits of candidates for any paid post than the large body of Fellows.

The proposed alterations were read to the Fellows at the General Meetings of 4 and 18 December 1873 and finally on 15 January 1874, when voting had to take place. Meanwhile, Trimen, who alone had opposed the proposals in Council, had discussed them with some of the Fellows, amongst them being undoubtedly his official superior, William Carruthers (1830–1922), Keeper of Botany in the British Museum.

When the President proposed these alterations as a whole at the General Meeting on 15 January 1874, Carruthers moved and H. G. Seeley, the palaeontologist, seconded that the various proposed alterations should be put to the vote separately. This was not unreasonable as the alterations were of very different importance and, according to Trimen, the Council had actually accepted the proposal that the two most important ones, already mentioned, should be voted on separately.

Bentham, although urged by several Fellows, including two members of his Council, declined to allow Carruthers's motion to be put to the meeting. "After some further discussion", as the *Proceedings* have it, or "after an hour's disagreeable talk", as Bentham's diary describes it, Bentham still remained obdurate, and the proposals were finally voted on as a whole. For the proposals to pass, two-thirds of the Fellows present had to vote in favour of them. There were 66 Fellows present, of whom one did not vote; 44 voted in favour and 21 against the proposals. So Bentham just had his way, and the meeting settled down as best it could to listen to papers about Japanese shells, fishes and brachiopods. The trouble, however, was by no means over, and Bentham's victory in passing a perfectly good piece of Society legislation was to prove a barren one for himself.

Bentham's attitude at this meeting exasperated not a few Fellows, including some of his supporters. Thus even Thiselton Dyer, in a letter to Trimen the day after the meeting, was constrained to write: "Bentham's proceedings in the Chair I thought quite indefensible. In fact I was strongly inclined to vote against the byelaws, as I suspect others actually did in consequence."

At the Council Meeting on 5 February 1874, Bentham intimated his intention of resigning the Presidency at the next Anniversary Meeting. Between the General Meeting of 15 January and this Council Meeting, Carruthers and other Fellows, who held that the alterations were contrary to the Charter and that Bentham had acted illegally at the

General Meeting, had consulted an "eminent Q.C.", who had supported their opinion and their intention of submitting the question to the Council for further consideration. Accordingly, at the Council Meeting of 5 February 1874, a letter signed by Carruthers and 12 other Fellows protesting against the proceedings of the General Meeting of 15 January and threatening to reopen the question at the General Meeting of that evening, 5 February, was presented. According to Trimen, who was present at the Council Meeting, Bentham received this letter very ungraciously and at first the Council was for ignoring it. However, it finally decided to inform Carruthers by letter immediately that the question could not be reopened at that evening's General Meeting, but that, if ten Fellows required it, the Council would call a special meeting of the Society. The General Meeting on 5 February was short and anything but sweet. The account, undoubtedly written by Bennett, was so incorrect and so ambiguously expressed that a letter of protest against it, signed by 20 Fellows, who gave their account of the meeting, was submitted to Council. From their account the following is taken.

Bentham was about to sign the Minutes of the previous meeting of 15 January when Carruthers rose to submit a question before the Minutes were signed. Bentham declared this to be irregular, as the President's duty was to sign the Minutes after they had been read. In this Bentham was right, as the Bye-Laws at that time required no confirmation of the Minutes. Bentham accordingly signed them. He then stated the Council's willingness to call a special meeting if ten or more Fellows desired it, but Carruthers insisted that he was entitled, under the Bye-Law regulating the business of the President, to put a question. Bentham held that the meeting could deal only with scientific reports and papers as laid down under another Bye-Law. Here Bentham was again strictly correct, but the Bye-Laws referred to by Bentham and Carruthers were not entirely consistent. Ultimately, Carruthers moved and J. E. Harting seconded a motion declaring the alterations in the Bye-Laws made at the meeting of 15 January illegal and the proceedings null and void. Bentham declined to allow this motion to be put, but demanded whether the meeting desired a discussion. Here Bentham made a tactical blunder, for he had had just declared, quite correctly, that the meeting could deal only with scientific matters. However, the question for or against a discussion was put, and on a show of hands Bentham claimed a majority against discussion. This was instantly challenged, and on a second show of hands the result was 15 for discussion and 11 against. Bentham then made his final blunder, for, instead of accepting the result of his own action in demanding the sense of the meeting, he abruptly left the Chair and the meeting broke up.

In this deplorable fashion Bentham's Presidency ended, for he sent in his resignation on the following day, and although he modified this hasty action in so far that his resignation did not take effect until 4 March, he never again occupied the Chair as President, although he did so several times as a Vice-President.

Bentham had been President for nearly 13 years. While giving of his best to the general welfare of the Society he took particular interest in the Library, as will appear later. His Presidential Addresses ranged over wide fields in a way that, owing to the vast growth of biological research since his time, would now be almost impossible. In his first Address (1862) he gave a review of the more important works that had recently been published in botany and zoology all over the world and of the explorations and investigations in progress. His first opinion as to the proper attitude of the Society towards Darwin's hypothesis has already been quoted. By 1863 he had so far relented or repented as to devote a considerable part of his Address to a discussion of the hypothesis. Other Addresses deal with such topics as the dispersion and migration of species, spontaneous generation, parthenogenesis, geographical biology, palaeontological investigations, hybridism, teratology, metamorphism and dimorphism, the history of the more important periodical publications in foreign languages and of those published in the United States of America. He expressed his views as to the composition of the Society in his first Address as follows:

> It has always appeared to me a mistaken idea that the Fellows of the Linnean Society should be limited to those who have shown proficiency in natural science; we should hope indeed to include all such in our body; but they require the encouragement of friends and patrons and work with increased zeal when aided by the association of those lovers of natural history who, having little leisure to devote to it, contribute nevertheless to our means, attend occasionally our meetings, glance over our proceedings and generally watch our progress.

This liberal policy has now long been accepted.

Bentham's sudden withdrawal shocked the Society and the contending parties within it for, although the latter differed over the Bye-Laws question and Bentham's attitude in this matter, they had great personal regard and admiration for him. A fresh effort was now made to settle this dispute and a letter signed by 17 Fellows requested the Council to call a special meeting of the Society to reconsider the question. Trimen had already in February, in a printed circular letter addressed to each member of Council, proposed that a committee should be appointed to consider the Bye-Laws and to suggest to the Council such alterations as might be thought desirable. The Council called a special meeting of the Society on 5 March 1874 with Busk, a Vice-President, in the Chair. At this meeting Carruthers moved the proposal that Trimen had already made to members of Council, but this was set aside in favour of an amendment made by Major-General Richard Strachey to the effect that the Council should obtain the opinion of some legal authority on the question; that if the legal authority considered the alterations in the Bye-Laws were legally binding no further steps should be taken; that if the legal authority considered that all or any of the alterations were illegal the Council should take steps to set aside the vote of 15 January 1874. It is pleasant to relate, after so much disagreeableness, that before the close of this meeting Sir John Lubbock proposed and the obstreperous Carruthers seconded a resolution expressing the Society's deep appreciation of Bentham's services both to the Society and to science during his long Presidency and it was passed unanimously. The whole question was then referred to Baron Hatherley, who had been Lord Chancellor from 1868 to 1872. He gave the opinion that the alterations in the Bye-Laws had been legally put to the General Meeting on 15 January 1874 and had been legally carried. This ended the dispute.

During the course of the dispute Hooker and Trimen were engaged in two successive epistolary duels over certain aspects of the latter's activity in the Society's affairs. The first, in which Thiselton Dyer intervened by way of elucidating Hooker's views, resulted from Trimen's discussion with some Fellows the proposed alterations in the Bye-Laws before the date of voting. Hooker strongly reprobated this action and even hinted at Trimen's conduct being officially reported to the Council. This last did not happen, but Trimen was very indignant and sent copies of Hooker's letter to members of Council. Details of the controversy are now unimportant, but the correspondence has historical interest in that it brings out two opposing views on the relation of the Council and of individual Councillors to the Society. Hooker held that the Council was of the nature of a "Cabinet", and that it was improper for any Councillor to discuss with Fellows not on the Council any topic under discussion or any resolution passed by the Council regarding which the Councillor was in a minority on the Council. Trimen held strongly that the Council was a "representative" body, as being elected by the Fellows, and that any member of it was not merely entitled but in duty bound to discuss with his constituents any proposal or resolution which he thought should be so discussed before it was voted on at a General Meeting. Neither view in its extreme form is tenable. Some items of Council business are fully given in its Minutes, which are open to inspection by any Fellow at reasonable times, so that he can easily find out what the Council has done or is doing. On the other hand, if the Council by an overwhelming majority is in favour of a certain course of action as it was in the matter of the alteration of the Bye-Laws, a minority member has no right to stir up merely factious opposition in the Society, for he is not elected by nor does he represent a special group or party in the Society. All members of Council are elected by the Society as a whole and represent the Society as such.

Trimen, although at that moment a thorn in the flesh of the Council, had a high sense of duty towards the Society, which was expressed in the above-mentioned printed circular letter sent by him to each member of Council individually after the General Meeting of 5 February 1874. In this letter, in addition to suggesting the appointment of a Committee to consider the Bye-Laws and the revival of a particular Bye-Law that had been long repealed, Trimen made three proposals that were adopted later. They were: "(a) Limitation of the office of the President to a definite short period, say, two or three years; (b) A paid resident Assistant-Secretary who shall be also Librarian and Editor of the Society's publications; (c) The recommendation of the Council for the removal of five of its members, annually submitted to the Fellows on May 24th of each year, to be based strictly on length of service and record of attendance of the Councillors; the custom of treating the Vice-Presidents as permanent officers and Councillors to be discontinued."

Hooker incautiously and incorrectly assumed that Trimen had distributed copies of his letter to Fellows as well as members of Council and again took Trimen to task. The ensuing correspondence towards its end began to be acrimonious.

In the original Charter of 1802, it was directed that on every Anniversary day the Fellows should "amove" any five members (i.e. one-third) of the previous year's Council and elect five other "discreet persons" to replace them. This of course did not mean that every three-year period was to bring about a complete change in the personal composition of the Council, including the honorary officers. In practice, the Council decided who were to be "amoved" and recommended to the Fellows who should replace them. What Trimen objected to was that certain members of Council had not been "amoved" within a reasonable number of years and that the same persons had been nominated Vice-Presidents annually for long periods. Since the foundation of the Society in 1788 there had been only seven Presidents, with tenures of office varying from three to 40 years. Bentham had been President for 13 years. As regards Vice-Presidents, J. D. Hooker had been one from 1861 to 1874, J. J. Bennett from 1860 to 1872, W. W. Saunders the Treasurer from 1861 to 1873, so that from 1861 to 1872 the Presidents and three out of the four Vice-Presidents had been the same Fellows. The cases of Bennett and Hooker were exceptional, for no other Fellows, except the Treasurer, had been Vice-Presidents for more than five consecutive years since 1853. Previous to 1853, Dryander was a Vice-President for 14 years, Lambert for 45, Goodenough for 6 and 22, Maton for 31, Lord Stanley for 12, Brown for 21 and 5, Horsfield for 15 and W. J. Hooker for 11 years. No Secretary, while such, has ever been a Vice-President but, since 1828, the Treasurer, except during the years 1860–61 and 1873–74, has always been one. The first Treasurer to be nominated a Vice-President was Thomas Marsham in 1811, but Edward Forster, who succeeded Marsham as Treasurer in 1816, was not nominated until 1828.

Trimen's proposal to have a paid Assistant-Secretary who should also be Librarian and Editor had much to recommend it. The honorary officers had and have not the time to conduct the ordinary executive work of the Society. The best arrangement is to have one paid officer in charge of all the Society's ordinary business, to make him responsible to the Council and honorary officers, and to give him enough assistance to allow him to do his share of the work and to see that the others do theirs. Trimen's remarks regarding the tenure of the Vice-Presidentships had an almost immediate effect, but his other proposals were set aside to be brought up again by other hands long after Trimen had left England in 1879 for Ceylon (Sri Lanka), where, among other services to botany, he prepared his *Handbook to the Flora of Ceylon* (5 vols, 1895–1900).

Amid the excitement over the alterations in the Bye-Laws the formality of presenting the certificates of recommendation of candidates for Foreign Membership on or before 7 March was forgotten, and the Council had to inform Filippo Parlatore (1816–77), the Italian botanist, and Alexander Agassiz (1835–1910), the American zoologist, that they were Foreign Members elect with confirmation delayed until 1875.

In April 1874, the Entomological Society, which had held its meetings in the Linnean rooms since 1866, applied for affiliation with the Linnean, suggesting that the members of the Entomological Society should become Entomological Associates of the Linnean Society on an annual contribution to be thereafter fixed. At first affiliation seemed certain, but the proposal fell through when the Linnean Society found it could not accommodate the library of the Entomological Society.

In May 1874, George James Allman was elected eighth President and St George Jackson Mivart Zoological Secretary. In May 1875, John Gwyn Jeffreys was elected Treasurer in place of Daniel Hanbury, who had died in March. Mercifully there were no more changes amongst the honorary officers until 1880.

George James Allman (1812–98) was a native of Cork and educated at Belfast for a legal career. However, he later chose to study law and became an MD of Dublin and of Oxford. He was speedily appointed Professor of Botany in Dublin University, whence after ten years he moved to Edinburgh as Professor of Natural History. There he taught and worked until his retirement in 1870, when he came to live in London. His name is associated more with zoological than botanical research and his monographs on Hydroids and Polyzoa are amongst the classics of zoology. He was an amiable man but not very effective as President. He had been elected FLS in 1872.

St George Jackson Mivart (1827–1900) was born in London and, after an education at Harrow and King's College, London, became a barrister. Like Allman he forsook law for natural history, and in 1862 was appointed Lecturer on Zoology at St Mary's Hospital, London. He wrote numerous zoological papers and became widely known as a writer of books, notably *On the Genesis of Species* (1871) and *Man and Apes* (1873), both anti-Darwinian, *Dogs, Jackals, Wolves and Foxes* (1890) and *A Monograph of the Lories* (1890) and of controversial religious articles. He tried to reconcile his Roman Catholic faith with evolutionary biology but failed to win assent. The Catholic Church excommunicated him shortly before his death. As his biographer, Jacob W. Grüber, states: "Mivart stands as an important symbol and victim of the deep conflicts in science and the intellectual milieu of the nineteenth century." Others, both Catholic and Protestant, within the Linnean Society had the same struggle of conscience in attempting to reconcile observed facts with theological pronouncements. Mivart had been a FLS since 1869 and received a doctorate from the intellectual stronghold of Roman Catholicism, the University of Louvain.

John Gwyn Jeffreys (1809–85), a native of Swansea, after practising as a solicitor in his native town, was called to the bar in London. He gave up his profession in 1866 and thereafter devoted himself to research in marine zoology, in which he had been interested since his schooldays. He was elected FLS in 1865. It is remarkable that all the four honorary officers of the Society at this time were or had been in the legal profession.

In March 1874, A. W. Bennett was formally appointed by the Council as Assistant-Editor of the Society's publications for the remainder of the session of 1873–74 at a remuneration of £50. Thereafter he was not reappointed, and the Secretaries had to struggle along by themselves, but not for long. At the Anniversary Meeting of 1875 Thomas Boycott suggested the appointment of a third Honorary Secretary. The Council accordingly, in December 1875, authorized the Honorary Officers to consider the question of appointing not an honorary but a paid Secretary. The Officers, however, persuaded the Council to lessen their own labours by stopping publication of the *Proceedings* and ceasing to print additions to the library and prepare obituary notices of deceased members of the Society. As information regarding the Society's finances could scarcely be withheld, they transferred the statement of the Society's accounts to the List of Members, an odd medium of publication. All this was a move in the wrong direction with no discernible justification. The Society was not in such financial straits as to make the small saving of expenditure worth while against the fact that the withholding of information led to dissatisfaction amongst the Fellows which smouldered for several years until it could no longer be ignored. The move had no influence on the question of increasing the Society's paid staff, for in the following month, January 1876, James Murie was appointed Sub-Editor at 60 guineas per annum. This was an annual appointment, but Murie continued to be reappointed with increasing salary, his designation being altered early in 1878 to Assistant-Secretary.

James Murie (1832–1925) was a native of Glasgow, where he had graduated in medicine in 1857. He then became successively Pathologist to the Glasgow Royal Infirmary; Assistant in the Museum to the Royal College of Surgeons, London; ship's surgeon, medical officer and naturalist to Petherick's expedition towards the sources of the White Nile; Assistant again in the Royal College of Surgeons; and, in 1865, Prosector to the Zoological Society. He held this last post for five years, during which he was rather a thorn in that society's side. He had been elected FLS in 1868. The Assistant-Secretary had to conduct all the current work of the Society, apart from the Library, and was expected to adopt such means as might suggest themselves or be suggested to him to make the General Meetings attractive.

The aid of the Society was invoked in 1880 by Dr (afterwards Sir) James A. M. Murray (1837–1915) in connection with biological terms and nomenclature for inclusion in the *Oxford English Dictionary*, and the Council advertised on the covers of the *Journal* appeals for assistance by members of the Society. To such collaboration that monumental dictionary owes its high scientific accuracy and coverage.

Considerable changes in the Society's staff took place in 1880. Both Jeffreys, the Treasurer, and Mivart, the Zoological Secretary, resigned and Richard Kippist, who had been Librarian since 1842, retired. Kippist, now an old and rather enfeebled man, had been ill during 1879; consequently the Society's accounts had fallen into such a muddle that the auditors could not present a financial statement for that year at the proper time, and an accountant had to be called in to put the accounts in order.

At the Council Meeting on 6 May 1880, it was agreed that the following changes should be recommended to the Fellows at the Anniversary Meeting: Currey, the Botanical Secretary, was to be Treasurer; Thiselton Dyer was to take Currey's place as Botanical

Secretary; and Edward Richard Alston (1845–81) was to succeed Mivart as Zoological Secretary. The election did not go according to plan, for B. D. Jackson was elected Botanical Secretary and not Thiselton Dyer.

Alston had been elected a Fellow in 1876. He was a native of Lanarkshire and practically self-educated. He had already made notable contributions to zoology, and his personal character endeared him to all who knew him, but he held the Secretaryship for less than a year, dying in March 1881.

In striking contrast with Alston's brief appearance on the Society's stage, the new Botanical Secretary's official connection with the Society was to endure for nearly half a century.

Benjamin Daydon Jackson (1846–1927) had been elected a Fellow in January 1868. He was London-born and educated at private schools, having at one time as a school-fellow Frank Crisp, who was to become his colleague as Treasurer in 1881. Jackson worked in the secretarial and accountancy business for some years, and, to begin with, was interested in field botany. Before long, however, he concentrated his attention on botanical literature. His first notable contribution to this study were reprints in 1876 of Gerard's *Catalogus Arborum* (1596) and in 1877 of Turner's *Libellus* (1538), both with biographical introductions, followed by a *Guide to the Literature of Botany* (1881) and *Vegetable Technology, a Contribution towards a Bibliography of Economic Botany* (1882). These revealed an acquaintance with botanical literature so unusual and extensive that he was appointed editor of the colossal *Index Kewensis* of botanical names (1893–95), financed by Darwin, the compilation of which occupied Jackson for over 13 years. Another reference work of lasting value is his *A Glossary of Botanic Terms* (1900; 4th edn, 1928). Within the Society he laboured more than anyone before him to facilitate the use of the Society's publications, collections and library. He particularly studied the library and collections of Linnaeus in the Society's possession, and his reputation as an authority on them became worldwide. Rather surprisingly he learned Swedish, an unusual accomplishment which enabled him to produce an abridged English version of T. M. Fries's monumental *Linné*, *Lefnadsteckning* (2 vols, 1903), published in 1923 as *Linnaeus, afterwards Carl von Linné*. Jackson had no university education and thus it was especially gratifying for him to receive an honorary doctorate from the University of Uppsala in 1905 and to be appointed a Knight of the Swedish Order of the Polar Star in recognition of his scholarship and his services to botany. He was to continue a member of Council for the unequalled period of 47 years, during which he served the Society for the first 22 years as Botanical Secretary, then 24 years as General Secretary, and the last year of his life as Curator of the Linnaean Collections.

Before the election of 1880 there was dissatisfaction in the Society over the alleged neglect of the Society's affairs by the honorary officers. A quotation from one letter of this time indicates the feeling that existed: "Allman's want of energy, Kippist's illness, Murie's unpopularity, at least in some quarters, and the most unfortunate composition of the present Council, are all evil influences affecting the Society more or less injuriously, and which it is easier to regret than remedy." There was undoubtedly some ground for grumbling. As if it were not enough that Jackson should have had to take up his duties under such depressing conditions, his own election to the Secretaryship by no means pleased all the botanical Fellows. Some of them took up the unreasonable attitude that, as Jackson had little or no standing in scientific research, he was unfitted to be Secretary and they discussed the question of addressing a memorial to the President. They overlooked the fact that eminence in research, although desirable, is not essential for the proper

(a)

(b)

(c)

(d)

performance of a secretary's duties. Their view was the converse of Goodenough's opinion, tactlessly expressed to Alexander McLeay in 1825, that Robert Brown was too eminent a botanist to be a secretary. The feeling against Jackson, after simmering for some time, at last subsided, and by 1885 his work as Secretary was so much appreciated that the resignation which he tendered that year was not accepted and he was asked to continue in office.

Since 1876 the Society's paid staff had consisted of a Librarian, an Assistant-Secretary and a Housekeeper or Messenger. On Kippist's retirement, the Council decided to abolish the Assistant-Secretaryship. The duties could not be abolished, but they got round this obstacle by adding them to those of the Librarian. The Council met in October 1880 to fill this post and practically to eject Kippist, who had been expected to leave in September but had not done so. Kippist finally left, but did not long enjoy his pension or endure his retirement, as he died in January 1882. Out of the 19 candidates for the Librarianship the choice lay between two: Murie, the Assistant-Secretary, and W. B. Hemsley, who had been for a short time Librarian of the Royal Horticultural Society's Lindley Library but was then working at Kew and later became the Keeper of the Herbarium there. Murie was chosen by 11 votes against four for Hemsley.

The year 1881 brought changes in all the honorary offices except the Botanical Secretaryship. At the Anniversary Meeting Sir John Lubbock, Bt, became ninth President and George John Romanes (not George James as given in the Society's lists for years) Zoological Secretary. In the following November, Frank Crisp was elected Treasurer in succession to Currey, who had died in September.

John Lubbock (1834–1913) was born in London, the son of Sir John William Lubbock, Bt (1803–65), a distinguished mathematician and astronomer, of the banking firm of Lubbock, Forster & Hotham. The Forster of the firm was that same Edward Forster who had been elected FLS in 1800 and was Treasurer from 1816 to 1849. When only 14 Lubbock was taken from Eton and placed in his father's business. The Lubbock family lived at Down, Kent; Darwin encouraged young John in his private studies and their friendship lasted for 40 years. Largely self-educated, the boy grew up to become a man of very wide interests, business, scientific, political, civic and social, and of great public spirit. He was elected FLS and FRS in 1858. His many papers on biological, anthropological and archaeological subjects, essays and articles on topics of the moment and popular books, together with his genial character, made him widely esteemed. He was an MP, Chairman of the London County Council, and in 1900 was raised to the peerage as Baron Avebury. In 1871, he sponsored the Bank Holidays Act; in 1880 the Wild Birds' Protection Act; and in 1882 the Ancient Monuments Act. No President has made a greater impact on public affairs and science in general.

Frank Crisp (1843–1919) was the most notable in the succession of the Society's Treasurers. He was born in London, the son of a member of the publishing firm of Ward & Co. After his schooldays in London he was articled in the legal firm of Ashurst & Morris, becoming in due time a partner, with his own name added to its title. Outside his legal work he developed a great interest in microscopes and microscopy. His ample means allowed him to indulge his horticultural fancies at Friar Park, his fine home at Henley-on-Thames, where he formed a magnificent alpine garden in the form of a miniature

Plate XI   (a) Benjamin Daydon Jackson, from the painting by Ernest Moore in the Society's collection. (b) John Lubbock, from the photograph in the Society's collection. (c) H W. Monckton, from a photograph taken in 1928 in the Society's collection. (d) Sir Frank Crisp, from a photograph in the Society's collection.

Matterhorn constructed out of 7000 tons of stone plus Portland cement and complete with alabaster snow and even porcelain chamois. He had a notoriously unsubtle sense of humour, not always appreciated by guests and other victims at Friar Park. His benefactions to the Society include the Crisp Fund for rewarding microscopical research, the table and clock in the Society's meeting room, the cost of the Supplementary Charter of 1903, and the cost of installing electric light. He also presented to the Society one of the only three bronzed-zinc copies in existence of the sculptor's model for J. F. Kjellberg's statue of Linnaeus in the Humlegarden at Stockholm, of which a copy stands outside the University of Chicago, Illinois. Of the other two copies, one belongs to the King of Sweden, the other is in the National Museum at Stockholm. Crisp was made a Knight in 1907 and a Baronet in 1914.

One of the first tasks of the new officers and Council was to allay dissatisfaction with the conditions into which the Society had drifted under Allman's Presidency. Publication of the *Proceedings* was resumed, and the *Proceedings* of the past five years (1875–80) were also published, but without the obituary notices, which the Secretaries had neglected to prepare during that period.

Until the 1930s paid advertisements were never admitted to the Society's publications. One request for insertion of an advertisement merits recording. In 1882 the manager of the Blue Ribbon Army Brain Restorative versus Alcohol Depot at Norwich sought an advertisement for his product. The Blue Ribbon Army was an organization formed to combat the use of alcoholic drinks. How the members of the Society would have regarded such an advertisement in their publications with its reflection on the state of their brains and the inference as to the cause thereof has to be left to the imagination. The Council rejected the opportunity of testing their reactions.

About that time also the Council resolved that the Treasurer should take entire charge of the accounts and collection of annual contributions, with such clerical help as he might think necessary. It was obviously a sensible arrangement for the Treasurer to do the Treasurer's work, but Murie, instead of being thankful to be relieved of this responsibility, took the resolution as a personal insult and at once became aggressive. The Council quailed at the spectacle and suspended the resolution, not Murie.

At the end of 1883 James West, who had been Collector, Messenger and Assistant in the Library, resigned on his appointment as Assistant-Secretary and Librarian to the Royal Microscopical Society, and Henry Wadey was appointed as Housekeeper in his place. Throughout 1884 there was a succession of temporary assistants in the Library. Murie himself was given two months holiday and a gratuity of £25 to allow him to attend the meeting of the British Association at Montreal. At the end of the year, out of a host of applicants, the Council appointed as Assistant in the Library August Wilhelm Kappel, who came from near Düsseldorf and was a relative by marriage of W. F. Kirby, FLS, then in the Zoological Department of the British Museum. This brought the number of paid staff up to three, and presently Murie indirectly brought about the addition of a fourth. Early in 1885 he sent in his resignation in a characteristic letter, but it did not take effect. The Council, however, decided to split up his hitherto double duties, to leave him as "Librarian and Sub-Editor", and to create a new salaried post, "Clerk to the Council". A Fellow, Arthur Rashdall Hammond, was appointed to this new post, which he held until 1906.

Romanes was succeeded in the Zoological Secretaryship by W. P. Sladen in June 1885. Walter Percy Sladen (1849–1900) came from an old Yorkshire family. He was especially interested in starfishes and other echinoderms and wrote the volume on the Asteroids in the *Challenger* reports. He held the Secretaryship for ten years, the longest period of any holder since its formal institution in 1861, and performed his duties with much zeal. Four years after his untimely death his widow founded in his memory The Percy Sladen Memorial Fund, the income of which is used to assist research in natural science and more especially in zoology, geology and anthropology. The President and Council of the Linnean Society are empowered to appoint a Trustee under certain conditions.

Sir John Lubbock resigned the Presidency in 1886, after a five-year tenure. The period of Presidency had hitherto been subject to no regulation, and had varied from the 40 years of the first President to the three years of the third, the Duke of Somerset. The Council then discussed the question of limiting the period of office, as had been suggested by Trimen in 1874, and in February 1886 decided that no future President should serve for more than four successive years. The first to come under this rule was William Carruthers, who succeeded Sir John Lubbock in May 1886.

William Carruthers (1830–1922) has already appeared as the leader of the revolt in 1874 that led to Bentham's abdication, and had been a Fellow since 1861. He was a native of Moffat, and was educated there and at Edinburgh University, with a view to entering the Church of Scotland, from which he was diverted to natural science, particularly the study of cryptogams. After a period of lecturing in Edinburgh, he became assistant to J. J. Bennett soon after the latter had succeeded Robert Brown as Keeper of the Botanical Department of the British Museum. He succeeded Bennett in 1871 and remained Keeper until his retirement in 1895.

In December 1887, Murie once more sent in his resignation to take effect after the usual period of notice, and this time the Council accepted it. He was granted a pension of £100 per annum. As he had served only two years that was very liberal on the part of the Council. At the Council Meeting of 19 January 1888, Murie laid before each member a long, printed statement in which he detailed, without excessive modesty, his achievements in the Society's service. The Council might have stomached this, but when it saw that the statement also made an utterly baseless attack on the President for having worked against Murie, the long-suffering Council resolved to end Murie's services on 31 January but to pay him to 24 May. The grant of the pension was not rescinded. Murie then betook himself to Leigh-on-Sea, where, except for occasional visits to London, he lived until his death on Christmas Day 1925.

At this same meeting in January 1888 the Council appointed James Edmund Fotheringham Harting (1844–1928), then sitting on the Council, to succeed Murie, with the difference that Harting's occupation of the residential flat was to be terminable by a resolution of the Council.

Harting was then a man of 47 who, in his younger days, had travelled extensively on the Continent. He was primarily an ornithologist, his publications including *The Ornithology of Shakespeare* (1871), *A Handbook of British Birds* (1872), *British Animals Extinct within Historic Times* (1880) and *Essays on Sport* (1883). He was also an authority on falconry and wrote *Hints on the Management of Hawks* (1884) and *Bibliotheca Accipitraria* (1891). At the time of his appointment to the Librarianship he was Natural History Editor of the *Field* and Editor of the *Zoologist*, posts he continued to hold after his appointment to the Society's service. Unfortunately, there was an inevitable pull between his work outside the Society and his duties within. Those latter were enough, if properly performed, to give full-time occupation, and the Council did not make this very clear. As it was, Harting interested himself too much in other work and studies outside his official duties to be an entirely satisfactory servant of the Society.

The principal event in 1888 was the celebration of the Society's centenary. Although the Council had from time to time excused the payment of entrance fee and annual contribution by specially distinguished botanists or zoologists elected as Fellows, the Society for the first 100 years of its existence had no overt means of showing its appreciation of eminence in scientific research. There had been three attempts to found a medal. In 1801, Richard Pulteney (1730–1801), a surgeon and historian of botany, bequeathed his collections of natural history to the Society on the conditions that either they should be kept distinct or, if sold, that the proceeds, made up to £200 if necessary, should be used to buy annually a medal of five guineas in value to be awarded to that member of the Society who should write within the year the best paper on any botanical subject. The non-incorporation of the Society at that time made the bequest invalid but, after incorporation in 1802, Pulteney's executors presented to the Society £200 of 3 per cent Consols as well as the collections. The Society sold the investment in 1805 or 1806 and the collections in 1863, but nothing more was heard of a medal.

In 1846, the legacy, also of £200 in 3 per cent Consols, left by Edward Rudge for the foundation of a gold "Linnean Medal" had to be declined for the reasons mentioned earlier in this history.

In 1887, the widow and son of Thomas Spencer Cobbold, FLS, distinguished for his researches on animal parasites, offered to institute a gold medal in his memory, but again the conditions were too hampering for the Society to accept.

In January 1888, J. Morley Dennis, FLS, of Grimsby suggested that a gold medal should be subscribed for and presented annually. The Council did not adopt this suggestion of a subscription, but resolved to institute at the Society's expense a Linnean gold medal free from all restrictions except that no one member of Council at the time of the award should be eligible. The medal was to be presented annually at the Anniversary Meeting alternately to an eminent botanist and an eminent zoologist selected by the Council irrespective of nationality or Society membership.

The medal had on the obverse the head of Linnaeus, with the legend "Carolus Linnaeus", on the reverse the arms of the Society, with the legend "Societas Linnaeana optime merenti", and an oval space for the medallist's name. The engraver of the medal, whose name is immortalized in small letters on the obverse under the shoulder of Linnaeus, was Charles Anderson Ferrier. A native of Dundee, he had lived in London for many years and was a Fellow from 1882 until his death in 1908. A silver copy of the medal was presented in 1906 to the national collection of coins and medals in the British Museum. To mark in a special manner the centenary year of the Society and the first year of the award two medals were given, one to a botanist and one to a zoologist. During the period 1888–1986 the medal has been presented to 48 botanists in the British Commonwealth, 18 foreign botanists, 49 zoologists in the British Commonwealth and 12 foreign zoologists. The award was suspended during the Second World War from 1942–45. In 1958 it became customary to present two Linnean medals annually, one to a botanist, the other to a zoologist. Agnes Arber (1879–1960), the Cambridge botanical morphologist, in 1948 became the first woman to receive it; she was also the third woman elected to the Royal Society. The last truly gold medal was awarded in 1976; thereafter it has been an alloy.

On Thursday, 24 May 1888, William Carruthers being President, Frank Crisp Treasurer, Benjamin Daydon Jackson Botanical and Walter Percy Sladen Zoological Secretaries, the formal celebration of the centenary of the Society's founding took place in the main Library on the first floor, with the presidential chair at the west end. Although on rare occasions women had been permitted to attend an ordinary meeting of the Society, they had never been allowed to be present at an Anniversary Meeting; but on this occasion the first row of chairs in the "front gallery" (probably the east gallery) was reserved for women. The official *Proceedings*, of course, ignore their presence.

Since 1865, after the death of Leopold I, King of the Belgians and uncle of Queen Victoria, there had been no Honorary Member of the Society until December 1886, when the Prince of Wales (afterwards Edward VII) was elected. At the Centenary Meeting, Oscar II, King of Sweden and Norway, was also elected, thus beginning an association which his successors to the throne of Sweden, Gustav V and Carl XVI Gustaf, have honoured the Society by continuing.

After the formal business of an ordinary Anniversary Meeting had been concluded, the Treasurer presented a brief synopsis of the financial history of the Society compiled by the Botanical Secretary, who also gave a not-so-brief account of the library and collections of Linnaeus, and the President delivered a historical sketch of the Society. Certain erroneous statements in those sketches regarding the early history of the Society suggest that they were rather hurriedly prepared, without verification from the Society's early records. After the Presidential Address four eulogia were pronounced: the first on Linnaeus written by Thore Fries, Professor of Botany at Uppsala, but read in his absence by Carruthers; the second on Robert Brown by Sir Joseph Hooker; the third on Darwin by W. H. Flower; and the fourth on Bentham by Thiselton Dyer. All were excellent tributes and can still be read for first-hand information. The Linnean Medals were then presented to Sir Joseph Hooker and Sir Richard Owen. The Centenary Dinner took place in the Victoria Hotel, Northumberland Avenue, and, on the following day, a Presidential Reception was held in the Society's rooms.

Carruthers might have risen better to the occasion in his address. He had spoken with more eloquence at the previous Anniversary Meeting in 1887, when he had proposed that the hundredth year of the Society should not pass away unnoticed, and with the words he then spoke this chapter well may end:

> The services we have, as a Society, rendered to biological science more than justify our right to exist. The story of the Linnean Society during the century is the history of Biology. That story would centre around three names which will ever be held in high honour by, I will not say all Linneans, but by all the world – the names, I mean, of our founder Sir James Edward Smith, of Robert Brown, and of Charles Darwin. These men represent the three great steps in Biological Science – the maintenance of the Linnean system, the philosophical illustration and establishment of the Natural System, and the study of the phenomena of life in the organism.

Chapter 6

From the Centenary to the admission of women
1888 to 1905

During the Society's first century there had been only ten Presidents and ten Treasurers, five sole Secretaries, two Botanical and six Zoological Secretaries. The resolution of 1886 to restrict the tenure of the Presidency to a maximum of four years started a comparatively rapid succession of Presidents, beginning with Carruthers. There was, and is, no definite term fixed for the Treasurership and the Secretaryships, but the changes in the Zoological have been more than in the Botanical Secretaryship since 1861 to the present day. During the period 1888–1905 there were six Presidents, one Treasurer, two Botanical and three Zoological Secretaries.

Carruthers was succeeded as President by Charles Stewart (1840–1908), the Conservator of the Hunterian Museum of the Royal College of Surgeons from 1884–1908. He was the son of a surgeon in Plymouth and trained for the medical profession at St Bartholomew's Hospital, London. Apart from his detailed catalogues of the Hunterian Museum collections he wrote little, but was considered one of the best lecturers in London. Jessie Dobson, a successor at the Royal College, has stated that "with his vast biological and anatomical knowledge, his artistic skill and his enthusiasm, no Conservator did more than he to carry on the great tradition of the Hunterian collection". Appreciation of these qualities led to his election as President from 1890 to 1894.

After him came Charles Baron Clarke (1832–1906), who held office only from 1894 to 1896. Although not a professional botanist, he had from his youth been interested in systematic botany. He was born at Andover and was a graduate of Cambridge, where he was Tutor of Mathematics at Queens' College for nine years before joining the Indian Educational Service. He made immense collections of plants from all over India and contributed notably to knowledge of the Indian flora through these and his publications on Indian *Commelinaceae*, *Gesneriaceae*, *Compositae* and *Cyperaceae*. He had multifarious interests outside botany and wrote on many topics of the day

The next President, from 1896 to 1900, was Albert Karl Ludwig Gotthilf Günther (1830–1914), for many years Britain's leading herpetologist and ichthyologist. He was a Württemberger who began his university education at Tübingen as a student of theology, changed to medicine and spent the greater part of his life as a zoologist in London studying fish and snakes. His father had died while the son was still a boy, and study of theology in preparation for the Lutheran Church provided the only means for such a boy of getting a free university education, but at Tübingen he came under the influence of Wilhelm von Rapp, who taught anatomy, physiology and zoology, and became a medical student. After further study at Berlin and Bonn he qualified as a physician in 1856. His

(a)

(b)

(c)

(d)

widowed mother had emigrated to England and he followed her there in 1857. An introduction to J. E. Gray, Keeper of Zoology in the British Museum, resulted in temporary employment cataloguing specimens of snakes at £40 per 1000, working in a gloomy, damp Museum cellar from 10 am to 10 pm. In four months Günther had examined 3100 specimens of Colubrine snakes, embarrassing Gray who had not enough Museum money to pay him! His *Catalogue of Colubrine Snakes*, a work of 281 pages, appeared early in 1858 as a British Museum publication. It was more than a catalogue; it was a thorough descriptive monographic survey. His *Catalogue of the Fishes* (8 vols, 1859–70) manifested the same combination of ability, industry and zeal. Not surprisingly, Günther was appointed Keeper of Zoology in 1875, retiring in 1895. Thereupon the Linnean Society took the opportunity of electing him President, honouring him as no other body did at the time. Despite his 38 years in the Museum, according to C. D. Sherborn, "He never lost his accent and I have often laughed to hear him talk about 'dese leedle frosches' when reading a paper ... (on one occasion) Günther beamed over his spectacles and said 'Would Professor Seely rebeat dat statement'. Seeley did so, and Günther said 'Den all I can say is dat all dose people who have said so is liars', and sat down". Günther was not unique in prodigious achievement; two other Victorian Presidents, Bentham and Lubbock, rivalled him. Unlike Lubbock, however, he was never an evolutionist; he was present at the historic meeting of the Society on 1 July 1858 but, as a taxonomist impressed by the constancy of specific characters manifested in the thousands of specimens he examined, he remained unconvinced of their change in accordance with the hypothesis of Darwin and Wallace. His presidential address of 1899 dealt with Linnaeus's collection of fish specimens and provided a catalogue published in *Proceedings*, sess. III (for 1898–99): 15–38 (1899).

The botanist who succeeded Günther as President was Sydney Howard Vines (1849–1934), the Sherardian Professor of Botany at Oxford. Vines was born in London and was educated partly in Germany and partly in England. He later entered Guy's Hospital Medical School, where T. H. Huxley chose him to help teach biology at the Royal College of Science. About the same time he entered Christ's College, Cambridge, and, in due course, was appointed Reader in Botany. He translated Karl A. E. Prantl's *Lehrbuch der Botanik* into English as *An elementary Text-book of Botany* (1880), which was so often mentioned as "Prantl and Vines" that a lady visitor to the British Museum (Natural History), being well acquainted with vines, asked Dr Rendle what kind of plant was a "prantl". In 1888, he was appointed to the Oxford Professorship, which he held until his retirement in 1919. Vines was one of the pioneers in England of the modern study of plant physiology and a founder of the *Annals of Botany*. His portrait (1905) by the Hon. John Collier hangs in the Society's rooms. He was President from 1900 to 1904.

William Abbott Herdman (1858–1925), the fifteenth President, from 1904 to 1908, was the last to preside over a Society composed of men only, for in the first year of his reign women began to be elected to Fellowship. He was born and educated in Edinburgh. After a brief period as Demonstrator in Zoology at the university there, he became at 23 Professor of Natural History at University College, Liverpool. After holding that post for

---

Plate XII   (a) Dunkinfield Henry Scott, from a photograph in the Society's collection. (b) Albert K. L. Günther, from a photograph in the Society's collection. (c) James Harting, from a photograph in the Society's collection. (d) William Herdman, from a photograph of a painting done in May 1906.

38 years he moved to the Chair of Oceanography. He was primarily a marine zoologist and a prolific writer on his subject. He was knighted in 1922.

The Treasurer throughout the period was Frank Crisp, of whom a brief account has already been given.

The two Botanical Secretaries were B. D. Jackson and D. H. Scott. Elected in 1880, Jackson held office until 1902, when he became General Secretary. His successor in the Botanical Secretaryship, Dukinfield Henry Scott (1854–1934), was the son of Sir Gilbert Scott, the celebrated architect. He was born in London and educated privately. At first a student of engineering, he reverted to botany, in which he had been interested as a boy. At this time the fame of Julius Sachs (1832–97), a brilliant botanical lecturer and experimentalist, and of his stimulating textbooks drew outstanding British students to his laboratory at Würzburg. They included F. O. Bower, Francis Darwin, H. Marshall Ward, S. H. Vines, Walter Gardiner and Scott. Back in England from Würzburg, Scott was appointed an assistant in University College, London, and then at the Royal College of Science. Finally, he became Honorary Keeper of the Jodrell Laboratory at Kew, and began, at first in association with Williamson, his masterly researches in palaeobotany, which gained him eminence and recognition. He was President of the Society from 1908 to 1912 and was awarded the Linnean Medal in 1921.

The three Zoological Secretaries were W. P. Sladen, already mentioned, from 1885 to 1895; T. G. B. Howes from 1895 to 1903; and the Rev. T. R. R. Stebbing from 1903 to 1907.

Thomas George Bond Howes (1853–1905) was a Londoner associated for his entire distinguished scientific career with the Royal College of Science, where he was successively assistant to T. H. Huxley, Demonstrator in Biology, Assistant Professor and Professor of Zoology. Ill-health ended his tenure of the secretaryship.

Thomas Roscoe Rede Stebbing (1835–1926) was also London-born. After a brilliant career as a student at Oxford he entered the Church, but took up tuition. Although he did not become a Fellow until 1895 he had been much earlier indirectly associated with the Society by his marriage in 1867 to an accomplished field naturalist, one of the daughters of W. W. Saunders, who was then the Society's Treasurer. Stebbing's special study was the Crustacea. He was the Linnean Medallist in 1908.

A demonstration of historical interest extending beyond the Society's domestic affairs took place at the General Meeting of 20 June 1889. To quote the *Proceedings* (1888–90: 53): "A demonstration on Animal Locomotion was then given by Mr. E. Muybridge, illustrated by projections on the screen by oxy-hydrogen light, of instantaneous photographs taken by him, to which motion was imparted by means of the zoopraxiscope." The audience in fact had seen one of the forerunners of the cinematograph. This was also the first recorded occasion on which a lantern had been used at a meeting, and it seems to have aroused a desire to possess one. In December 1891, the question of buying a lantern was referred to the officers for report, but their deliberations were speedily rendered needless by Richard C. A. Prior presenting in the following month £50 for the purchase of one. As none of the Society's staff could work the lantern, an outsider from the Royal Veterinary College had to be engaged to do so at £5 per session. In 1893, the means of illuminating the meetings were still further increased by the installation of electric light at the expense of Frank Crisp, the Treasurer.

In 1894, the Society expressed its views to the Colonial Office in favour of the retention of the Singapore Botanic Garden, the abolition of which as a scientific institution was being contemplated.

In 1897, the post of Assistant-Secretary, which had been nominally suspended since

1880, was revived, and J. E. F. Harting, who had been Librarian since 1888 in succession to Murie, was given the revived designation, while the title of "Librarian" was transferred to A. W. Kappel, who had been assistant in the library since 1884. At the same time, A. R. Hammond's original designation of "Clerk to the Council" was shortened to "Clerk". Those nominal changes had no effect on the work, although they may have lightened Harting's share of it; nonetheless, neither he nor Kappel overworked themselves in the Society's service.

At the Anniversary Meeting in 1898, Günther as President presented to Sir Joseph Hooker a gold medal that had been specially struck to mark the completion of the *Flora of British India* (1875–97) and to recognize Sir Joseph's great services to science during 60 years. Sir Joseph was then 80 years of age.

In February 1901, the Society submitted its Address of Condolence to King Edward VII on the death of Queen Victoria, who had been the Society's Patron for so many years. About this time the scheme for an International Catalogue for Scientific Literature was also under way. The Society undertook the preparation of the entries concerned with the botany of the British Isles and was represented at the Central Bureau of the Catalogue by Jackson, then still the Botanical Secretary.

Jackson did not remain Botanical Secretary much longer. Harting was not performing his duties as Assistant-Secretary with that zeal and exactitude that might have been expected of one who was a Fellow and had been a Councillor. Things could not go on as they were, and Harting found it expedient in 1902 to take the opportunity given him by the Council of devoting all his time to his outside interests.

With Harting's resignation, the Assistant-Secretaryship was once more abolished and the new paid post of General Secretary, at an annual salary of £250, was filled by Jackson. The work of the new post remained that of the old one, but with the difference that the General Secretary equalled in standing the two Honorary Secretaries. It was laid down that Jackson should remain a member of Council until the pending revision of the Bye-Laws was finished. Jackson did not relish this prospective exclusion from the Council on which he had sat for 22 years, and he stipulated that the General Secretary should continue on the Council. Knowing his worth, the Council accepted this stipulation, and Jackson entered his new duties on 24 May 1902 and served as a member of Council for the following 25 years. In his new post he gave of his best in Society affairs and wielded considerable influence on them.

At the Anniversary Meeting of 1902, the Prince of Wales, afterwards King George V, was elected an Honorary Member. His service as a Trustee of the British Museum, of which the British Museum (Natural History) at South Kensington was legally a part until 1963, brought him into close friendly relations with naturalists and men of varied learning, such as the other Trustees and the Directors, that he greatly valued. His election was thus in keeping with his general interests.

In 1903, the Council was somewhat nonplussed by the receipt of a letter from the philosopher Herbert Spencer (1820–1903) in which he thanked the Society for a congratulatory telegram on his eighty-third birthday. The Council had sent no congratulation by telegram or otherwise, but took care not to enlighten the philosopher. Spencer had never been a Fellow of the Society, although he had contributed a paper, "On circulation and the formation of wood in plants", which was published in the Society's *Transactions* in 1866. Spencer was more mindful of the Society than the Society had been of him, inasmuch as the Society became a beneficiary under his will: as late as 1936, £1241 came as payment of a bequest from him.

In his 1904 Presidential Address, Vines suggested that the Council should present an annual report on the Society's affairs. This suggestion has never been adopted, since the information given at the Anniversary Meetings serves as well as a special report.

While the events so far related in this chapter were happening, a revolution in the constitution of the Society had begun.

In April 1900, women, or rather one woman, began to knock at the Society's door, and the knocking continued, to the embarrassment of the Council, for the next few years until the door was opened. The question of the admission of women to scientific societies, although now presented for the first time to the Linnean Society, was not startlingly new. The Zoological Society had admitted women to Fellowship from its incorporation in 1829. The Royal Entomological Society had women members from the beginning in 1833. As far back as the 1860s the general question had been discussed in scientific circles. The *Life and Letters of T. H. Huxley*, I, p. 211, prints a letter from Huxley, dated 11 March 1860, to Sir Charles Lyell in which Huxley, who had married in 1855, gives his views. He advocated the "intellectual advancement and development of women", but was then of the opinion that women would be no better than "friponnes" in science. Twenty-two years later, however, he had observed "a wonderful change for the better". This change which Huxley had observed in women was not then paralleled by any corresponding change in the attitude to the admission of women by the men conducting the affairs of most of the scientific societies, notably the Royal and the Linnean. The Royal Microscopical Society in 1884 admitted women to its Fellowship, but without the rights or privileges of attending meetings. That society did not go so far, however, as to disdain accepting admission fees and annual contributions from their women Fellows, and this preposterous arrangement endured until 1909, when women were put on the same footing as men. In 1892, the Royal Geographical Society elected 15 women but repented its attitude in the following year, when the society was again closed to women and remained closed until 1913.

In the Linnean Society there is an early instance of a woman being present as a visitor at a Fellows' Meeting. Marsham, in his letter of 29 January 1797 to Smith, already mentioned in connection with the Fellows' Meeting of 17 January, gives the names of those present, beginning with Miss Goodenough and Dr Goodenough. No doubt the Treasurer had taken his daughter to the meeting to see the portrait of Smith by Rising. There is no recorded further visit of any woman for nearly 100 years.

Although the Society excluded women from membership, it had very occasionally published papers by women in both the *Transactions* and the *Journal*, the earliest paper being one by Anne Welch on "*Hemerocallis flava* from *H. fulva*", published in 1794 in Vol. II of the *Transactions*.

The first bold woman to seek entrance to the Society's rooms for scientific purposes was Miss Mary H. Beale of Stroud, who asked in November 1886 for permission to subscribe to the Society's publications and to use the library. The Council deferred consideration of this request and nothing more was heard of it. In the following month permission was given, "although contrary to custom" as the Minutes have it, to Francis Darwin (1848–1925), then Lecturer in Botany at Cambridge, for the attendance of Miss Anna Bateson at the General Meeting of 20 January 1887 to hear the reading of a paper of which she was joint author with Francis Darwin. In 1890, Miss Ethel Barton (1864–1922), later Mrs A. Gepp, and Miss Annie Lorrain Smith (1854–1937) were permitted to attend the General Meeting of 5 June during the reading of the algological papers of which they were in whole or part the authors. Both these ladies were distinguished cryptogamists. In 1898, a further stage was reached, when in May Miss Ethel Barton was actually allowed to demonstrate her own paper and to bring a woman friend with her. In November, Miss Dale was permitted to hear a paper of which she was part author, and in December H. J. Elwes brought two women to hear him discourse on the flora and fauna of the Altai Mountains.

So long as women were contented with such occasional snippets of permission, so long they were likely to remain outside the Society. Only a determined champion of their claims could overcome the inertia so well expressed in the phrase of the Council Minutes "contrary to custom". The champion presently appeared in the person of Mrs Marian Sarah Ogilvie Farquharson (1846–1912). As it is primarily more to her than to anyone else that women interested or engaged in biological studies owe their eligibility for membership of the Society, she merits special remembrance by women.

Marian Sarah Ridley was the eldest daughter of the Rev. J. Nicholas Ridley of Hollington, Hants, and was born at Privet, Northamptonshire, in 1846. Her scientific interests were botanical, and especially concerned with the higher cryptogams. She wrote *A Pocket Guide to British Ferns*, published in 1881. In 1883 she married Robert F. Ogilvie Farquharson (1823–90), a diatomist of Haughton, Aberdeenshire, and spent most of her life in Scotland.

On 9 October 1899, at the first Annual General Meeting of the Lady Warwick Agricultural Association for Women, held in Stafford House with the Countess of Warwick in the Chair, it was unanimously resolved that it was "desirable and important that duly qualified women should have the advantage of full fellowship in scientific and other learned societies, e.g. the Royal, the Linnean and the Royal Microscopical". At this meeting Mrs Farquharson submitted a humbly worded petition, dated 18 April 1900, to the President and Council of the Linnean Society, in which she craved that duly qualified women should be eligible for ordinary Fellowship and, if elected, there should be no restriction forbidding their attendance at meetings. She expressly did not ask for eligibility to "Executive posts in your Society". Mrs Farquharson was then a Fellow of the Royal Microscopical Society, which at that time did not allow its women Fellows to attend meetings. This explains the reference to restriction forbidding attendance at meetings.

In their earlier dealings with the question of the admission of women the Council of the Linnean Society was no better than a convocation of politicians seeking to evade the inevitable. It began badly. It returned Mrs Farquharson's petition with the intimation that communications of that nature could be received only through a Fellow. This action was neither courteous nor convincing. Nothing whatever in Charter or Bye-Laws prevented the Council either receiving the communication or discussing its subject. In any case, the Council was not going to be rid of the question in this fashion. Mrs Farquharson, rebuffed but undaunted, again submitted her petition at the Council Meeting of 7 June, this time through a supporter, Lord Avebury, who, as the far-sighted and public-spirited Sir John Lubbock, had been President from 1881 to 1886. The Council deferred consideration of the subject until its following meeting on 28 June, when it resolved that it was unable to accede to the proposal, as it was more than doubtful whether the Society's Charter could be held to apply to women. There the Council left the matter. Certainly, when the original Charter was granted in 1802, the possibility of women seeking election to the Society had not come within the bounds of thought. Nevertheless, there is no expressed discrimination in the Charter against them. The solitary masculine word, apart from proper names, in the whole Charter, the pronoun "he", refers only to the first President in connection with the appointment of Vice-Presidents for 1802–03. The difficulty was apparently that women had not yet legally become "persons".

The Council might have tried to leave the matter quiet, but the Council itself was not to be left in peace. Early in the following session, in November 1900, Marcus Manuel Hartog (1851–1924), then Professor of Natural History in University College, Cork, wrote to the Council, advocating the admission of women and urging that the interpretation of the Charter on the point should be defined. Thus prodded, the Council consulted early in 1901 a barrister, A. R. Kirby, who gave his opinion that the terms of the Charter precluded the admission of women. So once more the Council sat back and folded its hands, but this restful attitude was not to endure. In April 1901, Mrs Farquharson returned to the attack, this time submitting her case through F. DuCane Godman, then a member of Council, and G. B. Howes, then Zoological Secretary. Her letter "was laid on the table". In short, no notice was taken of it.

In June 1901, Miss Ethel Barton and Miss Annie Lorrain Smith were permitted to attend the General Meeting of 6 June, although they were not concerned with the sole paper discussed. However, when Mrs Farquharson applied in July for permission for herself and two other ladies to attend the first General Meeting in November she was informed that permission could not be considered as the programme for the next session had not been drawn up. The Council was entitled to refuse permission but the reason given remarkably resembled a pretext.

The Council might lay on the table Mrs Farquharson's application but it could not silence that disturber of its serenity. Early in the following session, Mrs Farquharson again assaulted the position, this time through Joseph Reynolds Green (1848–1914), the Pharmaceutical Society's Professor of Botany, who had been elected to the Council in May 1901. At the Council Meeting on 7 November 1901 another incantation was tried, the discussion being adjourned this time with the magical words "sine die". The magic did not work, for the Council had to deal with one not to be put off with "laid on the table", "sine die" or similar nonsense. Green re-submitted Mrs Farquharson's memorial on 19 December 1901 and stated that a considerable number of Fellows favoured it. The Council expressed a desire to see the signatures of those Fellows, thus beginning to weaken. Reynolds Green lost little time in gratifying, if that is the right word, the Council and produced enough signatures at the next meeting in January 1902 to shake the Council into referring the question to a committee of the honorary officers. In the multitude of councillors there was safety, but in the committee there was sense, and its report to the Council emboldened the latter to issue in March 740 copies of a circular to Fellows enquiring whether they were for or against the admission of women to the Society. There were 301 replies in favour, 126 against, with 313 not replying at all. The result of this referendum encouraged the Council to declare the General Meeting of 15 January 1903 a special one for considering and voting on proposals for obtaining a Supplementary Charter to embody certain alterations in the constitution of the Society. The two most important changes were provision for the admission of women and the enlargement of the Council from 15 to 20 members. Mindful, no doubt, of the trouble caused in 1874 by Bentham's insistence on a mixed lot of alterations in the Bye-Laws being taken en bloc, on this occasion the Chairman – Frank Crisp the Treasurer in place of Vines, the President, who was absent through illness – put the first proposed alteration embodying the admission of women separately to the vote. It was carried by 54 votes against 17. The remaining alterations, after a vain attempt to adjourn consideration of them, were carried by 43 votes against 3. The comedy was now drawing to a close, but not without a final tragic note.

Clearly, the Council had not exhibited enthusiasm over the prospect of women invading the Linnean rooms, and in his Presidential Address in 1903 Vines expressed his apprehension as to the future and described the Society as passing through a serious crisis. Still, if the Council had some sympathy with the crusted conservatives who had a vision of the Society falling under a "monstrous regiment", in both the Knoxian and modern sense of the term, there was a limit to that sympathy. When such a crusted one wrote to the Council requesting to have part of his composition fee returned to him in the event of women being admitted as Fellows and on his own consequent resignation, the Council was stony hearted – at least concerning the return of his money.

By the end of 1903, the petition for a Supplementary Charter was prepared and the Charter granted on 8 April 1904. The revision of the Bye-Laws was next undertaken and the revised Bye-Laws were passed on 3 November 1904. At last, after several years of hammering, the door was open. On 17 November 1904 the names of 16 women were presented to the meeting for election. They included the Duchess of Bedford; Mrs Catherine Crisp, the wife of the Treasurer; Mrs Mary Anne Stebbing, the wife of the Zoological Secretary; Mrs Constance Percy Sladen, the widow of a former Zoological Secretary; Dr Margaret Benson; Dr M. Ogilvie Gordon; Miss G. Lister; and Mrs Farquharson. At the ballot on 15 December, 15 out of the 16 women were elected. Lord Ripon, Lord Avebury, Sir Michael Foster, H. J. Elwes, W. C. McIntosh and J. Reynolds Green had signed the certificate of the one blackballed: she was Mrs Farquharson. The last exclusively masculine meeting of the Society exhibited no magnanimity. Her rejection was as disgraceful an act as the earlier treatment of J. E. Gray.

Mrs Farquharson, although grievously wounded at the moment of victory for her sex, was not slain. She reappeared as a candidate in March 1908 and that time was elected. Ill health, however, prevented this dauntless lady from ever being formally admitted. She died at Nice in 1912 and was buried at Alford in Aberdeenshire.

The first formal admission of women to Fellowship took place on 19 January 1905, when 11 signed the Book of Admission and Obligation. Frank Crisp, the Treasurer, gave a celebratory dinner on 18 May at Prince's Restaurant in Piccadilly for the women who had been elected during the session. He also commissioned and paid James Sant, RA, then aged 86, to paint a large picture of the scene, and the painting was exhibited in the Royal Academy exhibition in 1906. After Crisp's death in 1919 the picture, in accordance with his wishes, was presented to the Society by Lady Crisp. The picture shows the Presidential table with figures grouped about it. The figures from left to right, as the spectator views them, are: Miss E. L. Turner; Miss Annie Lorrain Smith; B. D. Jackson, the General Secretary; Miss S. M. Silver; Mrs L. J. Veley, who is signing the Book; Mrs Constance Sladen; D. H. Scott, the Botanical Secretary; Mrs (afterwards Lady) Crisp, who is receiving the hand of Fellowship from the President, W. A. Herdman; F. Crisp, the Treasurer. In the picture as it was exhibited in the Academy there were two other figures, the Rev. T. R. R. Stebbing, the Zoological Secretary, and his somewhat corpulent wife. Mrs Stebbing was standing in the right foreground, appearing between Herdman and Crisp. The Zoological Secretary was standing at the extreme right at the end of the table. A hand other than Sant's painted out those two figures before the Society received the picture. It hangs on the stairway above the Library. The two versions are reproduced in *The Linnean*, 1: 10 (1984).

Of these pioneering ladies, the most distinguished from a natural history standpoint

were Miss Smith and Miss Turner. Annie Lorrain Smith (1892–1937) belonged to a talented Scottish family; between 1892 and 1933 she worked at seaweeds, fungi and lichens in the British Museum (Natural History), was President of the British Mycological Society in 1907 and 1917, and wrote the standard *Handbook of British Lichens* (1921). Emma Louisa Turner (1866–1940) was a pioneer bird photographer who lived for many years on a houseboat on Hickling Broad, Norfolk, by "Miss Turner's Island", studying the habits of marshland birds. In 1928 she became warden of Scolt Head Island bird sanctuary; the island was cut off by strong seas for a time and she was afterwards acclaimed in newspapers as "the woman Crusoe", without, however, having any Man Friday. Her ornithological publications include *The Home Life of Some Marsh-birds* (1907), *Broadland Birds* (1925) and *Bird Watching on Scolt Head* (1928). Unfortunately, she was blind for the last two years of her life. It was preposterous that women of such talent and enthusiasm should have been so long excluded from membership of the Linnean Society. In extenuation it should be noted that the even more conservative Royal Society, with an image of elitism and exclusiveness to maintain, first elected women to membership in 1945; moreover, women were not granted full membership of the University of Oxford until 1920.

Comment must be made on the statement in Peter Chalmers Mitchell's *History of the Zoological Society of London*, 56 (1929): "It is of interest to recall that the Zoological Society a century ago admitted women as Fellows, although apparently not without heartsearching. The Linnean Society followed, but more than half a century later, and then, it is believed, chiefly from a reluctant compliance with financial needs." According to this, in 1929 there existed a belief that (a) the Linnean Society was unwilling to admit women to Fellowship and (b) the Society's reluctance to admit women was overcome chiefly because the Society wanted their money. Undoubtedly the Council of the Linnean Society was very reluctant either to discuss the question or to come to any decision about it, but the Council was not the Society. The Fellows, as soon as they were given the opportunity of declaring their views, showed that only about 17 per cent opposed the admission of women. In the referendum paper nothing whatever was said about the possible influence of the admission of women on the Society's income. In his Presidential Address in 1903, some months after the Fellows scattered all over the world had expressed their views and the Fellows assembled in the Society's meeting room had given their votes, Vines, who had been President throughout most of the period during which Mrs Farquharson and her supporters within the Society had been bombarding the Council, made the following remarks:

> Regarding the matter, as I am bound to do, from the point of view of the welfare of the Society, I must confess that I am not altogether free from apprehension as to the future. We are making a somewhat heroic experiment, with no precedent, no working hypothesis to suggest to us what the results are likely to be. If purity of motive can deserve success, then it should certainly be ours: for this revolution in our constitution is the expression of a sense of justice, of a desire to extend an equal recognition to all, whether men or women, who work in or for biological science.

Vines, in his first two sentences, expressed the attitude of the majority of the Council as well as his own; in the last sentence he expressed the feeling of the Society. Science has much benefited from the Society's women members, of whom one, Irene Manton, was the Society's President from 1973 to 1976 thanks to this "somewhat heroic experiment".

Plate XII   First admission of Women Fellows, from the painting by James Sant RA in the Society's collection: original version with Mrs Stebbing (right) included.

Chapter 7

From 1905 to 1936

At the beginning of the period 1905–36 the President of the Society was W. A. Herdman, D. H. Scott was Botanical Secretary and the Rev. T. R. R. Stebbing was Zoological Secretary. The paid staff consisted of B. D. Jackson, the General Secretary; A. W. Kappel, the Librarian; and A. R. Hammond, the Clerk. There were during the period eight Presidents and three Botanical and eight Zoological Secretaries.

Herdman gave way in 1908 to Dukinfield Henry Scott, who moved from the Botanical Secretaryship to the Presidency. Although Carruthers, who was President from 1886 to 1890, had done some research in palaeobotany, by electing Scott to the Presidency the Society first paid official tribute to the importance of the study of extinct plants. Scott held office until 1912.

Edward Bagnall Poulton (1856–1943) presided from 1912 to 1916. From 1893 to 1933 he taught as Hope Professor of Zoology in Oxford University, the Chair which had been founded in 1861 by the Rev. F. W. Hope, a Fellow of the Linnean Society. Poulton's contributions to zoology were numerous and various but important above all for emphasis on the protective colouring of the larvae and pupae of Lepidoptera in relation to their surroundings; in 1890 he published *The Colours of Animals, their Meaning and Use, especially considered in the Case of Insects*, followed in 1908 by *Essays on Evolution*. During Poulton's presidency Alfred Russel Wallace received from Boston, Mass., a pamphlet entitled *Shall we have Common Sense?* by a hitherto unknown American author, George Washington Sleeper (1826–1903). It was dated "1849" but put forward evolutionary views well ahead of those current in 1849. Poulton made it the subject of his presidential addresses in 1913 and 1914 and reprinted it in *Proceedings* 126 (1913–14) as an appendix (1914). This pamphlet had been found among Sleeper's papers after his death. Strangely enough it seemed neither to have been distributed nor even recorded during his lifetime. From its content in relation to the year 1849 the pamphlet appeared to be a work of genius anticipating that of Darwin and Wallace. In 1934, Howard Carter and Pollard's *An Enquiry into the Nature of certain Nineteenth Century Pamphlets* proved by refined bibliographical detective methods that a pamphlet dated "1847" of *Sonnets by E.B.B.*, i.e. by Elizabeth Barret Browning, a prized and costly collector's piece, was certainly a forgery printed after 1880 and now known to have been printed for the celebrated book collector and bibliographer Thomas James Wise (1859–1937). Application of such bibliographical methods for the Linnean Society some 20 years before Carter and Pollard had a similar result. The type used for Sleeper's pamphlet was not available before 1870; probably he had it printed about 1890. Thus George Washington S. was something of a liar. The Linnean Society could continue to honour Darwin and Wallace as it had always done.

The outbreak of the 1914–18 World War had little impact on the Society until much later (see page 103).

95

From 1916 to 1919 the Presidency was held by Sir David Prain (1857–1944), who had been Director of the Botanical Survey of India and Superintendent of the Royal Botanic Garden, Calcutta, from 1898 to 1905, and then was Director of the Royal Botanic Gardens, Kew, a post he held from 1905 to 1922. He was the second President to represent Indian botany, Charles Baron Clarke, President from 1894 to 1896, having been the first. Neither of them stayed the full course, Clarke being content with two years and Sir David Prain finding three enough. In this he anticipated by more than a decade what has now become the normal period of tenure of office. A genial well-liked man, unlike his predecessor as Director of Kew, Sir William T. Thiselton-Dyer, but nevertheless of as high administrative ability and greater botanical achievement, Prain helped to heal the animosity which had existed under Thiselton-Dyer between the British Museum (Natural History) and Kew.

The study of extinct plants having been recognized in 1908 by the election of D. H. Scott to the Presidency, it was now time to pay homage to research into the history of animals of the past. Appropriately the next President was Arthur Smith Woodward (1864–1944), the distinguished palaeontologist, then Keeper of the Geological Department of the British Museum. He held office for the full period of four years from 1919 to 1923. Woodward had studied palaeontology at Owens College, Manchester, obtained a post at the British Museum (Natural History) and became a leading authority on fossil fishes, consequently being promoted to Keeper in 1901; he retired in 1924. Before 1912 he seems to have given little or no attention to anthropological material. In that year Charles Dawson, a Sussex lawyer who was also an amateur antiquarian, invited him to an excavation of a gravel-pit at Piltdown, where, among a miscellaneous collection of fossils, they found some human remains, those of the famous and later notorious "Piltdown Man". This brought Woodward far more renown than any amount of high quality work on fossil fishes would have done. He enjoyed the prestige of it when President of the Society. In 1948 appeared, posthumously, his *The Earliest Englishman*, devoted to Piltdown Man. Death in 1944 spared him the traumatic experience of learning how completely he had been fooled and how futile had been his devoted attention to this ingenious fraud which was revealed by Weiner, Oakley and Le Gros-Clark in a British Museum (Natural History) publication of 1953 from his own department! Fortunately, his Presidential Address in 1922 was devoted to a subject in which he possessed extensive first-hand knowledge – Crossopterygian and Arthrodiran fishes.

Sir Arthur Smith Woodward was succeeded in 1923 by Alfred Barton Rendle (1865–1958), who was then Keeper of Botany in the British Museum (Natural History). He, like D. H. Scott in 1908, gave up the Botanical Secretaryship to become President. His period of service in the Museum lasted from 1888 to 1930, from 1906 to 1930 as Keeper of Botany. He joined the Linnean Society in 1888, was President from 1923 to 1927, and diligently and efficiently edited the *Journal of Botany* from 1924 to 1928. On his death, the Society gratefully put on record their high appreciation of his services to the Society during the 50 years of his Fellowship, which had included being a Council member for three triennial periods and Botanical Secretary from 1916 to 1923: "throughout his Fellowship of the Society he showed the greatest interest in its work, both by almost unvarying attendance at its meetings and by important botanical communications".

In 1927, Sir Sidney Harmer (1862–1950) became President: he had not long retired from the directorship of the British Museum (Natural History) which he held from 1919 to 1927 and was the last President to hold office for four years. After a distinguished academic career in Cambridge, he moved in 1907 to London as Keeper of Zoology in the British Museum (Natural History). Thanks to his initiative the Museum became the major centre of whale research. He directed attention in 1911 to the immense slaughter of whales which would endanger their existence. His Presidential Address in 1928 (*Proceedings* 140: 51–95) on the history of whaling showed how one stock after another of whales had been depleted by excessive killing; in his Presidential Address of 1930 (*Proceedings* 142: 85–163; 1931) on southern whaling he revealed alarming statistics demonstrating how high the killing had remained.

Frederick Ernest Weiss (1865–1953) followed Harmer as President. He belonged to one of the cultured German families who settled in the English Midlands in the nineteenth century and was Professor of Botany in the Victoria University of Manchester from 1892 to 1930. A versatile botanist, he made a contribution of note to everything he touched. During his Presidency, from 1931 to 1934, he delivered Presidential Addresses on the Stigmarian problem in fossil botany, on variegated foliage and the northward extension of the Mediterranean flora.

In 1934, the succession reverted again to the British Museum (Natural History) with the election to the Presidency of William Thomas Calman (1871–1939), Keeper of Zoology. Born in Dundee, he began his working life as a clerk in the Caledonian Insurance Company which indicated, on completion of his four-year apprenticeship, that he should find other employment. Fortunately, D'Arcy Wentworth Thompson (1860–1948), then professor of biology in Dundee, made him his laboratory assistant, then demonstrator, and so encouraged him that he gained a doctorate from St Andrew's University in 1903. Ray Lankester, equally impressed by his talent, put him in charge of Crustacea at the British Museum (Natural History). He became Keeper of Zoology in 1927 and retired in 1936, having not only revolutionized the study of Crustacea in the Museum but also its attitude to the employment of women as scientific staff; the only employment previously considered fit for them seems to have been as cleaners and lavatory attendants. Calman gave a Presidential Address in 1935 on the meaning of biological classification, in 1936 on the origin of insects, and in 1937 on a pioneer Antarctic naturalist, James Eights.

The first of the three Botanical Secretaries who came wholly within the period was Austrian-born Otto Stapf (1857–1933), who succeeded D. H. Scott in 1908 and was Secretary for eight years until 1916. He studied at Vienna University under Julius Wiesner and then became assistant to Anton Kerner von Marilaun. In 1885, having previously studied collections of herbarium specimens from Iran and Asia Minor, he travelled and collected plants in Iran, the cost paid by Jacob Eduard Polak, who had been personal physician to the Shah. Back in Vienna he found his efforts little appreciated. A letter of 21 July 1888 to J. D. Hooker indicates his growing dissatisfaction with conditions and attitudes in Vienna and the possibility of his seeking employment in a foreign country. Kerner had another brilliant student, Richard Wettstein (1863–1931), who married Kerner's daughter Adele. Stapf probably felt that this blocked the likelihood of his succeeding to Kerner's professorship in Vienna, which ultimately passed to Wettstein, and he gladly accepted in 1890 the post of Assistant for India, helping Hooker to complete *The Flora of British India*. Stapf's *Die Arten der Gattung Ephedro* (1889) had impressed Hooker as being the work of a very competent taxonomist. In 1909 he became Keeper of the Kew Herbarium. To the Botanical Secretaryship he brought a wide knowledge of languages, as well as of botany, and diligence in its affairs. After his retirement in 1922 he edited the *Index Londinensis* and *Curtis's Botanical Magazine* with the same care. In 1927 he received the Society's Linnean Medal. Stapf's successor,

Alfred Barton Rendle, served as Secretary for seven years until he was elected President in 1923.

The next Secretary was the mycologist John Ramsbottom (1885–1974), who at the time of his appointment was an Assistant in the Department of Botany in the British Museum (Natural History); he became Keeper in 1930. He held the Secretaryship until his election to the Presidency in 1937, when he was succeeded by Isaac Henry Burkill (1870–1965), Director of the Botanic Gardens, Singapore, from 1912 to 1925.

In the Zoological Secretaryship, the first change took place in 1907 when Arthur Dendy succeeded the Rev. T. R. R. Stebbing. Arthur Dendy (1856–1925), after an education at Owens College, Manchester, worked for a short time as a zoologist in the British Museum (Natural History). Thereafter he was, in succession, Assistant-Lecturer in Zoology at Melbourne University; Professor of Biology at Canterbury College, New Zealand; Professor of Zoology at Cape Town; and, from 1905 to his death in 1925, Professor of Zoology at King's College, London. His zoological work covered a wide field, but his chief studies were on sponges. He was Zoological Secretary for five years from 1907 to 1912.

Gilbert Charles Bourne (1861–1933), who followed Dendy, was educated at Eton and Oxford. He devoted himself particularly to marine zoology and was the first Director of the Laboratory of the Marine Biological Association at Plymouth. Later he returned to Oxford as assistant to Ray Lankester, and in 1906 became Linacre Professor of Zoology at Oxford, a post he held until his retirement in 1921. Apart from his eminence as a zoologist he was a celebrated oarsman. His Secretaryship came to an end in 1915 on account of the demands made upon his time by work in connection with the 1914–18 World War.

There seems to have been a sort of fatality attached to the Zoological Secretaryship about this time, for Bourne's intended successor, Richard Assheton, a brilliant zoologist, was struck down by an illness that prevented his name being put forward for election and killed him in October 1915; and Edward Alfred Minchin, also a man of great distinction, who actually was elected in May, died in September.

In November 1915, at the beginning of the following session, Edwin Stephen Goodrich (1868–1946), who was then in the Department of Comparative Anatomy, Oxford, was elected Secretary. He continued in office for eight years until 1923. In that year, the British Museum (Natural History) supplied the new President, A. B. Rendle; the new Botanical Secretary, John Ramsbottom; and the new Zoological Secretary, William Thomas Calman, then Assistant-Keeper and later Keeper of Zoology in the British Museum.

On Calman's resignation in 1928, George Parker Bidder (1863–1946) of Cambridge was elected, but ill health regrettably cut short his term of office at the end of three years.

John Stephenson (1871–1933), who came next in 1931, died in February 1933 before he had completed even two years of office. After a brilliant career in the Indian Medical Service, finishing up with the Vice-Chancellorship of the Punjab University, Stephenson had been for some years Lecturer in Zoology at Edinburgh University, and had come to London in 1929 as editor of the *Fauna of British India*. As well as being a zoologist of distinction, Stephenson was versed in the literature of Arabia and Persia.

He was followed as Secretary by Stanley Wells Kemp (1882–1945), who had been on the zoological staff of the Indian Museum, Calcutta, on the staff of the Zoological Survey of India, and was Director of Research to the *Discovery* expedition to the Antarctic. He resigned before the beginning of the session of 1936–37, on his appointment as Secretary to the Marine Biological Association of the United Kingdom and Director of the

Plymouth Laboratory. At the first General Meeting of the session of 1936–37, Martin Alister Campbell Hinton (1883–1961), Keeper of Zoology, British Museum (Natural History), was elected to succeed him.

The first formal admission of women to the Society having taken place in January 1905, the following month Queen Alexandra graciously consented to become an Honorary Member, the first Royal Lady to be one.

Muybridge's demonstration in 1889 of animal locomotion by the zooproxiscope has been mentioned. In March 1905, Mrs D. H. Scott, wife of the Botanical Secretary, showed a further development by exhibiting animated photographs of plants taken by the kammatograph.

At the Anniversary Meeting in 1905, Frank Crisp, who had been Treasurer since 1881, resigned. Horace Woolaston Monckton (1857–1931), his successor, had been educated at Wellington College and had become a barrister in 1880. From his early days he had been interested in rocks, plants and animals, and he soon joined the Geological Society; he became a Linnean Fellow in 1892. Outside the circle of his personal friends he was rather reserved and shy in manner, lacking the bluff geniality of his predecessor. Monckton held the Treasurership for 25 years. He was an able Treasurer and spared no pains in looking after the Society's general as well as financial interests. In the first year of his tenure of office the Society's accounts began to be audited by a professional accountant, but in spite of this precaution he had an unpleasant experience in connection with them a few years later.

At the International Botanical Congress in Vienna in June 1905, Alfred Barton Rendle, Keeper of Botany in the British Museum (Natural History), officially represented the Society. He gave a report at the General Meeting of 21 December 1905, and this was published in the *Proceedings* for 1905–06. The Congress was especially important in that it formulated the *International Rules of Botanical Nomenclature*, of which Rendle was an editor.

The bicentenary in May 1907 of the birth of Carl Linnaeus provided the occasion in Sweden for great celebrations at Lund, Uppsala and Stockholm, with all of which he had been associated. The Society's delegate as a guest of the University of Uppsala was William Carruthers, then aged 77. The choice of him as a delegate was appropriate, as he had long studied the history, work, portraits and personal relics of Linnaeus. Several other distinguished Fellows also attended the celebrations in other representative capacities. Jackson, the General Secretary, as a renowned authority on Linnaeana, as the Society's custodian of the Library and Collections of Linnaeus and as one acquainted with the Swedish language, was a specially honoured guest. He went to Sweden without academic or official recognition, neither of which he ever received from his own country. He returned as a Riddare av Kungl. Nordstjärneorden (R.N.O.) or Knight of the Swedish Royal Order of the Polar (Northern) Star and as an Honorary Master of Arts and Doctor of Philosophy (Fil. dr.) of the University of Uppsala. A Swedish knighthood of a British subject was, of course, not then recognized in Britain, as it had been earlier for Chambers and Hill, but there is no national discrimination against genuine academic distinctions, and the Society's General Secretary was henceforth always and properly called Dr Jackson. The dignity of Commander of the same order of knighthood was also conferred on Professor E. B. Poulton, the Hope Professor of Zoology at Oxford, who was to become the Society's President in 1912 and to receive a British Knighthood in 1935. The University of Uppsala also conferred the honorary degree of PhD upon Carruthers and Francis Darwin. For them, as for Jackson, this was a very high honour as the Swedish PhD (then equivalent to DSc in England) was the most difficult degree to gain in all Europe.

(a)

(b)

(c)

(d)

The Royal Swedish Academy bestowed its bicentenary medal upon the veteran Sir Joseph Hooker, who on account of his great age was unable to be present at the celebrations. Carruthers took with him a special copy of the Society's Linnean Medal for presentation to the University of Uppsala. An account of the celebrations is given in the Society's *Proceedings* for 1906–07. The Society at its Anniversary Meeting made no special occasion of the event beyond sending a congratulatory telegram to the University of Uppsala, but on 7 June the President and Council held an evening reception of commemoration in the Society's rooms, at which about 300 were present, including the Swedish Minister and his legation staff. A special feature of the exhibits at this commemoration was a display of manuscripts, books, medals and personal relics of Linnaeus. On the previous day, the Society had sent a congratulatory telegram to its Honorary Member, Oscar II, King of Sweden, on the occasion of their Majesties' golden wedding anniversary.

In 1907, the Society had joined in commemorating the birth of a great man. In 1908, it celebrated the jubilee of the presentation of a great idea. On the evening of Thursday, 1 July 1858, a small company of members had listened unexpectedly to the Secretary's reading of the papers by Darwin and Wallace on a hypothesis of organic evolution by natural selection (see Chapter 5). On the afternoon of Wednesday, 1 July 1908, a large and distinguished audience assembled in the theatre of the Institution of Civil Engineers, Great George Street, to celebrate the fiftieth anniversary of the reading of those papers. It was a Special Meeting of the Society and the first one since April 1788 held outside its own rooms. D. H. Scott, the President of the Society, was Chairman.

In the audience were representatives from Hertford Grammar School (associated with Wallace), Shrewsbury School and Christ's College, Cambridge (both associated with Darwin), from 17 universities, and 16 learned societies of the British Isles. The Danish and Swedish Ministers were present and the German Embassy was represented by Dietrich von Bethmann-Hollweg, not to be confused with Theobald of the same surname, who was German Chancellor in 1914. Some members of Darwin's family also came. Many of the universities and societies presented addresses by their representatives, and Professor Einar Lönnberg conveyed the greetings and felicitations of the King of Sweden as well as an illuminated address from the Royal Swedish Academy of Sciences at Stockholm.

Neither Darwin nor Wallace had been present at the meeting in 1858, at which Sir Charles Lyell and J. D. Hooker had introduced the papers. Of those four Darwin and Lyell had gone, but Wallace and Hooker still remained, Wallace then 85 and Hooker 91 years of age, and were present at the jubilee meeting.

The Council marked the occasion by having a special Darwin–Wallace Medal struck; it was designed by Frank Bowcher, with Darwin's head on one side and Wallace's on the other side. At the presentation of the medal in gold to Wallace he made clear his part in relation to Darwin in the conception of the hypothesis, the stimulus given to both by Malthus's *Principles of Population*, and the time for reflection both enjoyed during their travels. Silver copies of the medal were presented in person to Joseph Hooker, Eduard Strasburger of Bonn, Francis Galton and Edwin Ray Lankester. The medals for E. H. P. A. Haeckel of Jena and August F. L. Weismann of Freiburg im Breisgau were in their absence handed to the representative of the German Embassy.

Plate XIV   (a) Sir David Prain, from a photograph of a drawing by F. A. de Biden Footner, 1929. (b) Alfred Rendle, from a photograph in the Society's collection. (c) Frederick E. Weiss, from a photograph in the Society's collection. (d) Sir Sidney Harmer, from a photograph in the Society's collection.

In the evening a dinner, attended by 90 members and guests, was held in Prince's Restaurant, Piccadilly, and after the dinner a reception took place in the Society's rooms, at which there were exhibited, among other things, the certificates of recommendation of Darwin and of Wallace when they were candidates for Fellowship. A full account of the celebration was published in 1908 as a special volume, with portraits of Darwin and Wallace and the six silver medallists.

At the Anniversary Meeting of 1908, Gustav V, who had succeeded Oscar II on the throne of Sweden, was elected an Honorary Member. Two years later the Society lost its fourth successive patron, King Edward VII, and offered its Address of sympathy to King George V and its Honorary Member, the widowed Queen Alexandra.

As mentioned above, at the International Botanical Congress of Vienna in 1905, the Society had been represented by only one delegate, but at the following one held at Brussels in 1910 there were five delegates from the Society, representing the different branches of botany concerned with the discussions on taxonomy. The delegation presented its reports to the Society at the General Meeting of 15 December 1910. In the same month, the Council appointed a provisional committee to organize the next Congress which was intended to meet in London in 1915. That Congress never met.

In 1911, the audit of the Society's accounts revealed a very unsatisfactory state of affairs, which resulted in the dismissal of the Clerk concerned. Spencer Savage was appointed to succeed the defaulting Clerk, and remained in the Society's service until his retirement in 1951, apart from his service in the 1914–18 World War.

Sir Joseph Dalton Hooker, the most distinguished botanist of two generations, died on 10 December 1911 after a Fellowship of almost 70 years. Although he never served as President he, along with Thomas Bell and George Bentham, exercised great influence in the affairs of the Society and he was, after Darwin's death, its most illustrious Fellow. He bequeathed £100 to the Society, and this formed the nucleus of a special fund, the "Sir Joseph Hooker Memorial Lecture Fund", mentioned later. The many medals which had been awarded to him were lent to the Society, and on the death of Lady Hooker became its property. After his death his name was enrolled in Japan as one of the 29 heroes of modern times.

Hooker's Fellowship, although exceptionally long, fell short by five years of the membership of Thomas Garnier, but in this same year there died a Fellow who had been for many years the Father of the Society. He was Thomas Hodgson Archer-Hind of Newton Abbot, Devonshire, who was born in 1814, elected a Fellow in March 1834 and died in February 1911, having been a Fellow for 77 years; his principal interest had been gardening.

Nominally, the Library had had no assistant since 1897 when Kappel, who had been assistant since 1884, received the designation of "Librarian" transferred from Harting, who was appointed Assistant-Secretary. Now, in 1913, it was decided to have an assistant in the Library and W. H. T. Tams (1891–1980), later to become an Assistant-Keeper in the Department of Entomology, British Museum (Natural History), was appointed in the spring of that year, but at the end of it he resigned. In that same year the Society sold over half a ton of its old copper plates for nearly £40, happily ignorant of how the value of the metal would soar in the next few years.

Early in 1914, Tams was succeeded in the Library by Edwin Ephraim Riseley (1889–1917), who had been a Library Clerk to the Zoological Society. At the end of the session of 1913–14 the paid staff numbered five, the largest number in the service of the Society so far, and consisted of a General Secretary, a Librarian, a Clerk, an Assistant-

Librarian and a Housekeeper. Before the session ended, it was arranged to hold a Society Dinner on 12 November 1914, but by that date the younger members had begun to be scattered far and wide and the Society had other things to think about than feasting.

From its foundation the Society had seen a succession of wars in all parts of the world, from the wars of the French Revolution to the Balkan wars of 1912, and throughout them all had gone its way untroubled, but the war of 1914–18 altered all this. The Society's Officers, its paid staff, its members, its funds and its publications all suffered. Each of the two Presidents who held office during part of the war period suffered grievous personal loss. Of the paid staff, one had to be dismissed and two went on active service, one of them never to return. Seven Fellows were killed in action or died of wounds or exposure.

When the new session of 1914–15 opened on 5 November 1914 the First World War had been raging for three months. August Wilhelm Kappel, the Librarian, had left on 31 July to visit his relatives near Düsseldorf, but, although he became an enemy alien on 4 August, he managed somehow to get back to England about the middle of the month and was allowed to stay at Teignmouth. Meanwhile the Council, knowing that he had never become naturalized, suspended him, and later, additional causes having been discovered, dismissed him. He died at East Ham in December 1915. Kappel's duties were taken over by young Riseley in September 1914, and he was formally appointed Librarian in January 1915. He set himself energetically to bring the neglected Library into better condition, but soon the storm of war swept him to other duties and to death. He enlisted in the Rifle Brigade and was killed in France in August 1917. During his short time in the Society's service he so proved his worth that a tablet with a Latin inscription was placed in the Library to keep in memory his brief life. Spencer Savage, the Clerk, enlisted in February 1915 for overseas service, became a machine gunner on the Western Front and fortunately indeed for him, the Society and Linnaean scholarship he survived. He returned to duty in March 1919. It was difficult to believe this kindly scholarly man had once been a front-line soldier.

The dismissal of Kappel and the departure of Riseley and Savage left Jackson as the sole paid member of the Society's staff. This, of course, could not go on long, and in May 1916 William Shakespeare Warton, who was then one of the Library Clerks to the Zoological Society and who had been unfit for military service, was appointed Assistant Librarian, becoming Librarian in 1952. John William Windmill was appointed in March 1915 to perform temporarily the Clerk's duties, and was succeeded in March 1917 by Miss Mary Emily Bessie Smith, who died before she had completed two years' service.

As far back as 1901 Vines, who was then President, had suggested that the ordinary meetings of the Society should be held in the afternoon instead of in the evening as they had previously been. The Council discussed the same question again in 1906, but made no change on either occasion. Now the war brought about the change very quickly, for the darkening of the streets and the black-out of all house lights as a precaution against bombing by aircraft made evening meetings in the winter time undesirable. So meetings began at 5 pm from 17 December 1914.

The German invasion of Belgium caused the flight of many Belgians to England and the Society threw open its Library and meetings to the botanists and zoologists among the refugees.

On Monday, 7 January 1918, a most unusual meeting of part of the Society took place. Since the incorporation of the Society in 1802 there had been no meeting of Fellows only, but on this date Sir David Prain, the President, summoned such a meeting to pass a series of resolutions protesting against the reported intention of the Government to dismantle the exhibits of the British Museum, including the Natural History Museum, in order to use the buildings as offices. Copies of the resolutions were sent to the King, the Prime Minister (Mr Lloyd George), other members of the War Council, Lord Sudeley, the Trustees of the British Museum and the Press. The intention of the Government, if held, would have been quite in accordance with the larger lunacy of the time, but fortunately it was not carried out, and the Society played a part in achieving this result. This meeting does not appear as such in the Society's *Proceedings*, but a memorandum of it was read at the General Meeting of 17 January 1918. Some account of this potentially disastrous proposal will be found in Stearn, *The Natural History Museum in South Kensington* (1981).

In 1920, the Society commemorated the centenary of the death of Sir Joseph Banks, its friend and helper in infancy, by devoting the General Meeting of 19 June to papers on various aspects of his life: as a Traveller by B. D. Jackson; as a Patron of Science by A. B. Rendle; as a Botanist by J. Britten; and as a Trustee of the British Museum by A. Smith Woodward, the President. Portraits and relics of Banks were also exhibited.

In 1923, for the first time in its existence, the Society was honoured by the visit of a reigning sovereign. On 3 November the President and Council received His Majesty Gustav V, King of Sweden, an Honorary Member of the Society. His Majesty, after inspecting the Society's rooms and the collections and library of Linnaeus, signed the Society's Roll and Charter Book on a specially emblazoned vellum page. A photograph of this scene forms the frontispiece to the *Proceedings* for 1923–24.

By 1924, Jackson, who had been General Secretary since 1902, was verging on his eightieth year, and the Council therefore decided to give him some relief by once again resuscitating the post of Assistant-Secretary, in abeyance since 1902, uniting with it the designation of Librarian, which had not been used since Riseley's death in 1917. It was intended that Jackson should hand over part of his work to the new officer and should retire, after a reasonable time to allow the latter to become acquainted with the Society's business. The General Secretaryship was then to be replaced by the combined office of Librarian and Assistant-Secretary. In short, Trimen's proposal of 50 years before was at last to be put into force. Andrew Thomas Gage (1871–1945) was appointed in the autumn of 1924 to the new post, Jackson continuing as General Secretary until May 1926. Gage served the Society in this dual post from 1924 to 1929 and much improved its administration. A Scot, educated like Prain at Aberdeen, he had also joined the Indian Medical Service and in 1898 he followed Prain as Curator of the Herbarium of the Royal Botanic Gardens, Calcutta, and in 1905 as Director of the Gardens.

Some time before Jackson's resignation, the members of the Society had subscribed to have his portrait painted by Ernest Moore, and at the Anniversary Meeting in May 1926 Prain handed the portrait over to the Society. At the same time, cordial tributes of appreciation of his long and devoted service to the Society were paid to him. Simultaneously with the abolition of the General Secretaryship, the ad hoc post of "Curator of the Linnaean Collections" was created so that Jackson should still enjoy official association with the Society. Thus he continued to occupy his seat at his own desk at the window looking into Piccadilly at the southeast corner of the eastern Library Room until October 1927, when on his way home he was knocked down by a car in Buckingham Palace Road. He was taken to Westminster Hospital, where he died on 12 October. So passed one equalled in length of service only by Richard Taylor and unsurpassed in devotion to the Society.

In 1923, the Council considered the same question that had vexed Bell in the 1850s: how to counter the effect on the Linnean Society of the increase in number of smaller societies restricted to the study of special branches of biology. The same difficulties that confronted Bell 50 years before still existed and were now even more evident. Lack of money prevented younger scientific people from seeking the Fellowship of the Linnean in addition to membership of the smaller and less expensive societies that specially appealed to them, and the Linnean Society's lack of money and space made union impracticable. All that the Linnean Society could now do was to sacrifice a considerable part of its capital by exempting, from 1925, candidates under 35 at the date of their election from payment of Admission Fees.

In 1925, the Society lost its first lady Honorary Member of 20 years' standing, Queen Alexandra, and in its Address of sympathy to King George the Society expressed its own loss as well as that of His Majesty.

When the entire paid staff consisted of one man, in the early days of the Society, the only way in which he could be allowed a holiday was to close the Society's rooms for a month or so each year. This custom continued after the paid staff numbered more than one, but the reason then given for the closure was to allow the rooms to be cleaned. Consequently, all the paid staff went on holiday during August, when everybody else did, with the result that members, more particularly those in the provinces, could neither have books sent to them nor consult the Library during the month they were most likely to be free. The Council found that all members of the paid staff need not go on holiday at the same time and that the rooms could be cleaned without closing the whole place. Since 1927, the Society's rooms have therefore been open all the year round except on Saturdays, Sundays, Good Friday and the following day, Christmas Day, Bank Holidays and the day after a Bank Holiday.

There was another reason for the change that did not come before the Council. In 1926, the rooms were closed as usual on 1 August. Immediately afterwards a Fellow sent a postcard asking for a book to be sent to him, but there was no one to attend to this or the successive requests from the same Fellow. About a week before the end of the holiday, the Librarian had occasion to visit the rooms and he found a telegram on his table asking for attention to be given to previous requests and ending with the urbane enquiry, "Is the Librarian mad?" As the Assistant-Secretary he at once wrote to the Fellow, explaining the delay and asking whether the wording of the end of the telegram as received was the wording actually despatched by the Fellow. The latter sent an apologetic letter and explained that he had merely asked in the telegram whether the Librarian was dead! The correspondence then ceased, but it left the Assistant-Secretary feeling that it was undesirable for Fellows to continue to exhibit such a poverty of suppositions to account for the non-receipt of a book.

The part played by the Society in enlightening the Home Government concerned such proposals as the abolition of the Singapore Botanic Garden and the dismantling of the British Museum. It was much more agreeable for the Society to express by a unanimous resolution on 7 January 1926, after hearing a paper by Professor F. Wood-Jones on the Flinders Chase Reserve on Kangaroo Island, its appreciation of the act of the Government of South Australia in establishing that sanctuary for the flora and fauna of the island.

At the General Meeting of 28 April 1927, the President expressed the Society's appreciation of the good work accomplished by an Australian Fellow, Fred Turner (1852–1939) of Sydney, a Yorkshire man who was for many years Economic Botanist in New South Wales and who by his writings in the press had helped to bring about the passing by the New South Wales Legislature of an Act for the protection of the native plants of that state of the Commonwealth.

In 1929, a proposal was made to introduce blackbuck (*Antilope cervicapra*) into Ceylon (now Sri Lanka) for sport, and the Director of the Colombo Museum asked the opinion of the Society on the advisability or otherwise of the introduction. This seemingly simple question led to prolonged, animated and instructive debate at the two General Meetings of 21 November and 5 December 1929. The Society finally passed a unanimous resolution deprecating all attempts to introduce and naturalize wild animals or plants in countries where they are not native, unless such introduction is urgently needed for economic reasons, and until a thorough study has been made of the local conditions and of the likely ensuing results. The Trustees of the British Museum had long held the same views. The introduction of animals for sport or fur-farming has almost invariably had disastrous results for the local fauna and flora and in the long run economic ones, as is evident by the enormous sums annually expended in Europe to hold the introduced muskrat in check and the damage done by the coypu in East Anglia. The Society sent this resolution to the Colonial Office with a statement of the question that had brought it about. The Colonial Office sent the resolution on to the Government of Ceylon, and it appears to have influenced that Government in forming rules for issuing licences of acclimatization. In this same session of 1929–30 the Society also passed a resolution strongly deprecating the reported proposal to utilize Syon Park, on the bank of the Thames opposite the Royal Botanic Gardens, Kew, for a large scheme of sewage disposal. Objection by the nearby West Middlesex Hospital decisively defeated it.

Since the death of Queen Alexandra in 1925, the Society had been without a lady Honorary Member, but in November 1927 Queen Mary graciously consented to become one. In the following session of 1928–29 the Society had the honour of enrolling the Prince of Wales in the list of Honorary Members.

At the end of October 1929, Gage resigned the office of Librarian and Assistant-Secretary which he had held for five years. For the last two years of his service he had been allowed to occupy the top flat, which was originally intended for the Librarian but had been unoccupied from 1902. There, and after his retirement, he devoted much time to preparation of *A History of the Linnean Society of London* (1938). He was the last Librarian to reside there, for the ever-increasing pressure on the Library made it necessary to reserve the flat henceforth as an extension to the main Library and to provide a Council Room more convenient than the East Library. The new Librarian and Assistant-Secretary was Spencer Savage (1886–1966), who had been appointed Clerk in 1919 and who during his many years of service had acquired an intimate knowledge of the Society's history and its affairs. He was a very scholarly man who, under the influence of Jackson, became a distinguished Linnaean scholar in his own right and compiled for the Society *A Catalogue of the Linnean Herbarium* (1945), a remarkable piece of scholarship produced under very adverse conditions. His place as Clerk was filled by Robert Geoffrey Pugsley, son of the well-known amateur botanist William Herbert Pugsley (1868–1947).

In January 1931, the Treasurer, H. W. Monckton, died. Francis Druce (1873–1941), a Member of Council, undertook the duties and at the Anniversary Meeting in May was elected to succeed him and served until 1940, proving himself a wise and skilful Treasurer; he had already been Treasurer at the Royal Meteorological Society. Unfortunately he was killed, and his rich library and herbarium at his Chelsea flat destroyed, in an air-raid on 16 April 1941. He had not long been elected Master of the Worshipful Company of Innholders.

At the beginning of the session of 1931–32, the Roll of Honorary Members was enlarged by an accession that would have been unthinkable for more than the first century of the Society's existence. On 22 October 1931, His Imperial Majesty the Emperor Hirohito of Japan, having signified his wish to accept the invitation of the Council to become an Honorary Member, was by unanimous open vote elected one. This election was a tribute not only to His Majesty's exalted station but also to his personal interest in biological science, for the Emperor has a private botanical garden and laboratory, and, on his journeys before his accession, had studied the flora and fauna of the countries he had visited. He is the author of the beautifully produced *Nova Flora Nasuensis* (1972) and its *Supplementum* (1985). The elegance of the design surrounding the Imperial signature in the Book of the Charter and Bye-Laws has already been mentioned.

The General Meeting of 19 November 1931 commemorated the discovery of the cell nucleus a century earlier by Robert Brown, so closely associated with the Society from 1805 to 1858. Various appreciations of Brown and of his work appear in the *Proceedings* 1930–32: 17–54 (1932).

The Society's first Honorary Member, Sir Joseph Banks, had died in 1820 and in that same year the Society elected its first Royal Honorary Member, Prince Leopold (1790–1865) of Saxe-Coburg-Saalfeld, who married Princess Charlotte, the only child of George IV and, after her death in 1817, had continued to reside in England. His sister, Maria Louisa Victoria, wife of the Duke of Kent, was the mother of the infant Princess Victoria, who, 17 years later, as Queen Victoria, became the Society's third Patron. Prince Leopold was greatly interested in natural science, and his election as an Honorary Member was a recognition of this as much as of his position in the Royal Family. He refused the Crown of Greece but accepted that of Belgium. From 1831 until his death in 1865, he appears in the Roll of Honorary Members as Leopold, King of the Belgians, and after the death of the Prince Consort and of the King of Portugal he was, from 1862 to 1865, the Society's sole Honorary Member. One hundred and fifteen years after the name had first appeared, and 70 years after it had vanished from the Roll of living Honorary Members, it reappeared in 1935, when Leopold III (1901–83), King of the Belgians, as interested in natural history as his great-great-uncle Leopold I, became the Society's latest and youngest Honorary Member. Although the rise of Hitler in Germany was beginning to blight the stability of Europe, no one then could envisage how soon his kingdom would be invaded and he become a prisoner of war. In 1951 his unpopularity in Belgium forced him to abdicate.

Chapter 8

From 1937 to 1946

John Ramsbottom (1885–1974) became President of the Society in May 1937. Like his predecessor, he was a British Museum (Natural History) scientist. Born in Manchester, he entered the Museum's service in 1910 as a mycologist, became Deputy Keeper of Botany in 1928 and was Keeper of Botany from 1930 to 1951, a period which included the very difficult years of the 1939–45 World War. The Department of Botany was severely damaged by fire in an air raid on 9 September 1940. In addition, the war brought many calls upon his time as an expert on dry rot and moulds, notably in connection with *Penicillium*. A man of great ability, and procrastination, he much enjoyed the prestige of being prominent in learned societies without, however, giving associated duties all the attention expected. His resignation in 1935 as Botanical Secretary of the Linnean Society led to its editorial work being performed, with zeal and greater efficiency, by Isaac Henry Burkhill (1870–1965). Britain's most erudite botanist; he was author among much else of a *Dictionary of the Economic Plants of the Malay Peninsula* (2 vols, 1935) and *Chapters on the History of Botany in India* (1965); his distinctive style shows the influence of much reading in his youth of the Authorized English translation of the Bible and the works of Thomas Carlyle.

The most important events for the Society during Ramsbottom's Presidency were the celebration of the one-hundred-and-fiftieth anniversary; publication of A. T. Gage's *A History of the Linnean Society of London* in May 1938; and the outbreak of war in September 1939. The anniversary celebrations took the form of a symposium on 24–26 May, beginning with a Presidential Address by Ramsbottom on "Linnaeus and the Species Concept", scholarly like all his work, printed in *Proceedings*, Sess. 150 (1937–38): 192–219 (1938). Papers mainly concerned with the origin of species were given by E. B. Poulton, E. W. MacBride, O. Winge (Copenhagen), A. S. Woodward, Karl Jordan, Julian Huxley, P. A. Buxton, E. Fischer-Piette (Paris), B. Rensch (Münster) and Carl Skottsberg (Gothenburg). In the following discussion, H. J. Lam (Leiden), M. J. Sirks (Groningen), H. Boschma (Leiden), W. Robyns (Brussels) and the authors of the papers took part. The Society then possessed three of the wooden cases in which Linnaeus's herbarium had remained since being brought to England in 1784. Two of these were formally presented to the Svenska Linnésällskapet (Swedish Linnaeus Society), represented by Robert Fries, to be returned to Sweden. Spencer Savage provided a remarkable exhibition of portraits of Linnaeus and the first Fellows of the Society, together with historic documents and specimens which are listed in *Proceedings*, Sess. 150 (1937–38): 294–308 (1938). For all concerned, it was a memorable, informative, stimulating and happy occasion. Many years were to pass before anywhere in Europe there could again be such a co-operative international gathering. Francis Druce personally paid for most of the expenses of this celebration.

In 1938, the annexation of Austria by Nazi Germany and its threats to the

independence of Czechoslovakia made evident the high and dreadful possibility of a
European war, in which the destruction of cities by bombing could be expected, with
London as a primary target. Because of their international importance, the safeguarding
of the Linnaean collections received the Society's highest priority. Special cases were
made for their evacuation from London and they were packed and loaded ready for
transport on 30 September 1938. That day Chamberlain and Hitler signed the Munich
Agreement "to contribute to the peace of Europe", with the result that on 15 January
1939 German troops occupied Czechoslovakia; on 1 September 1939 they attacked
Poland; and on 3 September Britain became involved in war. Long before then, in April
1939, Hitler's aggressive intentions obliged the Society to evacuate the Linnaean
collections to Woburn Abbey, Bedfordshire, and there, by the co-operation of the eleventh
Duke of Bedford (1858–1940) and the twelfth Duke, a Fellow of the Society, they
remained for the duration of the war.

Ramsbottom's Presidential Address in May 1939 provided an historical survey of
mycology, with particular reference to its expansion since Linnaeus, the printed version of
which occupies *Proceedings*, Sess. 151 (1938–39): 280–367 (1941).

The black-out of street lighting necessitated by war conditions obliged the Society from
November 1939 onwards to meet between 2.15 and 2.30 pm. Although the Linnaean
collections and the Smith herbarium had gone, the Council decided to risk the retention
of the general library in London for the convenience of Fellows, although far from blind to
the risks. The meetings, despite most Fellows below middle age being recruited into the
armed forces or absorbed in war work, maintained their general interest. Thus, on 11
April 1940, there was a very interesting symposium on phylogeny and taxonomy (printed
in *Proceedings*, Sess. 152 (1939–40): 234–255; 1940), requested by the Association for the
Study of Systematics (later the Systematics Association) in which John S. L. Gilmour,
O. W. Richards, T. A. Sprague, Julian S. Huxley, W. B. Turrill, Ronald Melville, J. Burtt
Davy and M. J. D. White took part. The Society had lost, fortunately only temporarily,
the services of the Clerk, Theodore O'Grady, who was in the Army from 1939 to 1946.
Francis Druce retired as Treasurer in 1940 and Frederick Charles Stern (1884–1967), a
merchant banker particularly interested in lilies, peonies and snowdrops, who had been a
major in the 1914–18 War, was elected in his place. He served as Treasurer until 1958.

Edward Stuart Russell (1887–1954), who followed Ramsbottom as President in
1940, was a distinguished marine biologist, from 1921 to 1945 Director of Fisheries
Investigations. His philosophical views and interests extended into functional
morphology and animal behaviour, as is evident from his Presidential Addresses and his
books: *Form and Function, a Contribution to the History of Animal Morphology* (1916), *The Study
of Living Things* (1924), *The Interpretation and Development of Heredity* (1930), *The Behaviour of
Animals* (1934), *The Over-Fishing Problem* (1942) and *The Directiveness of Organic Activities*
(1945).

During Russell's first year of office, the persistent air raids on London compelled the
Council to alter its policy. Some 3000 of the most valuable books were sent to Oxford,
their selection being made by three specialist botanical librarians, J. Ardagh (British
Museum (Natural History)), E. Nelmes (Royal Botanic Gardens, Kew) and W. T. Stearn
(Lindley Library, Royal Horticultural Society), and by C. D. Sherborn, compiler of the
vast *Index Animalium*, who possessed an unrivalled knowledge of the older zoological
literature. Warren R. Dawson provided accommodation for the Society's records in his
country home. Although the Linnaean collections were away at Woburn, it by no means
followed that they were safe even there from German bombing. The Council, largely at

the instigation of Ramsbottom, sought ways of having a photographic record made for distribution to various centres of learning abroad. An appeal to the Carnegie Corporation of New York, supported by E. D. Merrill, received a typically generous American response: the Corporation made a grant of £2000 for the undertaking. Before the specimens of the Linnaean Herbarium were photographed by Messrs Wallace Heaton at Tring (to which they were transferred), Spencer Savage added numbers to the sheets for reference purposes. If the Herbarium had thereafter been destroyed, the microfilm would have been an invaluable record, even though it was inferior to the one made in 1959 for the International Documentation Centre with much better equipment. While handling the specimens, the photographer, Gladys Brown, was stung on the arm by a specimen of stinging-nettle (*Urtica*) which had been dried and mounted some 200 years earlier: the arm showed a definite blister, apparently similar to one produced by a fresh specimen (cf. *Proceedings*, Sess. 154 (1941–42): 50–57; 1942). The task took from early July to mid-November, the insects being photographed under the supervision of W. H. T. Tams, who succeeded in preparing all the 6000 Linnaean insects for photography during ten weeks of hard work day and night.

Russell's second Presidential Address in May 1941 was on "Biological adaptedness and specialization of instinctive behaviour" (*Proceedings*, Sess. 153 (1940–41): 250–268; 1941). The next major contribution to biology was a symposium in July 1941 on differences in the systematics of plants and animals (*op. cit.* 272–286; 1942); the speakers included W. B. Turrill, O. W. Richards, C. D. Darlington, Julian S. Huxley and A. J. Willmot. Another symposium, in April 1942, dealt with the biogeographic division of the Indo-Australian Archipelago (Malaysia), Wallace's Line, Weber's Line and other lines of faunistic demarcation suggested by various biogeographers as crossing eastern Malaysia. Geological, climatological, zoological and botanical aspects all came under consideration in papers by J. B. Scrivenor, I. H. Burkill, Malcolm A. Smith, H. K. Airy Shaw and F. E. Zeuner (cf. *Proceedings*, Sess. 154 (1941–42): 120–165; 1943).

At the Anniversary Meeting in May 1942, the President called attention to the tea enjoyed at meetings, the gift of two American friends, E. D. Merrill and Thomas Barbour. Later generations, happily unaccustomed to rigorous war-time rationing, cannot appreciate how welcome were such characteristic American acts of kindness. That year the Society did not award the Linnean Medal because it could not obtain the necessary gold. Russell's Presidential Address was on "Perceptual and sensory signs in instructive behaviour" (*Proceedings*, Sess. 154 (1941–42): 193–216; 1943). A symposium on intertidal zonation of animals and plants, with papers by T. A. Stephenson, John Colman, E. Marion Delf and V. J. Chapman, took place in June (*Proceedings*, Sess. 154 (1941–42): 219–253; 1943). Thus, despite the handicaps of war-time conditions, the Society continued to serve as a meeting place for the exchange of information over many biological fields. Russell concluded his period of office with a Presidential Address on "The stereotypy of instinctive behaviour" (*Proceedings*, Sess. 155 (1942–43): 186–208; 1944).

In 1944, papers of general interest were again presented to the Society. They included one on the theory of continental drift, increasingly favoured then by biological geographers but stated by geophysicists "quite definitely, and with obvious unanimity" to be mechanically impossible; this, after the paper by Thomas H. Holland, provoked lively discussion (*op. cit.* 112–125; 1944). Another by J. Pryce-Jones dealt with "Some problems associated with nectar, pollen and honey" (*op. cit.* 129–174; 1944). These General Meetings were held in association with the Zoological Society. The Council in revising the

Bye-Laws instituted two classes of Associates, those *honoris causa* of any age and others between the ages of 21 and 23, retaining their associateship no longer than five years and not beyond the age of 30.

Arthur Disbrowe Cotton (1879–1962), a mycologist who had collected flowering plants on Mount Kilimanjaro in 1929, including an endemic new species named *Senecio cottonii* in his honour, was Keeper of the Kew Herbarium from 1922 to 1946 and became President in May 1943. When asked, quite innocently, by a fellow botanist if he knew what had happened to one Enid M. Jesson, a Kew botanist whose name appeared briefly in the literature and then disappeared, he replied "I married her". The first notable happening of his Presidency was a symposium on the taxonomic value of the anatomical structure of the vegetative organs of the Dicotyledons (*Proceedings*, Sess. 155 (1942–43): 210–235; 1944), with contributions by C. R. Metcalfe, L. Chalk, B. J. Rendle, T. M. Harris, C. L. Hare, T. E. Wallis and T. A. Sprague. Later, in November 1943, to commemorate the centenary of Robert Fortune's first expedition to China, the Linnean Society, in association with the Zoological Society, held a symposium on the exploration of China (*Proceedings*, Sess. 156 (1943–44): 5–44; 1944), with contributions by E. Nelmes, F. C. Stern, Malcolm A. Smith and Hui-Lin Li.

Another such joint meeting took place in March 1944 on the difference in observance between botanical and zoological nomenclature (*Proceedings*, Sess. 156 (1943–44): 126–146; 1944), with contributions by M. L. Sprague, F. Hemming, E. Trewavas, T. A. Sprague, S. Neave and P. de Laszlo, the last-named a barrister who, being neither a botanist nor a zoologist, had the task of summarizing the discussion. He concluded "it was manifest that the Rules which existed to-day were a series of compromises with tradition and human frailties". They remain so.

After a lull in the German bombing of London, the city came under renewed attacks in 1944. They did not cease until the Allied forces had liberated northern France and Belgium. The last German rocket on England fell on 27 March 1945. The Council had removed early in 1944 some 3000 books to institutions outside London. As in previous sessions, the Society gladly placed its meeting room at the disposal of other Societies for their meetings. In the 1943–44 session these included the Aquinas Society, the British Mycological Society, the Botanical Society of the British Isles, the British Ecological Society, the British Association Committees, the South-Eastern Union of Scientific Societies, the Botanical Research Fund, the Society for the Promotion of Nature Reserves, the Genetical Society, the Society for Experimental Biology and the Association of Applied Biologists. It has remained the policy of the Society to further natural history by providing whenever possible such facilities to cognate groups and so promote their wellbeing in every way practicable. Cotton's Presidential Address dealt with "The megaphytic habit in the tree senecios and other genera" (*Proceedings*, Sess. 156 (1943–44): 158–168; 1944), the very remarkable species of *Senecio* subgenus *Dendrosenecio* on the East African mountains having engaged his attention since his visit to Mount Kilimanjaro. Later, in November 1944, the Society commemorated the bicentenary of the birth of the great French philosopher-naturalist and evolutionist J. B. A. de Monet, Chevalier de Lamarck (1744–1829), early elected as a Foreign Member of the Linnean Society. James Sowerby, Alexander McLeay, Edward Forster, Richard Taylor, Edward Sabine, Thomas F. Forster, Joseph Sabine and other prominent Fellows signed the certificate of his recommendation, but not the President, J. E. Smith. It was a tribute much too long delayed. Probably no one there then knew that Lamarck, desperately poor and scorned by contemporary French scientists, had become totally blind in 1818. His daughter

Rosalie is said to have comforted the sad old man with the words "La postérité vous admirera, elle vous vengera, mon père", which are inscribed on the touching memorial to them both in the Jardin des Plantes, Paris. One trusts that the Linnean Society's act gave them a little encouragement.

Meanwhile, on the continent of Europe the defeat of the German armies brought relief and hope to conquered peoples. The unconditional surrender of all German fighting forces came on 7 May 1945, only shortly before the Anniversary Meeting of 24 May under the Presidency of A. D. Cotton. The general mood was naturally one of relief and thankfulness and hope even though the war against Japan had yet to reach its dramatic and ominous end. The Society had survived the long war remarkably well. Despite the shattering of windows, the premises had been undamaged and it had maintained its meetings throughout, notwithstanding difficulties of travel, of heating and of organization. The library dispersed between the Bodleian Library in Oxford, the Zoological Museum, Tring, and the air raid shelters of the Royal Botanic Gardens, Kew; the records in the private hands of Warren Dawson in Buckinghamshire and T. A. and M. Sprague in Gloucestershire; the Linnaean collections at Tring. All had been kept safe. This was in marked contrast to the sad state of the British Museum (Natural History) scarcely two miles away, with many books, specimens and exhibits destroyed and the building badly damaged. Nevertheless, many difficulties lay ahead for the Society. During the war, in common with many other bodies and companies, it had been compelled to sell its overseas assets and to pay special war insurance; moreover, many Fellows outside Britain had been unable to pay their subscriptions. The interior of the building needed renovation, together with new bookshelves, before the evacuated material could be returned.

Cotton's Presidency ended in May 1945. Ramsbottom, Russell and he had had the difficult task of maintaining the Society through the war, which could indeed have been well nigh impossible but for the continuous support of the Botanical Secretaries, first I. Henry Burkill, then Bertie Frank Barnes (1888–1965), who also acted as Deputy Treasurer in F. C. Stern's absence on Home Guard duties, and the Zoological Secretary, Malcolm Arthur Smith (1876–1958), together with the Librarian and Assistant-Secretary, Spencer Savage. During Cotton's last session the Society held on 21 March 1945 a discussion on oceanography (*Proceedings*, Sess. 158: 78–93; 1947). About this time the Linnaean collections were brought back from Tring where they had been in store since 12 July 1941. The printing of Savage's *Catalogue of the Linnaean Collection* had been completed and published in an edition limited by paper restrictions to 250 copies. About 2000 volumes evacuated to Tring and about the same number to Kew had been returned, but there still remained some 3000 volumes at Oxford and the Society's records at Simpson House near Bletchley. Especially gratifying was the return to the Society's service of the Clerk, Theodore O'Grady, safe and sound after six and a quarter years in the Army. Upon him and Spencer Savage fell an increased burden of duties as the Society gradually settled to a peace-time existence bound by many war-time restrictions. The election of Gavin Rylands de Beer (1899–1972) as President began a new chapter in its history.

Chapter 9

From 1946 to 1961

At the Anniversary Meeting of 24 May 1946, Gavin Rylands de Beer (1899–1972) succeeded Cotton as President. Although professionally a zoologist and in the year of his election Professor of Embryology at University College, London, he had a breadth of interest and wide-ranging curiosity that took him into such diverse matters as Hannibal's crossing of the Alps, early Alpine travellers and the careers and works of Edward Gibbon and Jacques Rousseau, all supported by his many-sided and thorough erudition and fluent linguistic accomplishments in French, German and Italian. He interested himself not only in comparative anatomy, embryology, evolution and natural selection but equally in literature and biography, particularly relating to Switzerland. A prolific, but nevertheless scholarly, writer, he was the author of numerous articles and 30 books, among them *Growth* (1924), *Vertebrate Zoology* (1928), *Embryology and Evolution* (1930), *Early Travellers in the Alps* (1936), *Embryos and Ancestors* (1940), *Archaeopteryx Lithographica* (1954), *Alps and Elephants* (1955), *The Sciences were never at War* (1960) and *Charles Darwin* (1965). After years of teaching zoology at Oxford, he moved to University College, London, in 1938 and then in 1950 to the British Museum (Natural History), where he was Director from 1950 to 1960. His first contribution to the Linnean Society's *Proceedings* (159: 42–65; 1949) was a paper on "Edmund Davall, F.L.S., an unwritten English chapter in the history of Swiss botany", followed by supplementary articles in *Proceedings* 160: 179–185 (1949), 161: 56–63 (1949), 162: 185–188 (1951). Davall was admitted a Fellow in 1788; his friend and correspondent J. E. Smith dedicated the genus *Davallia* to him and Davall intended to produce a work on Swiss plants, some plates for which are in the Society's possession, but he died at the age of 35 before its completion. The bulk of his herbarium is in the Smith Herbarium belonging to the Society. De Beer's election as President seemed remarkably apt. Short, very industrious, learned, energetic, genial and likeable, eager and egotistic, with supreme self-confidence and a touch of justified vanity, he was almost a reincarnation of Linnaeus. His Presidential Address in May 1947 was on "How animals hold their heads" (*Proceedings* 159: 125–139; 1947). It gave him great pleasure to announce that Her Royal Highness the Princess Elizabeth (now Queen Elizabeth II) had accepted Honorary Membership.

In March 1948, the Society held another symposium, this time on the organization of taxonomic research. It included W. B. Turrill, E. Trewaras, J. W. Evans, E. Milne-Redhead and N. L. Bor who, as a one-time Indian forest officer, emphasized the disorganization of taxonomic research in India (*Proceedings* 160: 59–68; 1948). This was followed in May 1948 by one on the orientation of birds on migratory and homing flights by W. H. Thorpe, D. H. Cavendish, R. Wojtusiak, A. Landesborough Thomson, J. Fisher and others (*Proceedings* 160: 85–116; 1949). These aroused so much interest and attracted such distinguished audiences, with making available information and ideas from differently experienced workers so well demonstrated, that the Society resolved to make this kind of meeting a more or less regular part of the Society's programme. During the session 1947–48 a series of lectures was given by specialists, in conjunction with the Systematics Association, on the principles and methods of taxonomy subsequently published as a booklet, *Lectures on the Development of Taxonomy* (1950).

The Pilgrim Trust generously gave £2500 towards the restoration of the Library: a survey had shown that the cost of routine binding, purchase of arrears of war-time publications, repairs of existing books and provision of new shelving went high above the Society's available resources. Accordingly, this Pilgrim Trust contribution was much appreciated and most of it went on new shelving and structural alterations. Malcolm Arthur Smith (1876–1958), who had been Zoological Secretary for nine years, including the war period, resigned and Arthur Tindell Hopwood (1897–1969) took over from 1948 to 1954. He was a palaeozoologist in the British Museum (Natural History) in charge of fossil mammals but a man with broad interests, a philosophical turn of mind and a sense of humour. In Kenya he collected the skull of a fossil hominid which appeared to represent an ape related to, but earlier than, the chimpanzee and in 1933 he named it *Proconsul africanus*, not, as might be supposed, with a classical allusion in mind, but because it was before (pro) *Consul*, then a well-known performing chimpanzee! He certainly did not foresee its importance as representing a form ancestral to man and the apes.

The 1948–49 session exemplified the Society's policy of having joint discussions and symposiums with cognate bodies. Thus, on 10 February 1949, the Society held a joint meeting with the British Ornithologists' Union and the British Trust for Ornithology on the song of birds, with recordings by Ludwig Koch and spectograms by C. E. G. Bailey (*Proceedings* 161: 89–95; 1949). On 10 March 1949, there was a joint discussion with the Systematics Association on cytology as a factor in taxonomy, with W. B. Turrill, S. Muldel and F. C. Stern presenting papers. In the opinion of the geneticist Harland, "the first point that struck one was the fact that the earlier taxonomists were so often right in their classifications; how few were the mistakes which they made, while without the aid of cytology and genetics the taxonomist could make logical classifications of real validity; the final polish in many cases would perhaps have to be given by cytological and genetical data". Orthodox taxonomists doubtlessly felt encouraged and relieved. Turrill introduced two then unfamiliar terms: *taxon* (coined by Adolf Meyer in 1926 but made known by H. J. Lam) for "any taxonomic group" and *paramorph* suggested by J. R. Norman for "any taxonomic group below the rank of species" (*Proceedings* 161: 112–128; 1949). On 24 May 1949 de Beer devoted his second and last Presidential Address to "Caruncles and egg-teeth; some aspects of the concept of homology" (*Proceedings* 161: 218–223; 1949).

His successor as President in 1949 was the botanist Felix Eugen Fritsch (1879–1954), who had retired in 1948 from the Professorship of Botany at Queen Mary College, London. Like the earlier many-sided President F. E. Weiss, he was of German parentage and born in England. A temporary lectureship in 1902 at University College, London, led to his becoming Head of the New Botany Department of the East London College (later Queen Mary College), which was a one-man department until Edward James Salisbury (1886–1980) joined him as lecturer in 1914. Together they produced the popular Fritsch and Salisbury botanical text books, *An Introduction to the Study of Plants* (1914) and *An Introduction to the Structure and Reproduction of Plants* (1920). His major interest, however, was in the Algae, on which he published much, his major work being *The Structure and Reproduction of the Algae* (1935–45). Fritsch was elected to the Society in 1903, served on the Council 1922–26 and 1949–53 and was President 1949–52. He died on 23 May 1954, the day before he was to have received the Linnean Gold Medal.

The session of 1949–50 began with an alteration in the Bye-Laws raising the permitted number of Fellows to 1000, exclusive of Honorary Members, Foreign Members and Associates. The number of Fellows had been limited to 710 in 1919 but raised to 800 in 1923. Symposia and discussions on a single theme at a meeting having now become well established, six were held during the sessions: on heteroerism; on morphogenesis; on evolution of locomotory mechanisms in arthropods and worms; on succulent plants; on morphology and fine structure (*Proceedings* 162: 4–83; 1950); on time-rates in evolution; and on biometrics and systematics (*Proceedings* 162: 124–178; 1951). Fritsch devoted his Presidential Address to "The heterocyst, a botanical enigma" (*Proceedings* 162: 194–211; 1951). The success of earlier lectures on taxonomy led to another series in association with the Systematics Association, later published as a booklet, *Lectures on the Practice of Botanical and Zoological Classification* (1951).

Discussions were likewise a feature at the 1950–51 sessions, beginning with "What is Man?" (*Proceedings* 163: 9–16; 1951), continuing with "Taxonomic treatment of biological races" (*Proceedings* 163: 40–59; 1951) and "Australo-pithecines and their evolutionary significance" (*Proceedings* 163: 196–204; 1952). The session saw a number of changes in personnel: Bertie Frank Barnes (1888–1965), who had acted as Deputy Treasurer between 1942 and 1944 and was Botanical Secretary from 1944 onwards, retired and was succeeded by George Taylor, Keeper of Botany in the British Museum (Natural History), who had joined the Society in 1922. Spencer Savage (1886–1966) also retired; he had entered the Society's employment as Clerk in 1909 and had become Librarian and Assistant-Secretary in 1929. He had become greatly esteemed for his courteousness, his scholarship, his efficient management of the Society's affairs and his ever-ready helpfulness. He had acquired a remarkable first-hand knowledge of the Society's manuscripts, with a critical understanding of handwriting, had catalogued the Linnaean Herbarium and begun the cataloguing of the Smith Herbarium, which he completed during his retirement in Southampton. Everyone was sorry to see him move so far away. Since 1935, Theodore O'Grady had been Clerk, his major duties being concerned with the Society's accounts; he then succeeded Savage but with his post designated General Secretary and Miss M. P. Hamilton appointed as Clerk; she resigned in 1951 and was replaced by Mrs Edith Ziegler. Fritsch's Presidential Address was on "The evolution of a differentiated plant" (*Proceedings* 163: 218–233; 1952). The Hooker Lecture in 1951 was an especially interesting and characteristically erudite and comprehensive lecture by I. H. Burkill on "Habits of man and the origins of the cultivated plants of the Old World" (*Proceedings* 164: 12–42; 1953). Symposia were held on "Photoperiodism" (*Proceedings* 164: 134–148; 1953); "growth and systematics" and and "form and functions in the molluscs" (*Proceedings* 164: 140–181, 213–246; 1953). The Council appointed a committee for the care of the Society's collections which recommended that these should have two Honorary Curators of the collections. Noel Yvri Sandwith (1901–65), a Kew botanist, and Willie Horace Thomas Tams (1891–1980), a British Museum (Natural History) entomologist, were appointed the first Honorary Curators. A new Bye-Law authorizing removal of specimens by the Curators to Kew or the British Museum (Natural History) for special examination was submitted to the Society on 5 February 1953. Fritsch's Presidential Address on 24 May 1952 was on "Comparative studies in a polyphyletic group, the Desmidaceae" (*Proceedings* 164: 258–280; 1953).

Fritsch's successor as President, beginning with the 1952–53 session, was Robert Beresford Seymour Sewell (1880–1964). He first took a degree in zoology in Cambridge, then turned to medicine and qualified in 1907. He joined the Indian Medical Service in

1908 and, after service with two Punjabi regiments, became Surgeon Naturalist to the Marine Survey of Burma in 1910 aboard the survey ship *Investigator*. Thus began his long association with marine biology, giving attention to fish, molluscs, leeches and crustacea, especially the planktonic Copepoda on which his publications cover more than a thousand pages. From 1933 to 1936 he edited the *Fauna of India*. The session began with a symposium on the classification of Fungi (*Proceedings* 165: 3–10; 1954), then one on problems of the distribution of animals and plants in Africa (*Proceedings* 165: 24–85; 1954). The year 1953 being the bicentenary of the publication of Linnaeus's *Species Plantarum* (1753), the internationally accepted starting point of modern botanical nomenclature, the Society commemorated the occasion by a meeting with papers by T. A. Sprague, J. S. L. Gilmour, W. T. Stearn and J. Ramsbottom (*Proceedings* 165: 151–166; 1953). Sewell's Presidential Address on 28 May 1953 was "A study of the sea coast of Southern Arabia" (*Proceedings* 165: 188–210; 1955). His second address on 24 May 1954 discussed "The continental drift theory and the distribution of the Copepoda" (*Proceedings* 166: 149–177; 1956); his own work had led him to the conclusion that the present-day distribution of the Copepoda, a very old group, can better be accounted for by a process of fracturing and drifting of land masses rather than by the permanency of the ocean basins. The hypothesis of continental drift was at this time still opposed by many geologists, although the biologists had long favoured such heresy.

Hugh Hamshaw Thomas (1885–1962), the Cambridge palaeobotanist, presided from 1955 to 1958. His interest in fossils began when, as a schoolboy at Wrexham in Wales, he collected specimens from the local coal mines. This interest was strengthened at Cambridge by the Professor of Botany, A. C. Seward, and by E. A. N. Arber at the Sedgwick Museum, both distinguished palaeobotanists. In the 1914–18 War he served with the Royal Flying Corps, developing mapping techniques by aerial photography; he returned to aerial photographic interpretation, as head of a specialist unit in the Royal Air Force, during the 1939–45 War. Palaeobotany remained his life-long botanical preoccupation, a major contribution being his recognition and description of the Caytoniales in Jurassic rocks of Yorkshire published in 1925. From 1937 to 1950 he was Reader in Plant Morphology at the Botany School, Cambridge. He devoted his Presidential Address on 24 May 1956 to "Plant morphology and the evolution of the flowering plants" (*Proceedings* 168: 125–133; 1957), which was not so much concerned with plant morphology as with divergent morphological doctrines emphasizing the influence of Goethe and nature-philosophy.

During the 1956–57 session the Society again held several symposia: on the inheritance of acquired characters (*Proceedings* 169: 84–105; 1958); weed-killers (*Proceedings* 169: 105–110; 1958); cytotaxonomy (*Proceedings* 169: 110–134; 1958); biochemistry and taxonomy (*Proceedings* 169: 198–239; 1958). The last of these was held during the recess corresponding to the University Long Vacation, thus enabling overseas visitors to participate. The success of this experiment gave precedent for later "out of season" symposia. A notable event was the visit on 17 April 1957 of His Majesty Gustav VI Adolf King of Sweden (1882–1973), a scholar of repute with strong scientific interests who examined very thoroughly and with much appreciation exhibits selected from the collections of Linnaeus. He later gave £100 for the Society's Library Fund and a much larger sum towards the cost of the strongroom to safeguard the Linnaean collections. The Society celebrated on 30 May 1957 the two-hundred-and-fiftieth anniversary of the birth of Linnaeus with addresses by His Excellency the Swedish Ambassador in London, Gunnar Häglöf, on "Sweden in the time of Carl Linnaeus" and by W. T. Stearn on

"Botanical exploration to the time of Linnaeus" (*Proceedings* 169: 170–196; 1958). An important paper by A. J. Cain, "Logic and memory in Linnaeus's system of classification" (*Proceedings* 169: 144–163; 1958), made evident the theoretical considerations underlying Linnaeus's work, which had hitherto received scant attention. Thomas's Presidential Address was on "Palaeobotany and the evolution of the flowering plants" (*Proceedings* 169: 132–143; 1958). During this session the Society lost its oldest member, Henry Nicholas Ridley (1855–1956), elected in 1881, the virtual founder of the rubber industry of Malaya and, from 1888 to 1911, Director of Gardens at Singapore. He had been a Fellow for 74 years. In this he was, however, junior to William Stone (1857–1958), who at the age of 101 had been a Fellow for 79 years. A rich man, Stone settled at the Albany, Piccadilly, London, in 1893 and became known as *The Squire of Piccadilly*, under which title he published his reminiscences in 1905. The Society's third centenarian was Collingwood Ingram (1880–1981), who, however, was a Fellow for a mere 36 years. Isaac Henry Burkill (1870–1965), dying at the age of 94, did not achieve the longevity of these three but was nevertheless a Fellow for 71 years; his *Chapters on the History of Botany in India* (1966) sadly appeared posthumously.

At the Anniversary Meeting on 24 May 1957, the Kew botanist A. A. Bullock severely criticized the management of the Society's investments by F. C. Stern, who had been Treasurer since 1941. Stern tendered his resignation during the session and was succeeded by the Rt Hon. The Earl of Cranbrook (John David Gathorne-Hardy, 1900–78), a keen amateur naturalist. During the session the Society held symposia on the use of the electron microscope (*Journal*, Zoology) and water pollution (*Proceedings* 170: 159–172; 1959).

For many years the desirability of a Flora of Europe had been evident. A. H. R. Grisebach (1814–79) attempted such a work but achieved only a fragment, published posthumously in 1882; Werner Rothmaler put forward in 1944 plans for a comprehensive European Flora but the main impetus for the achieved *Flora Europaea* (5 vols, 1964–80) came from botanists in the British Isles after an informal meeting in Paris in 1954. In 1956, a meeting to consider the organization of a *Flora Europaea* project took place at the University of Leicester. Since the raising of funds was fundamental to the success of such a vast undertaking, the organizing committee needed a prestigious sponsor to guarantee its feasibility, its desirability and its standing, in other words its scientific respectability, to attract both money and international collaboration; no major British taxonomic institution had yet become involved in planning and participation. The Linnean Society agreed in 1957 to act as sponsor and the Royal Society made a grant of £750. At a meeting of the Linnean Society on 13 March 1958, T. G. Tutin and V. H. Heywood outlined its scope and some of the problems to be faced, then the work went ahead. By its completion in 1980, 187 botanists in 24 countries had contributed to it. Most of the British and Irish authors belonged to the Linnean Society. The *Flora Europaea*, covering 11 557 species, stands as the most successful major botanical achievement with which the Society has been actively involved. Some information regarding it will be found in *Flora Europaea* 5: xiii–xx (1980), *Taxon* 27: 3–13 (1978) and *Annales Musei Goulandris* 5: 122–129 (1982).

The President for the sessions 1958–61 was Carl Frederick Abel Pantin (1899–1967), Professor of Zoology in Cambridge from 1959 to 1966, earlier Lecturer and Reader in Zoology; he was President of the Marine Biological Association from 1960 to 1966. As the editorial introduction to his posthumous *The Relation between the Sciences* (1968) stated, Pantin was "a man of exceptional breadth and depth of mind. By profession he was a Zoologist, but the whole natural world inspired him with delight and wonder, and he had that curiosity of mind which is a rich gift to the possessor". Such qualities have indeed characterized most of the Society's Presidents. This interest in the world around led Pantin into sciences other than zoology, notably geology and physics. His major contribution to knowledge and understanding of the Invertebrates were "his electro-physiological and histological studies of the simpler types of nervous system, especially the nerve-net of the sea-anemone and the nervous system of some crustacea". To the affairs of the Linnean Society he brought "that gay and generous enthusiasm", backed by sound judgement and extensive learning, which made him so well liked and esteemed.

Two centennial celebrations came within Pantin's period of office in 1958: the centenary of the announcement of Darwin and Wallace's theory of evolution by means of natural selection (see p. 58) and the bicentenary of the publication of Linnaeus's *Systema Naturae*, tenth edition, which is the starting point for scientific zoological nomenclature. Pantin marked the first by unveiling on 1 July 1958 a plaque to Darwin and Wallace in the Society's Meeting Room and gave a memorable address (*Proceedings* 170: 219–226; 1959), then on 15 July 1958 presented Darwin–Wallace medals to 18 distinguished biologists; unfortunately, John Christopher Willis (1868–1958), author of *Age and Area* (1922) and compiler of a celebrated dictionary of flowering plants and ferns first published in 1897, had died on 21 March 1958 and a granddaughter had to accept his medal. This ceremony was followed by an address by A. T. Hopwood on "The development of pre-Linnaean taxonomy" and one by A. J. Cain on "The post-Linnaean development of taxonomy" (*Proceedings* 170: 230–244; 1959); Cain had earlier published a paper of the same philosophical nature, "Deductive and indirective methods in post-Linnean taxonomy" (*Proceedings* 170: 185–217; 1959).

Symposia had now become a regular feature of the Society's programme, particularly as various specialist groups had been formed within the Society, e.g. the Plant Anatomy Group and the Experimental Plant Taxonomy Group. On 19–20 December 1958 there was a symposium on "Experimental approach to problems of growth and form in plants" (*Journal, Botany*, 56: 153–302; 1959), and on 6 March 1959 one was devoted to the "Experimental taxonomy of vascular plants" (*Proceedings* 171: 122–134; 1960). At the conclusion of the 1958–59 session, Pantin gave his Presidential Address, "Diploblastic animals" (*Proceedings* 171: 1–14; 1960), after the usual annual review of the Society's activities. Previously, the task of editing the Society's publications had fallen upon the Botanical and Zoological Secretaries and, in consequence of their many other duties, there were sometimes grievous delays. The Council accordingly appointed an Editorial Committee and an Editorial Secretary, John Smart, their prime duty being "to ensure rapid and regular publication of scientific matter of the highest quality". N. Y. Sandwith, the Society's first Botanical Curator of the Linnaean collections, having retired in March 1959, W. T. Stearn, then at the British Museum (Natural History), was appointed to succeed him and remained Curator until 1985.

The first major event of the 1959–60 session was a symposium on quaternary ecology, held on 17 and 18 December 1959, its theme covering both plants and animals in Britain and Ireland (*Proceedings* 172: 25–89; 1961). There followed one on the reproductive phase in seed plants (*Proceedings* 172: 90–127; 1961) on 9 January 1960, and one on "The subspecies", in association with the Systematics Association, on 4 March 1960. During

Plate XV   (a) John Ramsbottom, from a photograph. (b) W. T. Calman, photograph of a drawing by W. T. Mornington, 1936. (c) Thomas Maxwell Harris, from a photograph taken around 1960. (d) C. F. A. Pantin, from the drawing by Juliet Pannett in the Society's collection.

(a)

(b)

(c)

(d)

July and August 1960 the International Documentation Centre photographed the Linnaean Herbarium under the supervision of W. T. Stearn, the Centre using special illumination and a film of very fine grain for reproduction on microfiche. An interest-free loan of £600 from the Nuffield Foundation made this possible. The task was slow and tedious, owing to the care with which the specimens had to be handled; the adjustments of camera and lighting were performed with great skill by Mrs H. de Mink; the excellence of the results is a tribute to her patience and fortitude. Pantin's Presidential Address on 24 May 1960 dealt with "Geonemertes: a study in island life" (*Proceedings* 172: 137–156; 1961). *Geonemertes* is a genus of small terrestrial worms inhabiting damp habitats and found only on oceanic islands and in Australia and New Zealand.

On 28 October the Society held a joint meeting with the British Mycological Society commemorating the centenary of the birth of Gulielima Lister (1860–1949), distinguished both as a mycologist and botanical artist. Elected to the Society in 1904, she was one of its first women members.

In November 1960, a letter to *The Times* by the President on the need for money to restore and maintain the Library brought a very welcome £4800. Henry Howard Bloomer (1866–1960) bequeathed £500 for the furtherance of natural history. The Council decided to institute an H. H. Bloomer Award to an amateur who had made a significant contribution to natural history. During the 1960–61 session there were symposia on 3 March 1961 on the experimental taxonomy of flowering plants (*Proceedings* 173: 92–113; 1963); on 6 April on language and classification, their use and abuse; and on 7 April on cell differentiation. Pantin concluded his Presidency with an Address, "On teaching biology" (*Proceedings* 173: 1–8; 1962), in which he emphasized that "an accepted science should be, as it were, a particular window opening upon the whole of the natural – and human – world"; "though a branch of learning may become unfashionable it does not mean that it is useless" and "what we consider useful and useless is very much a matter of fashion and emotion". Those were wise statements that an elitist body often tends to ignore.

The next President was Thomas Maxwell Harris.

Chapter 10

From 1961 to 1970

Thomas Maxwell Harris (1903–83), who on 24 May 1961 followed Pantin as President, was Professor of Botany at the University of Reading from 1935 to 1968 and was primarily a palaeobotanist and, like H. Hamshaw Thomas, a one-time student of A. C. Seward at Cambridge. He originally intended to study medicine but decided instead to specialize in botany. Seward put him to work on Triassic plant fossils from Greenland and so determined his life-long interest. From study of the Rhaetic flora of Greenland he passed to the Jurassic flora of Yorkshire, most of his material being collected by himself on excursions by bicycle with rucksack and hammer. He made a major contribution to palaeobotanical techniques by the use of cuticle characters. During his first year of office, the Society held a symposium on "The experimental taxonomy of flowering plants" on 2 March 1962; another on "Function and fine-structure in Protista" on 8 March 1962 (*Proceedings* 174: 31–52; 1965); and yet another on "The growth and development of the lower archegoniate plants" on 5 and 6 April 1962. It heard the Hooker Lecture by Theodosius Dobzhansky on "Species in Drosophila", in which he discussed the reality of species, their comparability and the diversity of biological situations covered by the species concept. As the President remarked, communications "ranged from the movements of *Nautilus* to the equally ponderous and mysterious movements of continents".

The 1962–63 session was notable for the institution of the H. H. Bloomer Award to be made to an amateur who had done distinguished work in natural history. Harry Howard Bloomer (1866–1960), a chartered accountant working near Birmingham, devoted his leisure to natural history, particularly shells and marine biology. It accordingly seemed fitting to the Council that his bequest to the Society should be used to express appreciation of work by an amateur naturalist. Its first recipient, in May 1963, was Job Edward Lousley (1907–76), an employee of Barclays Bank, from 1961 to 1965 President of the Botanical Society of the British Isles, author of *Wild Flowers of Chalk and Limestone* (1950) and many papers, notably on *Rumex*, and an authority on the British flora. The award medal was designed by Leo Holmgrén of the Royal Swedish Mint and portrays young Linnaeus examining *Trientalis europaea*, a native of Britain as well as of Scandinavia. Harris's Presidential Address on 24 May 1963 was on "The inflation of taxonomy" (*Proceedings* 175: 1–7; 1964), a plea against the splitting of families and genera. Symposia included one on the dating of post-glacial deposits on 21 February 1963 and another on the experimental taxonomy of the Pteridophyta on 1 March 1963. In 1863, the Society sold the major part of the botanical and zoological collections which had come into its hands but for which it lacked the staff to curate and study. There remained, however, various other collections, apart from those of Linnaeus and J. E. Smith. The Wallichian East Indian Herbarium, the largest of these, had been presented to the Society by the Hon. East India Company; in 1913 the Society transferred it to the Royal Botanic

(a)

(b)

(c)

(d)

Gardens, Kew. In 1963, the Council decided to reduce again its holdings and sold miscellaneous herbaria to Kew and the British Museum (Natural History). It retained the Linnaean and Smith collections. Spencer Savage had earlier catalogued the Linnaean Herbarium: during the year he completed a catalogue of the Smith Herbarium comprising 20 000 sheets, many of them with type or isotype specimens, these being taken to Southampton for his work there.

During the 1963–64 session the Bye-Laws were amended to abolish the Admission Fee and to extend the limit of Fellowship from 1000 to 1250 Fellows, exclusive of Honorary Members, Foreign Members and Associates; at the same time the Annual Contribution was raised from £5 to £7. The Library benefited from the appointment as Librarian of Sandra Raphael in September 1963. Previously the Society had been unable to spend on necessary binding the grants received from the Royal Society because it lacked the staff to prepare material for the binder; her appointment led to a doubling in the rate of binding. The Society also received the generous and much appreciated grant of £2000 from the Royal Society for the purchase of back numbers of some 20 German periodicals which the Society had been unable to afford since 1939. The second recipient of the H. H. Bloomer Award, on 24 May 1964, was Charles Earle Raven (1885–1964), Regius Professor of Divinity at Cambridge from 1932 to 1950, a field naturalist with extensive knowledge of British plants and British birds, almost all of which he had observed in the wild, and the author of *In Praise of Birds* (1925), *Bird Haunts and Bird Behaviour* (1929), *Natural Religion and Christian Theology* (1953), *John Ray, Naturalist, his Life and Works* (1942) and *English Naturalists from Neckam to Ray* (1947). He died on 9 July 1964, scarcely seven weeks after receiving this well-merited award.

Errol Ivor White (1901–83) followed Harris as President in May 1964. He began his Presidential Address, "A little on lung-fishes" (*Proceedings* 177: 1–10; 1966), with the observation that:

> It may not have escaped your notice that of the last four Presidents of this learned society three have had marked palaeontological leanings. Ten years ago we had Dr. Hamshaw Thomas, an eminent palaeobotanical authority, then after an interval for zoological refreshment with Professor Pantin, we had my illustrious predecessor Professor Tom Harris who, for all his activity as a professor of Recent botany, clearly had his heart in the right place and his eye on the Mesozoic; and finally myself whose tastes are even more archaic ... if you *will* call on palaeo-pipers you must expect to hear a fossil tune.

He accordingly chose a subject with its main interest, at least for him, in the Palaeozoic, some 300 million years ago, but with some remarkable Recent manifestations, the lung-fishes belonging to three living genera. Fossil fishes were White's life-long study. He graduated from King's College, London, as a petrologist, but a chance meeting with Arthur Smith Woodward on a geological field meeting in 1921 led him to apply for a vacancy in the Department of Geology (now Palaeontology), British Museum (Natural History). There Woodward initiated him in his own speciality, the study of fossil fishes, and he worked there for 44 years. From 1939 to 1955 he was Deputy Keeper of the Department; from 1955 to 1966 Keeper. The Linnean Society manifested its regard for Errol White by dedicating the volume *Fossil Vertebrates* (1967) to him.

During his first session (1964–65) the Meeting Room was redecorated and four of the

Plate XVI   (a) Errol White, from a photograph. (b) A. Roy Clapham, from a photograph in the Society's collection. (c) William T. Stearn, from a photograph taken by Ros Drinkwater in 1987. (d) P. Humphrey Greenwood, from a photograph by Godfrey Argent taken in 1986.

portraits restored. It was noted with much appreciation that over the last few years the Royal Society had allocated Libraries Assistance Grants-in-aid to the Society totalling £9500, of which £7500 was to enable the Society to bring its library bindings and repairs up to date. A symposium on 10 December 1964 dealt with "Patterns of distribution in Antarctic planktonic floras", another on 5 March 1965 with "The experimental taxonomy of flowering plants" and a third on 21 May 1965 with "Plant cells and cell walls", this celebrating the tercentenary of Robert Hooke's pioneer *Micrographia: or some Physiological Descriptions of minute Bodies made by magnifying Glasses* (London, 1665), of which, however, the best-known part is his illustration of the flea and his rapturous description of the strength and beauty of this small creature. The cataloguing of the Smith Herbarium by Spencer Savage, mentioned earlier, with the addition of numbers to the sheets for reference purposes, now made its photography practicable and this was done for the Society and published on microfiche by the International Documentation Centre which had earlier photographed the Linnaean Herbarium.

The first symposium of the 1965–66 session, held on 12 November 1965, dealt with "The Flora Europaea project", which the Society had effectively sponsored during its initial stages. There followed on 16 December one on "Factors influencing the distribution of *Amphioxus*", on 17 February 1966 "Intertidal studies at Scott Head Island, Norfolk", on 4 March "The experimental taxonomy of flowering plants" and on 17 March "Developmental morphology and anatomy of the shoot in cereals", a range of subjects clearly manifesting the diversity and modernity of the Society's extending biological coverage. At the Anniversary Meeting on 24 May 1966, the President presented the third H. H. Bloomer Award to David Lakin Harrison who, while serving as a medical officer with the RAF in western Asia, made a special study of the mammals of Iraq, Oman and Jordan, and through this experience and that of later expeditions produced *The Mammals of Arabia* (1963).

The precarious financial state of the Society resulting from increased running costs had been for some time a source of worry and indeed alarm; by May 1965 its deficit had risen to several hundred pounds. Much of this resulted from the high cost of producing its publications. For some years the receipts from subscriptions to the Society's publications had been between £1000 and £1300 less than the cost of producing them. The Council accordingly made a four-year publishing agreement with Academic Press whereby from 1 January 1966 the Press would advertise and promote the sales of the Society's publications at no cost to the Society and would share on a fifty–fifty basis the costs of producing them and the receipts from their sales. The first publications issued under this agreement were *Proceedings* 176 part 2 (for July 1966), *Journal, Botany* 59 no. 379 (for February 1966) and *Journal, Zoology* 46 no. 308 (for May 1966). It proved a pleasurably harmonious and satisfactory arrangement, thanks to the very co-operative attitude of the Academic Press management, and it helped to relieve the Society's Council of much worry, since the Society's utility and prestige depended so much on its publications. Nevertheless, there remained other grounds for concern and even misgiving, particularly over the Society's function in an ever-changing scientific world; the safeguarding of its collections in the event of sudden war; the overcrowding of the library; and the lack of adequate accommodation for office and council work. The Council accordingly appointed an Aims Committee in November 1966 under the Chairmanship of Dr Ronald W. J. Keay, Deputy Executive Secretary of the Royal Society. It submitted a constructive far-reaching report to the Council in March 1967. After much consideration, because its proposals envisaged expenditure high above the Society's resources, this report formed the basis of action in

1968 and 1969. The aims of the Society were concisely defined as "to promote all aspects of biology which are concerned with the diversity and inter-relationships of organisms", a statement in no way conflicting with, but expressing in modern fashion, the words of the Society's 1802 Charter: "the cultivation of the Science of Natural History in all its branches". The Council agreed that this brief statement might be supplemented when appropriate by a more detailed one as follows:

> The Society's activities have as their centre the promotion of the study of evolution, systematics and taxonomy. This requires the examination and collation of a wide range of scientific evidence from such subjects as genetics, ecology, anatomy, physiology, biochemistry and palaeontology. The role of the Linnean Society is therefore to serve as a meeting-point for many biological subjects and in this way the Society caters for biologists who wish to preserve a broad outlook on their science, as well as for those with more specialized interests.

There was nothing new in this, but it usefully made explicit what had long been the Society's traditional policy. As reported by the President in May 1968, in addition to various administrative changes, the Aims Committee urged strongly that the highest priority be given to making the Society's publications profitable; that policy with respect to the Library be reviewed; that a certain amount of reconstruction and modernization of the Society's rooms be undertaken without delay; and that an appeal for funds, to cover in particular the improvement of the accommodation and the reorganization of the Linnaean Collections and Society's Library, be launched in the near future.

The Council elected as White's successor in 1967 Arthur Roy Clapham (b. 1904), from 1931 to 1944 Botany Demonstrator in Oxford, from 1944 to 1969 Professor of Botany in Sheffield, joint author with W. O. James of *The Biology of Flowers* (1935), and with T. G. Tutin and E. F. Warburg of the well-known *Flora of the British Isles* (1952). A native of Norwich, birthplace of the Society's first President, J. E. Smith, Clapham was educated there and at Cambridge. Office as Pro-Vice-Chancellor and as Acting Vice-Chancellor of Sheffield University added to his administrative experience; his combination of tact, geniality and authority proved invaluable to the Society during the many negotiations associated with implementation of the Aims Committee's recommendations during his Presidency. This extended from 1967 to 1970 and was the most momentous in the Society's long history.

The session began with an Extraordinary General Meeting, presided over by Errol I. White, Vice-President, on 23 June 1967 to approve amendments to the Bye-Laws. One removed the restriction on the number of Fellows by the statement "the limit of the number of persons to be elected shall be determined by the Council". However, "the number of Fellows *honoris causa* shall not exceed twenty-five". A new group of Associates was instituted, student Associates, aged 18 to 23, as well as ordinary Associates, aged 21 to 28.

In April 1967, the Council appointed a Building Committee, under the chairmanship of J. C. Gardiner (later the Society's Treasurer), to give special consideration to the conservation of the Linnaean Collections and to the Library, the Meeting Room, cloakrooms, offices and accommodation for Gatekeeper and Housekeeper. The Committee's preliminary report was submitted to the Council in July 1967 and began a series of discussions on its implementation. In 1967, the Royal Society, which had occupied the east wing of Burlington House and rooms over the entrance archway, moved to spacious premises in Carlton House Terrace. In consequence the Linnean Society obtained three rooms above the entrance archway, formerly used by the Royal Society, and also the basement beneath the rooms of the Chemical Society. Thus there arose an immediate need for planning the Society's accommodation.

At the Anniversary Meeting on 24 May 1968, Clapham made the Fellows acquainted with these developments. He dealt first with the Society's publications. A meeting of the Society's officers with C. M. Hutt, then the managing director of Academic Press, later the Society's Treasurer, led to the following recommendations accepted by the Council in March 1968:

i.   that the Society's three series of publications each be issued quarterly, so as to reduce delays in publication and stimulate the intake of papers;

ii. that the present two Journals and Proceedings be renamed *Botanical Journal of the Linnean Society*, *Zoological Journal of the Linnean Society* and *Biological Journal of the Linnean Society* respectively, the aim being to give more emphasis than at present to the scope of each and to discard the now misleading title *Proceedings*;

iii. that the covers of the three publications be redesigned;

iv. that a complete volume of each series be issued each year with an agreed total number of pages per volume, so as to give subscribers a better indication of what they might expect to receive in one subscription year and to simplify accounting;

v.   that the present annual subscription of £5 for each series be increased from 1969, the future subscription to be the subject of discussion between the Treasurer and Academic Press;

vi. that consideration be given to relieving the Honorary Editors of some of the additional burden of work arising from quarterly publication of each series.

The issue of these three periodicals under their new titles began in 1969.

The Library Committee had had 19 members; following the recommendations of the Aims Committee the size of the Library Committee was reduced to nine and charged with considering future policy for the Library. This newly constituted committee submitted a report to the February 1968 meeting of the Council, at which the following proposals were approved:

i.   that the Society should continue to buy books to complete its coverage of subjects of historical importance to the Society and its interests, particularly those relevant to Linnaeus and the period of evolutionary controversy;

ii. that it should continue to buy books of high quality dealing with the fauna and flora of all parts of the world, but with the use of discretion regarding works on very restricted areas in more remote parts of the world;

iii. that it should continue to buy general works of natural history, but only those of high standard and sound scientific content;

iv. that it should not purchase student text books;

v.   that it should discontinue the purchase of journals specializing in electron microscopy and fine structure;

vi. that Library policy be kept under continuing review in the light of information on the demand for different categories of books and periodicals.

It was also agreed that the Society should make every effort to obtain the publications of British local natural history societies, the flora and fauna of northwestern Europe being of primary interest for the Library.

The reorganization and modernization of the Society's accommodation made possible by the accession of more rooms presented difficulties for which the Society's Curatorial

Committee and Building Committee lacked the requisite technical knowledge to tackle unaided. For the Library, the Building Committee recommended:

i. the rehousing of a large proportion, or all, of the books at present in the second floor rooms, in order to reduce the load on the floors and to enable these rooms to be used for other purposes;

ii. the rehousing of sufficient books from the main Library and elsewhere to eliminate all double stacking;

iii. the provision of sufficient shelving to house the probable additions to the Library for a period of, say, 15 years;

iv. the conversion of the present Council Room into an extension of the Library, with working bays and facilities for the Librarian.

For the Meeting Room the Building Committee recommended, and the Council approved, the provision of seating for 145–150 persons, this to be made possible by the removal of the Linnaean Collections, a smaller dais and better seating.

At that time, one room on the first floor had to serve simultaneously as Council Room, Committee Room, Executive Secretary's Office and part of the Library. The Council agreed that, in the reorganized building, that room should function exclusively as the east part of the Library. Space for a Council Room and a Committee Room, as well as for a Housekeeper's flat, could be found on the second floor when all books had been removed, and an Executive Secretary's Room, Staff Office and a Linnaean Collections examination area could be provided on the ground floor in rooms to the left of the main entrance. More adequate cloakroom and toilet accommodation could be made in the basement. To implement these proposed changes and to provide accommodation for storage of the Linnaean Collections the Society engaged the services of Pinkheard and Partners.

For the Linnaean Collections, which had hitherto been stored without any deterioration in wooden cases in the Meeting Room, from which they had been evacuated in war-time, there were two possibilities. In the sad event of a future war there would be no time or opportunity to remove them from Burlington House. Metal cabinets giving adequate protection against both fire and water would be so heavy that very costly strengthening of the floor above the basement would be needed if they were housed at ground level; moreover, windows would have to be blocked out on the Piccadilly side of the Society's premises and the Ministry of Public Buildings would almost certainly refuse permission for that. Hence it was agreed provisionally that suitable accommodation, ultimately a strongroom, proof against fire and water, should be provided in the basement. No one could then foresee the difficulties of humidity and temperature control there and the consequent high running costs.

The total cost of all this constructional work was estimated at about £55 000, an immense sum far beyond the Society's means. The Council accordingly set up an Appeals Committee with Dr R. W. J. Keay as Deputy Chairman.

After many preliminary enquiries, the Society launched its Appeal campaign with the publication and distribution of a brochure, *An Appeal for Development 1969*, in October 1968. A press conference led to notes about the Linnean Society and its Appeal appearing in various newspapers and magazines. An anonymous donor offered to match pound for pound of the donations from other sources. This generous benefactor was Stanley Smith from Australia, whose contribution ultimately amounted to £25 000. From the Royal Society, ever a generous helper of the Linnean Society, came £4970. The International Union of Biological Societies contributed US $3000. An exceptionally large gift was that of £5000 from the Drapers' Company, of which Frederick Claude Stern (1888–1967), the

Society's Treasurer from 1941 to 1958, had been Master. The Society was also much encouraged by a donation from its Patron, Her Majesty the Queen. By October 1969 a total of £12 098 had been received or promised by 279 Fellows and Associates out of a membership of 1054 in 1968, a disappointingly low number, and by 25 Foreign Members. People in 16 overseas countries made gifts. The Society's indebtedness to Sweden, Linnaeus's country, was particularly high, since the King of Sweden gave £2000 from a special fund for science and culture administered by him personally and the University of Uppsala £807; other donations came from the Royal Swedish Academy of Science, the Swedish Match Company and individual Swedes. Among gifts from the United States were $1200 from the Hunt Botanical Library, $1000 from the American Philosophical Society and $500 from the American Museum of Natural History; British Petroleum gave $1000. All these donations, which by May 1969 amounted to about £59 000 and by October to over £61 000, testified most gratifyingly to the esteem in which the Society was held and to international appreciation of the importance of the Linnaean Collections. The success of the Appeal owed much to the devoted work of Dr Keay, Mrs P. Baumann and the Society's permanent staff. Construction could now go ahead. By December 1969 the strongroom in the basement, its walls enclosed with tons of concrete, its fittings installed but no collections yet transferred, was open for inspection at the President's Reception. However, the general modernization of the Society's building remained to be done.

During this period of appeal and construction, which necessarily laid an extra burden on the Society's staff and officers, the normal business of the Society suffered little interruption. Again there were several symposia. One held in Liverpool in association with the Botanical Society of the British Isles on 11–12 September 1967 has its papers recorded in the volume edited by V. H. Heywood, *Modern Methods in Plant Taxonomy* (1968). On 2 January 1968 the Palaeobotany Group arranged a symposium on Devonian plants; on 1 March 1968 the Experimental Plant Taxonomy Group arranged one relating to *Cochlearia*, *Mentha*, *Potentilla*, *Papaver* and *Ranunculus* studied experimentally. At the Anniversary Meeting on 24 May 1968, Miriam Rothschild received the H. H. Bloomer Award for her work on fleas and on mimicry and protective adaptations of insects. Sandra Raphael, who had been Librarian and Archivist for six years, resigned in May 1969; she had efficiently reduced the arrears of binding and had elucidated the dates of publication of the Society's *Transactions*. Gavin Bridson was appointed to succeed her in July 1969. The first meeting of the 1969–70 session began with a symposium on "Modern developments in fern taxonomy" on 16 October 1969. Fortunately, more contributions came in answer to the Appeal, notably about £8000 from the Swedish Government and a second grant of $3000 from the International Union of Biological Sciences. On 6 January 1970 the differentiation of the reproductive cells of vascular plants was the subject of a symposium, followed on 15 January 1970 by the impact of industry on plants and animals; then on 6 March on infraspecific categories; on 19 March on biochemistry and phylogeny of plants and animals; and on 19 April on Mezozoic plants.

Clapham concluded his Presidency on 24 May 1970 with an address on "Arctic-alpine wanderers in Derbyshire" (*Biol. Journal*, 2: 327–231; 1970); awarded medals, including the H. H. Bloomer Award to Arthur Erskine Ellis, who had been head of the Botany Department at Epsom College for 32 years before retiring in 1963; and had written on many aspects of British natural history. Clapham also reviewed the Society's manifold activities before relinquishing office to Alexander James Cave, President for the session 1970–73.

Chapter 11

From 1970 to 1982

The 1970–71 session began in October under the Presidency of Alexander James Edward Cave (b. 1900), Professor of Human and Comparative Anatomy from 1941 to 1946 at the Royal College of Physicians and Professor of Anatomy at St Bartholomew's Hospital from 1946 to 1967. At the beginning of 1970, the Society's premises were in a somewhat chaotic state owing to the building work which was taking longer than anticipated; with that completed there remained countless tasks of cleaning and rearranging. Consequently, the President's Reception, hitherto held in December, was postponed until 14 May, a change of season so popular that it has been held in April or May ever since. The Library, closed in May 1970, was reopened in January 1971. To those who for many years had known the Society's rooms in their more or less Victorian state the change during the year was both surprising and welcome. Thus the cabinets formerly housing the Linnaean Herbarium, so familiar in the Meeting Room, had gone to the Executive Secretary's office. On the uppermost floor there was a large and elegant Council Chamber, to be reached, however, only by a long climb up stairs with ropes along the walls to aid the aged. The Society's portraits again adorned the walls; two of them, those of Sir James E. Smith and Sir Joseph Banks, had been restored through the generosity of an American Fellow, James W. T. Moody. At last, after all that dust-disturbing activity, the Council thought the Society now possessed rooms fittingly reflecting its dignity and pre-eminence and more efficient for its purposes.

In September 1970, the Society held a symposium on "New research in plant anatomy" honouring Charles Russell Metcalfe, who had retired in September 1969 as Keeper of the Jodrell Laboratory and had been Botanical Secretary from 1956 to 1962. In February 1971, the Chairman presented the printed record of this symposium to Metcalfe and at the Anniversary Meeting in May 1971 he received the Linnean Medal (*Biol. Journal* 3: 379; 1971). The H. H. Bloomer Award went to John Dony, an enthusiastic amateur botanist, the author of *Flora of Bedfordshire* (1953) and *Flora of Hertfordshire* (1967).

With the renovation of the Library and the cleaning of the books, which revealed that many considered "lost" had been simply misplaced, the Library Committee formulated a new policy regarding acquisition of periodicals. The increasing number and cost of these had now made it impossible for the Society to meet the needs of botanists and zoologists, as it had done much earlier before the founding of institutional libraries in the London area. The Library Committee recommended and the Council agreed that the Society should limit its acquisition of periodicals to those especially relevant to the natural history of the British Isles in particular and Western Europe in general, but continue to acquire non-European works essential to the scientific balance of the collection. Exchange of the Society's publications for those of other learned bodies continued for the time being but was later drastically curtailed.

(a)

(b)

The Society had received in 1859 from Lady Smith, the widow of Sir James Smith, a Chinese libation cup carved out of a rhinoceros horn, brought from China by Magnus Lagerström and given to Linnaeus. In view of the active interest in the Society and generous help towards the cost of the strongroom by H.M. King Gustav VI Adolf of Sweden, the President, Officers and some Council members formally presented this cup to His Majesty on 11 November 1970, his eighty-eighth birthday, during a short private visit to London. On another Linnaean occasion, 13 May 1971, the Society's rooms were officially reopened in the presence of His Excellency the Swedish Ambassador and the President expressed the Society's gratitude for Swedish generosity and that of other principal donors present.

Frederick Roger Goodenough, a descendant of the Society's original Treasurer, Samuel Goodenough, had taken over as Treasurer in succession to Lord Cranbrook, whose judicious management of the Society's investments had raised their annual income from between £600 and £700 to £3270. Nevertheless, there was in March 1971 still an excess of payments over income amounting to about £2800.

James Eric Smith, Director of the Marine Biological Association's Laboratory at Plymouth and eminent above all as a marine zoologist, received the Linnean Gold Medal on 21 October 1971, having been unable to attend the Anniversary Meeting in May 1971.

The most notable opening occasion of the 1971–72 session was the visit on 21 October 1971 of their Majesties the Emperor Hirohito and the Empress of Japan to view the Society's rooms and examine part of the Linnaean collections. The Emperor signed again the Roll and Charter Book he had originally signed in 1921 as Crown Prince of Japan. The Emperor, a keen investigator of marine biology but also a botanist, examined some Linnaean botanical and zoological specimens, but the Empress was more interested in the pearls cultured by Linnaeus. A photograph of this occasion with the President, Isabella Gordon and W. T. Stearn, all academically robed, receiving the Imperial party is given here. At the Anniversary Meeting on 24 May 1972, the Treasurer was happy indeed to report that the deficit of £2800 had been transformed into a surplus of £71, but not so happy next year to state that it was really a deficit of £161! During the past year the installation of a basement bookstore with some 1400 feet of shelving on sliding racks provided relief from congestion elsewhere. The major event, however, was a grant of £6500 from the Pilgrim Trust to enable the Society to have the Library recatalogued and classified in accordance with the Universal Decimal Classification; Gerda Semple was engaged for this task, to be undertaken under the supervision of the Librarian, Gavin Bridson. Unfortunately, while the external sandblasting of the building had given it a fresh clean appearance, the Library had received in consequence so much dirt and grit as to undo all the cleaning of two years before.

During the session there were, as usual, special meetings and symposia: "Behavioural aspects of parasite transmission" on 8–9 July 1971; "Taxonomy and phytogeography of higher plants in relation to evolution" at Manchester on "Crop evolution and plant breeding" on 20 January 1972; "Plants, a substratum for insect evolution" on 17

Plate XVII   (a) Visit by Emperor Hirohito. Their Majesties the Emperor and Empress of Japan photographed during their visit to the Society's Rooms on 7 October 1971. Also in the photograph are, from left to right, Dr Wm T. Stearn, Chairman of the Curatorial Committee; Dr Isabella Gordon; the President and the Emperor's Interpreter. (b) His Majesty King Carl XVI Gustaf of Sweden and Theodore O'Grady, Executive Secretary, during a visit to the Society's Rooms on 12 July 1975.

February 1972; "The ecological basis of conservation" on 20 April 1972; and "Interrelationships of fishes" on 27–28 July 1972.

At the Anniversary Meeting of 24 May 1972, the President presented the Trail–Crisp Award for Microscopy to Gordon Frank Leedale of the University of Leeds, primarily for his book *Euglenoid Flagellates* (1967), based on studies with both the light and the electron microscopes, and the H. H. Bloomer Award to Marie Åsberg, a Swedish psychiatrist at the Karolinska Sjukhuset, Stockholm, for her translation of Linnaeus's *Ölandski och Gothländska Resa* (1745), which after extensive revision and annotation by W. T. Stearn was published in *Biol. Journal* 5: 1–204 (1973).

The meeting of 19 October 1972 provided the opportunity for Arthur Roy Clapham, President of the Society from 1967 to 1970 and a Fellow since 1949, and Alfred Sherwood Romer, the American zoologist, author of *Vertebrate Palaeontology* (1947) etc., described metaphorically as epitomizing his subject by "a personal combination of archaic reptilian toughness and mammalian exuberance", to receive Linnean Gold Medals. Neither had been able to attend the Anniversary Meeting.

From 15 to 17 April 1973 a palaeobotanical group of the Society held a meeting at the University of Bristol which included a successful excursion in South Wales to find *Zosterophyllum, Gosslingia* and other fossil plants. The second awarding of medals within the 1972–73 session was at the Anniversary Meeting of 24 May 1973, when the President presented Linnean Gold Medals to George Ledyard Stebbins, the American botanical geneticist and systematist, and John Zachary Young, and the H. H. Bloomer Award to Ursula Katherine Duncan for her contribution to the study of British lichens. The Linnaean Collections were finally placed in the strongroom but already deficiencies which were to trouble the Curatorial Committee for years were becoming manifest; the running costs of the machinery to control humidity and temperature proved vastly greater than the original estimates. During the year the Society, for the sake of economy, terminated exchange agreements of periodicals with some 154 institutions. Nevertheless, the Society's costs continued to rise and the balance sheet for the year ended 31 March 1973 showed an excess of expenditure over income amounting to £3620.

This was Cave's last session as President, his Address being on "The primate nasal fossa" (*Biol. Journal* 5: 377–387; 1974), wherein he demonstrated that the form of the nasal fossa provided a criterion defining the primates – a group with vision-dominated life – separating them from other groups dominated by the sense of smell.

The first formal admission of women to Fellowship of the Society had taken place on 19 January 1905. In 1903, the President, S. H. Vines, had described their impending admission as "a somewhat heroic experiment, with no precedent". On 24 May 1973, the retiring President, A. J. E. Cave, manifested no such feelings of heroism when he formally handed the President's key to Irene Manton and invited her to take the Chair as the first woman to be elected President. It was certainly an historic even if not "heroic" occasion.

Irene Manton (b. 1904), a Cambridge graduate, Lecturer in Botany at the University of Manchester from 1929 to 1945 and Professor of Botany at Leeds from 1946 to 1969, had been a pioneer investigator of the cytology of ferns and other groups, notably the Cruciferae, and attained world renown for her use of electron microscopy, especially in the study of marine flagellates. She also had a reputation for "forthright and illuminating comments".

Her Presidency began with a special general meeting on 17 September 1973, an occasion of mourning owing to the recent death of the Society's generous benefactor and Honorary Member, King Gustav VI Adolf of Sweden. On 6 December 1973, the Society celebrated the bicentenary of the birth of one of its most distinguished members, Robert Brown (1773–1858), President from 1849 to 1853, with three papers: a survey of Brown's life and achievements by W. T. Stearn; one on the classification and phylogeny of the Proteaceae, a family to which Brown had given special attention, by L. A. S. Johnson and Barbara G. Briggs; and another on investigation of the plant cell since Brown's pioneer publications of 1828 and 1831 by J. Heslop-Harrison, who concluded that modern work on the same matters "serves only to increase respect for the precision and beauty of his observations and the quality of his thought". The Society's financial difficulties led to the regretted but unavoidable raising of a Fellow's annual subscription to £12 on 21 March 1974. Three symposia were held during the session: "The biology of the male gamete" in Cambridge on 5–7 September 1973 (*Biol. Journal* 7, supplement; 1974); "The biology and chemistry of the Cruciferae" on 7–9 January 1974 (*Biology and Chemistry of the Cruciferae*, 1976); and "The taxonomy and biosystematics of higher plants" on 30 April 1974. The awards of the Linnean Gold Medals in 1974 honoured the German entomologist and phylogenetist Emil Hans Willi Hennig, the pioneer of cladistics, and the Swiss botanical ecologist Josias Braun-Blanquet. The H. H. Bloomer Award went to two amateur specialists on spiders, Alfred Frank Millidge and George Hazelwood Locket, both professional chemists, and the Trail–Crisp Award for Microscopy to Brian Edgar Scourso Gunning. The grant of £2500 from the Pilgrim Trust to pay for a third year of recataloguing the Library was very welcome indeed. The rate of inflation produced an excess of expenditure over income of £4750 and would have been much higher but for increased sales of publications. To meet this difficulty the Council revived the Finance Committee with two qualified accountants, two trained bankers and three officers of the Society as members.

The session 1974–75 covered a diversity of biological matters manifesting the catholic interests and special knowledge of the Society's members. They ranged from the remarkable coelocanth fish *Latimeria* to the identification of old woodlands, oil pollution research, the Hookers of Kew as botanical imperialists and the biology of aphids. There were symposia on "The biology of bracken", *Pteridium aquilinum* (*Bot. Journal* 73: 1–302; 1976), on 3 September 1974; "The evolutionary significance of the exine" (*Linnean Soc. Symposium* no. 1; 1976) on 18–20 September 1974 and "Variation, breeding and conservation of tropical forest trees" (*Linnean Soc. Symposium* no. 2; 1976) on 17–20 April 1975; and "Applied plant anatomy" on 26 June 1975. His Majesty King Carl XVI Gustaf of Sweden honoured the Society with a visit and was formally admitted as an Honorary Member in succession to his late grandfather, King Gustav VI Adolf, on 12 July 1975; since 1888 the Head of the Swedish Royal House has been an Honorary Member.

At the Anniversary Meeting of 22 May 1975, the President awarded Linnean Gold Medals to Alexander Stuart Watt for ecological research and Philip Macdonald Sheppard for genetical research, and the H. H. Bloomer Award to Eric Smoothy Edees, a retired Classics schoolmaster, author of *Flora of Staffordshire* (1972) and an authority on *Rubus*. The Treasurer's report continued to emphasize the unsatisfactory state of the Society's finances under the pressure of inflation. In May 1974, the excess of expenditure over income amounted to just over £4750. The subscription had been raised to £12 and the number of Fellows increased from 1450 to 1508, with the result that by May 1975 the deficit amounted to £3176. During the year the Society sold by auction in November 1974 a number of duplicate books from the Library, the sale of which, after deductions of auctioneer's discount etc., realized £6844.

At the 4 December 1975 meeting of the next session (1975–76), the Council had the unpleasant task of recommending that the annual subscription of Fellows be raised to £16 and this was approved at the meeting of 15 January 1976. On 9–10 September 1975 the Society held a symposium on "Morphology and biology of living and fossil reptiles". There had already been many meetings held outside London, but on 5–10 April 1976 a joint meeting took place in collaboration with the German Arbeitskreis für Paläobotanik und Palynologie at Bonn and Wuppertal. It was followed on 29–30 June 1976 by a symposium on "Control of shoot form". William T. Stearn received the Linnean Gold Medal on 24 May 1976 at the Anniversary Meeting and Frederick Charles Stinton the H. H. Bloomer Award for palaeontological work as an amateur, principally on the otoliths of fish. The Society's financial state remained a matter of grave concern: from 31 March to 31 December 1975 the excess of expenditure over income, despite economies, increased to £6500. The Royal Society made a Library Assistance Grant of £1250 for binding and the British Library a grant of £4500 for book repairs and the purchase of multi-volume works and essential taxonomic works. From the estate of John James Lewis Bonhote (1875–1946) the Society received £4600 for furtherance of the study of heredity, thereby instituting the Bonhote Fund.

Irene Manton's term of office as President ended on 24 May 1976 and Peter Humphry Greenwood (b. 1927), a British Museum (Natural History) ichthyologist, succeeded her as President. Although born in Cornwall, he had been taken to South Africa when 18 months old. He served in the South African Navy from 1944 to 1946, then went to the University of the Witwatersrand, where reading J. R. Norman's *A History of Fishes* (1931) turned his attention to ichthyology. After seven years working on the fishes of the East African lakes he joined the staff of the British Museum (Natural History). He was the Society's Zoological Secretary from 1967 to 1976. A meeting at Leicester University on 29 October 1976 dealt with "Hybrids in botany, horticulture and agriculture"; others on 4 November 1976 with "Biology and taxonomy of round-cyst nematodes", on 18 November with "Botanical applications of numerical methods", and on 17 March 1977 with "Palaeoethnobiology". Symposia included "The biology and taxonomy of the Solanaceae" on 13–17 July 1976 at Birmingham; "The bestiary and animals in art" on 8–10 July, jointly with the Society of Antiquaries; "The ecological effects of pesticides" on 23–24 September, jointly with the Institute of Biology; "The biology of the Pycnogonida" on 7 October 1976; "Biological results of the Zaire River Expedition" on 6 January 1977; and "Plant–insect relationships with special reference to pollination" on 14–17 April 1977 at the University of Newcastle-upon-Tyne, jointly with the Botanical Society of the British Isles. Together they manifested the continuing wide scope of the Society's interests. The financial difficulties of the Society occasioned yet another regrettable but inevitable increase in the annual Fellow's subscription, which was raised to £20 in March.

The President presented Linnean Medals (because of cost no longer of gold) to Ernst Walter Mayr, the German-born American zoologist best known for his publications on evolution, and Thomas Gaskell Tutin, Professor of Botany at Leicester University from 1947 to 1967 and main editor and part-author of the *Flora Europaea* and of Clapham, Tutin and Warburg's *Flora of the British Isles*; the H. H. Bloomer Award went to Douglas Henry Kent, then an employee of the Gas Light and Coke Company but also the author, among much else, of *Historical Flora of Middlesex* (1975).

Another sale of duplicates from the Library brought in £5500. Nevertheless, the excess of expenditure for the calendar year amounted to £6600, much of it caused by the cost of journals supplied to Fellows.

To commemorate the bicentenary of the death of Linnaeus in 1778, the Council decided to institute a Bicentenary Medal, to be awarded only to persons under 40 years of age, for excellence in any field of biology.

The second year of Greenwood's Presidency began on 20 October 1977 with a meeting on "Application of *in vitro* methods to problems of plant hybridization", followed on 28 October by one in Sheffield on "Recent work in biosystematics" relating to *Allium*, *Dryopteris* and *Anacyclus*. Other meetings during the session took place in Southampton, Cardiff and Exeter. On 22–23 May 1978, the Society commemorated the two-hundredth anniversary of the death of Linnaeus on 10 January 1778 by an international symposium dealing with "Research on Linnaeus", to which W. T. Stearn, J. L. Larson (USA), J. J. Heller (USA), A. Wheeler, M. G. Fitton, M. C. Day, P. W. James, P. C. C. Garnham, H. Goerke (Germany), C. O. Von Sydow (Sweden), P. Smit (The Netherlands), J. E. Shillito, G. P. Broberg (Sweden) and B. Strandell (Sweden) contributed papers, most of them subsequently printed, together with others, in *Svenska Linnésällskapets Årsskrift 1978* (1979) as they were later delivered again in Uppsala and Stockholm. At the Anniversary Meeting on 24 May 1978, the President presented Linnean Medals to Karl Olof Hedberg, Professor of Systematic Botany at Uppsala, who has done especially notable work on the plants of the East African mountains, and Thomas Stanley Westoll for his diversity of contributions to zoological palaeontology; the Trail–Crisp Award for Microscopy to Tor Örvig, Professor and Head of the Palaeozoological Department of the Naturhistoriska Riksmuseet, Stockholm; the Bicentenary Medal, now first awarded, to the mycologist David Leslie Hawksworth; and the H. H. Bloomer Award to Donovan Reginald Rosevear (1900–86), one-time Inspector-General for Forests in Nigeria, for his work above all on West African mammals (bats, rodents and carnivores).

For the first time in many years the accounts of 1977 showed an excess of income, £201, over expenditure, very welcome indeed but overshadowed by the need for high expenditure on Library security and redecoration later. During the session the cataloguing of the Library was completed.

The 1978–79 session began with a special meeting on 28 September 1978 concerning the background to learning in Commonwealth countries, followed by another on 19 October on the impact of tree diseases on the British landscape, prompted by the dramatic and disastrous effects of the Dutch elm disease. A meeting in Liverpool revealed the unexpected ecological diversity and richness of industrial waste heaps. The Society's Library was the subject of four lectures on 7 December. Conservation of wildlife in the urban environment and chemical defence systems of plants against animals came under survey. There were also two symposia, each lasting three days: one on the skin of vertebrates, the other on monocotyledons of horticultural importance. The President, P. Humphry Greenwood, concluded his term of office at the Anniversary Meeting of 24 May 1979 with an Address on "Macro-evolution, myth or reality?" and the presentation of medals. They were the Linnean Medal for Botany to Paul Westmacott Richards, Professor of Botany at the University College of North Wales, Bangor, from 1949 to 1976, the author of *The Tropical Rain Forest* (1952) and much else; the Linnean Medal for Zoology to Robert McNeill Alexander, Professor of Zoology at Leeds University, noted for investigations on animal mechanics and the author of *Functional Design in Fishes* (1967) etc.; the H. H. Bloomer Award to Blanche Henrey, the author of *British Botanical and Horticultural Literature before 1800* (1975); and the Bicentenary Medal to Roger Laurence Blackman, an entomologist at the British Museum (Natural History) doing illuminating work on the cytology, genetics and biology of aphids, the author of *Aphids* (1974) widely used by students. During the session the Library benefited from generous grants from the

British Library. Surplus of income from sales of publications made it possible to set aside a further £7000 for providing security in the Library, redecorating and so on. At the Anniversary Meeting, J. G. Gardiner retired as Treasurer after four years of profitable service to the Society and was succeeded by Charles Hutt, formerly managing director of Academic Press. In July 1979, Theodore O'Grady, the Secretary since 1951, retired. He had entered the service as a clerk 44 years before, working with Spencer Savage and acquiring from him an abiding interest in the Society's history and well-being; all this was so warmly appreciated that he received on retirement a book with the signatures of some 630 Fellows and Associates and a subscribed sum of money to enable him and Mrs O'Grady to take a holiday in Sweden visiting places especially associated with Linnaeus. In his place the Council appointed Elizabeth Young, a keen botanist and a Fellow since 1972. Thus the Society began the activities of the 1979–80 session in June 1979 with a new President, a new Treasurer and a new Executive Secretary, changes in personnel but not in policy. Brian Gardiner agreed to serve a seventh year as Zoological Secretary.

William Thomas Stearn (b. 1911), formerly Librarian to the Royal Horticultural Society, then a botanist in the Department of Botany, British Museum (Natural History), later Visiting Professor at the University of Reading, followed Humphry Greenwood as President in 1979. Enquiry for taxonomic purposes into the precise application of Linnaean botanical names led him into the study of Linnaeus's life, methods and terminology, and of his cultural, historical and scientific background in eighteenth-century Sweden. This resulted in *An Introduction to the Species Plantarum and Cognate Botanical Works of Carl Linnaeus* (1957) and other publications relating to Linnaeus and his contemporaries. Stearn was elected a Fellow in 1934. In 1938, the Society published in the *Journal, Botany* his monographs of *Epimedium* and *Vancouveria* (Berberidaceae). He served on the Council from 1959 to 1963 and was Botanical Curator from 1959 to 1985.

The session 1979–80 began on 7 June 1979 with a lecture on the territorial habits of a blennid fish inhabiting shallow coral reefs of the Caribbean region. The Hooker Lecture on 18 October 1979 by J. Heslop-Harrison reviewed work on the digestive glands of insectivorous plants. Like its predecessors, the other meetings dealt with such diversity of subjects as blood groups, ethnobotany and experimental archaeology in southern England, Cucurbitaceae, natural history of the Shetland Islands in relation to the oil industry, ferns and fern allies (this meeting held at Newcastle-upon-Tyne), *Euphorbia* and *Aloe*. There were symposia on aspects of the plant cuticle, Antarctic biology and molluscan genetics.

During the session much work was done in renovating the Library: new lighting was installed, a new carpet laid, the walls painted and many grilles fitted to bookcases as a precaution against theft, an unfortunate reflection on contemporary morality. Students and children of Fellows gave invaluable help in shifting hundreds of books, Ethel Barrow continued to clean old manuscripts, while another volunteer helper, Margot Walker, catalogued the portrait prints, of which the Society possesses 1350. At the Conversazione on 25 April 1980 she and the Librarian mounted an exhibition of these, for which she provided a scholarly informative catalogue, *The Naturalist Delineated*. The sale of surplus books by Messrs Sotheby brought in approximately £40 000, which allowed the renovation of the Library to be done without drawing on capital. Unfortunately, the annual subscription by Fellows had to be raised again because of inflation. It was the President's happy duty to present the two Linnean Medals, the H. H. Bloomer Award and the Bicentenary Medal in appreciation of outstanding contributions to biology by the recipients. The Linnean Medal for Botany went to Geoffrey Clough Ainsworth, the author of important mycological works, *The Plant Diseases of Great Britain* (1932), *Medical Mycology* (1952) and, in collaboration with P. K. C. Austwick, *Fungal Diseases of Animals* (1959) and *Introduction to the History of Mycology* (1976), and the Linnean Medal for Zoology to Roy Albert Crawson, an entomologist concerned with disease-carrying beetles and the co-evolution of these beetles and fungi, whose publications include *The Classification of the Coleoptera* (1955) and *Classification and Biology* (1970). The recipient of the H. H. Bloomer Award, J. N. Eliot, had been both a lieutenant-colonel and a schoolmaster, but as an amateur entomologist had published important papers on Indo-Australian and Malayan butterflies. Christopher John Humphries, the recipient of the Bicentenary Medal, was the author of revisions of genera of Compositae, notably *Argyranthemum* and *Anacyclus*, and had taken a major part in acquainting botanists with the concepts and methods of the German entomologist Willi Hennig.

The 1981–82 session began on 15 October 1981 with lectures on the present and past plant life of the Lizard District, Cornwall, and the need for conservation – much of its once extensive lowland heath had been destroyed in the past 25 years. Later meetings dealt with matters as various as Robert Brown's microscope and the discovery of the cell nucleus, of which the one-hundred-and-fiftieth anniversary came in November 1981; the work of the Freshwater Biological Association; tsetse flies; cladistics, ecology of marine animals; dermatoglyphics in clinical medicine; mimicry in swallowtail butterflies; interaction of palymology and palaeobotany; and European plant taxonomy (this at Reading on 6 May 1982).

At the Anniversary Meeting on 27 May 1982, the President gave an Address on "Maria Sibylla Merian (1647–1717), pioneer artist of tropical natural history" and presented the session's medals. The Linnean Medal for Zoology went to Peter Humphry Greenwood, the Society's previous President, especially for his work on fishes of the great African lakes summarized in his *Fishes of Uganda* (1958), *The Cichlid Fishes of Lake Victoria* (1974) and *The Haplochromine Fishes of the East African Lakes* (1981), and the Linnean Medal for Botany to Peter Hadland Davis for his work on plants of the Near East, culminating in the monumental *Flora of Turkey* (9 vols, 1965–86), of which he has been the originator, editor and major author. The Bicentenary Medal was awarded to Harry John Betteley Birks (unfortunately not able to be present) for his work on vegetational history, palynology and ecology in Europe and North America; the Trail–Crisp Award (awarded every two to three years) to John Michael Pettitt for his work on the pollination and fertilization of marine flowering plants, as well as in the study of botanical fine structure and histochemistry; and the H. H. Bloomer Award to Lionel George Higgins, a medical man whose hobby had been the study of Lepidoptera which resulted in many publications, among them *The Classification of European Butterflies* (1975) with 402 line drawings, mostly of butterfly genitalia, by Higgins himself. In making that Award, the President noted that, in 1736, Johann Amman had sarcastically criticized Linnaeus's "lewd method" of classifying plants according to the number of their reproductive organs and had observed that "if the only true systematical disposition is to be taken from those parts, that are capable of producing their like, as the Doctor [Linnaeus] says, I can see no reason, why he should not proceed in the same manner with animals". This is exactly what Higgins and his colleagues have done.

The Presidential Address was on "Rabelais as a naturalist". His works contain many references to natural history and indicate the range of knowledge that such a studious physician as Rabelais gleaned from the literature of his time. An important appointment during the year was that of Charles Edward Jarvis (b. 1954) to undertake the typification of Linnaean plant names and the production of a catalogue, thanks to a grant from the Science and Engineering Research Council. Gavin Bridson, the Librarian and Archivist, having been granted leave of absence for one year to work at the Hunt Institute for Botanical Documentation in Pittsburgh, his duties were taken over by Gina Douglas.

Stearn's Presidency then ended. Robert James Berry (b. 1934), formerly Head of the Department of Biology at the Royal Free Hospital School of Medicine, Professor of Genetics at University College, London, since 1974, author of *Teach Yourself Genetics* (1965), *Ecology and Ethics* (1972), *Inheritance and Natural History* (1977) and joint author with J. L. Johnson of *The Natural History of Shetland* (1980), became President for the period 1982–85.

A notable out-of-season event during Stearn's Presidency was a visit to the Society's rooms on 28 July 1981 by the Crown Prince and the Crown Princess of Japan accompanied by members of the Japanese Embassy staff. Before formally admitting the Crown Prince to Foreign Membership as an ichthyological specialist the President referred to the Society's association with the natural history of Japan going back to 1794 when the Society published in its *Transactions* Carl Peter Thunberg's observations on Japanese plants. The Society may be the first learned body in Europe to have admitted a Japanese biologist to membership, namely Tokutaro Ito (1868–1941), elected in December 1886, who published in the Society's *Journal Botany* in 1887 a paper on Japanese Berberidaceae. In view of Crown Prince Akihito's main research interest, a display of literature on fishes beginning with the pioneer works by Rondelet and Salviani, both published in 1554, had been arranged in the library. He then examined and discussed the Linnaean fish specimens in the strong-room; the Crown Princess took pleasure in seeing the much more beautiful Linnaean specimens of butterflies. For all concerned it was a very pleasant occasion.

Chapter 12

From 1982 to 1987

Charles Darwin died on 19 April 1882 at the age of 73. Accordingly, the 1982–83 session, under the Presidency of R. J. Berry, gave prominence to Darwinian events. One was the filming by Thames Television of a programme, "The Evolution of Darwin", in the Society's Meeting Room; for this the furniture was rearranged with the dais on the north instead of west wall. Appropriately, at a special meeting on 24 June 1982, Ernst Mayr from Harvard gave an address on "The evolutionary synthesis, its history and subsequent fate". A symposium on "Darwin, a hundred years on", held as a joint meeting with the Systematics Association, took place on 16 and 17 September 1982. There were 18 papers presented during those two days, of which eight were published in full in *Biol. Journal* 20: 1–135 (1983) and abstracts of others in *The Linnean* 1 no. 2: 13–17 (1984). The intention was to explore disciplines other than evolution that Darwin had illuminated and to review subsequent developments. These included papers on Darwin's early interests, barnacles and coral reefs. A second Darwinian symposium, on 8 December 1982, held in association with the Charles Darwin Foundation for the Galapagos Isles, provided 17 papers on "Evolution in the Galapagos Islands" published in *Biol. Journal* 17: 1–135 (April 1982). The Post Office commemorated the centenary with the issue of gloomy postage stamps on which the heads of Galapagos creatures look at a ghostly aged Darwin, not the youthful naturalist of the *Beagle* who first saw them and whom George Richmond portrayed. They were particularly disappointing because the Linnean Society had earlier proposed the issue of commemorative stamps and had offered assistance, which the Post Office had ignored. Nevertheless, the Press, television and the Post Office together ensured that no one escaped learning something about Darwin that year even if what they learned from some articles was misleading, incorrect and prejudiced.

However, Darwin did not monopolize the Society's programme. Thus, on 21 October 1982, a set of lectures on "The rehabilitation of the Thames Estuary" dealt with the increased oxygen level and general improvement of the Thames resulting from pollution control and gave encouraging reports on the consequent recovery of algae, annelids, crustaceans, fish and waterfowl. Later meetings were on the preservation and physiology of seeds; the origin of dinosaurs; leaf cuticles; the flora and fauna of the Madeiran islands; and taxonomic data-bases. Moreover, the Society held a regional meeting at Bristol on 25 to 27 June 1982 on "The role of the local naturalist in conserving our threatened plants".

In 1982, the Society made an agreement for the British Ecological Society to receive accommodation in the Linnean Society's rooms from January 1983 onwards. The Conversazione on 29 April 1983 was the first in which the British Ecological Society participated. Biologically the relations of the two societies can be described as commensal and symbiotic.

At the Anniversary Meeting on 21 May 1983, the President presented the Linnean Medal for Botany to Terence Ingold, Professor of Botany at Birbeck College from 1944 to

1972, primarily for his mycological work, and the Linnean Medal for Zoology to Michael James Denham White, Professor of Zoology and then of Genetics at the University of Melbourne from 1958 to 1971. Ingold's research has been basically on the formation and discharge of spores, their dispersal and subsequent fate, the subject of his *Spore Discharge on Land Plants* (1939), but in his other activities he has taken a major part in the expansion of university education in Africa. He served the Linnean Society as Botanical Secretary from 1962 to 1965. White intended to become a botanist, but found Edward Salisbury's botanical lectures at University College so dull and unimpressive and D. M. S. Watson's zoological lectures so dynamic and inspiring that he became instead an evolutionary zoologist specializing in entomology and thence genetics. Thus he came to produce *The Chromosomes* (1937) and *Animal Cytology and Evolution* (1945), both works with significant impact.

The Bicentenary Medal was awarded to John Richard Krebs, University Lecturer in Zoology at Oxford, for ecological studies on territoriality, flocking, vocal communication and feeding strategies in birds. The H. H. Bloomer Award went to Oleg Vladimirovitch Polunin (1914–85), a biology master at Charterhouse School, Godalming, from 1938 to 1972 and the author of popular, carefully prepared botanical guides for tourists to plants of the Mediterranean, Western Europe, the Balkan Peninsula and the Himalayas based on his own travels and collecting, some in collaboration with Anthony Huxley, B. E. Smythies and Adam Stainton.

The President's Address on 24 May 1983, entitled "The evolution of British biology" (*Biol. Journal* 20: 327–352; 1984), was far from being purely historical. It pointed out that "British biology is multiply divided between 115 national societies and 900 local ones, as well as divisions between amateurs and professionals, pure and applied, universities and research institutes". In 1981, there were 2160 biologists on the staff of 39 universities and, of course, a vast number of others employed as biology teachers in schools. The Institute of Biology had 15000 members in 1982, all professional biologists. This contrasts markedly with the situation, for instance, in 1818 when the Linnean Society was almost the only biological society in Britain. The 450 members represented a high proportion of the country's practising biologists and were almost all well-to-do amateurs, for Britain had only five universities and no biological employment outside them. It raises the question of whether there should be amalgamation between groups to counter long-term inefficiency and what the place should be of the Linnean Society amid the multitude of specialist groups. Undoubtedly, for what seemed good reasons at the time, the Society failed at crucial occasions to meet the expanding needs of British biology. Indeed, Berry commented, "A cynical reading of Gage's (1938) *History of the Linnean Society* portrays a status-conscious Society exchanging expressions of mutual admiration with other venerable bodies, but spending an inordinate amount of time threshing around in bewilderment and pique at the existence and success of other biological societies, all of which had directly or indirectly broken away from the Linnean parent". He concluded, however, that "the Linnean Society has the desire to look forward and to accept the logic of the changing forces in British biology. In some ways the Linnean has survived as a living fossil, occupying a niche but in a state of what has come to be known as evolutionary stasis. There seems no intrinsic reason why the Society should not go through a period of rapid change". With minor change of wording Berry's comments could equally be applied to the Royal Society and other long-established societies conscious of their honourable traditions.

During the 1982–83 session, Elizabeth Young retired as Executive Secretary after three years of unstinting service; Commander John Fiddian-Green, RN (retired), was appointed in her place and took office in November 1982; there were over 60 applicants for this post.

The excess of income over expenditure in 1982 was £4700. The Treasurer in recording this pointed out that the cost of the Society's publications received by members amounted to 74 per cent of their subscriptions which was thus returned to them.

His Royal Highness The Duke of Edinburgh attended the meeting on 17 March 1983, examined Linnaean material in the strongroom with the critical eye of a naturalist, and signed the Roll and Charter Book to become an Honorary Member.

The 1983–84 session began on 22 June 1985 with a lecture by Eviatar Nevo from Haifa, Israel, on "The evolutionary significance of genetic diversity in plants and animals". "The biology of Pteridophytes" was the subject of an international symposium in Edinburgh on 12–16 September 1983, held jointly by the Linnean Society, the British Pteridological Society and the Royal Society of Edinburgh, and brought together over 120 participants from 24 countries. Such co-operative undertakings help to compensate for the fragmentation of biological endeavour by specialization. A symposium on 17 November considered "Co-evolution, resistance and nematodes". The whole of 16 February 1984 was directed to 11 papers on "The future ecology of the Norfolk Broadlands" dealing with the deleterious effect of pollution, recreational damage, drainage and the introduction of the coypu (*Myocaster coypus*). This was a joint meeting with the British Ecological Society.

At the Anniversary Meeting of 24 May 1983, the President presented the awards for the year. The Linnean Medal for Botany went to John Gregory Hawkes, Professor for 20 years at Birmingham, whose life's work had centred on potatoes and their allies, to which he has devoted some 80 publications and for which he has travelled extensively in Latin America, collecting material, however, not only of *Solanum*. John Stodart Kennedy, who received the Linnean Medal for Zoology, had early in his career been engaged in applied research on locust control; later he worked on aphid behaviour, insect migration and female pheromone location by moths. The Trial–Crisp Award went to Karl Fredga, Professor of Genetics at Uppsala, for research on the exceptional sex chromosomes systems in various genera of mammals. Richard Ford, recipient of the H. H. Bloomer Award, ran the natural history firm of Watkins and Doncaster for many years but devoted his spare time to palaeontology, specializing on the fossil mammalia of the Isle of Wight. The Bicentenary Medal went to another palaeontologist, Peter Roland Crane, whose earlier work was also on Isle of Wight fossils but of plant origin. Subsequently he has studied American early angiosperms.

The Treasurer looked on 1983 as a good financial year with an excess of £5500 of income over expenditure but, owing to increasing expenditure on publications, stated that the yearly subscription of a Fellow receiving two journals would have to be raised to £35 in 1985. During the year the Society received a donation of £9000 from the estate of John Ramsbottom, former Botanical Secretary and President.

The Presidential Address by R. J. Berry on "Ethics in biology and for biologists" (published in *Biologist*, *J. Inst. Biol.* 31: 262–264; November 1983) recognized and discussed three main types of ethical questions likely to be faced by biologists: environment, care and treatment of animals, and biomedical problems. An especially valuable donation came in 1984 from Isabella Gordon, who presented a large part of her library relating to Crustacea, on which she had devoted so many years of study at the

British Museum (Natural History). A particularly pleasing occasion was a reception on 12 July 1984 in honour of the eightieth birthday of Irene Manton, the Society's first woman President.

The importance of study of the biology of fresh water, which involves a variety of interacting disciplines, received special recognition by the Society through the formation of the Freshwater Group in 1985, the hope being expressed that it will bring together not only biologists but also chemists, hydrologists and engineers concerned with the use and management of freshwater resources. The inaugural meeting took place on 3 October 1985.

In the 1984–85 session there were four symposia held in association with other bodies, now a usual and welcome procedure against the danger of scientific isolation by specialist groups. The first was on "Insects and the plant cuticle" on 15 to 17 July 1984 at Oxford with the co-operation of the University's Botany School and Department of Zoology; it ranged from the finer details of the plant surfaces to the co-evolution of plants and insects. For an international symposium on "Contemporary issues in systematics", held on 16 to 21 July 1984, the Society, the Systematics Association and the Willi Hennig Society collaborated so successfully as to attract 255 participants from 18 nations; cladistics, philosophy, evolutionary theory and much else came into the 54 papers presented. The third, on "Pollen and spores: forms and function" on 27 and 28 March 1985, and the fourth, on "Systematic and taxonomic approaches in palaeobotany" on 1 to 3 April, were held in association with the Systematics Association. The meeting arranged for 17 January 1985 was completely disarranged by snow impeding travellers by car and a strike those coming by rail, so, at very short notice, the President provided an alternative lecture on mouse genetics and J. S. Jones one on habitat choice and genetic diversity.

At the Annual General Meeting on 24 May 1985, the Treasurer reported an excess of income over expenditure of £7000 after transferring £45 000 to a contingency fund for repairs and improvements, an almost unbelievably happy state of solvency for those who remembered such lean years as 1974 when excess of expenditure over income was a little over £4750 and 1975 when it was £3176.

The President presented the Linnean Medal for Botany to Jeffrey Barry Harborne, the Linnean Medal for Zoology to Arthur James Cain, the H. H. Bloomer Award to Bertram Evelyn Smythies and the Bicentenary Medal to Nicholas Hamilton Barton. Harborne's work has been in the field of biochemistry, notably in relation to plant taxonomy and ecology, at the Universities of Bristol, California (Los Angeles), Liverpool and Reading, and at the John Innes Institute. He is the author of numerous papers on plant phenolics and the textbook *Introduction to Ecological Biochemistry* (1977), now available in Japanese, Russian and Spanish translations. Evolutionary biology in general, but especially in relation to birds and snails, has been a major interest for Cain, over many years Professor of Zoology at Liverpool, but he has also made notable contributions to understanding of Linnaeus's methods. He is the author, among much else, of *Animal Species and their Evolution* (1954). After education at both Cambridge and Oxford in mathematics, natural sciences and forestry, Smythies joined the Burma Forest Service in 1934, from which he retired in 1948 but served in the forest service of Sarawak from 1949 to 1964. Field observations provided material for publications on the birds of Burma and Borneo. From 1964 to 1979 his residence in Spain led him into study of the flora of Spain and the Balearic Islands and preparation of a detailed checklist of their vascular plants. He is thus, like Raven, the first recipient of the H. H. Bloomer Award, well fitted to receive it both as a zoologist and a botanist. Barton is a zoologist with considerable mathematical expertise who has given special attention to hybrid zones between races of the Alpine grasshopper (*Apodisma pedestris*) and between species of toads.

The Presidency of R. G. Berry then ending, William G. Chaloner took office as President for the 1985–88 sessions.

Presidents distinguished for research in palaeontology have included the botanists D. H. Scott, H. Hamshaw Thomas and T. M. Harris and the zoologists S. H. Woodward and Errol E. White. Two other Presidents, W. Carruthers and F. E. Weiss, also had strong palaeobotanical interests. The election of William Gilbert Chaloner (b. 1928) added another botanist to this select group. After graduating at the University of Reading, he studied palaeontology there for a PhD, spent two years in the Royal Artillery, then from 1956 to 1972 was Lecturer and Reader in Botany at University College, London. He was Professor of Botany at Birkbeck College, London, from 1972 to 1979, then at Bedford College, London, from 1979 to 1985; when this was united with Royal Holloway College, he became Professor at the combined institution. When admitting new Fellows, he made it his pleasant custom to introduce them to the meeting with a few words on their work and interests.

With the forthcoming bicentenary of the Society's foundation in 1988, preparations for this became an important activity during Chaloner's Presidency. The Council decided that, instead of crowding all commemorative events within the commemorative year, it would be better to spread them over three years and to hold special joint meetings with other societies having closely allied interests. Another decision was to issue more than one publication relevant to the Society's history and possibly facsimiles of a few rare and important works on the Society's Library.

Meetings in 1985 included an all-day one with eight speakers on the Humber Estuary, its features and management, the area being internationally important for waders and wildfowl in winter. Later meetings dealt with environmental problems in Siberia; plants and animals as sources of pharmaceuticals; research on the Linnaean Collections; and communication in biology with special reference to television nature films and the balancing of entertainment against instruction. In 1986, they involved lectures on the biological effects of ozone and the evolutionary genetics of the house sparrow (*Passer domesticus*). The first of the bicentenary special meetings was a three-day symposium in June held at the Royal Botanic Gardens, Kew, in association with the Phytochemical Society on the "Chemistry, taxonomy and economic botany of the Euphorbiales". Its proceedings form *Botanical Journal* vol. 94 (1987).

Lady Nora Barlow, the last surviving grandchild of Charles Darwin and the editor in 1958 of an unexpurgated edition of his *Autobiography*, celebrated her hundredth birthday on 22 December 1985 and received the Society's congratulations from the President. She was elected a Fellow in 1925.

At the Anniversary Meeting on 22 May 1986, the President announced that His Royal Highness The Prince of Wales had been made an Honorary Member; His Imperial Highness Akihito, the Crown Prince of Japan, already a Foreign Member, was elected as an Honorary Member. The President then presented the Linnean Medals for Botany to Arthur Cronquist and that for Zoology to Percy Cyril Claude Garnham. Cronquist's early taxonomic interests were in the Compositae (Asteraceae) and Sapotaceae of America. Later he became especially interested in the phylogeny and classification of the angiosperms as a whole, culminating in his massive *Integrated System of Classification of Flowering Plants* (1981). He is a Californian by birth but has spent most of his life since 1949 on the staff of the New York Botanical Garden. Garnham, after many years of research in Kenya on protozoan infections of animals including man, was appointed Reader in Medical Parasitology at the London School of Hygiene and Tropical Medicine in 1947 and five years later Professor, publishing in 1966 *Malaria Parasites and other Haemosporidia*. His numerous publications, about 400, based on detailed research have given him a world-wide repute as an outstanding parasitologist.

The H. H. Bloomer Award was presented to Walter J. Le Quesne, originally from Jersey and professionally a nuclear chemist. Over many years he has devoted his attention as an amateur entomologist to the leaf-hoppers, plant-hoppers and their relatives constituting the Auchenorrhyncha, producing keys to the British species of all the families, these published between 1960 and 1986. He has also made major contributions to the theoretical development of numerical taxonomy.

The Bicentenary Medal went to David William Minter, primarily for his research on *Lophodermium* species attacking pines, in which he demonstrated that what was generally considered to be a single variable species *Lophodermium pinastri* was in fact a complex of four species distinguished not only morphologically but also physiologically and in pathogenicity. He joined the staff of the Commonwealth Mycological Institute at Kew in 1977 as a mycologist and published in 1981 a world monograph of *Lophodermium* on pines.

The Treasurer happily reported that income had exceeded expenditure by £6700, of which £25 000 had been set aside for premises repairs and improvements and £25 000 for bicentenary expenses.

The meetings of the 1986–87 session covered the now usual diversity of subjects. In 1986, they included "Water quality and health" by the Freshwater Group founded in 1985, with special reference to sewage treatment and microbiological problems; "Nomadic DNA"; "Visual communication in biology", which should have been valuable to inexperienced lecturers; "Man-directed evolution of crop plants", this being a bicentenary joint meeting with the Association of Applied Biologists; and "Dynamic responses to the environment", a bicentenary joint meeting with the Society for Experimental Biology. Those for 1987 included "Nature, natural history and ecology", a bicentenary joint meeting with the Field Studies Council; "Horizons in lichenology", a bicentenary joint meeting with the British Lichen Society; "Rare breeds of cattle and their conservation"; "Changing attitudes to nature conservation", a bicentenary joint meeting with the Royal Society for Nature Conservation; "Phylogeny and classification of the Tetrapods", a two-day international symposium jointly with the Systematics Association and the Palaeontological Association; and "Bryology, modern research and the way forward", a bicentenary joint meeting with the British Bryological Society. A lecture by Roy Porter on "The social and intellectual climate for natural history in 18th-century England" constituted a bicentenary joint meeting with the Society for the History of Natural History.

Bicentenary joint meetings of the 1986–87 session included "The management of fertility in domestic feral and zoo populations of mammals" in association with the Zoological Society; "Novel approaches to the systematics and identification of Fungi" with the British Mycological Society; "Biota and palaeoatmospheres" with the Geological Society and the Palaeontological Society; "Problems arising from the profusion of insects" with the Royal Entomological Society; and "Natural products as pharmacological probes" with the Pharmaceutical Society of Great Britain.

At the Anniversary Meeting on 21 May 1987, the President awarded the Linnean Medals for Botany to V. H. Heywood and for Zoology to C. Fryer, the Bicentenary Medal to A. J. J. Jeffreys, the H. H. Bloomer Award to M. C. Clark and the Trail–Crisp Award to S. Blackmore.

Vernon Hilton Heywood, while an undergraduate at Edinburgh, made his first expedition to Spain in 1947, when he had the interesting experience of being captured by bandits but given a safe-conduct as an innocent botanist, and a second with Peter H. Davis in 1948. Thus began his long-sustained interest in the Spanish plants. In 1953 he was awarded a PhD for his thesis on the mountain flora of Spain. He then returned to Spain to work for the Consejo Superior de Investigaciones Científicas, from which many papers resulted. Returning to Britain in 1955, he was appointed to a Lectureship in Botany at the University of Liverpool on condition that he took over the Secretaryship of the then embryonic *Flora Europaea* organization. Thus during the next 25 years he played a major part in bringing to triumphant conclusion the *Flora Europaea* in five volumes. This is not the place to list the 41 books with which he has been associated and his nearly 200 papers, but of far-reaching importance has been *Principles of Angiosperm Taxonomy* (1963) in collaboration with Peter H. Davis, manifesting the multidisciplinary approach characteristic of many of his publications. These have included studies of Umbelliferae, Compositae and Cruciferae. He was appointed Professor and Head of the Department of Botany at the University of Reading in 1963. His increasing involvement with problems of plant conservation led to his being seconded, after 18 years at Reading, to Kew in 1987 to direct the Conservation Monitoring Centre and Botanic Garden Conservation Secretariat.

Geoffrey Fryer, after service in the Royal Navy as an electrical artificer, began his research career as a member of the Joint Fisheries Research Organisation working in an ill-equipped laboratory on the western shore of Lake Malawi, Central Africa. His study of the cichlid rock fishes of Lake Nyasa, Malawi, later earned him a PhD as an external student of London University. His publications include a catalogue of the crustacea of Lake Malawi and detailed studies of feeding mechanisms and feeding behaviour in a wide range of crustacean groups. From the Colonial Research Service he moved to his final position with the Freshwater Biological Association Laboratory on Lake Windermere, Cumbria, in 1960 and there began painstaking studies of the microdistribution of British freshwater entomostracans.

The award of the Bicentenary Medal to Alec John Jeffreys was in recognition of his outstanding work as a molecular geneticist, with particular reference to mitochondrial protein synthesis, detection of single genes in mammalian DNA and development of the DNA fingerprint technique so important in cases of disputed paternity. In these he is undoubtedly a pioneer. His initial studies were at Oxford, then continued in Amsterdam; thence he moved to the Department of Genetics at the University of Leicester.

Malcolm Charles Clark, the recipient of the H. H. Bloomer Award, although interested in natural history from his boyhood onwards, first became involved in botanical recording in 1954 and contributed more to the *Computer-mapped Flora of Warwickshire* (1971) than any other single contributor. He subsequently took an important part in collecting data for *A Fungus Flora of Warwickshire* (1980), covering 2600 species and a splendid example of successful work by a team of self-taught enthusiasts. Through his own major contributions and his ability to organize surveys and bring them to completion, he has come to occupy a distinguished position in British mycology.

The work in microscopy which has earned for Stephen Blackmore the Trail–Crisp Award would have highly pleased and amazed its two founders, since palynology as a major botanical discipline, the invention of its major tools, the transmission and the scanning electron microscopy have all come since that time. Blackmore's research for his PhD at Reading was on the pollen morphology of Compositae Cichoriene. He then spent a year at the Royal Society Aldabra Research Station in the Indian Ocean. In 1980 he was appointed Head of the Palynology Section, Department of Botany, British Museum (Natural History). Here he tackled some fundamental problems of pollen function, ornamentation and its relative phylogenetic importance, and pioneered the application to plant material of freeze fractures and cytoplasmic maceration followed by high resolution scanning microscopy.

On 19 January 1988, the Post Office issued a set of postage stamps designed by Edward Hughes to commemorate the Society's Bicentenary and based on illustrations and manuscripts by Fellows in the Society's collections. They depicted the short-spined sea-scorpion or bull-rout (*Mixocephalus scorpius*), a northern spiny sea fish, from an illustration by Jonathan Couch (1789–1870); the yellow water lily (*Nuphar lutea*), widespread in the British Isles, from an illustration by Joshua Reynolds Gascoigne Gwatkin (1855–1931); Bewick's swan (*Cygnus columbianus bewicki*), the smallest of northern swans, from an illustration by Edward Lear (1812–1888); the morel (*Morchella esculenta*), an edible fungus appearing in Spring, from an illustration by James Sowerby (1757–1822).

Throughout its history the Linnean Society has been a non-political and non-sectarian body existing purely for the furtherance of natural history; the criteria for acceptance of papers to be published are their quality, scientific relevance and interest, not their country of origin or the politics of its government. This view was challenged in 1987 and made it necessary for the President to state unequivocally on behalf of the Council the Society's adherence to its traditional policy of keeping politics out of science (*The Linnean* 3 no. 3: 45; 1987).

Chapter 13

Meetings

Except for groups concerned exclusively with the issue of publications, the meetings at which persons of like or related interests can talk about their scientific or literary activities, exchange information, exhibit specimens and listen to lectures together provide the main justification for a society's existence, indeed its mainstay. Accordingly, even in the dark days of the 1939–45 World War, the Linnean Society strove to maintain a succession of such meetings.

From 1788 until the first week of May 1802 there were two sets of meetings: General Meetings held on the first Tuesday and Fellows' Meetings held on the third Tuesday of every month except August and September. Both sets of meetings were held at 6 o'clock in the evening until April 1792, thereafter at 7 o'clock. The General Meetings lasted about an hour. All classes of the Society could attend the General Meetings, at which papers were read, but only Fellows had the right to attend the Fellows' Meetings dealing with the business of the Society. The procedure for elections of members of any class of the Society and for new Rules and Orders or change in those existing was such as to give information to all classes but to keep the decision in the hands of the Fellows.

The Anniversary Meeting, at which the President, the Treasurer and the Secretary were annually elected, was held on the third Tuesday in April up to 1794, but thereafter on 24 May or, if that were a Sunday, on 25 May. The Anniversary Meeting was a Fellows' Meeting and the Minutes were inscribed in the Book of Minutes of Fellows' Meetings. It was held at 1 pm and the ballot closed at 3 pm, so that the meetings with a declaration of the elections lasted over two hours. How the Fellows occupied themselves during that time is a mystery, but if one were to rely on Marsham's picture of their habits given in his letter of 22 September 1796, already quoted, probably they were not entirely silent and their talk not purely scientific. Having spent over two hours in electing the same old triumvirate, they reassembled at 4 or 4.30 pm to enjoy the Anniversary Dinner, then a purely Fellows' feast.

The first and fourteenth sessions were exceptional. As the first session lasted from April 1788 to July 1789, it contained 16 General Meetings. The second to thirteenth sessions extended from the first week of October to the first week of July and, in each, ten General Meetings were held. In short, the Society as a body spent only ten hours per annum in scientific meetings. The fourteenth session was of the usual duration, from the first week of October 1801 to the first week of July 1802, but the obtaining of the Royal Charter, the incorporation of the Society and the resulting convocational activities of the 15 members mentioned in Chapter 2 made it one of mixed meetings. From 6 October 1801 to 4 May 1802 there were the usual monthly Fellows' and General Meetings. Then the old Society was dissolved. Fifteen members then held five meetings as Fellows, the last two of those being on 24 May 1802, and immediately before the first Anniversary Meeting of the new

Society on that day. The following session of 1802–3 was the first complete session under the new dispensation.

As the new Council of 15 Fellows henceforth conducted most of the Society's business, the general body of Fellows no longer needed to meet once a month, and their meetings ceased. The Fellows, however, did not surrender all their powers to the Council, nor was their right to hold their own exclusive meetings definitely abolished, although it has been exercised only once since 1802, in 1918. The powers retained by the general body of Fellows were:

i.   the election of all members of Council from 1802–3 onwards;
ii. the election from members of Council of the President, the Treasurer and the Secretary, and the appointment – the word used in the Charter is "appoint" – of such other Officers as the Fellows might think proper and necessary for the Society's business;
iii. the election of members of all four classes of the Society;
iv. the confirmation or rejection of any Bye-Laws or alterations in them proposed by the Council.

The Society, however, has seldom allowed itself to be entangled in a too strict or quibbling interpretation of its Charter and Bye-Laws, and at the very first meeting of the 15 as Fellows on 11 May 1802 it was ordered that "the Society [not Fellows only] be summoned to attend the Anniversary Meeting on Monday the 24th instant at one o'clock and to dine at five o'clock precisely on that day at the Thatched House Tavern in St. James's Street". So in the very first set of Bye-Laws it was directed that "In case of a vacancy in the Council or among the Officers of the Society happening during the Intervals of the Anniversary Elections, the Council shall appoint a Special General Meeting for the purpose of filling up such vacancy...". This is the only Bye-Law from 1802 to 1936 in which the expression "Special General Meeting" occurs, and in this Bye-Law the calling of such a meeting is restricted to a special purpose.

The Fellows not only provide the financial support of the Society but are also by far the largest proportion of its members, so that, despite the pre-Charter distinction between Fellows' Meetings and General Meetings, even at the latter Fellows greatly predominated. The first Council, in May 1802, had to all intents two days a month at its disposal for General Meetings. As at all these the chief business henceforth was, or should have been, the reading of scientific papers, the Council, to judge from its action, thought that two meetings a month for ten months every year was too much of a good thing. So the session was lopped at both ends and henceforth began in the first week of November and ended usually in the third week of June, the General Meeting days being the first and third Tuesdays in November, December, February, March, April and June. In January and May only one General Meeting was held, on the third Tuesday in January and the first Tuesday in May. This normally gave a total of 14 General Meetings in a session, exclusive of the Anniversary Meeting. The hour of meeting was advanced from 7 to 8 pm. The Anniversary Meeting remained unchanged.

This arrangement of ordinary or General Meetings continued up to and including the hundred-and-sixteenth session (1903–4) with only one change. The General Meeting day was shifted to Thursday, with effect from 5 November 1857, except for two meetings in the session of 1877–78 which were held for some unstated reason on a Tuesday.

In 1861, the hour of the Anniversary Meeting was altered from 1 to 3 pm. During this period of 101 years there were a few exceptional sessions in which the regular order or number of General Meetings was upset by an event such as the death of a member of the Royal Family, the death of Sir Joseph Banks and deaths of Officers or members of Council.

In 1802, Bank Holidays were unknown but, in 1871, the Bank Holidays Act was passed in which Sir John Lubbock (later Lord Avebury), then a Fellow of the Society and destined ten years later to become its President, took a prominent part. Whit-Monday became a Bank Holiday. 24 May had fallen on Whit-Sunday in 1795, 1801, 1863 and 1874, and the Society had held its Anniversary Meeting on Whit-Monday in each of those years. In 1885, when 24 May was Whit-Sunday and in accordance with the Charter the Anniversary Meeting should have been held on Whit-Monday, the Council issued a statement that only a pro forma Anniversary Meeting would be held on that day and that it would then be adjourned to 11 June at 8 pm. On this occasion the moon seems to have affected not merely the date of the meeting but also the recording, for the Minutes and the Proceedings concerned with it make an irresolvable muddle. According to the Minutes, the pro forma meeting, at which only three Fellows were present, was held on 26 May. The election of Council and Officers took place at an intercalated meeting on 11 June 1885. This session therefore had 14 General and nominally two Anniversary Meetings.

In the session of 1895–96, when 24 May again fell on Whit-Sunday, a pro forma Anniversary Meeting was held on Whit-Monday, when only seven Fellows attended. The new Charter of 1904 got rid of the Whit-Monday difficulty by directing that, if 24 May should be a Sunday or Bank Holiday, the Anniversary Meeting should be held on the following day or on a day within that week.

When war broke out in 1914, reasonable assurance that meetings would continue to be held in strict accordance with the existing Bye-Laws ceased; so, in December 1914, the Bye-Law that had regulated from 1904–5 the days and hour of the General Meetings was replaced by one directing that the General Meetings be held on the afternoons or evenings of such Thursdays from November to June inclusive as the Council might decide.

Special General Meetings are mentioned in the Bye-Laws only in connection with elections. In 1918, when it became necessary to hold a meeting on Monday 7 January to protest against the reported intention of the Government to dismantle the British Museum, Sir David Prain, who was then President, called a Meeting of Fellows for the first, and so far the only, time since the incorporation of the Society in 1802.

When the session was curtailed at both ends in 1802, the result was not very neat, as it left two General Meetings in June straggling after the Anniversary. This did not matter so much when the same Fellow remained President year after year, but when a new President was elected it was unseemly that he should enter his duties at the very end of a session. In June 1900, the Council endeavoured to make the change of Presidents less unceremonial by resolving that in future at each Anniversary Meeting when a change of President occurred the new President should be inducted by his predecessor and a vote of thanks proposed to the outgoing President

The outbreak of World War I caused the hour of the ordinary Meetings to be changed from 8 to 5 pm in December 1914, but not until 1923 was the hour of the Anniversary Meeting, which had been 1 pm from 1788 to 1860 and 3 pm from 1861 to 1922, changed to 5 pm. In 1927, the straggling ends of the session were cut off and from that year the Anniversary Meeting has ended every session. In 1930, the Society once more began to start the new session in October, just 129 years after it had last met in that month.

The Bye-Laws in force up to 1914 laid down that the General Meetings should last about an hour "at the Discretion of the President". The Bye-Laws since 1914 mention neither duration nor "Discretion", and on later occasions the duration of the meetings and the endurance of the members has extended to two hours and sometimes more. Probably the practice of discussing papers, helped by the change of hour from 8 to 5 pm, gradually brought about the elongation of the meetings.

Out of all this tedious and trivial chronicle there emerges the one significant fact that, despite the shortening of the session, the Society in its General Meetings gives nearly twice as much time as it did for many years to the observance of its motto.

Chapter 14

Papers and publications

The Linnean Society began its extensive and varied series of publications with the issue on 13 August 1791 of volume I of its *Transactions* in impressive quarto format. This volume contained J. E. Smith's Presidential introductory discourse on the rise and progress of natural history, together with ten zoological and 14 botanical papers and one on some fossils of Switzerland. They made known species new to science, for which until then there existed no British periodical available for their publication. Gage's census of papers in the *Transactions*, first series (1791–1875), revealed 410 as botanical, 353 as zoological and 17 as general. Between 1875 and 1936, the *Transactions*, then divided into a botany and zoology series, contained 112 botanical and 253 zoological papers. In the *Journal, Botany* and *Zoology* 1857–1936, there were 1098 botanical and 936 zoological papers.

Until 1856, these quarto *Transactions* remained the Society's only medium of publication of papers in full, apart from a few systematic papers in the *Proceedings* between 1838 and 1856. The quarto format was expensive and unnecessary except for large-scale illustrations. In 1839, the Society began publication of *Proceedings* which contained abstracts of papers, obituaries and reports of meetings. After the issue of two volumes in 66 parts (1839–55), they were in 1856 divided into *Journal of the Proceedings (Zoology)* and *Journal of the Proceedings (Botany)*. The titles of these were shortened in 1866 to *Journal (Zoology)* and *Journal (Botany)*. In 1868, the *Proceedings* became an independent journal separate from these two, which henceforth were devoted purely to scientific communications. So matters continued for a century. In 1968, the Council decided to rename its three periodicals. The effect of this minor revolution was that the *Journal of the Linnean Society (Botany)* ended with vol. 61 (1968) and continued as *Botanical Journal of the Linnean Society* vol. 62 (1969); the *Journal of the Linnean Society (Zoology)* ended with vol. 47 (1968) and continued as *Zoological Journal of the Linnean Society* vol. 48 (1969). The *Proceedings* ended with vol. 179 (1968) and were replaced by *Biological Journal of the Linnean Society* vol. 1, of which nos 1–2 (1969) were entirely devoted to "Speciation in tropical environments".

Between 1973 and 1981 the Society issued a *Newsletter*, a small informal publication containing news of Fellows etc. Meanwhile the *Biological Journal* became more and more restricted to papers relating to evolution, which provided common ground for botanists and zoologists and gave less room to papers of an historical nature. This led to the creation in 1984 of a further periodical, *The Linnean, Newsletter and Proceedings of the Linnean Society of London*.

Apart from these the Society has increasingly published independent works. In 1866–77 it issued a *Catalogue of the Library* in three parts. A new edition was issued in 1896, after earlier incompetent and costly attempts had been scrapped. For compilation of the next *Catalogue of the Printed Books and Pamphlets in the Library of the Linnean Society of London* (1925), the Society had the devoted and diligent services of its learned General Secretary,

B. Daydon Jackson, and Clerk, Spencer Savage, both bibliographically skilled. Despite the passage of time, this volume of 860 pages remains a valuable reference work, especially as the books which were in Linnaeus's own library are listed and distinguished by the letter $\mathscr{L}$. This does not include manuscripts which were to be dealt with in special publications. Four parts of the *Catalogue of the Manuscripts* were published between 1934 and 1948, the first (1934) on the Smith papers by Warren R. Dawson, the other three (1937, 1940, 1948) by Spencer Savage. In 1945, the Society published Savage's *A Catalogue of the Linnaean Herbarium*, issued in 250 copies, which has become an indispensable reference work for anyone concerned with the typification of Linnaean botanical names. Another new publishing venture began in January 1944 with the issue as a pamphlet of *Synopses of the British Fauna – No. I Opiliones* by Theodore M. Savory, the first of 13 published between 1944 and 1969. *Synopses of the British Fauna (New Series)* was initiated by Doris Kermack in 1970. Beginning with accounts of British ascidians, prosobranchs, marine isopods, harvestmen, sea spiders and land snails, this series had reached 37 volumes by 1987. They are concise, profusely illustrated practical field and laboratory handbooks on animal groups designed to meet the needs of amateur and professional naturalists, sixth-form pupils and undergraduates; their authors are all zoological specialists. "A history of *Synopses of the British Fauna*" by Doris Kermack will be found in *The Linnean* 2 no. 2: 9–13 (1986).

The holding of symposia on particular biological themes begun during World War II proved so informative and stimulating that their organization has become part of the Society's programme for the promotion of biology. They have a lasting value only if published. Originally, their papers were issued in volumes forming supplements to the Society's botanical and zoological journals, later (1976) as an independent Symposium series. Their range has covered subjects as diverse as plant anatomy, early mammals, biology and chemistry of the Umbelliferae, parasite transmission, tropical trees, pollination, exine of pollen, biology of the male gamete, morphology of reptiles etc.

Could those first Fellows of the Society who began its immense number of publications with their 1791 *Transactions* have contemplated what has now been achieved during two centuries since the Society's founding, they would undoubtedly be filled with pride and amazement. On opening at random the *Biological Journal* they would also be more than a little bewildered to read:

> Six proteins showed no evidence of allozymic variation in any of the samples. These were guanine deaminase, albumin, superoxide dismutase, cathodal malate dehydrogenase, α-glycerophosphate dehydrogenase, and haemoglobin – controlled by a total of nine monomorphic loci. The allele frequencies at the remaining 14 autosomal loci are given for each sample in Table 1. We have not given the full phenotypic data, since very few samples show any departure from the Hardy–Weinberg expectations, and there is no evidence of consistent excess of deficiencies of heterozygotes at any locus (see below). Neither is there any evidence of linkage disequilibrium when the loci are examined in pairs. Since Bulatova *et al.* (1972) have shown there to be 38 pairs of chromosomes in *P. domesticus*, this is not unexpected.

Such has been the linguistic if not literary progress of modern biologists and chemists.

With such passages and the following they would find their familiar Samuel Johnson's dictionary quite unhelpful:

> Similarity between BCAL-based and SL-based transforms in viverrids is as expected because viverrine viverrids, a significant proportion of the family sample, provide the Y-intercepts for the master equations, and thus by definition would average 1.00 in all transforms. However, the lack of significant difference between BCAL- and SL-based transforms in the felids was

surprising because felids have relatively short tooth rows, like mustelids although not quite as extreme, and for that reason one would expect reduced BCAL (compared to SL)-based transforms in the Felidae.

It is only fair to believe that Darwin, Wallace and Huxley would be equally bewildered.

PAPERS

A draft of proposed Rules shows that the founders of the Society had had in mind that it should consist of Ordinary Members and Corresponding Members. One draft Rule laid down that "Every Ordinary Member within one year after his admission shall communicate a dissertation upon some subject in Natural History under the forfeiture of one guinea". Another Rule expressed the expectation "that every Corresponding Member should send some communication to the Society within one year after he has been admitted a member". Further consideration seems to have led to the conclusion that this was not the best way to ensure a flow of either members or papers. So the first printed "Rules and Orders" contain neither monetary nor other stimuli to the production of papers.

Until 1802, all papers had to be delivered to the President, who laid them before the Fellows at their meetings, and the Fellows decided whether the papers should be read at a General Meeting and whether they should be published. The first Bye-Laws published in 1802 do not specify any particular Officer as the receiver of papers nor do they direct that papers should be passed by the Council for reading at a General Meeting. This latter omission left open the possibility of an unsuitable paper being read at a General Meeting and, although the Officers very seldom allowed such a thing to happen, a resolution passed by the Council on 19 March 1844 indicates that by then some unsatisfactory paper or papers had been read. In 1806, Salisbury had made a savage attack on J. E. Smith's work at a General Meeting. Not until 1904 did the Bye-Laws empower the Council to decide whether or not papers communicated to the Society should be read at a General Meeting. By tradition, presidential addresses are not refereed.

The Council has always exercised the power of authorizing or refusing publication, as distinct from mere reading, of papers. The Bye-Laws of 1802 direct the entire Council to be a Standing Committee to consider the publication of papers read or communicated at General Meetings; three members, one of whom had to be either the President or a Vice-President, formed a quorum. The Standing Committee could co-opt other Fellows not members of Council but specially skilled in the subject matter of any paper to aid in a decision. Detailed instructions are given regarding procedure. In 1861, all those elaborate instructions were swept away, and the new Bye-Laws simply empowered the Council to refer papers to referees, whether members of Council or not, but any member could call a ballot of the Council on any question concerning publication. The new Bye-Laws of 1904 widened the Council's choice of referees to persons outside the Society. In 1878, a form of report was devised on which referees had to express their opinion of papers submitted to them.

For more than the first 100 years of the Society's life members received no information of what papers were to be read at a General Meeting. William Robinson (1838–1935), the distinguished horticulturist, suggested in 1880 that printed copies of agenda for the General Meetings should be posted to Fellows before each meeting. The Council put such an intolerable amount of resolution into deferring consideration of this proposal that it was not until 1893 that an experimental issue of postcards announcing the papers to be read at each General Meeting was sanctioned. Those postcards were distributed only to the Fellows, about 260, resident in or near London. A. P. Hammond, the Clerk, received an increase of £10 in salary for the dreary job of writing all those postcards. Many years later the Council decided to post printed advance notices of each meeting to all members resident in the British Isles.

Thus, up to 1893, no members, except the Officers, knew what awaited them at a General Meeting. Certainly those who came to the celebrated meeting of 1 July 1858, when the Darwin and Wallace papers on evolution were presented, must have been taken completely by surprise and thus were quite unprepared to comment. This was not all: for the first 50 years only those who attended the General Meetings knew what took place at them. All others received no information beyond what was vouchsafed in occasional brief snippets printed at the end of the volumes of the *Transactions*, and even the *Transactions* were delivered only at the Society's rooms. When the *Proceedings* were started in 1838 the situation was not much better, as they also were given out only at the Society's rooms. Not until 1911 was it decided to send out reports of all meetings to all members everywhere.

Most of the papers submitted to the Society have been either purely botanical or purely zoological, but the Programme Committee aims also to include papers of general biological interest, particularly with reference to expeditions. An especially noteworthy development has been the holding of symposia.

The statistics show that during the first 50 years the average number of papers read at meetings did not reach two. In fact the Society was too often at a loss for papers and, up to 1820, no papers were forthcoming at six meetings. The record would have been even worse during the succeeding years had not the work of a long-dead Dutchman and of a Scotsman, who was alive at the beginning of the period but dead before the end of it, been ruthlessly used to save the Society's face. The *Hortus Indicus Malabaricus* of Hendrik Adriaan van Rheede tot Draakestein (1637–91) was published in 12 volumes at Amsterdam between 1678 and 1703. He was a Dutch soldier and colonial administrator, from 1669 to 1676 governor of the Dutch East India Company's territory in Southern India. Under his supervision three Brahmins and their slaves, knowledgeable about plants, collected a vast number of specimens and provided valuable local information about their medicinal and other properties, local names etc. Local artists drew these plants and engravings were made in Holland from the drawings. This immense work is of lasting importance for the study of the Indian flora on account of the use made of it by Linnaeus, who based at least ten specific names on Rheede's illustrations, and by others. There have been several attempts to provide his plants with binomial names, beginning with one by Dennstedt in 1818, but the most elaborate was Hamilton's, partly published from 1822 to 1837 in the Society's *Transactions*. Francis Buchanan (1762–1829), afterwards Hamilton, had been elected an Associate in 1788 and a Fellow in 1816, after his retirement from India, where he served in the Bengal Medical Service from 1794 to 1815. He wrote an erudite and prodigious "Commentary on the Hortus Malabaricus", which he presented as a paper to the Society. Although very learned, the work could not be said to be of enthralling interest to the ordinary member of the Society. Very occasionally, the reading of a paper occupied the whole or part of the hour at more than one meeting, but Hamilton's "Commentary" stands by itself, for the Society was doped with it at 31 meetings, the first dose being given in May 1821 and the last in April 1852. On 14 occasions it was the only fare provided and on ten was one of the two papers read. But it is going too far to drag the "Commentary" even indirectly into connection with the formation of the Zoological Club, as Vines did in his first Presidential Address in 1901, when he said "and wearied perhaps by meetings in which the only compensation for the absence of discussion seems to have been interminable commentaries on the Hortus Malabaricus, certain Fellows in 1882 founded the Zoological Club". In fact only four instalments of the "Commentary" had been read before 27 November 1882 when it was resolved to form the Club. Although the first published part of the "Commentary" appeared in 1822 in Vol. 13 of the *Transactions* and the last in 1837 in Vol. 17, the paper continued to be read at intervals during the following 15 years. Bell as President speedily stirred the Society out of its lethargy, and if mere number of papers is any indication the Society has never been more energetic than it was from 1853 to 1888, when the average figure for papers read at meetings is more than three.

The total number of papers read at meetings is not the same as the total number considered by the Fellows or Council for publication, as not all papers read were intended for publication and parts of a long paper read at different meetings are considered as separate papers.

PUBLICATIONS

Transactions

As mentioned above, the quarto *Transactions* were the Society's only medium for publication of papers in full, except for a few systematic papers from 1838 to 1856 in Volumes 1 and 2 of the *Proceedings*, until 1856. The first series (Vols 1–30; 1791–1875) contained purely botanical or purely zoological papers and a few papers pertaining more or less to both botany and zoology and here called general papers. Both botanical and zoological papers appeared in each volume with the same continuous paging, except in Volume 29 which is entirely botanical. A General Index to Vols 1–25 was published in 1866 and one to Vols 26–30 in 1876. Sandra Raphael in *Biological Journal* 2: 61–76 (1970) has elucidated the dates of publication of the *Transactions* from 1791 to 1875 (see Appendix 1).

In the new series (1875–1936) botanical and zoological papers are in separate sets of volumes. Seven volumes and part of Volume 8 of the botanical series had appeared when the World War of 1914–18 broke out. The consequent general upheaval and the great rise in the price of commodities and services made it impossible for the Society to continue publishing on the pre-war scale. Volume 8 was finished in 1915; the sole paper constituting Volume 9 appeared in 1916 and its title-page, contents and index in 1922, and with this the botanical series, but not all the botanical papers in the *Transactions*, came to an end.

Up to August 1914, Volumes 1 to 9 and 12 to 15 of the zoological series had appeared complete and all the parts of Volumes 10 and 16, except the final index parts, and all of Volume 11, except one paper and the index. Probably the zoological series would have had to end about as summarily as the botanical if the Society had not been helped with grants from the Trustees of the Percy Sladen Memorial Fund and from the Fund administered by the Royal Society. In 1905, the Trustees of the Percy Sladen Fund organized an expedition under the scientific leadership of John Stanley Gardiner (1872–1946) to explore the Indian Ocean, the Admiralty placing at their disposal the surveying ship HMS *Sealark*. The 141 separate reports published on the expedition and its

TRANSACTIONS

OF THE

LINNEAN SOCIETY.

VOLUME I.

LONDON:

PRINTED BY J. DAVIS.

SOLD BY BENJAMIN WHITE AND SON, FLEET-STREET.

M.DCC.XCI.

(a)

INTRODUCTORY DISCOURSE

ON THE

RISE AND PROGRESS

OF

NATURAL HISTORY.

DELIVERED BY THE PRESIDENT, APRIL 8, 1788.

THE Study of Nature, that is an attention to the ground on which we tread, the vegetables which clothe and adorn it, and the boundless variety of living creatures presenting themselves to our notice on every side, must have been one of the first occupations of man in a state of nature. In no country hitherto discovered, however barbarous and unenlightened, is the human race found so negligent and helpless as not to have investigated the natural bodies around them, so far at least as from thence to supply

B their

(b)

(c)

collections occupy eight volumes, forming Volumes 12–19 (1907–36) of the zoological series of the *Transactions*. Those eight volumes contain a bibliographical snare. Although the volumes are nominally zoological, six purely botanical papers are unostentatiously tucked away amongst the zoological. Four out of the six had already been published in the botanical series and were reprinted in the Reports of the expedition, as they were concerned with plants collected by the expedition. The other two were published for the first time in part 2 (August 1931) of Volume 19 (Volume 8 of the Reports).

The greater part of Vine's Presidential Address in 1901 dealt with the scientific value of the Society's publications up to 1900. He recognized the difficulty of the task and the impossibility of enumerating all the important papers but, even with that restriction, his analysis "in little more than bare outline" occupies ten pages of the *Proceedings* for 1900–1. The additional mass of papers in the succeeding years have made vain any attempt feebly to imitate or extend Vine's evaluation in this history, but a less ambitious analysis is possible if only the number and general character of papers are considered.

Of the 523 botanical papers in the *Transactions*, 375 are taxonomic, 56 anatomical, 20 physiological, 16 cytological and embryological, 12 morphological, 13 palaeobotanical. The remainder come under such headings as economics, classification in general, evolution, geography, history and biography, institutions and collections, instruments and methods, nomenclature, pathology, phenology, philosophy, terminology and teratology; the number of papers under those heads varying from one to five. Apart from the taxonomic papers the above classification is more or less tentative, for some of the papers fit into more than one pigeon-hole, as will be readily understood. Of the 375 taxonomic papers, 270 are entirely predominantly concerned with Phanerogams and 105 with Cryptogams. Of the 270 phanerogamic papers, 27 deal with the general phanerogamic flora of a particular area and 243 are monographs of families or genera or merely descriptive of species or genera, whether new or not. Of the 105 cryptogamic papers, five are more or less floristic and the rest monographic or merely descriptive.

Of the 606 zoological papers in the *Transactions*, 447 are taxonomic, 120 anatomical, 12 physiological, 10 morphological and the remainder under similar headings to those under botanical series, except that palaeontology takes the place of palaeobotany, the papers under such headings varying in number from one to four. Of the 447 systematic papers, 347 are either monographs of or descriptive of Invertebrates, nine are concerned with the invertebrate fauna of definite areas, 85 are either monographs of or descriptive of Vertebrates and six are on the vertebrate fauna of definite areas.

Proceedings

In December 1838, the Council ordered the Secretary, then Francis Boott, to prepare and publish from time to time an abstract of the Proceedings of the Society. The session of 1838–39 began on 6 November, and Boott started his abstracts from that date. From then, until the end of the session of 1847–48, 37 numbers paged continuously were issued independently at irregular intervals and those, with contents and index completed in 1849, form Volume 1 of the *Proceedings*. From November 1848 to June 1855, 29 more numbers appeared to form Volume 2. The paging in both volumes is in arabic numerals. Volume 2 has nominally 444 pages but actually 448, as there are two sets of pages 333–36. In those two volumes under each meeting are given the Chairman, new

Plate XVIII (a) Title page of Vol. I of *Transactions*. (b) First page of Smith's Presidential Address. (c) Recent publications members elected, specimens exhibited and by whom, titles and authors of papers read, fairly full abstracts of the papers, the taxonomic ones being practically unabridged. Obituary notices of members who had died while in membership are included but not otherwise, and the elections of Officers and Council are given under the Anniversary Meetings.

In May 1855, J. J. Bennett, then Secretary, and J. D. Hooker submitted a motion to the effect that in future papers communicated for the *Proceedings* should be printed in full; that the *Proceedings* should be given a printed cover and registered as a periodical; that every Fellow not in arrear should receive a copy free; and that copies should be sold to the public at an annual subscription. After a committee on these proposals had submitted its report, the Council accepted them with the modifications that the title *Proceedings* was to be altered to *Journal of the Proceedings* and that the Minutes of the meetings and other parts, except the papers and abstracts of papers, were to be paged in Roman numerals continued from number to number.

The outcome of Bennett and Hooker's resolution was the appearance on 1 March 1856 of a new octavo publication entitled *The Journal of the Proceedings of the Linnean Society*, a somewhat cumbrous and confusing name. Their publication, judged bibliographically, was likewise cumbrous and confusing, as will be evident from the following account. From 1856 until 1865, 32 numbers were published, forming Volumes 2–8. There were three separate sets of the numbers, distinguished by the colour of their covers and the character of their contents: a set with dark-blue covers; a set with green covers; a set with pink covers. The numbers of the first set contained both botanical and zoological papers and sometimes the Proceedings proper. If a number contained all three the order was: I. Proceedings, with independent roman paging; II. Zoology, with its own arabic paging; III. Botany, with its own arabic paging. The green set of numbers contained only Botany, and the pink set only Zoology. The dark-blue set was ordinarily only for free distribution to Fellows. The green and pink sets were ordinarily for sale to the public or to members who desired extra copies or back copies of any particular purely botanical or purely zoological number. The *Proceedings* for the sessions 1855–56 to 1863–64 were published either in instalments or complete for a session as Part I of whatever number of the dark-blue set was ready. The *Proceedings* of each session of the period formed section 1, with its own roman pagination and index, of a volume of the *Journal of the Proceedings*, except that the Proceedings for the two sessions 1860–62 were continuously paged, with an index covering both sessions. Volume 8 started with No. 29 entitled as before, but with No. 30 the title was shortened to *The Journal of the Linnean Society*, which also appeared on the title-page of the complete volume (Nos 29–32). Also with Volume 8 the dark-blue set of numbers ceased to appear, so that thereafter Botany and Zoology were confined to two separate series of numbers and volumes.

From 1864–65, the *Proceedings* were intended to be distributed to members with whatever number of either the Botanical or the Zoological *Journal* was ready but, as far as can now be discovered, they were distributed up to 1867–68 only with the numbers of the Zoological *Journal*, presumably because they had formerly always been in front of the Zoology section of the dark-blue numbers. The *Proceedings* for 1864–65, 1865–66 and 1867–68 were thus distributed either in instalments or complete for a session, but those for 1866–67 were sent out independently as a blue booklet.

From the session of 1868–69, the *Proceedings* resumed their original independence of issue which they had possessed from 1838 to 1855. Although they had ceased to be an integral part of the *Journal* in 1864 and were now entirely disentangled from it, the force of custom ensured that not until 1880 did they revert to their original arabic pagination. From 1868–69 to 1871–72 they were issued in instalments, with or without the specially paged "Additions to the Library". From 1872–73 to 1929–30, the *Proceedings* for each session were published some time after the session as a single green-covered booklet, except that those for each of the groups of sessions 1875–80, 1880–82, 1883–86 and 1888–89 formed a continuously paged volume. With the session of 1930–31 a reversion was made to the practice of 1868 to 1872 of issuing the *Proceedings* in instalments without wrappers during each session, but from 1935–36 they have been issued in numbered parts clad in covers advertising their contents. In 1882 they were first sold to the public. The sessions began to be numbered with the *Proceedings* of the hundred-and-tenth session (1897–98).

Since 1855, the *Proceedings* have varied in bulk, character and arrangement. The bulk has varied from the 11 pages of the *Proceedings* for 1875–76 to the 252 of those of 1929–30. Certain items, except in a few abnormal years, have always been included, such as reports of the meetings, elections of members and officers, Presidential Addresses, obituary notices of members, annual financial statement from 1860 onwards, additions or donations or both to the Library and, up to 1863, donations to the Museum.

Reports of the General Meetings were for many years very brief. Occasionally they included abstracts of certain papers, sometimes collected at the end of the volume, sometimes under the accounts of meetings, this latter practice becoming more general in later years. In the 1920s the reports began to include more regularly the discussions of papers as well as their abstracts. From 1867–68 to 1871–72, the arrangement was very muddled: the additions or donations to the Library, and in some years an analytical catalogue of the biological papers in the periodicals received in the Library, were mixed up with reports of the General Meetings. In later years, special papers have been published in full in the *Proceedings*, especially during the Second World War when paper was rationed.

From 1906 to 1919, the *Proceedings* included a list, supposedly arranged by calendar years, of benefactions to the amount or value of £25 and over, received from 1790 onwards, but since 1920 only such benefactions received during the calendar year in which a session ends and during the preceding 19 years are given. These lists are not to be implicitly trusted as they have not always been prepared in accordance with their headings. During the period 1888 to 1911 there was also given annually a list of the donations, irrespective of amount, received during the financial year. There were thus in the *Proceedings* during that period three sets of years: the sessional, from November to June; the financial, from 1 May to 30 April; and the calendar year.

From 1854 to 1936 there were 81 Presidential Addresses, none being given in 1874 and 1915. The six Addresses delivered by Allman from 1876 to 1881 were printed in the *Journal*, five in the zoological series and one in the botanical. Lubbock's Address in 1886 appeared in the *Journal (Botany)*. All the other Addresses are printed in the *Proceedings* or the *Biological Journal*. Most of the Addresses from 1875 have been mainly devoted to the elucidation of either predominantly botanical or predominantly zoological subjects, but a few are of general interest, such as: Carruther's Address in 1889 on the portraits of Linnaeus; Poulton's Addresses in 1913 and 1914 on an extraordinary literary forgery by George Washington Sleeper pretending to anticipate the Darwin–Wallace hypothesis of organic evolution and later scientific discoveries; Calman's Address in 1935 on the meaning of Biological Classification; and Prain's philosophic discourse in 1918 on the effects of the business of life on the beginnings of the science of natural history.

Almost all Addresses make some reference to the Society's affairs, but only a few make those affairs their main topic. Such were the Addresses by Carruthers in 1887 and 1888, by Vines in 1901 and 1902, and by Rendle in 1925, 1926 and 1927. In his Address in 1917 on "The relationship between the pursuits of the Society and the business of life" Prain treated his subject in the spirit of a scientific humanist – to use the language of one of his successors in the Presidential Chair. It is possible to infer from his last Address, in 1919, on "The relationship of the existing Statutes of the Society to our present needs" that he did not consider either the Statutes or the Society's observance of them to have been always the quintessence of wisdom.

The small economical size of the *Proceedings*, approximately 21 cm × 14 cm, with narrow margins, was invaluable during the Second World War years of paper rationing but, after the completion of the *Proceedings* for session 157 (1944–45), published in 1946, the Council decided to increase its size to approximately 25 cm × 16 cm, so as to be equivalent to that of the *Journal*. Henceforth the *Proceedings* were given volume numbers corresponding to the sessions. Thus Volume 158 (1947) containing the Proceedings of the hundred-and-fifty-eighth session (1945–46) began the new format.

Journal

The idea of starting a journal was, as mentioned in Chapter 3, first expressed by William Kirby in 1822. Although the formal motion to extend the scope of the *Proceedings* was made by J. J. Bennett and J. D. Hooker in May 1855, the project of starting a Journal was discussed, according to B. D. Jackson's *George Bentham*, by Bell, the President, Bentham and Hooker at a dinner party in Bentham's flat in Victoria Street on 2 March 1855.

The Committee appointed in June 1855 to consider Bennett and Hooker's motion met in November, and amongst its members were Robert Brown, the ex-President, and J. J. Bennett, then Brown's Assistant in the British Museum. Those two apparently objected to any modification of the original motion in the way of starting a Journal, for an extract from Bentham's diary reads "Brown and Bennett attempting to defeat the plan by side-winds but all was satisfactorily carried". The result was the combination of *Proceedings* and *Journal* both in title and, so far as distribution to Fellows was concerned, in contents as already described.

Each of the Volumes 1–8 (1856–65), made up of the dark-blue covered set of numbers for distribution only to Fellows, contained four numbers of Zoology and four of Botany, in addition to the Proceedings. Thereafter, the Botanical and Zoological numbers were distributed to Fellows, as from the beginning they had been sold to the public, in separate series, but each volume of each series was now intended to be made up of eight numbers, and up to Volume 15 in Botany and Volume 17 in Zoology this was so. Succeeding volumes have varied from two to nine numbers in Botany and three to eleven in Zoology. Occasionally, two or more numbers have been run together to form one part. The two separate series that remained after 1865 began at once to get out of step.

During 1859 to 1861, while Volumes 3–6 of the combined series were in course of publication, there was also a confusing additional issue in Botany only of one supplementary volume and three supplementary numbers or parts in that series, the volume and the numbers having each its own paging, title and index. It was evidently intended at first that those supplementary numbers should form supplementary volumes, as the single supplementary volume of two numbers is described on its title-page as "Supplement to Botany – Vol. I". Those supplements were as follows:

Supplement to Botany – Vol. 1. 1859	No. 1. Musci Indiae Orientalis. By William Mitten. Pp. 1–96. 21 Feb. 1859.
	No. 2. Ditto. Pp. 97–171. 1 May 1859.
Supplement to Vol. 4 – Botany	Synopsis of Dalbergieae. By George Bentham. Pp. 1–134. 7 March 1860.
(First) Supplement to Vol. 5 – Botany	Florula Adenensis. By Thomas Anderson. Pp. i–xxxiv and 1–47, with 6 plates. 31 Dec. 1860.
Second Supplement to Vol. 5 – Botany	Notes on Aurantiaceae. By Daniel Oliver: pp. 1–44; Notes on Menspermaceae, Tiliaceae, Bixaceae and Samydaceae. By George Bentham: pp. 45–99. 24 May 1861.

In Zoology there was no corresponding issue of supplementary numbers, but on 18 July 1860 there was issued an unnumbered part inexactly described on its pink cover as "Supplemental to Vol. V – Zoology". It is actually an extra part (pp. 57–168, with one plate) inserted between No. 17, which forms the first part (pp. 1–56) of the Zoological section of Volume 5, and No. 18 (pp. 169–216). Although issued separately from Nos 17 and 18 of the dark-blue cover combined set of Botany and Zoology, it is not a supplement to Vol. 5, but an integral part of that volume.

In 1888, a General Index to Volumes 1–20 (1857–84) of the Botany series was published, and in 1896 a similar index to Volumes 1–20 (1857–90) of the Zoology series. B. D. Jackson, then Botanical Secretary, prepared the Botany Index and A. W. Kappel, the Assistant-Librarian, the Zoology Index. In addition to the indexes proper, each General Index gives a table of dates of publication of the *Proceedings* and parts of the appropriate *Journal*.

In 1907, beginning with Volume 38 (Botany) and Volume 30 (Zoology), the page size of the *Journal* was enlarged and its general format improved.

In Volume 2 (Botany) the contents mention only one plate, but there are actually two plates. In Volume 8 (Zoology) the contents mention only eight plates, but there are actually ten.

As in the *Transactions* so in the *Journal* several botanical papers have invaded the Zoological volumes. In addition to the three botanical papers that were first published in the Zoological series, a fourth, that had been first published in the Botanical series, was reprinted in the Zoological, and a fifth, that had also first been published in the Botanical series, was given in title only in the contents of a Zoological number.

In some of the earlier volumes of both series many papers are little more than brief notes, extracts from letters and so forth, with the result that volumes such as 14 and 20 in the Botanical series contain over 50 papers.

As might be expected, an analysis of the papers gives results generally similar to those yielded by the *Transactions*. Thus, to 1936, of 1098 botanical papers, 712 are taxonomic, 109 physiological, 81 morphological, 48 anatomical, 32 palaeobotanical, 24 teratological, 18 distributional and the rest concerned with a variety of subjects such as bibliography, classification in general, ecology, cytology and embryology, evolution, nomenclature, economic and medicinal, dispersal, hybridization, Mendelism, phenology etc. Some of those numbers express merely a personal judgement and should be accepted as such, for some papers so combine anatomy, morphology and physiology as to make the placing of them quite arbitrary. Of 712 taxonomic papers, 312 are monographic or descriptive of Phanerogams, 162 are phanerogamic or floristic and the rest concerned with Cryptogams, either monographic or descriptive or floristic as regards certain divisions such as Ferns or Mosses or Algae.

Of 936 zoological papers, 610 are taxonomic, 78 deal with invertebrate and 71 with vertebrate anatomy, 29 are palaeontological, 28 physiological, 23 are concerned with distribution and the remainder with such subjects as embryology and cytology, evolution, food habits, heredity, nomenclature, plankton, teratology, terminology etc.

The Linnean

The *Biological Journal*, as successor in 1969 of the *Proceedings*, continued to carry records of the Society's business, annual reports etc. until 1983. Its increasing restriction thereafter to papers relevant to the theory of evolution made it necessary for papers of general interest and records of the Society's activities to be published elsewhere. In 1984, the Council accordingly instituted a new journal, *The Linnean*, containing the proceedings, general news, announcements of meetings, obituaries and short miscellaneous papers. Volume 1 (1984–85) consisted of six numbers; volume 2 (1986) and volume 3 (1987) each with three numbers, all with their own pagination.

Distribution

The distribution of the Society's publications to members was during many years effected by the simple process of delivering them in the Society's rooms only to members who called or sent an agent for them. Later the printers distributed them. Now the Society has a joint publishing arrangement with Academic Press for the three journals, Biological, Botanical and Zoological.

The inevitable accumulation over many years of undistributed and unsold copies led to confusion both in storage and in recording. A certain proportion of the stock was stored with the two firms who were the Society's selling agents. In 1861, a great part of the stock of *Transactions* with Messrs Longman, Green, Longmans and Roberts was destroyed by a fire in that firm's premises. In 1862, the Council made a drastic and ill-judged reduction of the Society's stock by selling to the other firm of agents $2\frac{3}{4}$ tons of *Transactions* as waste-paper, for which the Society received over £50.

In January 1883, Frank Crisp and J. D. Hooker proposed that 55 complete sets of the first series of the *Transactions* and 20 complete sets of the *Journal* should be made up. An attempt to do so revealed that the old stock-books had been very inaccurately kept and that the stock was in great confusion. Only a few complete sets of *Transactions*, only one or two complete sets of the *Journal* and not one complete set of the *Proceedings* could be made up. In 1929, the stock was thoroughly overhauled and rearranged by complete volumes and odd parts in the hope of making up a complete set or two, but not even one complete set of any of the publications emerged from the mass.

Chapter 15

Medals, awards and special funds

The Linnean Society awards medals for distinguished biological achievement and possesses a number of special funds providing for the promotion of biology. These, in order of their founding, are:

1888   Linnean Medal
1894   Westwood Fund
1908   Darwin–Wallace Medal
1909   Trail Award
1910   Crisp Award
1913   Hooker Lecture
1919   Goodenough Fund
1926   E. A. Minchin Fellowship Fund
1963   H. H. Bloomer Award
1965   Flora Europaea Fund
1966   Jane Jackson Endowment
1968   Appleyard Fund
1972   Denis Stanfield Award
1973   Omer-Cooper Bequest
1975   Bonhote Fund
1978   Bicentenary Medal
1987   Jill Smythies Award

Applications for grants from the Society's funds have to be made on the appropriate forms obtainable from the Executive Secretary. A memorandum on the history and constitution of medals as the gift of the Council was published in *Proceedings* 127 (1914–15).

THE APPLEYARD FUND

The Appleyard Fund was established in 1968 with a capital sum of £4200 from the estate of Percy Appleyard, FLS (d. 1943). An annual income of approximately £200 is available from which grants are made towards the expenses of research projects in the fields of botany or zoology by Fellows and Associates of the Society who are not in full-time employment as biologists. The Fund is administered by a Committee appointed by the Council.

THE BICENTENARY MEDAL

The Bicentenary Medal was struck in silver in 1978 to commemorate the two-hundredth anniversary of the death of Carl Linnaeus (1707–78). It is awarded, normally annually, to a person under the age of 40. Any biologist not at the time a member of Council is eligible. One side of the Bicentenary Medal, portraying young Linnaeus examining *Trientalis*

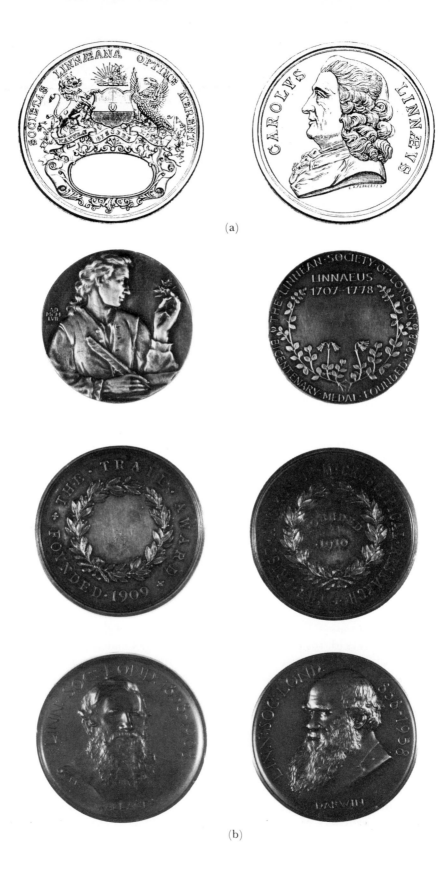

(a)

(b)

europaea, is the same as that of the H. H. Bloomer Award medal but the obverse is almost encircled by *Linnaea borealis* and has the marginal inscription *The Linnean Society of London Bicentenary Medal Founded 1978* and *Linnaeus 1707–78* above the name of the recipient.

1978	D. L. Hawksworth
1979	R. L. Blackman
1980	C. J. Humphries
1981	R. S. K. Barnes
1982	H. J. B. Birks
1983	J. Krebs
1984	P. R. Crane
1985	N. H. Barton
1986	D. W. Minter
1987	A. J. J. Jeffreys

THE BONHOTE FUND

This Fund was established in 1975 with a capital sum received from the estate of the late John James Lewis Bonhote (1875–1922), a Fellow since 1904. An annual income of approximately £400 is available from which grants are made to British-born subjects towards the cost of projects related to furthering knowledge of heredity. The Fund is administered by a Committee appointed by the Council.

THE DARWIN–WALLACE MEDAL

The Darwin–Wallace Medal was struck in 1908 and 1958 to commemorate the fiftieth and one-hundredth anniversaries of the reading of the joint paper by Charles Darwin and Alfred Russel Wallace, "On the Tendency of Species to form Varieties; and the Perpetuation of Varieties and Species by Natural Means of Selection", which was read on 1 July 1858 and published.

The recipients of the Darwin–Wallace Medal in 1908 were: the medal in gold to Alfred Russel Wallace, and in silver to Joseph D. Hooker, Ernst Haeckel, Eduard Strasburger, August Weisman, Francis Galton and E. Ray Lankester.

The recipients of the Darwin–Wallace Medal in 1958 were: Edgar Anderson, Maurice Caullery, Ronald A. Fisher, C. R. Florin, J. B. S. Haldane, Roger Heim, John Hutchinson, Julian Huxley, Ernst Mayr, H. J. Muller, E. Pavlovsky, Bernhard Rensch, G. Gaylor Simpson, Carl Skottsberg, E. A. Stensio, H. Hamshaw Thomas, G. V. Turesson, V. van Straelen, D. M. S. Watson and J. C. Willis (posthumously).

The Medal has a profile of Darwin on one side and of Wallace full-face on the other with the marginal inscription "LINN. SOC. LOND. 1858–1908" on both sides.

THE DENIS STANFIELD AWARD

The Denis Stanfield Memorial Fund was established in 1972 to commemorate Denis Percival Stanfield (d. 1971) with capital sufficient to allow an Award from income to be

---

Plate XIX Medals: (a) Linnean Medal. (b) Bicentenary Medal. Trail Crisp Medal. Darwin–Wallace Medal.

made at three-year intervals; the Award should be recognized as a mark of real distinction and take the form of a sum of money to assist persons of scientific merit to undertake botanical research on tropical African plants. The recipients of the Award are selected by a Committee appointed by the Council and composed of persons having special knowledge of tropical botany.

THE E. A. MINCHIN FELLOWSHIP FUND

This Fund was established in 1926 with a gift of £100 from a Fellow who desired to remain anonymous and it is in memory of Edward Alfred Minchin (1866–1915), the distinguished zoologist, who was Zoological Secretary for a short time before his untimely death. The income is used to pay for a period of years the annual contribution of a young student of science who would not otherwise be able to become a candidate for Fellowship. Nomination, which is not published, is in the hands of the President.

THE FLORA EUROPAEA FUND

The Linnean Society encouraged the preparation of the *Flora Europaea* (5 vols, 1964–80) by agreeing to act as the sponsor of this great undertaking when it was no more than a project. In consequence, a trust deed of 1965 set up a *Flora Europaea* Fund into which all royalties received from the sales of this work should be paid, the Fund to be administered by a Committee appointed by the Council, and that for a period of 20 years this money should be available for the preparation and revision of the *Flora Europaea* and for continuation of research in plant taxonomy associated with it.

THE GOODENOUGH FUND

Early in June 1910, the Council adopted a motion by Professor (later Sir Edward) Poulton that a circular should be drawn up inviting donations to a fund for assisting in certain cases the payment of annual contributions, but decided later in the same month not to issue the circular. No more was heard of the scheme until 1919, when Sir David Prain in his Presidential Address suggested an "Admission Fee Reduction Fund", and conjured up an entrancing vision of the distant future when no admission fees and only reduced annual contributions would be payable. He considered that when the proposed Fund had reached £4000 it would be possible to debit all admission fees against it, but that £20 000 would be necessary before beginning to reduce the rate of annual contributions. An eminent Fellow, whose name unfortunately is not given, had suggested that the Fund should be called after Samuel Goodenough (1745–1827), the Society's first Treasurer who played so conspicuous a part in the formation and early guidance of the Society. It is a most appropriate name in one sense, for he laid stress, even before the Society had been formed, on the importance of money to "carry matters into effect". In 1920, a circular inviting donations was distributed, but the Fund has increased very little and very slowly. The income is used to pay the annual contribution of one or more Fellows who merit assistance. The President, the Treasurer and the Secretaries administer the Fund. Details of distribution are not published.

THE H. H. BLOOMER AWARD

A legacy of £500 by Harry Howard Bloomer, FLS (1866–1960), an accountant with both botanical and zoological interests and a President of the Birmingham Natural History and Philosophical Societies, enabled the Council in 1963 to establish the H. H. Bloomer Award to an amateur naturalist who has made an important contribution to biological knowledge (including biological bibliography), the recipients being alternately a botanist and zoologist. C. E. Raven qualified as both, but was classified as a zoologist for the purpose of the Award. This may be given to any person not at the time a member of Council. The recipient receives a donation provided out of the Fund and a silver medal designed by Léo Holmgren and struck in 1957 by the Swedish Royal Mint, Stockholm. The medal portrays Carl Linnaeus at the age of 25 when he made the Lapland journey, quill pen in hand, examining the flowers of chickweed wintergreen (*Trientalis europaea*).

Recipients of the H. H. Bloomer Award

1963	J. E. Lousley
1964	C. E. Raven
1965	E. C. Wallace
1966	D. L. Harrison
1967	A. G. Long
1968	Miriam L. Rothschild
1969	T. D. V. Swinscow
1970	A. E. Ellis
1971	J. G. Dony
1972	Marie Åsberg
1973	Ursula K. Duncan
1974	A. F. Millidge and G. H. Locket
1975	E. S. Edees
1976	F. C. Stinton
1977	D. H. Kent
1978	D. R. Rosevear
1979	Blanche Henrey
1980	J. N. Eliot
1981	D. E. Allen
1982	L. G. Higgins
1983	O. V. Polunin
1984	R. L. E. Ford
1985	B. E. Smythies
1986	W. J. Le Quesne
1987	M. C. Clark

THE HOOKER MEMORIAL LECTURE FUND

The veteran Kew botanist Sir Joseph Dalton Hooker died in 1911 and bequeathed £100 to the Society. Early in 1913, the Council decided to make this sum the nucleus of a Fund to endow a Sir Joseph Hooker Memorial Lecture to be delivered every second, third or fourth year, and invited contributions. In June of that year, before the Fund had been properly established, the distinguished botanist, zoologist, traveller and sportsman Henry John Elwes (1846–1922), who was a friend of Sir Joseph and had recently returned from revisiting the eastern Himalaya, asked the Council to allow him to give the first Hooker

Lecture. The Council agreed, somewhat hesitatingly one gathers, and Elwes delivered on 20 November 1913 a lecture on "The travels of Sir Joseph Hooker in the Sikkim Himalaya", Lady Hooker being amongst the audience. Elwes never submitted a manuscript and his lecture was never published. On 7 June 1917 the Society met first in its own rooms at 5 pm and then reassembled, for the second time in its history, outside its own rooms at 8 pm in the lecture theatre of the Civil Commission, Burlington Gardens, to hear a lecture by Professor Frederick Orpen Bower (1855–1948) of Glasgow University on "The natural classification of plants". In his introductory remarks, the President, Sir David Prain, stated that, owing to the fact that the scheme had not matured in 1913, the lecture delivered by Elwes was not a "Sir Joseph Hooker Memorial Lecture". The scheme aimed at a Fund with a minimum capital of £600, but in 1917 the capital was still less than £400. Notwithstanding the incompleteness of the Fund, it was thought desirable that the first lecture under it should be delivered in the centenary year of Hooker's birth. The 7 June 1917 was actually the seventy-fifth anniversary of Hooker's election as a Fellow. According to Prain, this lecture by Bower was the first Hooker Lecture. Since 1920–21, however, the Society's annual Lists show Elwes as the first Hooker Lecturer. The lecture has to be "on some subject especially associated with the name of Sir Joseph Hooker", which in view of his interest in plant distribution, classification, evolution and travel provides ample scope. The lecturer is not necessarily a member of the Society. From 1917 to 1980, 16 lectures were delivered and published either in the *Journal* or *Proceedings*. The income of the Fund in hand is applied to the publication of the lecture with a donation to the lecturer.

The Hooker lecturers

1913	H. J. Elwes
1917	F. O. Bower
1922	A. C. Seward
1926	C. Schroeter
1929	E. J. Allen
1933	William Wright Smith
1936	F. Kingdon-Ward
1939	R. Lloyd Praeger
1943	W. H. Lang
1948	D. M. S. Watson
1951	I. H. Burkill
1958	W. B. Turrill
1962	T. Dobzhansky
1966	A. S. Romer
1974	C. T. Ingold
1980	J. Heslop-Harrison

THE LINNEAN MEDAL

The Linnean Medal is the Society's highest award and was instituted in May 1888 to mark the centenary of the Society's founding. The Council Minutes for May 1888 state that "It has been a matter of not a little anxiety to the Council that in selecting the first recipients of the Medal, they should choose men not only worthy in themselves to receive this honour, but men so universally esteemed for their scientific labours that their choice would testify to the world the great importance attached by the Linnean Society to the award of the Linnean Medal''. The Council annually awards it alternately to an eminent botanist and an eminent zoologist or to both simultaneously as an expression of the Society's estimate and appreciation of service to science. Any biologist, irrespective of nationality, not at the time a member of Council is eligible to receive the Medal. The President bestows it on the recipient at the Anniversary Meeting and specifies the grounds for which it has been awarded.

The Medal has the arms of the Society, the wording SOCIETAS LINNAEANA (earlier "Linnaeensis") OPTIME MERENTI and the year and name of the recipient on the one side and on the obverse a portrait of Linnaeus in profile with the wording CAROLUS LINNAUS; this bears a close resemblance to a medal by Durand in 1818, which in turn was obviously influenced by C. F. Inlander's medallion of 1773. The Medal was of gold up to 1976, since then it has been of alloy.

Recipients of the Linnean Medal

1888 Sir Joseph D. Hooker and Sir Richard Owen	1925 F. W. Oliver
1889 A. L. P. P. de Candolle	1926 E. J. Allen
1890 T. H. Huxley	1927 O. Stapf
1891 J. B. E. Bornet	1928 E. B. Wilson
1892 A. R. Wallace	1929 H. de Vries
1893 D. Oliver	1930 J. P. Hill
1894 E. H. P. A. Haeckel	1931 K. R. von Goebel
1895 F. J. Cohn	1932 E. S. Goodrich
1896 G. J. Allman	1933 R. Chodat
1897 J. G. Agardh	1934 Sir Sidney Frederick Harmer
1898 G. C. Wallich	1935 Sir David Prain
1899 J. G. Baker	1936 J. S. Gardiner
1900 A. Newton	1937 F. F. Blackman
1901 Sir George King	1938 Sir D'Arcy Wentworth Thompson
1902 R. A. von Kolliker	1939 E. D. Merrill
1903 M. C. Cooke	1940 Sir Arthur Smith Woodward
1904 A. C. L. G. Günther	1941 Sir Arthur George Tansley
1905 E. Strasburger	1942–45 Award suspended
1906 A. M. Norman	1946 W. T. Calman and F. E. Weiss
1907 M. Treub	1947 M. Caullery
1908 T. R. Stebbing	1948 Agnes Arber
1909 F. O. Bower	1949 D. M. S. Watson
1910 G. O. Sars	1950 H. N. Ridley
1911 H. zu Solms-Laubach	1951 T. Mortensen
1912 R. C. L. Perkins	1952 I. H. Burkill
1913 H. G. A. Engler	1953 P. A. Buxton
1914 O. Butschi	1954 F. E. Fritsch
1915 J. H. Maiden	1955 Sir John Graham Kerr
1916 F. E. Beddard	1956 W. H. Lang
1917 H. B. Guppy	1957 E. A. Stensio
1918 F. Du C. Godman	1958 Sir Gavin de Beer and W. B. Turrill
1919 Sir Isaac Bayley Balfour	1959 H. M. Fox and C. Skottsberg
1920 Sir Edwin Ray Lankester	1960 Libbie H. Hyman and H. Hamshaw Thomas
1921 D. H. Scott	1961 E. W. Mason and F. S. Russell
1922 Sir Edward Bagnall Poulton	1962 N. L. Bor and G. Gaylord Simpson
1923 T. F. Cheeseman	1963 Sidnie M. Manton and W. H. Pearsall
1924 W. C. McIntosh	1964 R. E. Holttum and C. F. A. Pantin

1965	J. Hutchinson and J. Ramsbottom	1976	W. T. Stearn
1966	G. S. Carter and Sir Harry Godwin	1977	E. Mayr and T. G. Tutin
1967	C. S. Elton and C. E. Hubbard	1978	K. O. Hedberg and T. S. Westall
1968	A. Graham	1979	R. McN. Alexander and P. W. Richards
1969	Irene Manton and Ethelwyn Trewavas	1980	G. C. Ainsworth and R. A. Crowson
		1981	B. L. Burtt and Sir Cyril A. Clarke
1970	E. J. H. Corner and E. I. White	1982	P. H. Davis and P. H. Greenwood
1971	C. R. Metcalf and J. E. Smith	1983	C. T. Ingold and M. J. D. White
1972	A. R. Clapham and A. S. Romer	1984	J. G. Hawkes and J. S. Kennedy
1973	G. L. Stebbins and J. S. Young	1985	A. J. Cain and J. B. Harborne
1974	E. H. W. Hennig and J. Braun-Blanquet	1986	A. Cronquist and P. G. C. Garnham
		1987	G. Fryer and V. H. Heywood
1975	A. S. Watt and P. M. Sheppard		

THE OMER-COOPER BEQUEST

A bequest of £5000 was made by Professor Joseph Omer-Cooper, FLS (1893–1972). Under the terms of the will the money is "to be used for the furtherance of the study of Isopod Crustacea and/or the Hydrophagous Coleoptera". The income is made available when appropriate:

1. for the purchase of books relating to water beetles and isopods (and/or related crustacea) for the Library;
2. to subsidize the preparation and publication of monographs or other suitable works on water beetles and isopods (and/or related crustacea);
3. to assist the financing of symposia concerned with water beetles and isopods (and/or related crustacea).

THE TRAIL–CRISP AWARD AND MEDAL

Up to 1966 the Society made two independent awards relating to microscopy, the Trail Award and the Crisp Award. In 1966, the Council amalgamated them into a single award, the Trail–Crisp Award, in recognition of an outstanding contribution to biological microscopy published in the United Kingdom with preference to that of a younger worker. Before 1972 these awards were made at intervals of not less than 5 years. The recipient receives a bronze medal and the balance of income from the Fund in hand at the time.

In 1909, James William Helenus Trail (1851–1919), who was a Fellow from 1875 and Professor of Botany in the University of Aberdeen from 1877 until his death, presented £100 for the foundation of a Fund to encourage research on protoplasm. An accompanying memorandum explained his views, which gave a wide interpretation to such research and great freedom to the Council in forming or reforming regulations for the use of the Fund. Trail's memorandum was published in the *Proceedings* for 1914–15 p. 52. From 1910 to 1930 the Fund was used to make every fifth year an award of a bronze medal with the balance of the income of the Fund in hand at the time. When no award was made, as in 1935, the sum held over was invested and added to the capital. There were no restrictions beyond that the Award may not be given to a member of the Council in being. This Medal has the portrait of Linnaeus facing left, as in the Linnean Medal, on one side and on the obverse the marginal inscription THE TRAIL AWARD FOUNDED 1909 and within this a laurel wreath.

In 1910, Sir Frank Crisp (1843–1919) presented £200 to establish a Fund for the encouragement of microscopical research. Crisp was particularly interested in microscopy and microscopes, one of his hobbies being the formation of a large and historically interesting collection of microscopes.

The terms of the Crisp Award were less wide than those of the Trail Award, for, unlike the latter which could be bestowed irrespective of membership of the Society or medium of publication, the Crisp Award was confined to papers contributed to the Society's publications only by Fellows. Otherwise, the provisions regarding it were similar to those regulating the Trail Award and, like it, the Crisp Award consisted of a bronze medal and whatever balance of income available. The Medal has the portrait of Linnaeus facing left, as in the Linnean Medal, on one side and the marginal inscription THE CRISP AWARD FOR MICROSCOPICAL RESEARCH and a laurel wreath encircling FOUNDED 1910.

Recipients of the Trail Award and Medal

1910	E. A. Minchin
1915	L. Doncaster
1920	Dame Helen Gwynne-Vaughan
1925	R. Chambers
1930	Kathleen B. Blackburn
1937	C. F. A. Pantin
1948	C. D. Darlington and Honor B. Fell
1954	Irene Manton
1960	L. E. R. Picken

Recipients of the Crisp Award and Medal

1912	C. F. U. Meek
1917	R. J. Tillyard
1927	H. G. Cannon
1940	D. J. Scourfield
1957	Mary Agard Pocock

Recipients of the Trail–Crisp Award and Medal

1967	J. Heslop-Harrison
1972	G. F. Leedale
1974	B. E. S. Gunning
1978	T Ørvig
1982	J. M. Pettitt
1984	K. Fredga
1987	S. Blackmore

THE WESTWOOD FUND

John Obadiah Westwood (1805–93), a native of Sheffield, forsook the law for the pursuit of entomology, in which he became a prominent investigator; he was elected to the Linnean Society in 1827 and was an original member and thrice President of the Royal

Entomological Society of London founded in 1833. Keeper of the Entomological Collection and Library presented to the University of Oxford by the Rev. F. W. Hope, he was the first to hold the Hope Professorship founded by Hope in 1861. He bequeathed £500 New Zealand 4 per cent stock jointly to the two societies, the interest to be applied in paying for entomological illustrations in the *Transactions* of each society in alternate years. This was an inconvenient arrangement, and with the consent of the testator's nieces, Emma and E. Lucy Swann, the original terms were modified to allow each society £250 in cash. In 1926, the Misses Swann gave consent for the expression "entomological" to be extended in meaning to include all Arthropoda, so that income from the Fund could be used to pay for illustrations in papers on Arthropoda published by the Linnean Society.

THE JILL SMYTHIES AWARD

This Award was established in 1987 by Bertram E. Smythies, FLS, the recipient in 1985 of the H. H. Bloomer Award, in honour of his wife, Florence Mary ("Jill") Smythies, whose career as a botanical artist was cut short by an accident to her right hand. The Award is for published illustrations of high-quality, drawings or paintings in aid of plant identification, with emphasis on botanical accuracy and the portrayal of diagnostic characteristics. Illustrations of cultivars of garden origin are not eligible. It consists of a silver medal and a purse and is to be awarded at the Council's discretion usually, but not necessarily, annually, as advised by the Awards Committee. The Award may be made to anyone not a member of Council and for work published at any date.

THE JANE JACKSON ENDOWMENT FUND

In 1930 the Society was made the residual legatee of the estate, valued at about £4000, of the late Jane Jackson, widow of Benjamin Daydon Jackson, this being subject to certain life-interests. The money, which came into the possession of the Society in 1966, forms the Jane Jackson Endowment Fund for increasing the remuneration of the Society's staff.

Chapter 16

Botanical and zoological collections

The Linnean Society in the late eighteenth century, like the Royal Society earlier that century, began to accumulate miscellaneous collections which ultimately became an encumbrance.

The records of the Society give no clear exposition of its motive in attempting to form a museum of natural history. Probably the general idea that one of the functions of a philosophical society was to create such a museum incited the Society to begin accepting gifts of specimens and collections. For example, the Spalding Gentlemen's Society established a museum in 1727 (cf. *The Linnean* 3 no. 2: 18–22; 1987). The Linnean Society never had space enough or sufficient staff for the proper exhibition and care of its collections, and this speedily became apparent; witness Marsham's comment in September 1796: "the Museum in a state of confusion. No one knows what is in it". Gifts of specimens and of whole collections continued to pour in until 1802. Donations and names of donors began to be printed in Volume 10 (1811) of the *Transactions*, and continued to be printed in every volume up to Volume 21 (1855), when they were transferred to the *Proceedings*, in which they appeared up to 1863.

No useful purpose would be served by endeavouring to analyse the heterogenous mass of material received during about 70 years, the bulk of which was stowed away in attics and storerooms, where few ever entered. Certain special collections, however, call for mention: the British and exotic Herbarium and the collection of minerals and shells bequeathed by Richard Pulteney in 1802; the collection of insects and shells presented by Sir Joseph Banks previous to 1815; a large collection of Indian and Cape plants presented by William Roxburgh previous to 1815; the George Caley collection of quadrupeds, birds and reptiles of New South Wales, purchased by 41 members and presented to the Society in 1818; the herbarium of Sir J. E. Smith, purchased by the Society in 1829; the East Indian Herbarium presented by the Hon. East India Company (H.E.I.C.) in 1832 and stated to comprise about 8000 species collected by König, Roxburgh, Röttler, Russell, Klein, Hamilton, Heyne, Wight, Finlayson and Wallich; the herbarium of about 12 000 sheets of British and foreign plants bequeathed by Nathaniel John Winch in 1838; the herbarium of William Withering presented by his grandson, Beriah Botfield, in 1852; the collection of British birds' eggs bequeathed by John Drew Salmon in 1861.

By the 1850s, the absurdity of the Society continuing to accumulate material that it could neither store nor catalogue properly became clear, but not until Bell was President were steps taken to discourage donations. In 1857–58 a British Herbarium was made up from the collections of Pulteney, Winch and Withering. In 1863 it was decided to retain the Smithian and East Indian Herbaria, the Javan collections of Thomas Horsfield, the Society's British Herbarium, the Australian Herbarium, the Carpological Collection, the Salmon Collection of eggs, Mrs Griffith's Algae and the Acharius Collection of Lichens, but to get rid of the rest.

The British Museum received the Banksian Collection of insects and shells, a collection of Australian mammals and birds and types of insects described by McLeay, Curtis and others. Winch's Herbarium, after it had contributed to the formation of the Society's British Herbarium, was presented to the Natural History Society of Northumberland, Durham and Newcastle-upon-Tyne (now the Natural History Society of Northumbria), which had asked in vain for that Herbarium when it was bequeathed to the Linnean Society in 1838; it is now in the Hancock Museum, Newcastle-upon-Tyne. All the other collections and specimens were sold by auction in 268 lots in the "great rooms" of J. C. Stevens, 38 King Street, Covent Garden, on 10 November 1863; these included "shells, birds, insects, horns, herbariums from all parts of the world, and a variety of other natural history specimens". Among the herbaria were those of Pulteney, Relham, Murray, Maton, Davies, Don and Thomas Watts. Apart from the Linnean and Smith Collections the Society now possesses almost none of the collections retained in 1863. Thus the extensive East Indian or Wallichian Herbarium is now at the Royal Botanic Gardens, Kew. The collections of Nathaniel Wallich (1768–1854), Superintendent of the Hon. East India Company's Botanic Garden near Calcutta, formed much the greater part of the East Indian Herbarium, and he worked assiduously in sorting out the collection while he was in England on furlough from 1828–32. The correspondence concerning the gift of this Herbarium by the H.E.I.C. to the Society, printed in Volume 17 (1837) of the *Transactions*, conveys to the unbiased reader the conviction that the Herbarium was unreservedly presented to the Society. According to Bentham's diary the Directors of the Company also allowed £200 for mounting paper. Nevertheless, in 1905, Sir William Thiselton-Dyer, then nearing the end of his service as Director of Kew, applied for transfer of the Herbarium to Kew on the ground that he believed that it was only deposited with the Society and was actually the property of the Secretary of State for India. The Council declined to accept Thiselton-Dyer's belief as a valid reason for parting with the Honourable Company's gift but, in 1913, the Fellows, by a Resolution based on wider grounds, authorized the Council to offer the Herbarium along with Horsfield's and some other collections to the Royal Botanic Gardens, Kew, then under the unaggressive direction of David Prain.

Although the Society has not accepted any collections for its own keeping since 1863, it did accept as Trustees a collection of British Mollusca bequeathed to it in 1888 by Hunter Jackson Barron, to be placed in some institution where the collection could be utilized. This collection was handed over in 1889 to the Mason Science College, later merged with the University of Birmingham.

In 1962, the Society still possessed about 45 herbarium collections other than those of Smith and Linnaeus. The Royal Botanic Gardens, Kew, acquired the mycological specimens for £250 in August 1962 and the British Museum (Natural History) the algae, lichens, mosses and various phanerogams for £250 in January 1963 and the British Herbarium comprising between 3000 and 3500 specimens for £300 in April 1963.

THE COLLECTIONS OF LINNAEUS

The Linnean Society holds in trust for the benefit of science the botanical and zoological collections, the library and the correspondence of Carl Linnaeus and has always been strongly conscious of its responsibility for their safe keeping. As mentioned earlier (Chapter 3), the Society burdened itself with a heavy debt and was somewhat financially handicapped for many years in order to buy them and keep them available for study. Their importance lies in their use by Linnaeus when drafting his publications, notably *Species Plantarum* (1753) and *Systema Naturae*, 10th edn (1758), and subsequent editions and dissertations, which are the basis of modern scientific nomenclature for plants and animals. At the time James Edward Smith acquired the Linnaean collections from Linnaeus's widow they comprised:

Herbarium of ca. 14000 plants
Birds in glass boxes, 45 specimens
Dried fishes, 158 specimens
Insects, 3198 specimens
"Conchylia", 1564 specimens
Corallia, large number – but not counted
Minerals, 2424 specimens
Library, ca. 1600 volumes
Manuscripts and papers relating to almost every aspect of his scientific work, together with ca. 3000 letters.

Smith must have disposed of the birds, for nothing more is known of them. He sold the minerals in 1796 (as recorded in the sale catalogue *Linnean Cabinet of Minerals – A Catalogue of the genuine and entire Collection of the late celebrated Sir Charles Linné ... which will be sold by Auction, by Mr. King, at his Great Room, King Street, Covent Garden, on Tuesday, March 1, 1796 etc.*).

The Linnaean collections, somewhat diminished in content, came to the Linnean Society when the library and collection of James Edward Smith were purchased in 1829 from Smith's widow. The Linnaean collections in the Society's possession, apart from the printed books and manuscripts of both the elder and younger Linnaeus, consist of: 1. Herbarium; 2. Insects; 3. Shells; 4. Fishes; 5. Miscellaneous zoological specimens. The Herbarium, much the most important of the collections when received by the Society, was contained in three upright, narrow, dark-green painted wooden cabinets, as originally used by Linnaeus. From 1857 to 1873 these cabinets and the other collections were placed in mahogany cases in the Library. From 1873 to 1914 they occupied the north wall of the Meeting Room. During 1914 to 1916 the collections were removed to a cellar for safety from bombs, but this was such an inconvenient place that the collections were replaced in the Meeting Room in 1916, the original Linnaean cabinets being discarded for the Herbarium, which then was stored in 21 steel boxes in a steel and asbestos-lined mahogany case. The original Linnaean cabinets, after resting in a lumber-room for ten years, were transferred in 1926 to the East Gallery of the main Library. In 1938, the Society returned two of them to Sweden as a gift to the Swedish Linnaeus Society.

These specimens are now housed in a special basement strong-room constructed in 1970 with very generous Swedish, American and other financial aid, especially from an Australian businessman, Sidney Smith, and designed to resist both flooding and a heavy fall of masonry. Unfortunately, as mentioned before, the thickness of the concrete used to ensure this has created unforeseen problems as regards the control of temperature and humidity. The collections were moved into the strong-room in 1971.

As regards the purchase of the Linnaean and Smith Collections, the Society's *Transactions* 16: 755–760 (1833) provides an extract from the Minutes of the General Meeting, on 24 May 1828, which actually gives a list of subscriptions "entered into", amounting to a total of £1593 8s. Entering into a subscription is not the same as paying it, and the total actually received from 1829 to 1836 was £1509 8s. The total amount raised by loans or bonds was £1500 raised at intervals between 1829 and 1837. Towards the total, William Horton Lloyd lent £400, Robert Brown £300, S. H. Sterry, who was not a member, £200, and six other Fellows, including Edward Forster and Richard Taylor, the Under-Secretary, £100 each. Interest on the loans was at 5 per cent until 1848 and thereafter at 4 per cent until 1861, when the last bond (Richard Taylor's) was paid off. The Society never had to pay interest on the total borrowed, as bonds began to be paid off or cancelled from 1832. The Society had to repay only £1200, as Sir Thomas Gery Cullum's bond was cancelled in 1831 after his death and the £200 out of Brown's £300 remaining unpaid was cancelled at his death in 1858, in accordance with the testamentary directions of these two Fellows. As the subscriptions actually paid came to less than half the net purchase amount another subscription was started in 1842, mainly by the efforts of Joseph Janson, who was a Fellow from 1831 to 1846. This subscription closed in 1846–47 and brought in £1015 18s.

The amounts spent directly and indirectly on the purchase of the Linnaean and Smithian natural history collections, books and manuscripts are as follows:

	£	s.	d.
Net cost	3150	0	0
Interest on unpaid balances	140	19	6
Total of interest paid on loans	1197	19	8
Total	£4488	19	2

THE LINNAEAN HERBARIUM

Linnaeus was justly proud of his library and his natural history collections and regarded them as valuable financial assets for his heirs. He declared in his "Voice from the grave to her who was my dear wife" that "invaluable as they [his herbaria] are, they will increase in value as time goes on. They are the greatest the world has ever seen. Do not sell them for less than 1000 ducats". As regards the herbarium, the Sloane Herbarium assembled by Sir Hans Sloane (1660–1753) was, however, much larger than Linnaeus's. On Linnaeus's death in 1778 his son Carl received his library and natural history collections but not the herbarium. Relations between Mrs Linnaeus and the son were far from happy and she locked the herbarium in the unheated and damp little museum at Hammarby to prevent his access to them. When the herbarium came ultimately into his hands, he found that rats, mice and mould had caused much damage. It seems probable that Linnaeus kept his collection of Swedish plants apart from his general herbarium and that this was almost totally destroyed, possibly by Linnaeus himself in his disturbed mental state before his death, for there are surprisingly few wild Swedish specimens in the Linnaean Herbarium.

On the death of Carl the younger in November 1783, the Linnaean collections became the property of his mother, who needed money to provide dowries for his four sisters. Unable to find a Swedish buyer willing to pay as much as the 1000 guineas sterling offered by James Edward Smith of Norwich (see Chapter 1) for the Linnaean collections, J. C. Acrel, acting for Mrs Linnaeus, sold them to Smith and they were shipped to London in

September 1784, to the dismay of many Swedes who naturally considered the sale a national disgrace.

The older herbaria consisted of specimens mounted on sheets bound into volumes; thus the Sloane Herbarium consists of 265 volumes, with specimens of a species dispersed through more than one volume. Thus comparison of such permanently fixed specimens for taxonomic study was difficult and time consuming. Linnaeus mounted his specimens on loose sheets that could be easily rearranged to suit any system of classification; thus all specimens referred to a particular genus could be placed together and compared. Moreover, other specimens could be added to them when necessary. All the world's herbaria use this Linnaean method. Linnaeus's example and teaching probably led to its general adoption in the second half of the eighteenth century.

Smith maintained the Linnaean Herbarium in the same state as received, although he gave away a few specimens to friends, in particular Sir Joseph Banks.

In 1836, i.e. not long after the acquisition by the Society of the Linnaean Collections, David Don and Richard Kippist made a manuscript catalogue of the Herbarium, giving a list of the genera, numbered from 1 to 1292, in the Linnaean order, with the number of sheets under each genus and an index to the genera. This catalogue was printed in the *Proceedings* for 1906–7 as an appendix to a paper by B. D. Jackson on a manuscript list of the Herbarium written by Linnaeus himself, presumably in 1755. A much more extensive Index to the Herbarium by B. D. Jackson, prefaced by much interesting information regarding the collection, forms a Supplement (1912) to the *Proceedings* for 1911–12. This Index gives the genera in alphabetical order and under each genus the species, also alphabetically. The prefatory information to this Index was reprinted in revised form, with additions and corrections to the Index and a photograph of the case containing the Herbarium, as a Supplement to the *Proceedings* for 1921–22; and further corrections were included in Part 2 of the *Catalogue of Manuscripts* (1937). Jackson left also in manuscript form a Catalogue of the Herbarium, which amounts to about 14000 sheets. Jackson's *Index to the Linnean Herbarium* (1912) contains a valuable biographical list of contributors to the Herbarium and a bibliography. To specific epithets Jackson added numbers 1, 2 or 3, according to when the name occurred in three lists by Linnaeus, which Jackson considered to be enumerations of the Herbarium, "in 1753 by the figure 1, in 1755 by the figure 2, in 1767 by the figure 3". Spencer Savage pointed out in 1937 the difficulties in accepting the dates assigned by Jackson to these lists and stated that "it is mere presumption to suppose that the markings had the intention of registering the specimens in the Herbarium". The numbers in Jackson's *Index* should be ignored because potentially misleading. Thus, because Jackson's *Index* under *Aristolochia* has the entry "longa.1", Nardi in *Webbia* 38: 267 (1984) concluded that a specimen (L.H. 1071.10) labelled "longa 12" *is* "to be considered the type specimen of the species" because "this according to Jackson (1912) was in Linnaeus's possession prior to 1753" when Linnaeus published the name *Aristolochia longa*. In fact, this specimen belongs to an endemic Algerian species *A. fontanesii* and was evidently sent to Linnaeus after April 1754 by Erik Brander (1720–1845), who was Swedish Consul in Algiers from 1753 to 1765. It is important to bear in mind that a specimen in the Linnaean Herbarium is not necessarily the primary element of his protologue and may have no relevance as regards selection of a lectotype.

When in 1941 Spencer Savage numbered the sheets of the Linnaean Herbarium he found so many errors and omissions in Jackson's manuscript catalogue that the Committee appointed to arrange for photographing of the Herbarium requested Savage to prepare a revised catalogue. The Society published his *A Catalogue of the Linnaean*

Herbarium in 1945 in an edition of 250 copies. The enterprise of the American botanist E. D. Merrill and a generous grant from the Carnegie Corporation of New York made possible this photographing of the Herbarium to provide a record which would have been invaluable had the Herbarium been destroyed during the course of the Second World War.

This war-time microfilm did not reveal on enlargement all the details needed for critical study. Accordingly, as mentioned before, the Society entered into association with the International Documentation Centre in 1958 for making a new photographic record of high quality. This was done between 11 July and 29 August 1959. It produced a set of 856 microfiches which throughout the world have made known the contents of the Linnaean Herbarium. An account of this new photographic record was published in *Taxon* 10: 16–19 (1961).

THE LINNAEAN ZOOLOGICAL COLLECTIONS

The Linnaean zoological collections consist chiefly of Lepidoptera and Coleoptera, dried fishes and shells, all of which have received much study by specialists.

On 1 April 1856, under the Presidency of the reforming and innovative Thomas Bell, the Council appointed a Committee consisting of Bell, George Bentham, Wilson Saunders and J. J. Bennett "to examine the Books, Manuscripts and Collections, forming the Library and Museum of Linnaeus and to report to the Council:— What they respectively consist of; Where they are now respectively deposited; In what state they are respectively; and whether any suggestions may occur to the Committee with reference to their preservation and exhibition to the Fellows of the Society and visitors".

The Committee devoted several meetings to their task. They found the manuscripts in excellent preservation and recommended that the Linnaean correspondence should be mounted on guards and bound in volumes. The plants and insects were likewise excellently preserved. William Yarrell, author of *History of British Fishes* (1835–39), helped with the examination of the specimens consisting of half-skins pasted upon paper, "generally in fair condition". As regards shells, the Committee, with the help of Silvanus Hanley, author of *Catalogue of recent bivalve Shells* (1842–56), regretted "to state that serious injury has resulted to the Linnean collection of shells from the careless mode in which they have been occasionally referred to by visitors and from the attempt of a former sub-curator to arrange them according to a modern method. Many of the specimens have been displaced from their original receptacles, and other difficulties have been created to the complete identification of the Linnaean species, and their discrimination from the specimens added by Sir J. E. Smith". The sub-curator incriminated could only have been Henry Sowerby, who was assistant in the Library and Museum from 1842 to 1853. Hanley offered to revise the collection, and his offer was gladly accepted. Hanley was a far from rapid worker, for it was reported to the Council in 1879 that he had not completed his revision, and an exhortatory letter had to be sent to him. Unfortunately, Hanley removed the shells from the small metal cases in which Linnaeus had placed them and which bore the numbers corresponding to the MSS catalogue of the "Museum Ulricae", the museum formed by Queen Ulrica, the Consort of King Adolf Fredrik of Sweden. A "Report on the Linnaean shell collection" by S. P. Dance in *Proceedings* 178: 1–24 (1967) gives the consequences of Hanley's intervention.

B. D. Jackson's "Catalogue of the Linnean specimens of Amphibia, Insecta and

Testacea noted by Carl von Linné" in *Proceedings* 125 (1912–13), *Supplement* (1913), provides a partial catalogue, with historical introduction, of zoological specimens. Earlier, the celebrated ichthyologist and herpetologist Albert C. L. G. Günther listed the fish specimens of the Linnaean collection in *Proceedings* III (1898–99): 15–38 (1899).

Other publications relating to Linnaean zoological material include C. H. Brunton *et al.*, "Brachiopods in the Linnaean collection", *Proceedings* 178: 161–183 (1967); M. C. Day and M. G. Fitton, "Discovery in the Linnaean collection of type material insects described by Johann Reinhold Forster", *Biol. Journal* 9: 31–43 (1977); and those listed by W. T. Stearn in W. Blunt, *The Compleat Naturalist*, 250–51 (1971).

THE SMITH HERBARIUM

James Edward Smith began to form his herbarium of British plants in 1777 when he was 18 and living in Norwich. To this he added many specimens gathered or given to him during his tour of 1786 to 1787 in The Netherlands, France, Italy and Switzerland, as well as specimens from British gardens at varying dates. Like his contemporaries with private herbaria such as Sir Joseph Banks and A. B. Lambert, he bought specimens but the greater part of his herbarium consists of material which came by gift or bequest. It includes the bequeathed East Anglian herbarium of the Norwich apothecary Hugh Rose (c. 1717–92) comprising 3573 specimens and the bequeathed Swiss herbarium of Edmund Davall (1763–98) comprising 4854 specimens. Smith was on friendly terms with many fellow botanists in Britain and abroad and he received numerous specimens as gifts from them. In all, 490 collectors are represented in his herbarium. Smith described many new species detected during the preparation of the text of *English Botany* (1790–1814), *Flora Britannica* (1800–4), *A Specimen of the Botany of New Holland* (1793), *Exotic Botany* (1804–7), 3348 articles contributed to *Rees's Cyclopaedia* (1802–20) and 52 papers in the *Transactions of the Linnean Society* (1791–1822). The types of these, as well as isotypes of species described by Olof Swartz from the West Indies, give the Smith Herbarium an especial importance.

In 1963, Spencer Savage numbered and catalogued all the sheets with his customary care as a preliminary to the photographing of the herbarium for the International Documentation Centre. The latter have made its contents available on microfiche. An account of the Smith Herbarium by W. T. Stearn will be found in the *Botanical Journal* of 1988.

SAVAGE'S CATALOGUE OF THE LINNAEAN HERBARIUM

Users of Savage's *Catalogue of the Linnaean Herbarium* can have no conception of the difficult war-time conditions under which he compiled this scholarly work. He could not refer directly to the sheets of the Herbarium itself, then safely out of London and unavailable. He had to base his catalogue entirely on a copy of the Carnegie Corporation's 1941 microfilm. There was no microfilm viewer at his disposal, so W. H. T. Tams ingeniously devised one out of a cigar box, a pocket lens of 8 × magnification, and an electric light bulb and flex. Using this contraption Savage patiently scrutinized the microfilm centimetre by centimetre, evening after evening, for nearly two years, despite air-raid alarms, and recorded the particulars visible on every photograph. This was a demanding task, needing high concentration and tenacity and imposing considerable eye-strain, probably only he could have accomplished it so well with equipment so cheap and simple.

Chapter 17

The Library

University and other scientific institutions and museums throughout Britain nowadays possess libraries devoted to their special interests and essential for their work. This was not so at the founding of the Linnean Society in 1788. Before then, naturalists, such as John Ray and Hans Sloane in the second half of the eighteenth century, assembled large private working libraries, but the increase of natural history literature then became such that only a few wealthy individuals, such as Banks, Smith and Lambert, could maintain libraries with adequate coverage. Becoming inevitably beyond the means of private individuals in the early nineteenth century, library formation and upkeep then became the task of such co-operative bodies as the Linnean Society and provincial literary and philosophical societies. The Linnean Society from its beginning set out to make natural history works available to its members. It first purchased a bookcase as early as 1790 for books were already being presented, notably by Banks and his curator, Dryander, to form a library.

During the first decade the Society relied almost entirely on donations of books for the growth of its Library and has always been grateful for them. The records of accessions to the Library in the Society's Minutes have proved very helpful to natural history bibliographers seeking to ascertain precise dates of publication of works, particularly those issued in parts, containing new scientific names. Only £26 was spent on it during the first decade, but in 1798 the first "Library Fund" was started by making every Fellow elected after May of that year contribute £1 to the Fund in addition to his Admission Fee of £1 11s. 6d. After the Fee was raised to £5 5s. in 1823 and to £6 in 1829 the Fund continued to have allocated to it £1 of the Fee until 1836, when this stopped and the Fund ceased to be mentioned.

During the depressed period of 1838–58 the average annual expenditure on the Library dropped to £18, the lowest amount since the first decade. Under Bell and Bentham the expenditure rose from an annual average of £12 12s. during 1848–58 to £62 in 1858–68 and £82 in 1868–78. Then, in 1879, the Council, after much discussion at five meetings and the usual reference to a committee, resolved to form "The Library Fund of the Linnean Society of London", to be established by voluntary contributions, and to start it voted £100 from the Society's common funds. Thus little came out of so much talk and Bentham, who was not then a Councillor but again became one in May 1880, had another plan, which he set forth in a printed letter distributed to members of Council in June 1880. Both the Council's Resolution and Bentham's plan came to nothing.

Bentham died in 1884. He left in his will £1000 to the Society, with the expressed desire that it should be used to open a Library Fund, but the Society received only £567 11s. 2d., the reason being, to quote the phraseology of the legal firm explaining it, that "the amount was not payable out of Bentham's Pure Personalty, and as it was in the nature of a charitable bequest, it could be paid only in proportion that the Pure

(a)

(b)

(c)

(d)

Personalty bore to the Realty and the Impure Personalty"! Presumably the lawyers did better out of such distinctions than the Society. In 1885 the Council, on a motion by Thiselton-Dyer and Carruthers, once again resolved to establish a formal "Library Fund" with £500, the first instalment of Bentham's legacy, as a beginning. The Fund was to form a separate item in the Society's accounts. This "Fund" never appeared as a separate item in the published accounts, but in the financial statements published in the *Proceedings* for 1885–86, 1887–88 and 1889–90 the words "Mr. Bentham's Bequest as a Library Fund" appeared in brackets opposite the item in the table of investments of £450 Forth Bridge Railway Stock, which was purchased with £500 of Bentham's legacy. After 1890 even this indication vanished, to reappear in the same context as "Library Fund" in 1925. Although it ceased so speedily to appear even nominally in the published accounts the Fund retained a sort of cryptic existence, for it is mentioned in the Council Minutes now and then, as in 1886, when it was resolved to add the balance – £67 11s. 2d. – of Bentham's legacy to it, and in 1894 when the legacy of £100 left by Algernon Peckover was ordered to be included in it.

In 1911, once more the Society received a legacy of £500, this time left by Francis Tagart, and on this occasion the sum was invested as a distinct "Tagart Fund", with the interest used exclusively for the purchase of books, and the Fund appearing as a separate item in the financial statement for 1911–12 and succeeding years.

In the session of 1923–24 the Council made yet another attempt, the fourth since 1798, to create a Library Fund, and sent out a circular to members inviting contributions. As an inducement to subscribe it was stated that one Fellow had undertaken to contribute a sum, subject to a maximum of £250, equal to 10 per cent of the subscription raised within six months. In the circular no reference was made to any existing or previous Library Fund except the Tagart Fund, which looks as if the Council in 1923, as in 1911, was unaware of the history of the Fund.

The appeal yielded the paltry sum of £21 2s., but the Fund was more or less formally established, for in the financial statement in the *Proceedings* for 1924–25 the words "Library Fund" reappeared as just mentioned. In the 1926–27 session half of the legacy of £200 left by Alfred Osten Walker, £100 bequeathed by Frank Morey and £90 by Mrs Mary Anne Stebbing were invested as additions to the Fund. Finally, in the published accounts for 1927–28 the Library Account was separated from the General Account, but has subsequently been united with it.

The first catalogue of the Library was strictly not a catalogue but a succession of lists of additions and donations printed in the *Transactions*, the first instalment in Volume 5 (1800) and the seventeenth and last in Volume 21 (1855). Up to Volume 20 the entries were numbered consecutively and had then reached 2977. The entries in Volume 21 were not numbered but occupy 29 pages. This was most inconvenient for discovering the contents of the Library and, after the Society had been installed in the central block of Burlington House, the Council directed Richard Kippist, who with the Porter constituted the entire staff, to prepare a separate catalogue. He was supposed to have it ready by 1862, but the task proved too much for him and he had to be allowed a temporary assistant. Even then not until 1866 did the catalogue begin to appear. It was published in three

Plate XX   Staff: (a) Richard Kippist, from a photograph in the series "Literary and Scientific Portrait Club", begun in 1854. (b) A. R. Gage, from a photograph in the Society's collection. (c) W. G. Chaloner. (d) Spencer Savage, from a drawing by E. J. Savage, 1929, in the Society's collection.

parts: Part I (1866), pp. 1–289, containing separate papers and works and completed Journals; Part II (1867), pp. 1–85, containing Transactions and such-like publications of Societies and Supplement to Part I; Part III (1877), pp. 1–109, containing additions from 1866 to 1876.

After the Centenary it was resolved to prepare a new catalogue in two parts, to be issued free to Fellows. The preparation was entrusted to J. E. F. Harting, the Librarian, and A. W. Kappel, his assistant. Although nearly £200 was spent in hiring external assistance for them, they did the work so badly that, after Part II had been issued in proof in 1893 and Part I likewise in 1895, it had to be taken out of their hands altogether, the proofs scrapped and the services of an expert bibliographer called in. Ultimately, the catalogue appeared in 1896 as a single volume of 727 pages, with periodicals included in the general alphabetical arrangement.

In pleasing contrast to the expense incurred and the incompetence displayed in the preparation of the 1896 catalogue, B. D. Jackson, then General Secretary, and Spencer Savage, then Clerk, bore entirely the much heavier labour of preparing the much more scholarly fourth and current catalogue, published in 1925. The catalogue is a single volume of 860 pages.

Facilities for proper use of the Library developed but slowly. Up to 1805, the Library and Museum were open only from noon to 4 pm on Tuesdays, the meeting days, but on Robert Brown's appointment in that year as Clerk, Librarian and Housekeeper the Library was open on two days a week during the same hours. In 1806, the Council permitted borrowing of books, but only on written application. From 1822 both Library and Museum were open from Monday to Friday from noon to 4 pm, and from 1826 members could borrow up to two books at a time on written application to the Council. In 1829, probably as the purchase of the Linnaean Collections compelled economy, the Library was open only on three days a week and the Museum on the other two days for the same four hours. Later on Kippist, who had succeeded David Don as Librarian in 1842, disregarded the restriction and kept both places open each of the days. When the Society received in 1857 free quarters in Burlington House, one condition was that members of all Societies housed there should be allowed to consult each other's libraries, and that men of letters and science should be admitted for reference and study on orders given by Fellows of the Societies.

Since 1857, the Society has from time to time widened facilities so as to permit not merely consultation but also borrowing of books by certain recognized Scientific Societies not resident in Burlington House, by the British Museum, by any Government Department and by the Science Museum. In 1928, the Society's Library became one of the Outlier Libraries of the (National) Central Library for Students, whereby students who are not members of the Society may, by applying through the National Central Library, borrow from the Linnean Society books which they might not otherwise be able to consult, and members of the Society may obtain through the National Central Library books not in the Society's Library. This alliance brought to the Society a grant of £2000, spread over the years 1928–30, from the Carnegie United Kingdom Trust. The grant had to be spent as received on the purchase of books, and this explains the steep rise in Library expenditure during 1928–36 already mentioned.

In 1852, it was estimated that the amount of shelving space likely to be required by the Society, allowing for additions up to 1882, was 2500 square feet. In 1936, the Library filled approximately 6000 square feet of shelving and had overflowed into the former residential flat. Movable racks in the basement have eased this.

Although the Society has bought important reference books throughout its history and continues to do so, the Library has benefited greatly from the generosity of Fellows who, in accordance with tradition, have presented copies of their works to the Library. The bulk of the Library consists of the periodical publications issued by other scientific societies or academies or published independently. Between 600 and 700 periodicals, representing over 50 countries and about 20 different languages, were received; over 500 of them by exchange or gift and the rest by purchase up to the Second World War. Before 1800 fewer than ten were received by exchange. The latest information appears in periodicals and much information remains available only in them.

During the nineteenth century the Library met an evident need by Fellows. During the twentieth century the establishment of so many other libraries, particularly in the London area, obtaining the same periodicals as the Library, lessened its utility as regards these. After the Second World War the cost of purchasing some journals and the cost of printing and posting the Society's publications in exchange for others together with storage space problems led to a drastic curtailment in acquisition. At one time the Library acquired works relating to the natural history of any part of the world. By the mid-twentieth century this was leading to costly and unnecessary duplication with the British Museum (Natural History) and the Royal Botanic Gardens, Kew.

Hence, in 1979, the Society decided on a drastic reduction of its exchanges for periodicals and to concentrate its acquisitions to works on the natural history of northwestern Europe and to a lesser extent on the northern hemisphere.

The Society has seldom suffered serious loss in books, but a bad case occurred in 1854 when 166 volumes were reported as having been stolen from the Smithian Library, purchased in 1829, and stored in 1854 in an attic in the Society's house in Soho Square, and apparently sold as waste paper. The culprit was suspected to be the Society's Porter, who had lived in the house but had died in June 1854. More recent losses from many London libraries, including that of the Society, have led to the installation of metal grilles in the Reading Room.

For nearly thirty years the Society paid no particular attention to the Library of Linnaeus, numbering about 1500 volumes that were distributed amongst the ordinary volumes in the Library and even lent out to members. Fortunately, Smith had inscribed their title pages with the note "E. Bibl. Linn. propria". One result of the report of the special committee of 1856 was the segregation of the books of Linnaeus, the placing of them alongside his Collections and the prohibition of lending them. There is no special published catalogue of the Linnaean Library, but in the General Catalogue of the Library the Linnaean volumes are distinguished by the letter $\mathscr{L}$. The Linnaean Library was moved into the basement strong-room, along with the Linnaean specimens, in 1971–73.

In 1881, a beginning was made with the binding of the Linnaean correspondence, which finished in 1900, to form 17 red leather-bound volumes. The collection of non-biological Linnaean Theses was bound in 13 volumes in 1928–29 under the supervision of R. W. T. Gunther.

At least from 1859, and possibly earlier, a Library Committee has supervised the work of the Library and submits its recommendations to the Council.

Sale of duplicates and other material

From time to time, a few duplicates have been put on sale to Fellows. However, in June 1963, to the dismay of some Fellows, the Society put on sale at Messrs Sotheby and Co. a collection of 64 water-colour drawings of Indian birds, mammals and plants executed between 1774 and 1782 by three Muslim artists for Lady Impey. Later, in November 1974, Messrs Christie, Manson & Woods sold by auction a large collection of duplicate books. A further sale of books took place in June 1976 by Messrs Sotheby, with Edwards's *Natural History of Uncommon Birds* (1743–51) and *Gleanings in Natural History* (1758–64) going for £2200. A few more were sold by Sotheby's in May 1978 and others in July 1979.

The decay of public morality has unfortunately made it necessary to spend part of this money on library security measures, instead of books.

Chapter 18

Portraits and busts

On the walls of the Society's rooms hang many impressive gilt-framed portraits commemorating former Presidents and other worthies distinguished in natural history, their diversity of pose, dress, facial type and expression reflecting the diversity of character and period. A social historian or a psychologist would find ample material here for study and speculation. Certainly they deserve much more than a passing glance. The Society's acquisition of portraits began with the gift by R. A. Salisbury in 1807 of Zoffany's portrait of Daniel Solander (1736–82) which hangs in the Library. The following notes unavoidably repeat some information scattered throughout the chronological record in this volume.

In the Entrance Hall is a copy by Lorens Pasch the younger of the portrait of *Carl Linnaeus* (1707–78) at Versailles by the celebrated Swedish painter Alexander Roslin. The original was painted in 1775 and is recorded in Tycho Tullberg, *Linnéporträtt*, nos 116, 119, pl. 14 (1907). It depicts Linnaeus in purple dress, seated at a table, wearing the prized decoration of the Royal Order of the Northern Star and a sprig of *Linnaea borealis*, the twinflower, in his left hand. Robert Brown presented this to the Society.

In the Lobby at the foot of the stairs hangs a copy of the "Bridegroom portrait" of *Linnaeus* by J. H. Scheffel, made in 1739 and now at Hammarby. Dressed in a red coat, Linnaeus rests his right arm on a copy of the octavo *Systema Naturea* and holds a sprig of *Linnaea borealis*. This portrait is recorded in Tullberg, *Linnéporträtt*, no. 30, frontispiece (1907), and reproduced in colour there and in W. Blunt's *The Compleat Naturalist* 138 (1971). Nearby is a portrait of the celebrated German-born flower painter *George Dionys Ehret* (1708–70), shirt informally open, intently examining a shoot of *Cestrum diurnum*. This was made by George James about 1767 and was bequeathed to the Society in 1941 by Sir Arthur Evans, reputed to be a descendant of Ehret. It is reproduced in Greta Calmann, *Ehret*, pl. 6 (1977); she notes that, in common with another portrait, it shows "a pronounced chin with a dimple, full lips and somewhat heavy bone structure and very strong hands". Ehret began as a gardener at Heidelberg but spent most of his life as an artist in England. Both he and Linnaeus were employed by George Clifford at the same time in 1736 at Hartekamp in Holland, the one as artist, the other as botanist, and became life-long friends. Ehret contributed 21 plates to Linnaeus's *Hortus Cliffortianus* (1738) and published independently in 1736 a plate illustrating Linnaeus's sexual system of plant classification. Next to this is a portrait of Ehret's patron, the wealthy Nürnberg physician and bibliophile *Christoph Jacob Trew* (1695–1769), the author of sumptuous botanical works with many plates by Ehret. He went to Nürnberg in 1733 to meet Trew, who gave him some instruction in floral structure and encouraged him thereafter by purchasing and publishing his coloured drawings of plants. This portrait is a copy of one at Erlangen and was given by Trew to his English correspondent, the Quaker merchant and plant collector Peter Collinson in 1752.

In the office by the lift is a portrait of *Daniel Oliver* (1830–1916), a faithful copy by Miss Zilera of the original done in 1894 by J. W. Forster. Oliver was Keeper of the Kew Herbarium from 1864 to 1890 and also Professor of Botany at University College, London, from 1861 to 1888 in succession to John Lindley. He was an accomplished artist and this portrait shows him intently painting. His son, Francis Wall Oliver (1864–1951), followed him as a Professor of Botany at University College, which from 1829 to 1929 had only three botanical professors, all highly distinguished.

The portrait of *Francis Masson* (1741–1805) is by George Garraud. He was born in Aberdeen and died in Montreal. Trained as a gardener, he spent most of his life as a plant collector for the Royal Garden at Kew, being at the Cape of Good Hope from 1772 to 1774, then in the Canary Islands and Azores, the West Indies, Spain and Portugal from 1776 to 1785 and out again in South Africa from 1786 to 1795. In 1796 he became a Fellow. Sent out to eastern North America in 1798, he evidently found the harsher winter conditions uncongenial and he died in 1805. Masson published *Stapeliae novae* in 1796 to 1799 with plates drawn by himself. He introduced innumerable plants into cultivation.

Edward Stanley (1779–1849), for many years rector of Alderley, became in 1837 Bishop of Norwich. Like many clergymen then he devoted part of his leisure to the study of natural history, particularly birds. His association with the Linnean Society began with his election as a Fellow in 1828 and he was President from 1837 to 1849. The portrait is by J. H. Maguire.

Somewhat out of the way, in the Executive Secretary's Office, hangs a portrait of the barrister and botanist *James Ebenezer Bicheno* (1785–1851), Secretary of the Society from 1825 to 1832, looking down upon his present successor. In the same room is a portrait of an unidentified ornately dressed young gentleman in the past unacceptably identified as Sir Joseph Banks or William Curtis; the Office has a pastel portrait by Helen Monostorn of *Theodore O'Grady* (b. 1919), Executive Secretary for 28 years.

The portraits in the Meeting Room naturally come most often to the gaze if not the curiosity of Fellows. Above the presidential chair, presiding as it were over the meeting, is a copy of the 1774 portrait of *Linnaeus* by P. Krafft the elder, belonging to the Royal Swedish Academy of Sciences, Stockholm, and recorded in Tullberg, *Linnéporträtt*, no. 107, pl. 11 (1907). Dressed in dark blue, Linnaeus holds both a large book and a sprig of *Linnaea borealis* in his left hand and wears the decoration of the Royal Order of the Northern Star.

To the right of the doorway on entering the Meeting Room is a portrait of the Rev. *Miles Berkeley* (1803–89), one of the many English clergymen who have notably contributed to natural history, his speciality being mycology. A classical scholar, he checked the latinity of Bentham and Hooker's *Genera Plantarum* (1862–83), the descriptions in which are models of botanical Latin. *Archibald Menzies* (1754–1842), whose portrait hangs nearby, was a Scottish naval surgeon who served as naturalist on Vancouver's voyage round the world in the *Discovery* (1791–95) and among much else introduced the Chilean monkey puzzle tree, *Araucaria araucana*, into cultivation. He climbed Mauna Loa on Molokai, Hawaiian Islands, in 1794 and David Douglas found in 1833 that he was still locally remembered as the red-faced man who cut off the limbs of men and gathered grass! The painting of *Charles Darwin* (1809–92) by John Collier, son-in-law of T. H. Huxley, has been mentioned earlier. *Nathaniel Wallich* (1786–1854) was painted by Lucas. A Dane by birth, he became surgeon to the Danish settlement at Serampore, Bengal, in 1807 and then from 1815 to 1841 superintendent of the Calcutta Botanic Garden; he made immense botanical collections in India.

On the wall behind the rostrum are portraits of *Robert Brown* (1773–1858) by H. W. Pickersgill; of *John Joseph Bennett* (1801–75) by Eddis; of *John Lubbock* (1834–1913), Lord Avebury, by Leslie Ward; and of *Walter Percy Sladen* (1849–1900) by Wels. *Robert Brown's* remarkable contributions to botany earned him the designation of "Botanicorum facile princeps" from Alexander von Humboldt. He was the Society's President from 1849 to 1853. Outside botany he is best known for his investigation of the Brownian movement. *J. J. Bennett*, for many years Brown's assistant, followed him as Keeper of the Botanical Department of the British Museum and served the Society as Secretary from 1840 to 1860. The services of *John Lubbock*, President from 1881 to 1886, by profession a banker, to botany, entomology, anthropology, education and the well-being of the general public were many, varied and important. As a Member of Parliament he sponsored bills relating to the protection of open spaces, ancient monuments and wild birds, limitation of working hours for shop assistants and institution of bank holidays (once called St Lubbock's Days). No President of the Linnean Society has contributed more to the general good of the British people or contributed to more branches of biology than this highly talented, public-spirited, largely self-educated amateur naturalist. *Percy Sladen*, a distinguished zoologist with wide cultural interests, the Society's Zoological Secretary from 1885 to 1895, is remembered chiefly through the Percy Sladen Trust instituted by his widow Constance (1848–1906), who was one of the first woman Fellows elected in 1904.

Other portraits in the Meeting Room are those of *Richard Pulteney* (1730–1801) by T. Beach; *William Jackson Hooker* (1785–1866) by Gambarella; his son, *Joseph Dalton Hooker* (1817–1911), by H. Herkomer; *George Bentham* (1800–84) by Lowes Dickinson; *Nathaniel Bagshaw Ward* (1791–1868) by J. P. Knight; and *Aylmer Bourke Lambert* (1761–1842) by John Russell. *Richard Pulteney*, a medical man and amateur naturalist, here portrayed in 1783 wearing a red négligée cap, wrote two major works, *A General View of the Writings of Linnaeus* (1784), which preceded the founding of the Linnean Society, and *Historical and Biographical Sketches of the Progress of Botany in England* (2 vols, 1790), both still valuable sources of information. *W. J. Hooker*, having failed as a brewer in Suffolk, became a successful Professor of Botany in Glasgow from 1820 to 1841 and then, from 1841 to 1865, the first director of the newly nationalized Royal Botanic Gardens, Kew; an immense number of important publications, with over 640 illustrations drawn by himself, stand to his credit. The artist has noted his shrewdness. *J. D. Hooker*, as distinguished a botanist as his father, followed him as director of Kew. His collaboration with Bentham resulted in their monumental *Genera Plantarum* mentioned above. *George Bentham*, one of the most industrious and perceptive botanists of all time, was President from 1861 to 1874 when his Presidency ended abruptly. As Carruthers, who had been an opponent, wrote in 1891: "no man ever occupied the Chair who was more whole-hearted in his devotion to the Society, more unceasing in his labours on its behalf, or more liberal in its support". *Nathaniel Ward*, a doctor in the smoky East End of London, is best known for his invention of the Wardian case which enabled plants to be grown indoors under the uncongenial atmospheric conditions of Victorian London and to survive long sea voyages for introduction from one country to another. His portrait indicates a little of his "singularly charming manner, utterly free from all vanity, self-interest and self-love and ever ready to encourage anything good or true in others" which impressed his contemporaries. *A. B. Lambert*, an original member of the Society and a Vice-President for nearly 50 years, amassed an enormous private herbarium intended as a bequest to the British Museum but which, owing to mismanagement of his financial affairs, had unfortunately to be sold by auction and dispersed widely after his death to satisfy his creditors (cf. N. S. Miller in *Taxon* 19: 489–553; 1970).

Portraits likewise ornament the Stairway from the Lobby to the Library. Near the bottom is a somewhat crude copy of the portrait at Oxford of *Johann Jacob Dillenius* (1687–1747), first Sherardian Professor of Botany in Oxford and the author and illustrator of *Hortus Elthamensis* (1732). He was born in Darmstadt, came to England in 1721 and became a founder and first President of the Botanical Society. He is depicted with bulging rubicund cheeks and a look almost foretelling his death from apoplexy. His right hand points to a drawing of *Sprekelia formosissima*. Next comes a painting by John Linnell of *John Claudius Loudon* (1783–1843), the extraordinarily industrious and well-informed Scottish writer on horticulture and dendrology, author of *Arboretum et Fruticetum Britannicum* (8 vols, 1838) and much else, and a noted landscape architect. He was elected a Fellow in 1806. Beside this hangs a portrait of *William Yarrell* (1784–1856), the ornithologist and ichthyologist, Treasurer of the Society from 1849 to 1865. A monument in St James's Church, Piccadilly, commemorates him. *Thomas Bell* (1792–1880), portrayed by H. W. Pickersgill, was a distinguished dental surgeon and zoologist, President from 1853 to 1861, who took a very important part in reforming the administration of the Society and promoting its utility. According to Carruthers, "he was greatly beloved by all who knew him; his gracious presence in the Chair was, as I well remember, singularly encouraging to the younger and more diffident Fellows to take part in the business of the Meetings". He retired to Selborne, Hampshire, and produced in 1876 and 1877 the standard edition of Gilbert White's *The Natural History and Antiquities of Selborne* (first published 1788). The portrait of *George Busk* (1807–85) was painted by his daughter, Miss E. M. Busk. A naval surgeon who became a distinguished zoologist, he served the Society as Zoological Secretary from 1857 to 1868. The pioneer marine biologist *William Carmichael M'Intosh* (1838–1931) of St Andrews, who looks with his long beard a typical Victorian Scottish Professor of Zoology, was from 1913 to 1932 President of the Ray Society which published his *Monograph of the British Marine Annelids* (4 vols in 9 parts, 1873 to 1923). His publications included *The Life-histories of the British Marine Food-fishes* (1897) and about 300 medical, biographical and zoological works and papers.

The Library has high on the wall at its west end a portrait by Thomas Phillips of the masterful *Joseph Banks* (1743–1820), "the autocrat of the philosophers", companion of Cook on his voyage round the world in the *Endeavour* (1768–71), President of the Royal Society from 1778 until his death in 1820 and the Linnean Society's first Honorary Member. This lofty position, while in keeping with Banks's station in life, leads to its being unjustly disregarded. Below this is the portrait of *Daniel Carlsson Solander* (1736–82) by Johann Zoffany, Banks's Swedish librarian and Linnaeus's one-time favourite student, who by accompanying Banks and Cook on the *Endeavour* voyage became the pioneer investigator of Pacific natural history. Near the entrance is a 1789 engraved portrait of *Linnaeus*, published by J. & J. Boydell based on Roslin's portrait, with an ornate crimped paper surround.

The historic meeting of 10 January 1905 when women were first formally admitted to the Fellowship of the Society is the subject of the large painting by James Sant on a wall of the Stairway (see Chapter 6). The figures from left to right are: Miss *Emma Louise Turner* (1866–1946), ornithologist; Miss *Annie Lorrain Smith* (1854–1937); *Benjamin Daydon Jackson* (1846–1927), the General Secretary; Miss *Sarah Marianne Silver* (d. before 1965); Mrs *Lilian Jane Veley* née Nutcomb (d. 1936), zoological microscopist, signing the Book of Admission and Obligation; Mrs *Constance Sladen* (1848–1901), widow of the zoologist

Percy Sladen; *Dukinfield Henry Scott* (1854–1934), the Botanical Secretary; Mrs (later Lady) *Crisp*, wife of Frank Crisp, taking the hand of fellowship from *William Abbott Herdman* (1858–1924), the President; *Frank Crisp* (1843–1919), the Treasurer. The original painting as exhibited at the Royal Academy in 1906, which had been commissioned by Crisp, portrayed at the right-hand side Mrs Stebbing and her husband, the Rev. Thomas R. Stebbing (1835–1926), the Zoological Secretary. When the Society received this painting from Lady Crisp in 1919, after Crisp's death and in accordance with his wishes, these two figures had been painted out. The original and later version are reproduced by Margot Walker in *The Linnean* 1: 10 (1982). At the east end of the Library is a portrait of *James Edward Smith* (1759–1828), the purchaser of the Linnaean collections from Linnaeus's widow, one of the three founders of the Linnean Society and its President for 40 years; he is probably best known as the author of Sowerby and Smith's *English Botany* and the collector of the Smith Herbarium now in the Society's keeping.

Anyone who toils up the stairs to the Second Floor will find another array of portraits. Outside the Council Room is one of *William Kirby* (1759–1850), rector of Barham, Suffolk, celebrated for his entomological works, notably *Monographia Apum Angliae* (2 vols, 1815–26). Next to this is one of *St. George Jackson Mivart* (1827–1900), at first a barrister, later a zoologist and for a time a professor at Louvain, Zoological Secretary of the Society from 1874 to 1880. A devout Roman Catholic, he was excommunicated for his heretical belief in evolution and, like several contemporaries, became a mentally tortured victim of theological and scientific conflict.

Within the Council Room hangs a further collection of impressive large gilt-framed portraits, beginning on the east wall with that of *Alexander McLeay* (1767–1848) by Lawrence. He served the Society as Secretary from 1798 to 1825, when he was appointed Colonial Secretary of New South Wales and emigrated to Sydney. His entomological studies led him to propose an ingenious quinary system of biological classification accepted by a few naturalists but later rejected by all. Next comes a portrait by Eddis of *Edward Forster* (1765–1849). He and two brothers, Thomas Furly Forster (1761–1825) and Benjamin Meggot Forster (1764–1829), were keen Essex amateur botanists. Edward, a banker, was the Society's Treasurer from 1816 to 1849. The adjoining portrait is of *Benjamin Daydon Jackson* (1846–1927), first Editor of the *Index Kewensis* (1893–95), General Secretary of the Society from 1902 to 1926 and an industrious botanical bibliographer and Linnaean scholar. *George James Allman* (1812–98), the Society's President from 1874 to 1881, here portrayed by Miss E. M. Busk, was Professor of Botany in Dublin from 1844 to 1855 and Professor of Natural History in Edinburgh from 1855 to 1870.

On the west wall the portrait of *Sydney Howard Vines* (1849–1934) by Collier, the Society's President from 1900 to 1904, Professor of Botany at Oxford from 1888 to 1919, depicts him resplendent in Cambridge University scarlet and grey doctorial robes. His English translation (1886) of K. Prantl's German elementary text book of botany was once usually known as "Prantl and Vines". This led to a lady's enquiry at the Natural History Museum: "Dr. Rendle, I know what vines are, but, please, what is a prantl?". *Henry Seymer* (1745–1800), whose portrait was presented by a relative, A. B. Lambert, never belonged to the Linnean Society but knew many eighteenth-century naturalists, among them Pulteney and Solander, and amassed in his home at Hanford, Dorset, a natural history collection especially of insects, shells and minerals; the genus *Seymeria* (Scrophulariaceae) commemorates him. By the entrance is a portrait of *William Carruthers* (1830–1922). He joined the botanical staff of the British Museum in 1859 and was Keeper from 1871 to 1895 of the Department of Botany in the British Museum, which he doughtily defended against annexation by the Royal Botanic Gardens, Kew. Carruthers specialized in the study of cryptogamic plants. He served the Society as President from 1886 to 1890 and held strong views on the conduct of the Society's affairs. His "Catalogue of the portraits of Fellows etc. belonging to the Society" published in *Proceedings* 1888–1890: 30–46 (1891) has proved most helpful in preparing this chapter, especially as he himself had known many of those portrayed.

Some of the plaster casts of busts listed by Carruthers were discarded some years ago but five remain. The Society, however, still possesses six marble busts, three by the well-known sculptor Francis Chantrey (1781–1814). These are the subject of an article by Margot Walker in *The Linnean* 1 no. 3: 9–11 (1984). The bust by Chantrey of *James Edward Smith* stands in a corner on the stairway. His busts of *Joseph Banks* and of *Charles Hatchett* (1765–1847), a Fellow of the Society, renowned not for work in natural history but in analytical chemistry especially on organic substances, are both in the Library. Here also are busts of *Robert Brown* and *Thomas Bell*, both by Peter Slater. The other bust, downstairs, at the entrance of the Meeting Room is of *William Sharp MacLeay* (1792–1865) by Charles Summers. He was the eldest son of Alexander McLeay and, like him, a zoologist.

In addition to the framed portraits on public view, the Society possesses a large collection of prints and drawings of naturalists catalogued by Margot Walker. A selection of 78 of these, with a catalogue entitled *The Naturalist delineated* by Mrs Walker, was exhibited at the Presidential Conversazione of 25 April 1980. The collection amounts to over 1360 items portraying about 850 individuals; 766 of portrait prints, together with a separate collection of 89 portraits of Count Georges-Louis Buffon (1707–88), came to the Society by bequest from Arthur Russell, FLS (1824–92), Member of Parliament for Tavistock, Devon, from 1857 to 1885, a keen naturalist with a private menagerie. This gift attracted other gifts of portraits, notably a large one from William Rushton Parker (1853–1943), for many years a general practitioner in Kendal. Thus over the years the Society has come to own one of the world's most extensive collections of portraits of naturalists.

Chapter 19

Membership

As mentioned in Chapter 2, the Linnean Society began with three Honorary Members, 20 Fellows, 39 Foreign Members and 11 Associates. Like the Royal Society, it had an elitist concept of itself, with inclusion in its select company regarded as a privilege and honour to be coveted. However, even smug exclusive groups cannot survive on self-esteem alone and must necessarily seek money from membership subscriptions, donations and grants, usually by increasing the number of members.

FELLOWS

Fellows constitute a class many times larger than all the other classes put together and are the main scientific and financial support of the Society. The scientific work of Fellows has been a subject in not a few Presidential Addresses, but only once has an Address been devoted almost entirely to the relation of the Fellows to the Society. This critical and illuminating Address was delivered by David Prain in 1919 and published in *Proceedings* 131 (1918–19): 22–37 (1919); it still merits attention. Some of the reforms anticipated in this Address were embodied in the revised Bye-Laws of 1920.

The qualifications for Fellowship are a declared active interest in a branch of natural history, supported if possible but not necessarily by publications and a signed recommendation by a Fellow or Fellows, and the capacity to pay the current annual subscription, followed by approval of the Council and balloting by Fellows at a General Meeting. The Council has the power to refuse approval of, and the Fellows to blackball, a candidate considered unsuitable, but have rarely used these powers; the disgraceful exclusion on petty grounds of J. E. Gray and Mrs F. M. Farquharson, both very suitable (see pp. 21, 91), is particularly notorious because so very exceptional. On being admitted at a General Meeting, the new Fellow signs the obligation book and takes the hand of the President, who then declares "By the authority and in the name of the Linnean Society of London I admit you a Fellow thereof". For these occasions Stearn revived during his Presidency (1979–82) the former traditional wearing of an old-fashioned tricorn hat, but later Presidents have not followed this antique practice (see pp. 14, 15).

Most Honorary Members, Foreign Members and Associates remain so for life. No Fellow is elected for life, but any Fellow of long standing having reached a certain age may, by paying a Composition Fee, become thereafter a Fellow for life, notwithstanding possible but extremely improbable ejection. Those who do not compound ordinarily remain, or should remain, Fellows only so long as they continue to pay within a specified period of grace their annual contributions. Of course undesirable Fellows may be, and in the past have been, removed for reasons other than failure to pay their dues. There have been a very few instances of a Fellow dying so soon after election and qualification that his name never appeared in a printed List, and also one instance, in 1897, of a candidate being elected nearly a month after his death; he had died in New Zealand and news of his death did not reach the Society in time. The names of a few Fellows occur more than once in the chronological list, owing to their withdrawal and re-election at a later date. A very few Fellows have ceased to be so, only to be elected as Associates. All these circumstances are minor difficulties in the compilation of an accurate census either of annual members or of the total Fellowship. The great difficulty, that only an inordinate expenditure of time and toil could overcome, is caused by the past neglect for many years to carry out the Bye-Laws regarding the "rejection", as it was called up to 1904, or "removal", the present more delicate term, of Fellows who had ceased to pay their annual dues, whereby the names of Fellows, useless to the Society, remained on the List year after year. Accordingly, in the first table given below only the numbers of elections are given, which exceed the true number of qualified Fellows by a small and indefinite percentage comprising candidates who did not qualify after election and Fellows elected more than once.

Census of Elections of Fellows from 1788 to May 1986

Period	Number of Elections	Period	Number of Elections
1788–98	196	1888–98	316
1798–1808	202	1898–1908	306
1808–18	217	1908–18	268
1818–28	306	1918–28	412
1828–38	225	1928–36	255
1838–48	157	1936–46	251
1848–58	149	1946–56	559
1858–68	265	1956–66	483
1868–78	328	1966–76*	1285
1878–88	415	1976–86	

* Including student members.

The first Charter gave no power either to limit the number of Fellows or the number of elections to be held in a session. The Charter of 1904 conferred the power lacking in the first, but it was not until 1919 that the first limitation of number to 710 Fellows was made. Four years later financial considerations compelled the raising of the limit to 800. In 1943, the limit of the number of Fellows was raised to 1000. Later it was made more flexible by a Bye-Law stating "the limit of the number of persons to be elected shall be determined from time to time by Council".

The descriptions of candidates are occasionally quaintly expressive, such as "parochial botanist" and "indigenous botanist". Elections have seldom caused trouble but, in 1810, there was an unusual occurrence. William Bullock (fl. 1795–1840), the proprietor of "The Liverpool Museum", London, had been proposed as a candidate in 1809, but his certificate was withdrawn. He was again proposed in 1810 and the ballot was to take place in November. Early in that month William Elford Leach, who had been elected in 1809, wrote to the Fellows resident in London, entreating them "if they are friends to Science and Enemies to Quackery to attend the Linnean Meeting on Tuesday next Nov. 6th for the purpose of blackballing Mr. Bullock (Proprietor of the Liverpool Museum) who by puffs with which he daily fills the newspapers is likely to bring that hitherto respectable body into disrepute". At the meeting one of the recipients of Leach's exhortation carried a motion that the letter should be read, with the result that the meeting resolved that Leach should be reprimanded from the Chair. Thereupon the Chairman, William George Maton, the founder of the Linnean Club, administered a solemn three-cornered hat rebuke to the misguided Leach, and the proprietor of the museum was elected. Before the next meeting took place some of the Fellows on further reflection considered that they had treated Leach with unnecessary severity and gave notice of motion to rescind the resolution of reprimand. Leach also sent a letter of apology to the President, disclaiming any personal enmity to Bullock and explaining that zeal for the welfare of the Society was the sole motive of his action. This letter was read at the next meeting and the resolution of reprimand was rescinded.

Robert John Thornton, MD (c. 1768–1837), the author of *New Illustration of the Sexual System of Linnaeus* (including *Temple of Flora*) and other botanical works, was rejected, according to Alexander McLeay in a letter to Smith, "because he was considered a Quack in Botany as well as in Medicine and chiefly because he published himself as F.L.S. before he was even proposed to the Society, as if his Election were a mere matter of course".

Election and payment of dues qualify only for nominal Fellowship, and formal admission as above is necessary before a Fellow can vote at any election or on any question concerned with the management of the Society. This condition regarding formal admission led to an extraordinary claim in 1872. Charles Herne was elected on 7 March, paid his Composition Fee and died exactly three weeks after his election without having been formally admitted. His executor, Frederick Halsey Janson, who was a lawyer and also a Fellow and who lived to be a centenarian, demanded the return of Horne's Composition Fee on the ground that he had not been admitted formally to Fellowship. The Council declined to accept Janson's reason as valid, stating that many Fellows widely scattered over the world would never have an opportunity of being admitted and that the Council considered that scientific men who join the Society do so from a wish to benefit science and not merely for their personal advantage. Janson appears not to have pursued the matter further.

The roll of about 4000 Fellows includes almost all the notable botanists and zoologists of the British Empire down to the Second World War, but it may not be amiss to mention the names of not a few distinguished in other fields of human endeavour.

In addition to those trained in the medical profession such as J. E. Smith, the chief founder of the Society, Robert Brown, Thomas Bell, Sir Joseph Hooker, Sir Richard Owen, T. H. Huxley and Sir William Henry Flower, that profession has been more directly represented in the Society by: Edward Jenner, the discoverer of vaccination; Sir Charles Bell, famous for his discoveries in the functions of the nervous system; Sir William Bowman and Sir James Paget, eminent surgeons; Sir Michael Foster, the physiologist; Sir Thomas Clifford Allbutt, the celebrated physician; and Sir Marc Armand Ruffer, the pathologist and bacteriologist who lost his life in the 1914–18 War.

Amongst explorers were Sir John Franklin, Sir James Clark Ross, who explored both the Arctic and Antarctic, was an investigator of terrestrial magnetism and whose last voyage was in search of Sir John Franklin; and Sir John Richardson, the medical officer and naturalist on the first two of Sir John Franklin's Arctic voyages, who, when in charge of Haslar Naval Hospital, was instrumental in sending T. H. Huxley as medical officer and naturalist on HMS *Rattlesnake*. Admiral Philip Parker King, the surveyor of the coast of Australia after Flinders and of the South American coast, had as second in command on the latter survey Captain Fitzroy, under whom Darwin afterwards sailed on HMS *Beagle*. There was also Heinrich Barth, the African explorer; Sir John Kirk, the medical officer and companion of Livingstone on his Zambesi journey and later Consul-General at

Zanzibar; James Augustus Grant, the Nile explorer; Sir Clements R. Markham, the introducer of Cinchona into India; and Captain Charles Sturt, the "Father of Australian Exploration".

Other activities are represented by General Sir Thomas Macdougall Brisbane, after whom the city of Brisbane, Australia, is named. He was distinguished as a soldier in the Napoleonic wars, as a civil administrator in Australia – he was Governor of New South Wales – and as an astronomer. Sir John Bennett Hearsey was in command of the Bengal Division when the Indian Mutiny broke out and saved Calcutta by his firm handling of the dangerous situation at Barrackpore. Another soldier was Field-Marshal Sir Arthur Arnold Barrett. Sir Thomas Stamford Raffles was the founder of Singapore and one of the founders and first President of the Zoological Society of London; George Bellas Greenough, one of the founders of the Royal Astronomical Society; and Jacob Bell, the founder of the Pharmaceutical Society. Sir William Macleay, nephew of Alexander McLeay, the Society's second Secretary, was chief founder and a munificent benefactor of the Linnean Society of New South Wales. Further variety is represented by Sir Roderick Impey Murchison and Sir Charles Lyell, eminent geologists; Captain Frederick Marryat, the novelist; Charles Kingsley, the writer and novelist; Robert Chambers, the founder of *Chambers Journal* and author of the anonymously published *Vestiges of the Natural History of Creation*; Sir Joseph Henry Gilbert, the partner of Sir John Bennett Lawes in the famous Rothamstead agricultural investigations; Sir Joseph Paxton, the celebrated horticulturist and designer of the 1851 International Exhibition building, which afterwards became the Crystal Palace; and John Rennie, the great civil engineer and builder of bridges.

ASSOCIATES AND FELLOWS HONORIS CAUSA

Prior to 1943 Associateship was an honour restricted to those financially unable to offer themselves as candidates for Fellowship but whose work as naturalists deserved recognition and who were likely by their attendance at meetings or their papers to benefit the Society. Up to 1929, residence within the British Empire was also a necessary qualification, but between 1930 and 1968 anyone, irrespective of nationality or residence, was, *ceteris parabus*, eligible both for Associateship *honoris causa* and Ordinary Associateship. Associates have no voice in the Society's affairs, but otherwise they enjoy the privileges of Fellows. Associateship is no bar to candidature for Fellowship and, in the past, many Associates have been elected Fellows.

When the Society was formed there were 11 Associates and 50 years later there were 49. The maximum number remained unspecified until 1861, when it was fixed at the present number of 25; but it was not until 1864 that the number actually reduced to that figure. The total number of Associates appointed or elected from 1788 to May 1936 is 236, of whom 77 have been elected since 1864. An election, other than that of a member of the Royal Family, is valid only if at least two-thirds of the Fellows present vote for the candidate. Fellows, Foreign Members and Associates are elected by ballot, but no election for Fellowship or Foreign Membership is valid unless the candidate gains two-thirds of the number voting. Until 1903, the election of Associates had followed the same lines as that of Fellows, except that, for some inscrutable reason or by inadvertence, reference to the clause requiring a minimum of two-thirds of the votes was omitted from the Bye-Laws concerning Associates. There was no explicit direction that Associates, in distinction to all the other classes, were to be elected by a simple majority of votes, however small. Consequently, on 18 February 1904, when one of two candidates for election to two vacancies was found to have received less than two-thirds of the votes, the President (S. H. Vines) and the other Officers on the platform were nonplussed, but shelved the difficulty for the moment by withholding any declaration regarding the doubtful candidate's success or failure. The President, after consulting the Council, declared at the meeting of 17 March that the candidate in question had been duly elected by a simple majority of votes. This raised fresh trouble. Since 1874, when Bentham could sign the Minutes of a General Meeting without confirmation, it had been laid down that approval of the Minutes by the Fellows was a prior condition to the President's signature of them. At the meeting of 7 April, confirmation of the Minutes of the meeting of 17 March was refused after much discussion on the point that, as the election of an Associate had not been declared at the time of election, it could not be declared at a later meeting. The President then took the opinion of Sir Edward Fry, QC, a distinguished lawyer and a Fellow. He gave it that a bare majority of votes was sufficient; that delay in declaration did not affect the validity of the election; and that, as the Council was charged with the Society's business, it was competent for the President, with the Council's approval, to act as he did. At the meeting of 21 April the President submitted this opinion to the Fellows and, after discussion, the disputed Minutes of 17 March were confirmed and all was well. This incident led to the election of Associates thereafter being brought into line with that of the election of Fellows and Foreign Members, but even this did not provide for a contingency which became reality nine years later.

On 18 December 1913, two candidates were up for election for one vacancy. One candidate received a majority of the votes but not two-thirds of them, so that strictly both candidates had failed. This impasse was got over by immediately submitting the less unsuccessful candidate to a second ballot, when he was declared to have been elected.

Amongst past Associates have been, for part or all of their time as members of the Society, such distinguished men as Mungo Park, the explorer of Africa; Robert Brown; Francis Hamilton; David Douglas, the botanical explorer of western North America; William Mitten, the bryologist; Philip Henry Gosse, the zoologist and father of Sir Edmund Gosse, the poet and critic; Charles Barter, the botanist to the Niger Expedition under Dr Bailie in the 1850s; Frederick Welwitsch, the African explorer; W. B. Hemsley, later Keeper of the Kew Herbarium and part author of *Enumeration of Plants known from China*; M. C. Cooke, the mycologist and one of the Society's Linnean Medallists; Charles Davis Sherborn, the zoological bibliographer and indexer; Richard Spruce, botanical collector in South America and helper in the introduction of Cinchona to the eastern countries of the British Empire; and Otto Stapf, later Keeper of the Kew Herbarium and editor of *Curtis's Botanical Magazine* and another of the Linnean Medallists.

In 1943, the Bye Laws of the Society were changed to distinguish two groups of Associates, Associates *honoris causa*, equivalent to the former Associates, and ordinary Associates, "who upon election shall pay an annual contribution". The second category of ordinary Associate also carried an age or time limit, being valid for five years only or until the age of 30, whichever period be the shorter. It was aimed at providing a junior membership of the Society. In 1968, a further change was made under which the former Associates *honoris causa* were renamed Fellows *honoris causa*, with future membership being restricted to citizens of the British Commonwealth. There remained two different types of Associate for, at the same time, a Student Associate category was introduced for those between 18 and 24 years old, Associates being limited to those between 21 and 29, as being eligible for election to Fellowship after the age of 30.

HONORARY MEMBERS

At first the number of Honorary Members was limited to four without exception. Later on this limit was extended to permit inclusion of such members of the British Royal Family as might wish to honour the Society, but in fact, until recent years, there have never been more than four Honorary Members at a time, and since 1840 all have been either members of the Royal Family or foreign sovereigns. The complete list is as follows:

Years of
Membership

1788–1820	Sir Joseph Banks, Bt., P.R.S.
1788–93	Duc de Noailles
1789–97	Earl of Gainsborough
1794–98	Thomas Pennant
1797–1809	The third Duke of Portland
1798–1839	Marquis of Blandford (sixth Duke of Marlborough from 1817)
1800–20	Brownlow North (Bishop of Winchester)
1812–25	Shute Barrington (Bishop of Durham)
1820–65	Prince Leopold (Leopold I, King of the Belgians from 1831)
1840–61	Prince Albert, Prince Consort
1843–54	Frederick Augustus II, King of Saxony
1856–61	Pedro V, King of Portugal
	(1866–86 No Honorary Members)
1887–1901	Edward, Prince of Wales (King Edward VII and Patron, 1901–10)
1888–1907	Oscar II, King of Sweden and Norway (King of Sweden from 1905)
1903–10	George, Prince of Wales (later King George V, Patron, 1910–36)
1906–25	Queen Alexandra
1909–73	Gustav V, King of Sweden
1927–53	Queen Mary
1929–72	Edward, Prince of Wales (King Edward VIII and Patron, 20 Jan. 1936 to 10 Dec. 1936), later Duke of Windsor
1931	Hirohito, Emperor of Japan
1935–83	Leopold III, King of the Belgians (abdicated 1951)
1936–52	George VI, Patron
1938	Queen Elizabeth the Queen Mother
1947	The Princess Elizabeth, later Queen Elizabeth II, Patron
1975	Carl XVI Gustaf, King of Sweden
1983	Prince Philip, Duke of Edinburgh
1986	Charles, Prince of Wales
1986	Akihito, Crown Prince of Japan

FOREIGN MEMBERS

Election to Foreign Membership is the Society's method of honouring eminent foreign biologists by other than the award of the Linnean Medal. At first there was no numerical limit, so that in 1802 the roll increased from the original 39 to 82, or more than a fifth of all classes of the Society. In that year the newly established Council decided that no more should be elected until the total should fall below 50 and that the total thereafter should never exceed 50. Since 1818, this has remained the maximum number, the apparent exception of 51 in the List for 1926–27 being caused by the inadvertent inclusion of Giovanni Battista Grassi, who had died in May 1925. Election is accordingly a very high honour.

Foreign Members ordinarily remain so for life, but there are at least two instances of Foreign Members becoming Fellows: David Hosack of the United States in 1794 and Joseph Correa de Serra of Portugal in 1796.

Bell, in his earlier Presidential Addresses, gave accounts of the Foreign Members elected during the session, but the Lists and Proceedings have not always in the past been precisely informative regarding this distinguished class of members. The minimum of information is contained in such lists as those of 1864 and 1874, which give merely dates of election, names, not always correctly, and cities of residence.

Up to 1863 the names and addresses of Foreign Members were printed in the Lists in latinized form, thus Carl Ludwig Blume of Leiden was listed as "D. Carolus Ludovicus Blume – Lugduni-Batavorum", John Torrey of New York as "D. Johannes Torrey – Novi-Eboraci" and Johan Wilken Hornemann of Copenhagen as "D. Janus Wilken Havniae". From 1788 to May 1936 the total number elected was 383 and from 1818 the total was 289, on average equivalent to a complete renewal of the List every 20 years. This seems a rather horrifying mortality, but it becomes less alarming by remembering that scientific eminence of biologists is seldom gained in youth and that few Foreign Members could be called young at the time of election.

The Lists conceal a commentary, obviously limited in its scope but interesting so far as it goes, on the relative distinction in biological investigations, as judged by the Society, of foreign countries. Here is a census of elections compiled by Gage during a hundred years ending May 1936:

Census of Elections of Foreign Members from May 1837 to May 1936

Countries	Botanists	Zoologists	Total
Argentina	—	1	1
Austria	7	3	10
Belgium	4	4	8
Chile	—	1	1
Czechoslovakia	2	1	3
Denmark	7	6	13
Egypt	1	—	1
Estonia	1	—	1
Finland	1	—	1
France	26	15	41
Germany	33	21	54
Italy	10	4	14
Japan	1	1	2
The Netherlands	4	4	8
Norway	1	2	3
Portugal	—	1	1
Russia	8	4	12
Sweden	10	6	16
Switzerland	14	3	17
United States	14	16	30
	145	93	238

The boundaries of the countries are the political ones existing in 1936, which are not in every case what they were when elections took place. Thus Dorpat, where Alexander von Bunge lived when elected in 1863, was then under Russia but in 1936 was Tartu in

Estonia. Under the various countries are included their colonies, if any. Thus Melchior Treub of the Buitenzorg Botanic Garden is included amongst the botanists of The Netherlands. William Nylander, one of the representatives of Finland, was actually living in Paris at the time of his election in 1876. The elder Agassiz, who is included under the United States, was a professor at Neuchâtel when he was elected in 1844. Giovannibattista Amici of Modena, elected in 1845, is included amongst the Italian botanists, but he was more particularly distinguished as a mathematician and astronomer and for his improvements to the reflecting telescope and the microscope. The representatives of Argentina, Chile and Egypt were of German origin.

In 1987 the Foreign Membership was as follows:

Argentina	1	The Netherlands	2
Austria	3	Norway	1
Belgium	2	Peru	1
Canada	1	Poland	1
Denmark	1	Portugal	1
Eire	1	South Africa	2
France	5	Sweden	4
Germany	3	Switzerland	4
Israel	1	USSR	3
Italy	2	United States	10

In 1985, the Bye-Laws were amended to make residence in the United Kingdom the only excluding factor for a Foreign Member, thus opening the way to the election as Foreign Members of British citizens resident outside the United Kingdom.

Chapter 20

Finance

The costs of a learned society such as the Linnean, with premises and library to maintain, staff to pay and publications to print, can be met only by adequate subscriptions from its members and these subscriptions must necessarily rise as the society's commitments increase, even though supplemented by donations, grants and bequests, usually infrequent; by income from investments, which may be small; and by the sale of publications, which may be underpriced. Thus keeping an excess of income over expenditure has always provided the Treasurer with problems, especially since the end of World War II. He presents the balance sheet giving details of the Society's assets and liabilities, income and expenditure, together with grants and awards from special funds, at the Anniversary Meeting, when the Fellows have the right to question them and request explanations. These accounts are now published in *The Linnean*.

For the first 75 sessions (1788–1859) ordinarily only members attending Anniversary Meetings received information regarding the Society's finances, but since 1860 a financial statement has been published annually; at first in the *Proceedings*, except during 1875–80 when no *Proceedings* were published, then in their successors, the *Biological Journal* and *The Linnean*. The account has all along been a simple statement of annual receipts and expenditure but these have increased in complexity over the years. At first there was merely the single general statement, then in 1886 a separate statement of investments appeared and in 1911 the first separate account of the special funds.

Inflation has rendered meaningless a collective statement of the Society's income and expenditure from the beginning to the present time. Gage painstakingly tabulated that from 1788 to 1936, a period during which the buying power of the pound declined but slowly, and this was as follows.

General Statement of Receipts and Expenditure from
26 February 1788 to 30 April 1936

Receipts				Expenditure			
Heads	£	s.	d.	Heads	£	s.	d.
Admission Fees	18,653	3	0	Herbarium & Museum	4,344	1	$1\frac{1}{2}$
Annual Contributions	132,463	8	2	Library	23,949	10	7
Composition Fees	29,069	16	0	Rent, Rates, Taxes,			
Sale of Investments	11,158	1	3	Insurance	14,189	11	4
Bequests, Donations, Grants,				Investments	23,114	2	5
Loans, Subscriptions	20,508	18	10	Staff	57,833	2	2
Sale of Publications	23,537	3	5	Publications	88,179	10	1
Interest & Miscellaneous	21,028	2	0	Miscellaneous	43,848	19	$3\frac{1}{2}$
Total	£256,418	12	8	Total	£255,458	17	0
				Bal. on 30 April 1936	959	15	8
					£256,418	12	8

Admission fees

Although no fees are now paid by Fellows on election to the Society, these long constituted a useful addition to the Society's funding. The original admission fee, from 1788 to 1798, was £1 11s. 6d., then raised to £2 12s. 6d. in 1798, with a further increase to £5 5s. in 1823. The £2 12s. 6d. paid by Fellows elected between 1798 and 1823 included a contribution of one guinea to the Library Fund until the session of 1835–36. After 1924, Fellows under the age of 35 at date of their election were exempted from paying an Admission Fee. It was totally abolished in 1964.

Composition fees

A payment of ten guineas, equivalent to ten annual subscriptions of a guinea, exempted Fellows from 1788 to 1802 from any further contribution to the Society however long they continued as members; but since botanists and zoologists tend to be long-lived, such composition fees were not ultimately to the Society's benefit. So many Fellows took advantage of the small amount required for composition up to 1802 that during the first 20 years the receipts from Compositions exceeded the income from Annual Contributions. In 1802, the newly established Council altered this, and from the third decade Annual Contributions have formed much the largest percentage of the Society's receipts. The Society was early aware of the desirability of saving at least a proportion of the Composition Fees, and between 1790 and 1804 rather more than half the Fees received during that period were invested in Consols. Unfortunately, by 1806, almost the whole amount had to be sold to meet the rapid increase in expenditure on publications and the cost of the lease of and repairs to No. 9 Gerrard Street.

From 1804 to 1858 almost the entire sum of £10 900 received during that period was spent. Bell held strong views regarding this misuse of the Composition Fees, which in fact could not then be avoided, and urged that all such Fees should be invested. Bentham favoured investing half those Fees. After the time of Bell and Bentham, the receipts from Composition Fees steadily decreased and finally ceased to have any bearing on the purchase of investments. From 1788 to 1912 the Composition Fee, although raised three times during that period, made no allowance for age or length of Fellowship of a compounder, but the amount payable was that in force at the time of the compounder's election to Fellowship, not at the time of his composition. From 1878 to 1912, when the annual contribution was £3, the composition fee was £45. In 1912, a sliding scale of compositions was established according to the age of the compounder and length of Fellowship. This endured until 1919, when the privilege of compounding was suspended until 1935; then it was reintroduced on a sliding scale which takes the compounder's age and length of Fellowship into consideration.

Annual contributions

The annual subscription to the Society increased but little over the years, starting at one guinea in 1788; it was still only £4 in 1935. The subsequent fall in the value of money has necessitated much more drastic increases as the following table indicates.

Scales of Payments by Fellows in Successive Periods

Periods	Admission Fees			Annual Contributions			
	£	s.	d.	£	s.		
1788–98	1	11	6	1	1		
1798–1802	2	12	6	1	1		
1802–23	2	12	6	2	2		
1823–29	5	5	0	2	2		
1829–78	6	0	0	3	0		
1878–1912	6	0	0	3	0		
1912–19	6	0	0	3	0		
1919–20	6	0	0	3	0		
1920–24	6	0	0	4	0		
1924–35	4	0	0	4	0		
1935–64	4	0	0	4	0		
1964–68	discontinued			7	0		
1968–70				7	0 (UK)	5	0 (overseas)
1970–75				8	0 (UK)	6	0 (overseas)
1975–76				12	0 (UK)	10	0 (overseas)
1976–77				16	0		
1977–79				20	0		
1979–85				25	0		
1985–				30	0		

Up to 1838, the receipts from Annual Contributions steadily increased, but during the next ten years they declined from an annual average of £458 to £426; the receipts from Admission Fees falling during the same period from an annual average of £121 to £88. Those two decades mark a distinct ebb in the Society's prosperity; about half the Society consisted of compounders who contributed nothing beyond their comparatively small Composition Fee. Too many Fellows had failed to pay their Annual Contributions and, in 1807, arrears stood at £536. In 1823, they had risen to nearly £900. An enquiry that year into the Society's finances revealed that the Library Fund had been diverted to general purposes and that the Treasurer had advanced money out of his own pocket to enable the Society to meet all its immediate expenses. Edward Forster, Treasurer from 1816 to 1849, certainly had a difficult time and in the latter years of his period of office was too old to act with vigour. The only result of the 1823 investigation was the raising of the Admission Fee to five guineas, which added an insignificant amount of the annual income. Nothing was done to prevent the accumulation of arrears of Annual Contributions. Six years later the purchase of the Linnaean and Smithian Collections worsened even more the Society's financial condition, and the scale of all payments by Fellows had to be increased. In 1842, the arrears of more than £2300 drove the Council to face the situation: there were then 556 Fellows, of whom 300 were compounders; of the 256 annual contributors, exactly half were in arrear for various periods. One Fellow, a Captain Thomas Brown, had been in arrear for 23 years!

At last the Council began a systematic drive against defaulters. Three sets of letters, marked A, B, C respectively and worded in increasing degree from mild reminder to threat of removal, were sent out during succeeding years, but only with moderate success. In 1848, a fourth form of letter, appropriately marked D, was prepared, threatening legal proceedings, and was sent to the worst defaulters. This threat caused some to pay up; others paid after being taken to court. Those four series of letters continued to be sent out for about the following 20 years, by the end of which the Society had made a wonderful recovery in every direction.

It is the duty of Fellows who recommend candidates for Fellowship to make reasonably sure *inter alia* that candidates are able and willing on election to pay their dues to the Society. Every Fellow on his election is also informed of his privileges and his obligations. There is thus no excuse for a Fellow continuing without special permission of the Council to enjoy the former while evading the latter; but the Linnean, like most similar societies, has always endured a small proportion of ignorant, careless, even downright dishonest Fellows, and its records preserve some fine specimens of all types.

Most defaulters are either careless, postpone withdrawal in the hope of being able to pay up arrears within a reasonable time, or may be hampered by currency restrictions if living outside Britain. The Council has always recognized this and has never erred on the side of harshness in dealing with Fellows in arrear. Only in bad instances has the Council called in the aid of the Law. It must be emphasized that the printing of the Society's publications becomes ever more costly and the Society cannot afford to supply them to Fellows failing to pay their subscriptions.

Under Bell's Presidency (1853–61) income from Annual Contributions began to increase and has continued to do so, from an annual average of £426 during the decade 1848–58 to £1073 during 1878–88, to £2188 during 1918–28, to £2586 during 1928–36, rising to £37 091 in 1983. Although the later figures look splendidly high, they reflect more a fall in the purchasing power of money than a rise in real income.

Bequests, donations etc.

The Society has been fortunate in having a few Fellows able and willing to contribute more than their legal dues, as well as some who have made munificent bequests. Thus Charles Lambert bequeathed £500 in 1876, George Bentham £567 in 1885, Francis Tagart £400 in 1912 and John Ramsbottom £9000 in 1985. The Society has also received large grants from the Government Grant administered by the Royal Society, from the Percy Sladen Fund and the Carnegie United Kingdom Trust.

Publications

As members have always been entitled to free copies of those Society's publications issued after their election and to buy extra copies at reduced rates, and as the public demand for scientific publications was small for many years, the receipts from sales were much below the expenditure on their production. A purely cash account, however, does not take into consideration the fact that by exchanging its publications for those of other societies the Linnean Society saved much direct expenditure on periodicals for its Library. The average annual receipts were about £8 during the Society's first ten years; the cost of production was about £50 a year, i.e. about 26 per cent of the Society's total annual income.

The financial situation as regards publications has changed very much for the better since the Society entered into association with Academic Press for publication of its journals.

Herbarium and Museum

The total expenditure on these down to 1935 was £4344 1s. 1½d. The Society in its corporative capacity did not spend much either on the acquisition or on the care of its collections, apart from the Linnaean and Smithian. Excluding £215 6s. subscribed privately by Fellows to purchase the Caley Collection in 1817–18, the Society up to 1828 spent only about £303 on its collections. From 1829 to 1835 the Society spent directly £3290 19s. 6d. in purchasing the Linnaean and Smithian Collections, including interest on unpaid balances of the price. Thereafter, until 1860, the annual expenditure seldom exceeded £6, and from 1860 until 1928 no direct expenditure on collections is shown in the accounts. During 1928–30, £66 14s. 5d. was spent on the Linnaean Collections and, since then, only small amounts, until the building of the basement strong-room with its high maintenance costs.

Library

For the first 90 years less than 5 per cent of the total annual expenditure was on the Library, but it nevertheless increased through gifts from authors and other generous well-wishers. The average annual expenditure per decade varied during that period from £2 12s. 3d. in the first decade to nearly £82 in the ninth decade. In 1848–58 the average sank to £12 12s. In the tenth decade the average annual expenditure was more than double the previous highest, and it continued to increase with slight fluctuations until 1918–28, when the grant of £2000 from the Carnegie United Kingdom Trust sent it up during that decade to an annual average of nearly £500.

During the Second World War the purchase of books published outside Britain virtually stopped; with the coming of peace the purchase of missed periodicals and books imposed a heavy burden on the Society's limited financial resources, alleviated, however, by generous grants from the Royal Society.

Rent, rates, taxes, insurance

From 1788 until 1857 the Society paid rent for its rooms at the following rates:

1788–95	Great Marlborough Street	£20 p.a.
1795–1805	Panton Square	£40 p.a.
1805–21	Gerrard Street	£105 p.a.
1821–51	Soho Square	£140 p.a.
1851–57	Soho Square	£200 p.a.

During the last period Brown paid £80 per annum to the Society as rent for his part of the house. Until 1795, the Society paid no rates or local taxes, but thereafter seems to have paid them until 1843. In the Parliamentary session of 1843–44 George William Wood, MP for Kendal and a Fellow of the Society, introduced a Bill to exempt scientific societies from local taxation, and in November 1843 the Society was certified by John Tidd Pratt, the Barrister authorized, under 6th and 7th Victoria, Ch. 36, as exempt from County, Borough, Parochial and other local taxes. This did not prevent the Overseers of the Poor of St Ann's, Westminster, demanding payment of rates in 1853, but the Society contested the demand and, on 31 May 1854, the case was decided in the Court of Queen's Bench in favour of the Society on all points raised.

The Society continued to pay certain general taxes, such as Property Tax and Inhabited House Duty, as the Minutes show that in 1870 and in 1881 the Society appealed against the assessments on the Librarian's and Porter's quarters. When the Society after 1858 again began to hold investments, it paid Income Tax on the interest, and it was not until 1900 that Henry Groves suggested steps should be taken toward recovering this tax.

The Society has never had to insure its homes, although as already mentioned the Office of Works in 1873 applied unsuccessfully to the Society to bear the cost of the insurance of its present rooms.

The first mention of insurance of the Society's own possessions is in 1841, when the Council ordered insurance of the Library and Collections for £3000. In 1858, the sum was raised to £6000, distributed to: Furniture and Fixings, £800; General Library, £2000; Linnaean Library and Collections, £2000; East Indian Herbarium and Cases, £500; New Holland Collections, £200; and Miscellaneous Collections, £500. The sum insured remained at £6000, with a slight readjustment of the details in 1864, until 1884, when it raised to £10 000, distributed to: Furniture and Fixings, £500; General Library, £5000; Linnaean Collections, £3000; East Indian and other Herbaria, £500; and Portraits and Busts, £1000. In 1936, the amount insured was £43 500, distributed to: Household Furniture and Fixtures, £1500; Printed Books and Stock of Publications, £25 000; Linnaean Library and Collections, £10 000; Smithian and the smaller Collections, £500; and Collections of Portraits, Busts and Engravings, £6500.

From 1788 to 1858, when the Society had to pay rent, the average annual expenditure on Rent, Rates, Taxes and Insurance varied from over £30 during the first decade to over £238 in 1818–28. After the Society's removal from its rent-free rooms in Burlington House, the average annual expenditure on all four items between 1858 and 1918 varied from over £8 in 1868–78 to nearly £18 in 1908–18. Since 1918, the average has increased from a little over £29 during 1918–28 to over £52 during 1928–36.

Chapter 21

Epilogue

Attainment of a bicentenary by a learned society largely dependent on its own resources naturally gives rise to thanksgiving for its survival during times of crisis and to congratulations on its achievements. Such an occasion also provokes thoughts on the Society's future role in a rapidly changing world. Primarily, this role continues to be to provide a service to its members and through them to the community. The aims of the Linnean Society, as stated in the Charter of 1802, must remain "the cultivation of natural history in all its branches". The meaning of this phrase has changed much since then, as the content, for example, of Society publications makes evident when examined over a long period.

The papers in Volumes 1 (1791) and 2 (1794) of the Society's *Transactions* are indeed varied and include J. E. Smith's admirable introductory discourse on the rise and progress of natural history. Mostly, however, they are taxonomic in accordance with contemporary interest and need; thus they include descriptions of new species of lichen, fish, leech, seaweed, sedges, grasses, Japanese and other exotic plants, etc. During this period, the quarto *Transactions* provided the only means available for the publication of such papers and its existence undoubtedly stimulated their production. The Linnean Society, like the Royal Society and the Horticultural Society of London, took a long time to learn that such information could be conveyed to the public more quickly, more conveniently and at less cost by octavo *Proceedings* or *Journals*. Publication of *Transactions* continued until 1936, but from 1856 onwards the Society's other periodicals carried most of the original and other information presented to the Society as well as records of its activities. The men responsible for these publications may have been forgotten but the publication of so much work of lasting value to biology has provided, and still provides, a major justification for the Society's continuity of effort; it remains a gift to posterity.

A society, however, needs also to serve the present interests of its members, which are ever changing. Over a long period the meetings in London for the hearing of lectures held the Society together; they were probably as valuable for personal contacts and informal discussions as for information gained from the papers read. The Society at times resented the founding of other more specialized societies, even though the depletion of its resources through the purchase of the Linnaean and Smith collections prohibited the Society from fulfilling their functions. The later, wider extension of biological science has made the existence of these societies with their own publications essential for progress. The Linnean Society now happily co-exists with these more recent societies and supports them whenever it can. The bicentenary joint meetings and indeed many earlier joint meetings have convincingly shown that all can profit from making specialized knowledge available to a wider audience. This co-operation in "the furtherance of natural history" within such domains of special enquiry as the anatomy, biochemistry, cytology, evolution, genetics and physiology of plants and animals, as well as into their classification and naming, was inconceivable at the Society's founding but is welcome now. All this accords with the wise remarks of a former President of the Linnean Society, Carl F. A. Pantin: "Because it prevents the sterile restriction of the sciences, the collection together of people with very varied sorts of learning is one of the most valuable features of learned societies of any kind ... the maintenance of a broad tradition of learning is essential to scientific progress." The fragmentation of science has made that difficult; zoologists tend to ignore meetings on botanical subjects and botanists those on zoological subjects, of course to their mutual loss. "In these days of specialised studies," wrote Agnes Arber, a Linnean Medallist, in 1950, "the different branches of biology cannot but lead existences which are, to a great extent, isolated from one another. The aims which they pursue, and the highly technical methods by which these aims are pursued, differ so widely that one reminds oneself, with something of a shock, that all the branches are concerned with the same living world, and that their disjunction arises, not out of differences of content but out of the divergent treatment which the mind accords to the same phenomena, when seen from different standpoints – thinking makes it so. The different branches should not indeed be regarded as so many fragments which, pieced together, make up a mosaic called biology, but as so many microcosms, each of which, in its own individual way, reflects the macrocosm of the whole subject." Such a perception of the basic wholeness of biology, though rarely stated so explicitly, underlies the existence of the Linnean Society. As the Society enters its third century, with the biological sciences becoming ever more complicated, their terminology understandable only by the initiated or even arcane, their literature overwhelmingly extensive and unwieldy, and their practicians narrowly specialized, the Society's fostering of interdisciplinary contacts becomes ever more important. The maintenance of a broad tradition of biological learning accords not only with the Society's past but is vital for its future if it is to remain creatively "a society for the cultivation of the science of natural history in all its branches" and be true to its motto *Naturae discere mores*.

Appendix 1

Publication dates of Transactions

The dates below are those ascertained by Sandra Raphael and published in the Society's *Biological Journal* 2: 61–76 (1970).

Volume 1	13 August 1791
Volume 2	1 May 1794
Volume 3	25 May 1797
Volume 4	24 May 1798
Volume 5	20 February–22 February 1800
Volume 6	24 May–27 May 1802
Volume 7	8 November–21 November 1804
Volume 8	9 March 1807
Volume 9	23 November 1808
Volume 10, part 1, pp. 1–228	8 March 1810
Volume 10, part 2, pp. 229–414	7 September 1811
Volume 11, part 1, pp. 1–178	20 May 1813
Volume 11, part 2, pp. 179–430	24 January 1816
Volume 12, part 1, pp. 1–290	25 February 1818
Volume 12, part 2, pp. 291–598	2 July 1819
Volume 13, part 1, pp. 1–274	23 May–21 June 1821
Volume 13, part 2, pp. 277–637	3 December–19 December 1822
Volume 14, part 1, pp. 1–170	28 May–12 June 1823
Volume 14, part 2, pp. 171–394	15 November 1824
Volume 14, part 3, pp. 395–604	31 May 1825
Volume 15, part 1, pp. 1–334	9 February 1827
Volume 15, part 2, pp. 335–533	11 December–20 December 1827
Volume 16, part 1, pp. 1–150	12 February–19 February 1829
Volume 16, part 2, pp. 151–454	27 May 1830
Volume 16, part 3, pp. 455–796	Before 19 March 1833
Volume 17, part 1, pp. 1–146	26 April–8 May 1834
Volume 17, part 2, pp. 147–314	25 May 1835
Volume 17, part 3, pp. 315–464	21 June–9 July 1836
Volume 17, part 4, pp. 465–600	18 July–8 August 1837
Volume 18, part 1, pp. 1–132	21 June 1838
Volume 18, part 2, pp. 133–246	7 May–30 May 1839
Volume 18, part 3, pp. 247–482	25 June 1840
Volume 18, part 4, pp. 483–728	29 July–11 August 1841
Volume 19, part 1, pp. 1–80	21 May–28 May 1842
Volume 19, part 2, pp. 81–170	5 August 1843
Volume 19, part 3, pp. 171–302	6 November 1844
Volume 19, part 4, pp. 303–542	5 November 1845
Volume 20, part 1, pp. 1–162	29 August 1846
Volume 20, part 2, pp. 163–358	11 December 1847
Volume 20, part 3, pp. 359–510	24 May 1851
Volume 21, part 1, pp. 1–84	After 18 May 1852
Volume 21, part 2, pp. 85–184	23 June 1853

Volume 21, part 3, pp. 185–242	7 November–21 November 1854
Volume 21, part 4, pp. 243–354	10 November 1855
Volume 22, part 1, pp. 1–112	23 October–8 December 1856
Volume 22, part 2, pp. 113–154	21 November 1857
Volume 22, part 3, pp. 155–288	4 November–24 December 1858
Volume 22, part 4, pp. 289–430	12 November 1859
Volume 23, part 1, pp. 1–250	After 1 November 1860
Volume 23, part 2, pp. 251–422	14 December 1861
Volume 23, part 3, pp. 423–612	13 November 1862
Volume 24, part 1, pp. 1–48	30 January 1863
Volume 24, part 2, pp. 49–210	17 November 1863
Volume 24, part 3, pp. 211–532	8 November 1864
Volume 25, part 1, pp. 1–72	27 May 1865
Volume 25, part 2, pp. 73–360	30 November 1865
Volume 25, part 3, pp. 361–570	After 1 November 1866
Volume 26, part 1, pp. 1–352	5 March–11 April 1868
Volume 26, part 2, pp. 353–496	4 September–12 September 1868
Volume 26, part 3, pp. 497–662	2 March–13 March 1869
Volume 26, part 4, pp. 663–716	21 May 1870
Volume 27, part 1, pp. 1–94	24 December 1869
Volume 27, part 2, pp. 95–304	9 July 1870
Volume 27, part 3, pp. 305–464	22 April 1871
Volume 27, part 4, pp. 465–654	11 November 1871
Volume 28, part 1, pp. 1–188	Before 13 January 1872
Volume 28, part 2, pp. 189–432	After 17 May 1872, possibly 8 June
Volume 28, part 3, pp. 433–506	3 May 1873
Volume 28, part 4, pp. 507–562	After 3 July 1873, possibly 23 August
Volume 29, part 1, pp. 1–68	8 June 1872
Volume 29, part 2, pp. 69–106	23 August 1873
Volume 29, part 3, pp. 107–190	11 September 1875
Volume 30, part 1, pp. 1–156	4 July 1874
Volume 30, part 2, pp. 157–334	14 November 1874
Volume 30, part 3, pp. 335–670	10 April 1875

Appendix 2

Publication dates of Proceedings and Journals

The information below is reprinted from B. D. Jackson's *General Index* (1888) for the *Journal (Botany)* and from A. W. Kappel's *General Index* for the *Journal (Zoology)*; the information for the *Proceedings* occurs in both indexes.

Proceedings of the Linnean Society of London

VOL. I.—From Nov. 1838 to June 1848. (1849.)
Pp. xv, 401.

VOL. II.—From Nov. 1848 to June 1855. (1855.)
Pp. xiii, 448.

No.		Pp.					No.		Pp.				
	1. Pp.	1–8,	issued	March	9, 1839.			38. Pp.	1–16,	issued	Nov.	6, 1849.
	2. Pp.	9–16,	issued	April	27, 1839.			39. Pp.	17–32,	issued	Nov.	6, 1849.
	3. Pp.	17–32,	issued	May	16, 1839.			40. Pp.	33–48,	issued	Nov.	6, 1849.
	4. Pp.	33–40,	issued	Nov.	5, 1839.			41. Pp.	49–64,	issued	April	16, 1850.
	5. Pp.	41–48,	issued	Dec.	17, 1839.			42. Pp.	65–80,	issued	Oct.	18, 1850.
	6. Pp.	49–56,	issued	March	3, 1840.			43. Pp.	81–96,	issued	Oct.	30, 1850.
	7. Pp.	57–64,	issued	April	7, 1840.			44. Pp.	97–112,	issued	April	15, 1851.
	8. Pp.	65–72,	issued	Nov.	10, 1840.			45. Pp.	113–128,	issued	Nov.	4, 1851.
	9. Pp.	73–80,	issued	Dec.	17, 1840.			46. Pp.	129–144,	issued	Nov.	4, 1851.
	10. Pp.	81–88,	issued	April	6, 1841.			47. Pp.	145–160,	issued	April	19, 1852.
	11. Pp.	89–96,	issued	April	22, 1841.			48. Pp.	161–176,	issued	July	23, 1852.
	12. Pp.	97–112,	issued	June	12, 1841.			49. Pp.	177–192,	issued	Oct.	28, 1852.
	13. Pp.	113–120,	issued	Jan.	18, 1842.			50. Pp.	193–200,	issued	Oct.	28, 1852.
	14. Pp.	121–128,	issued	April	5, 1842.			51. Pp.	201–220,	issued	June	23, 1853.
	15. Pp.	129–152,	issued	Nov.	14, 1842.			52. Pp.	221–236,	issued	Nov.	8, 1853.
	16. Pp.	153–160,	issued	Feb.	16, 1843.			53. Pp.	237–252,	issued	Nov.	8, 1853.
	17. Pp.	161–168,	issued	May	23, 1843.			54. Pp.	253–268,	issued	Feb.	7, 1854.
	18. Pp.	169–176,	issued	Aug.	9, 1843.			55. Pp.	269–284,	issued	May	2, 1854.
	19. Pp.	177–184,	issued	Feb.	7, 1844.			56. Pp.	285–300,	issued	Sept.	19, 1854.
	20. Pp.	185–196,	issued	May	— 1844.			57. Pp.	301–316,	issued	Sept.	19, 1854.
	21. Pp.	197–212,	issued	Sept.	— 1844.			58. Pp.	317–332,	issued	Nov.	7, 1854.
	22. Pp.	213–220,	issued	?	1844.			59. Pp.	333–348,	issued	Feb.	6, 1855.
	23. Pp.	221–228,	issued	Feb.	— 1845.			59*Pp.	333*–336,*	issued	Feb.	27, 1855.
	24. Pp.	229–236,	issued	May	6, 1845.			60. Pp.	349–364,	issued	May	1, 1855.
	25. Pp.	237–252,	issued	May	6, 1845.			61. Pp.	365–380,	issued	Sept.	5, 1855.
	26. Pp.	253–260,	issued	May	6, 1845.			62. Pp.	381–396,	issued	Sept.	5, 1855.
	27. Pp.	261–268,	issued	May	6, 1845.			63. Pp.	397–412,	issued	Sept.	5, 1855.
	28. Pp.	269–284,	issued	May	— 1846.			64. Pp.	413–428,	issued	Oct.	19, 1855.
	29. Pp.	285–304,	issued	Aug.	— 1846.			65. Pp.	429–436,	issued	Oct.	19, 1855.
	30. Pp.	305–312,	issued	Feb.	16, 1847.			66. Pp.	437–448,	issued	{ Oct. 31, 1855. / Title & Index. }	
	31. Pp.	313–320,	issued	April	30, 1847.							
	32. Pp.	321–328,	issued	May	13, 1847.							
	33. Pp.	329–340,	issued	Sept.	9, 1847.							
	34. Pp.	341–364,	issued	May	2, 1848.							
	35. Pp.	365–380,	issued	July	14, 1848.							
	36. Pp.	381–388,	issued	Oct.	2, 1848.							
	37. Pp.	389–401,	issued	{ May 15, 1849. / Index, Title, &c. }								

From this date the 8vo series of publications became divided into the *Journal of Proceedings*, and the *Proceedings*; the latter containing the record of business at the General and Anniversary Meetings.

Journal of the Proceedings of the Linnean Society (Zoology)

Vol. I. (1857).   Pp. iv. 182.

No. 1. Pp.   1–48, issued   March   1, 1856.
     2. Pp.   49–96, issued   June   1, 1856.
     3. Pp.   97–140, issued   Nov.   1, 1856.
     4. Pp.   141–182, issued   March   21, 1857.

Vol. II. (1859).   Pp. iii. 176.

No. 5. Pp.   1–40, issued   June   21, 1857.
     6. Pp.   41–88, issued   Nov.   2, 1857.
     7. Pp.   89–136, issued   Feb.   20, 1858.
     8. Pp.   137–176, issued   May   20, 1858.

Vol. III. (1859).   Pp. iv. 204.

No. 9. Pp.   1–62, issued   Aug.   20, 1858.
    10. Pp.   63–110, issued   Nov.   1, 1858.
    11. Pp.   111–158, issued   Feb.   1, 1859.
    12. Pp.   159–204, issued   April   11, 1859.

Vol. IV. (1860).   Pp. iii, 189.

No. 13. Pp.   1–48, issued   July   1, 1859.
    14. Pp.   49–96, issued   Sept.   19, 1859.
    15. Pp.   97–144, issued   Dec.   8, 1859.
    16. Pp.   145–189, issued   Feb.   10, 1860.

Vol. V. (1861).   Pp. iv. 320.

No. 17. Pp.   1–56, issued   June   5, 1860.
    17b. Pp.   57–168, issued   July   18, 1860.
    18. Pp.   169–216, issued   Nov.   14, 1860.
    19. Pp.   217–264, issued   March   27, 1861.
    20. Pp.   265–320, issued   May   24, 1861.

Vol. VI. (1862).   Pp. iv, 206.

No. 21. Pp.   1–48, issued   Nov.   1, 1861.
    22. Pp.   49–96, issued   March   1, 1862.
    23. Pp.   97–152, issued   May   15, 1862.
    24. Pp.   153–206, issued   Nov.   1, 1862.

Vol. VII. (1864).   Pp. iii, 249.

No. 25. Pp.   1–48, issued   March   4, 1863.
    26. Pp.   49–108, issued   May   13, 1863.
    27. Pp.   109–180, issued   Oct.   29, 1863.
    28. Pp.   181–238, issued   April   5, 1864.
Title, &c. Pp.   239–249, issued   Sept.   3, 1864.

Vol. VIII. (1865).   Pp. iv, 215.

No. 29. Pp.   1–52,   Title and Contents to Vol. VII., issued Sept. 3, 1864.
    30. Pp.   53–108, issued   Jan.   13, 1865.
    31. ⎰ Pp. 109–215, issued ⎰ Dec.   5, 1865.
    32. ⎱   ⎱ Index, Title, &c.

From **Vol. IX.** onwards the Zoological and Botanical Journals were published independently, with the title slightly altered.

The Journal of the Linnean Society (Zoology)

Vol. IX. (1868).   Pp. iv, 496.

No. 33. Pp.   1–48, issued   April   30, 1866.
    34. Pp.   49–112, issued   Oct.   11, 1866.
    35. Pp.   113–180, issued   Jan.   30, 1867.
    36. Pp.   181–244, issued   Sept.   14, 1867.
    37. Pp.   245–308, issued   Nov.   14, 1867.
    38. Pp.   309–372, issued   Dec.   13, 1867.
    39. Pp.   373–436, issued   Feb.   18, 1868.
    40. Pp.   437–496, ⎱ issued April   23, 1868.
Title & Contents. ⎰

Vol. X. (1870).   Pp. iv, 514.

No. 41. Pp.   1–68, issued   May   30, 1868.
    42. Pp.   69–132, issued   Aug.   7, 1868.

    43. Pp.   133–196, issued   Sept.   25, 1868.
    44. Pp.   197–260, issued   Nov.   26, 1868.
    45. Pp.   261–330, issued   Jan.   8, 1869.
    46. Pp.   331–394, issued   Aug.   10, 1869.
    47. Pp.   395–458, issued   Jan.   17, 1870.
    48. Pp.   459–514, ⎱ issued May   20, 1870.
Title & Contents. ⎰

Vol. XI. (1873).   Pp. iv, 556.

No. 49. Pp.   1–89, issued   Oct.   12, 1870.
    50. Pp.   90–153, issued   Feb.   16, 1871.
    51. Pp.   154–218, issued   June   8, 1871.
    52. Pp.   219–284, issued   Sept.   14, 1871.
    53. Pp.   285–348, issued   Oct.   16, 1871.

Journal of the Proceedings—Zoology (continued)

54. Pp.   349–425, issued   Dec.   20, 1871.
55. Pp.   426–492, issued   Oct.   29, 1872.
56. Pp.   493–556, } issued July   18, 1873.
Title & Contents, &c. }

VOL. XII. (1876).   Pp. v, 600.

No. 57. Pp.   1–99, issued   Feb.   11, 1874.
58. Pp.   100–195, issued   Nov.   3, 1874.
59. Pp.   196–251, issued   May   22, 1875.
60. }
61. } Pp. 251–407, issued   Feb.   25, 1876.
62. }
63. Pp.   408–514, issued   May   25, 1876.
64. Pp.   514–600. } issued Sept.   19, 1876.
Title & Contents. }

VOL. XIII. (1878).   Pp. viii, 530.

No. 65. Pp.   1–46, issued   Sept.   19, 1876.
66. Pp.   47–109, issued   Dec.   15, 1876.
67. Pp.   110–185, issued   Feb.   28, 1877.
68. Pp.   185–260, issued   June   5, 1877.
69. Pp.   261–334, issued   June   20, 1877.
70. Pp.   335–384, issued   Aug.   20, 1877.
71. Pp.   385–457, issued   Sept.   25, 1877.
72. Pp.   457–530, } issued Feb.   27, 1878.
Title & Contents, &c. }

VOL. XIV. (1879).   Pp. viii, 761.

No. 73. Pp.   1–64, issued   Oct.   24, 1877.
74. Pp.   65–186, issued   May   23, 1878.
75. Pp.   187–311, issued   Aug.   31, 1878.
76. Pp.   312–417, issued   Oct.   31, 1878.
77. Pp.   418–505, issued   Jan.   31, 1879.
78. Pp.   506–606, issued   Apr.   23, 1879.
79. Pp.   607–688, issued   May   20, 1879.
80. Pp.   689–761, } issued Sept.   2, 1879.
Title & Contents, &c. }

VOL. XV. (1881).   Pp. viii, 509.

No. 81. Pp.   1–73, issued   Mar.   30, 1880.
82. Pp.   73–137, issued   July   31, 1880.
83. Pp.   138–187, issued   Sept.   3, 1880.
84. Pp.   187–241, issued   Nov.   20, 1880.
85. Pp.   241–290, issued   March   25, 1881.
86. Pp.   291–332, issued   Sept.   29, 1881.
87. Pp.   333–412, issued   Oct.   4, 1881.
88. Pp.   413–509, } issued Nov.   3, 1881.
Title & Contents, &c. }

VOL. XVI. (1883).   Pp. viii, 623.

No. 89. Pp.   1–88, issued   Dec.   23, 1881.
90. Pp.   89–183, issued   Jan.   26, 1882.
91. Pp.   184–254, issued   March   8, 1882.
92. Pp.   255–323, issued   April   6, 1882.

93. Pp.   324–392, issued   June   12, 1882.
94. Pp.   393–478, issued   July   31, 1882.
95. Pp.   479–545, issued   Sept.   26, 1882.
96. Pp.   546–611, issued   March   10, 1883.
Title, &c. Pp.   613–623, issued   March   24, 1883.

VOL. XVII. (1884).   Pp. viii, 456.

No.   97. Pp.   1–40,
Titlepage, Index, and Contents
to Vol. XVI., pp. i–viii, and pp.
613–623 inclusive, issued
March 24, 1883.
98. Pp.   41–108, issued   April   17, 1883.
99. Pp.   109–174, issued   July   31, 1883.
100. Pp.   175–269, issued   Aug.   14, 1883.
101. Pp.   270–346, issued   Oct.   20, 1883.
102. Pp.   347–394, issued   Feb.   29, 1884.
103. Pp.   395–456, } issued Sept.   18, 1884.
Title & Contents, &c. }

VOL. XVIII. (1885).   Pp. vi, 345.

No. 104. }
105. } Pp.   1–204, issued   Aug.   13, 1884.
106. Pp.   205–291, issued   Dec.   19, 1884.
107. Pp.   292–345, } issued Mar.   31, 1885.
Title & Contents, &c. }

VOL. XIX. (1886).   Pp. viii, 419.

No. 108. Pp.   1–57, issued   May   22, 1885.
109. Pp.   58–116, issued   Aug.   13, 1885.
110. }
111. } Pp. 117–161, issued   Nov.   13, 1885.
112. Pp.   161–229, issued   Dec.   31, 1885.
113. Pp.   230–284, issued   April   7, 1886.
114. Pp.   284–336, issued }
Title & Contents, pp. viii,   } Sept.   30, 1886.
& Index, Pp. 412–419.   }
115. Pp.   337–411, issued   July   23, 1886.
Title, &c. Pp.   412–419, issued   Sept.   30, 1886.

VOL. XX. (1890).   Pp. vii, 592.

No. 116, Pp.   1–61, issued   Oct.   27, 1886.
117. Pp.   61–107, issued   June   30, 1887.
118. Pp.   107–117, issued   Oct.   29, 1887.
119. Pp.   118–188, issued   Nov.   1, 1888.
120. Pp.   189–274, issued   Sept.   15, 1888.
121. Pp.   275–298, issued   Jan.   31, 1889.
122. Pp.   299–394, issued   Aug.   31, 1889.
123. Pp.   395–472, issued   Dec.   31, 1889.
124. { Pp. 473–592, issued } July   31, 1890.
125. { Title & Contents.   }

Journal of the Proceedings of the Linnean Society (Botany)

Vol. I (1857). Pp. iv, 203.

No. 1. Pp.   1–48,   issued   March   1, 1856.
     2. Pp.   49–96,   issued   June   1, 1856.

     3. Pp.   97–144, issued   Nov.   1, 1856.
     4. Pp.   144–203, issued   March   21, 1857.

Vol. II. (1858). Pp. iv, 205.

     5. Pp.   1–48,   issued   June   21, 1857.
     6. Pp.   49–96,   issued   Nov.   2, 1857.
     7. Pp.   97–144, issued   Feb.   20, 1858.
     8. Pp.   145–205, issued   May   20, 1858.

Vol. III. (1859). Pp. iv, 214.

No. 9. Pp.   1–64,   issued   Aug.   20 1858.
    10. Pp.   65–112, issued   Nov.   1, 1858.
    11. Pp.   113–160, issued   Feb.   1, 1859.
    12. Pp.   161–214, issued   Apr.   11, 1859.

Vol. IV. (1860). Pp. iv, 209.

    13. Pp.   1–48,   issued   July   1, 1859.
    14. Pp.   49–100, issued   Sept.   19, 1859.
    15. Pp.   101–156, issued   Dec.   8, 1859.
    16. Pp.   157–209, issued   Feb.   10, 1860.

Vol. V. (1861). Pp. iv, 200.

No. 17. Pp.   1–52,   issued   June   5, 1860.
    18. Pp.   53–108, issued   Nov.   14, 1800.
    19. Pp.   109–156, issued   March   27, 1861.
    20. Pp.   157–200, issued   May   24, 1861.

Vol. VI. (1862). Pp. iv, 220.

No. 21. Pp.   1–48,   issued   Nov.   1, 1861.
    22. Pp.   49–96,   issued   March   1, 1862.
    23. Pp.   97–150, issued   May   15, 1862.
    24. Pp.   151–220, issued   Nov.   1, 1862.

Vol. VII. (1864). Pp. iv, 254.

No. 25, Pp.   1–56,   issued   March   4, 1863.
    26. Pp.   57–110, issued   May   13, 1863.
    27. Pp.   111–169, issued   Oct.   29, 1863.
    28. Pp.   169–244, issued   April   5, 1864.
Title &c., Pp. 245–254, issued   Sept.   3, 1864.

Vol. VIII. (1865). Pp. iv, 279.

No. 29. Pp.   1–74,   issued   June   30, 1864.
    30. Pp.   75–126, Title and Contents to Vol.
                         vii, issued Sept. 3, 1864.
    31. Pp.   127–210, issued   Dec.   12, 1864.
    32. Pp.   211–274, issued   Feb.   17, 1865.

The Journal of the Linnean Society (Botany)

Vol. IX. (1867). Pp. iv, 530.

Nos. 33, 34. Pp. 1–128 (Title to Vol. viii, pp. iv,
      275–279), issued June 12, 1865.
No. 35. Pp.   129–200, issued   Oct.   12, 1865.
    36. Pp.   201–263, issued   Feb.   14, 1866.
    37. Pp.   263–326, issued   June   14, 1866.
    38. Pp.   327–390, issued   Nov.   29, 1866.
    39. Pp.   391–454, issued   April   6, 1866.
    40. Pp.   455–526, issued   Aug.   23, 1867.
  — { Pp.   527–530, issued }   Mar.   19, 1868.
    { Title & Contents.   }

Vol. X. (1869). Pp. iv, 510.

No. 41. Pp.   1–64,   issued   Sept.   5, 1867.
    42. Pp.   65–128, issued   Feb.   21, 1868.
    43. Pp.   129–192, issued   March   19, 1868.
    44. Pp.   193–256, issued   May   14, 1868.
    45. Pp.   257–320, issued   May   23, 1868.
    46. Pp.   321–392, issued   June   16, 1868.
    47. Pp.   393–454, issued   June   23, 1868.
    48. Pp.   455–510, issued   Jan.   20, 1869.

Vol. XI. (1871). Pp. iv, 572.

No. 49.   Pp. 1–64   (1½ blank pages),
                        issued April 9, 1869.
Nos. 50–51. Pp. 65–183, issued Aug. 2, 1869.

No. 52.   Pp. 185–252, issued Dec.   30, 1869.
    53.   Pp. 253–348, issued May   10, 1870.
Nos. 54–55. Pp. 349–468, issued Sept. 17, 1870.
No. 56.   Pp. 469–572, issued May   23, 1871.

Vol. XII. (1869). Pp. 659.
Issued complete, June 1869.

Vol. XIII. (1873). Pp. iv, 582.

No. 65. Pp.   1–64,   issued   Aug.   17, 1871.
    66. Pp.   65–144, issued   March   5, 1872.
    67. Pp.   145–203, issued   May   29, 1872.
No. 68. Pp.   203–266, issued   Dec.   4, 1872.
    69. Pp.   267–334, issued   March   21, 1873.
    70. ⎫
    71. ⎬ Pp. 335–582, issued   June   20, 1873.
    72. ⎭

Vol. XIV. (1875). Pp. vi, 641.

No. 73. Pp.   1–64,   issued   Oct.   9, 1873.
    74. Pp.   65–140, issued   Dec.   3, 1873.
    75. Pp.   141–208, issued   April   25, 1874.
    76. Pp.   207–310, issued   July   31, 1874.
    77. Pp.   311–390, issued   Oct.   17, 1874.
    78. Pp.   391–483, issued   Feb.   1, 1875.
    79. Pp.   483–546. issued   April   24, 1875.
    80. Pp.   547–641, issued   July   5, 1875.

The Journal of the Linnean Society (Botany) (continued)

Vol. XV. (1877). Pp. ix, 548.

No. 81. Pp.	1–40,	issued	Oct.	11, 1875.
82. Pp.	39–89½,	issued	March	3, 1876.
83. Pp.	90–159,	issued	May	11, 1876.
84. Pp.	159–252,	issued	July	11, 1876.
85. Pp.	253–363,	issued	Sept.	14, 1876.
86. Pp.	363–422,	issued	Oct.	23, 1876.
87. Pp.	423–480,	issued	Dec.	15, 1876.
88. Pp.	481–548,	issued	Feb.	28, 1877.

Vol. XVI. (1878). Pp. vi, 772.

No. 89. Pp.	1–60,	issued	May	31, 1877.
90. Pp.	61–140,	issued	July	14, 1877.
91. Pp.	141–196,	issued	Aug.	21, 1877.
92. Pp.	197–280,	issued	Sept.	25, 1877.
93. Pp.	281–376,	issued	Nov.	29, 1877.
94. Pp.	377–472,	issued	Jan.	10, 1878.
95. Pp.	473–568,	issued	Feb.	27, 1878.
96.⎫ 97.⎭ Pp.	569–772,	issued	June	17, 1878.

Vol. XVII. (1880). Pp. viii, 607.

No. 98. Pp.	1–86,	issued	July	31, 1878.
99. Pp.	87–172,	issued	Nov.	5, 1878.
100. Pp.	173–268,	issued	Dec.	31, 1878.
101. Pp.	269–332,	issued	May	20, 1879.
102. Pp.	333–404,	issued	Aug.	20, 1879.
103. Pp.	405–510,	issued	Oct.	1, 1879.
104.⎫ 105.⎭ Pp.	511–607,	issued	March	30, 1880.

Vol. XVIII. (1881). Pp. vii, 551.

No. 106.⎫ 107.⎭ Pp.	1–122,	issued	Aug.	3, 1880.
108. Pp.	123–194,	issued	Oct.	15, 1880.
109. Pp.	195–263,	issued	Dec.	31, 1880.
110. Pp.	263–367,	issued	Feb.	21, 1880.
111. Pp.	367–419,	issued	April	29, 1881.
112. Pp.	419–472,	issued	June	3, 1881.
113. Pp.	473–526,	issued	July	9, 1881.
— Pp.	527–551,	issued	Sept.	30, 1881.

Vol. XIX. (1882). Pp. vii, 394.

No. 114. Pp. 1–13, issued Sept. 30, 1881.
(Title, Index, and Contents of Vol. xviii.)

115.⎫ 116.⎭ Pp.	13–138,	issued	Dec.	24, 1881.
117–⎫ 119.⎭ Pp.	139–200,	issued	April	13, 1882.
120. Pp.	201–261,	issued	June	26, 1882.
121. Pp.	261–334,	issued	Aug.	28, 1882.
122. Pp.	335–394,	issued	Nov.	29, 1882.

Vol. XX. (1884). Pp. vii, 532.

No. 123.⎫ 124.⎭ Pp.	1–24,	issued	Dec.	18, 1882.
125. Pp.	25–86,	issued	Feb.	28, 1883.
126. Pp.	87–158,	issued	March	24, 1883.
127. Pp.	159–236,	issued	April	16, 1883.
128. Pp.	237–312,	issued	June	6, 1883.
129. Pp.	313–416,	issued	Sept.	24, 1883.
130. Pp.	417–464,	issued	April	26, 1884.
131. Pp.	465–532,	issued	April	28, 1884.

Proceedings

Session 1855–56. Pp.	1–16,	issued	March	1, 1856, with Journ. No. 1.
Pp.	17–64,	issued	Nov.	1, 1856, with Journ. No. 3.
1856–57. Pp.	1 57,	issued	Nov.	2, 1857, with Journ. No. 6.
1857–58. Pp.	1–72,	issued	Nov.	1, 1858, with Journ. No. 10.
1858–59. Pp.	1–88,	issued	Sept.	19, 1859, with Journ. No. 14.
1859–60. Pp.	1–56,	issued	March	27, 1861, with Journ. No. 19.
1860–61. Pp.	1–52,	issued	Nov.	1, 1861, with Journ. No. 21.
1861–62. Pp.	53–62,	issued	March	1, 1862, with Journ. No. 22.
Pp.	61–134,	issued	Nov.	1, 1862, with Journ. No. 24.
1862–63. Pp.	1–9,	issued	May	13, 1863, with Journ. No. 26.
Pp.	9–53,	issued	Oct.	29, 1863, with Journ. No. 27.
Pp.	53–87,	issued	Sept.	3, 1864, with Journ. No. 29.
1863–64. Pp.	1–48,	issued	Sept.	3, 1864, with Journ. No. 29.
Pp.	49–71,	issued	Jan.	13, 1865, with Journ. No. 30.

The above Proceedings were issued only in the *complete* numbers of the Journal, that is, neither separately, nor with the separate issues of Zoology and Botany.

Session 1864–65. Pp.	1–112,	issued	Dec.	5, 1865, with Journ. No. 31 & 32.
Session 1865–66. Pp.	1–90,	issued	Oct.	11, 1866, with Journ. No. 34.
Pp.	91–124,	issued	Jan.	30, 1867, with Journ. No. 35.

Proceedings (continued)

Session 1866–67. Pp.   1–47, } issued Nov. 14, 1867
Addns. to Library Pp.   1–24, }
Session 1867–68. Pp.   1–16,   issued Dec. 13, 1867, with Journ. No. 38.
           Pp. 17–32,   issued Feb. 18, 1868, with Journ. No. 39.
           Pp. 33–48,   issued April 23, 1868, with Journ. No. 40.
           Pp. 49–112,   issued Aug. 7, 1868, with Journ. No. 42.
Addns. to Library Pp. 113–132, } issued Nov. 26, 1868, with Journ. No. 44.
           Pp.   1–27, }
Session 1868–69. Pp.   1–24,   issued Jan.   1869.
           Pp. 25–40,   issued April   1869.
           Pp. 41–64,   issued Aug.   1869.
           Pp. 65–134, } issued Oct.   1869
Addns. to Library Pp.   1–22, }
Session 1869–70. Pp.   1–32,   issued Dec.   1869.
           Pp. 33–96,   issued June   1870.
           Pp. 97–120, } issued Oct.   1870.
Addns. to Library Pp.   1–26, }
Session 1870–71. Pp.   1–28,   issued Feb.   4, 1871.
           Pp. 29–121, } issued Aug.   1871.
Addns. to Library Pp.   1–24, }
Session 1871–72. Pp.   1–28,   issued Dec. 20, 1871.
           Pp. 29–112, } issued Aug.   1872.
Addns. to Library Pp.   1–32, }
Session 1872–73. Pp.   1–95, } issued Aug. 11, 1873.
Addns. to Library Pp.   1–25, }
Session 1873–74. Pp.   1–62, } issued March 14, 1874.
Addns. to Library Pp.   1–26, }

There was a preliminary issue of the above, for temporary use, in 6 parts containing from 3 to 11 pages each, but the General Index refers only to the complete Sessional account.

Session 1874–75. Pp.   1–79, } issued Nov.   20, 1875.
Addns. to Library Pp.   1–16, }
Session 1875–80. Pp.   1–84,   issued July   1882.
Session 1880–82. Pp.   1–80,   issued March   1883.
Session 1882–83. Pp.   1–54,   issued Oct.   1883.
Session 1883–86. Pp.   1–172,   issued Oct. 10, 1886.
Session 1886–87. Pp.   1–65,   issued July   1887.
Session 1887–88. Pp.   1–129,   issued May   1890.
Session 1888–90. Pp.   1–122,   issued Aug.   1891.

Appendix 3

Officers of the Society

LIST OF PRESIDENTS

		Elected	Died (†) or resigned	Years of service
1.	Smith, Sir James Edward	26 Feb. 1788	†17 Mar. 1828	40
2.	Stanley, Edward Smith (Lord Stanley)	24 May 1828	24 May 1834	6
3.	Seymour, Edward Adolphus (Duke of Somerset)	24 May 1834	21 Nov. 1837	$3\frac{1}{2}$
4.	Stanley, Edward (Bishop of Norwich)	2 Dec. 1837	6 Sept. 1849	$11\frac{3}{4}$
5.	Brown, Robert	4 Dec. 1849	24 May 1853	$3\frac{1}{2}$
6.	Bell, Thomas	24 May 1853	24 May 1861	8
7.	Bentham, George	24 May 1861	4 Mar. 1874	$12\frac{3}{4}$
8.	Allman, George James	25 May 1874	24 May 1881	7
9.	Lubbock, Sir John	24 May 1881	24 May 1886	5
10.	Carruthers, William	24 May 1886	24 May 1890	4
11.	Stewart, Charles	24 May 1890	24 May 1894	4
12.	Clarke, Charles Baron	24 May 1894	4 June 1896	2
13.	Günther, Albert Carl Ludwig Gotthilf	4 June 1894	24 May 1900	4
14.	Vines, Sydney Howard	24 May 1900	24 May 1904	4
15.	Herdman, (Sir) William Abbott	24 May 1904	25 May 1908	4
16.	Scott, Dukinfield Henry	25 May 1908	24 May 1912	4
17.	Poulton, (Sir) Edward Bagnall	24 May 1912	24 May 1916	4
18.	Prain, Sir David	24 May 1916	24 May 1919	3
19.	Woodward, (Sir) Arthur Smith	24 May 1919	24 May 1923	4
20.	Rendle, Alfred Barton	24 May 1923	24 May 1927	4
21.	Harmer, Sir Sidney Frederic	24 May 1927	28 May 1931	4
22.	Weiss, Frederick Ernest	28 May 1931	24 May 1934	3
23.	Calman, William Thomas	24 May 1934	24 May 1937	3
24.	Ramsbottom, John	24 May 1937	24 May 1940	3
25.	Russell, Edward Stuart	24 May 1940	24 May 1943	3
26.	Cotton, Arthur Disbrowe	24 May 1943	24 May 1946	3
27.	de Beer, Gavin Rylands	24 May 1946	24 May 1949	3
28.	Fritsch, Felix Eugen	24 May 1949	24 May 1952	3
29.	Seymour Sewell, Robert Beresford	24 May 1952	24 May 1955	3
30.	Hamshaw, Hugh Thomas	24 May 1955	24 May 1958	3
31.	Pantin, Carl Frederick Abel	24 May 1958	24 May 1961	3
32.	Harris, Thomas Maxwell	24 May 1961	28 May 1964	3
33.	White, Errol Ivor	28 May 1964	24 May 1967	3
34.	Clapham, Arthur Roy	24 May 1967	28 May 1970	3
35.	Cave, Alexander James Edward	28 May 1970	24 May 1973	3
36.	Manton, Irene	24 May 1973	24 May 1976	3
37.	Greenwood, Peter Humphry	24 May 1976	24 May 1979	3
38.	Stearn, William Thomas	24 May 1979	27 May 1982	3
39.	Berry, Robert James	27 May 1982	24 May 1985	3
40.	Chaloner, William Gilbert	24 May 1985		

LIST OF TREASURERS

	Elected	Died (†) or resigned	Years of service
1. Goodenough, Samuel	26 Feb. 1788	24 May 1798	10
2. Marsham, Thomas	24 May 1798	24 May 1816	18
3. Forster, Edward	24 May 1816	†21 Feb. 1849	32
4. Yarrell, William	24 May 1849	†1 Sept. 1856	$7\frac{1}{4}$
5. Boott, Francis	4 Nov. 1856	24 May 1861	$4\frac{1}{2}$
6. Saunders, William Wilson	24 May 1861	24 May 1873	12
7. Hanbury, Daniel	24 May 1873	†24 Mar. 1875	2
8. Jeffreys, John Gwyn	24 May 1875	24 May 1880	5
9. Currey, Frederick	24 May 1880	8 Sept. 1881	$1\frac{1}{4}$
10. Crisp, Frank	17 Nov. 1881	24 May 1905	$23\frac{1}{2}$
11. Monckton, Horace Woollaston	24 May 1905	14 Jan. 1931	$25\frac{1}{2}$
12. Druce, Francis	28 May 1931	24 May 1941	10
13. Stern, Frederick Claude	24 May 1941	24 May 1958	17
14. Cranbrook, The Earl of	24 May 1958	28 May 1970	12
15. Goodenough, Frederick Roger	28 May 1970	22 May 1975	5
16. Gardiner, John Campbell	22 May 1975	24 May 1979	4
17. Hutt, Charles Maurice	24 May 1979		

LIST OF SECRETARIES

Sole Secretaries

	Elected	Resigned	Years of service
1. Marsham, Thomas	26 Feb. 1788	24 May 1798	$10\frac{1}{4}$
2. McLeay, Alexander	24 May 1798	24 May 1825	27
3. Bicheno, James Ebenezer	24 May 1825	24 May 1832	7
4. Boott, Francis	24 May 1832	25 May 1840	8
5. Bennett, John Joseph	25 May 1840	24 May 1860	20
6. Busk, George	24 May 1860	Zoological Sec. from 1861	

Sole Under-Secretaries

	Elected	Resigned	Years of service
1. Taylor, Richard	24 May 1810	25 May 1857	47
2. Busk, George	25 May 1857	24 May 1860	3
3. Currey, Frederick	24 May 1860	24 May 1861	1

Botanical Secretaries

	Elected	Resigned	Years of service
1. Currey, Frederick	24 May 1861	24 May 1880	19
2. Jackson, Benjamin Daydon	24 May 1880	24 May 1902	22
3. Scott, Dukinfield Henry	24 May 1902	25 May 1908	6
4. Stapf, Otto	25 May 1908	24 May 1916	8

5. Rendle, Alfred Barton	24 May 1916	24 May 1923	7
6. Ramsbottom, John	24 May 1923	24 May 1937	14
7. Burkill, Isaac Henry	24 May 1937	24 May 1944	7
8. Barnes, Bertie Frank	24 May 1944	24 May 1951	6
9. Taylor, (Sir) George	24 May 1951	24 May 1956	5
10. Metcalfe, Charles Russell	24 May 1956	24 May 1962	6
11. Ingold, Cecil Terence	24 May 1962	24 May 1965	3
12. Brenan, John Patrick Michlethwait . . .	24 May 1965	24 May 1972	7
13. Perring, Franklin Hugh	24 May 1972	24 May 1978	6
14. Cutler, David Frederick	24 May 1978	24 May 1984	6
15. Bisby, Frank Ainley	24 May 1984		

Zoological Secretaries

	Elected	Died (†) or resigned	Years of service
1. Busk, George	24 May 1861	24 May 1869	8
2. Stainton, Henry Tibbats	24 May 1869	25 May 1874	5
3. Mivart, St George Jackson	25 May 1874	24 May 1880	6
4. Alston, Edward Richard	24 May 1880	†7 Mar. 1881	9 mths
5. Romanes, George John	24 May 1881	11 June 1885	4
6. Sladen, Walter Percy	11 June 1885	24 May 1895	10
7. Howes, Thomas George Bond	24 May 1895	3 Dec. 1903	7½
8. Stebbing, Thomas Roscoe Rede	3 Dec. 1903	7 Mar. 1907	3¼
9. Dendy, Arthur	7 Mar. 1907	24 May 1912	5
10. Bourne, Gilbert Charles	24 May 1912	29 May 1915	3
11. Minchin, Edward Alfred	29 May 1915	†30 Sept. 1915	4 mths
12. Goodrich, Edwin Stephen	18 Nov. 1915	24 May 1923	7½
13. Calman, William Thomas	24 May 1923	24 May 1928	5
14. Bidder, George Parker	24 May 1928	28 May 1931	3
15. Stephenson, John	28 May 1931	†2 Feb. 1933	1 + 8 mths
16. Kemp, Stanley Wells	16 Mar. 1933	29 Oct. 1936	3 + 7 mths
17. Hinton, Martin Alister Campbell . . .	29 Oct. 1936	23 May 1939	3
18. Smith, Malcolm Arthur	24 May 1939	24 May 1948	8
19. Hopwood, Arthur Tindell	24 May 1948	24 May 1954	6
20. Hewer, Humphrey Robert	24 May 1954	*24 May 1960	6
21. Vevers, Henry Gwynne	24 May 1960	24 May 1967	6
22. Greenwood, Peter Humphry	24 May 1967	28 May 1970	3
23. Purchon, Richard Denison	28 May 1970	17 Sept. 1973	3
24. Gardiner, Brian George	17 Sept. 1973	22 May 1980	7
25. Kermack, Doris Mary	22 May 1980		

* No nominations for Officers given in 1960 A.M. Minutes (Bk 18).

Editorial Secretaries

	Elected	Resigned	Years of service
1. Smart, John	28 May 1959	24 May 1966	7
2. Alvin, Kenneth Leonard	24 May 1966	24 May 1968	2
3. Kermack, Doris Mary	24 May 1968	24 May 1974	6
4. McClintock, David Charles	24 May 1974	24 May 1978	4
5. Patterson, Colin	27 May 1982	*24 May 1985	3
6. Pye, John David	24 May 1985		

* J. D. Pye: Acting Editorial Secretary from 17 Jan.–24 May 1985.

LIST OF SALARIED STAFF

Clerk, Librarian and Housekeeper

1795–1805   Benjamin Price
1805–22   Robert Brown
1822–41   David Don

Brown was nominally only Librarian from 1820–22.

Housekeeper

1924–44   George Brown
1945   F. Browning
1946–51   Major M. Cyyg
1951–56   B. Wislaski
1957–79   Mrs J. Wislawska (died in service)
1979   Gordon Read
1979–80   Cyril Costello
1980–83   Mrs Y. Hoang
1983–   Mrs Shirley Theobald

Librarian (and Clerk up to 1885)

1842–80   Richard Kippist
1880–88   James Murie
1888–97   James Edmund Fotheringham Harting
1897–1914   August Wilhelm Kappel
1915–17   Edwin Ephraim Riseley (died on active service)
1917–24   Vacant [? William Shakespeare Warton, also Assist. Sec. (O'Grady info.)]
1924–29   Andrew Thomas Gage (also Assistant Secretary)
1929–51   Spencer Savage (also Assistant Secretary)
1952–56   William Shakespear Warton
1956–63   Vacant
1963–69   Sandra Raphael
1968–83   Gavin Douglas Ruthven Bridson
1983–   Georgina Lundy Douglas

General Secretary

1902–26   Benjamin Daydon Jackson
1951–66   Theodore O'Grady

Executive Secretary

1966–79   Theodore O'Grady
1979–82   Mary Elizabeth Young
1982–   John Haywood Fiddian-Green

Curator of Linnean Collections

1926–27   Benjamin Daydon Jackson

Sub-Editor or Assistant Editor or Assistant Secretary

1874	Alfred William Bennett
1875–76	Vacant nominally
1876–80	James Murie
1880–97	Vacant nominally
1897–1902	James Edmund Fotheringham Harting
1902–24	Vacant (General Secretaryship in being)
1924–29	Andrew Thomas Gage (was also Librarian)
1929–51	Spencer Savage (also Librarian)

Clerk to the Council (later Clerk)

1885–1905	Arthur Rashdall Hammond
1906–11	P. F. Visick
1911–15	Spencer Savage [war service 1915–19]
1915–17	John William Windmill [temporary Clerk]
1917–18	Miss Mary Emily Bessie Smith [temporary Clerk]; died in the Society's service
1919	Miss Agnes Marney [temporary Clerk]
1919–29	Spencer Savage
1929–38	Robert Geoffrey Pugsley [resigned]
1939–51	Theodore O'Grady [war service 1939–46]
1951	Mary Patricia Halberton
1952–63	Mrs Edith Ziegler
1963	Mrs M. Westlake
1963–65	Miss Jacqueline Kyle (later Mrs Smith)
1970–78	Mrs Patricia Baumann (part-time)
1971	Miss Ricarda M. Chepmell (temporary Clerk)
1971	Miss Monica Allen (temporary Clerk)
1971	Miss L. M. Kale (temporary Clerk)
1971–76	Mrs B. Lorraine Russell
1976–78	Miss Eleanor M. Dunphy
1978–79	Mrs Martha P. Lingard
1979–83	Mrs Eve Williams
1983–86	Miss Eve Hickey
1986	Miss Alexandra Myers
	Mrs Jacqueline Elliott (Bicentenary Secretary)
1987	Miss Marie Joanna Polius

Administrative Officer

1979–	Miss Susan Darell-Brown

Assistant Librarian

1830–41	Richard Kippist
1842–53	Henry Sowerby (part-time only)
1853–58	Frederick Yorke Brocas (part-time only)
1858–72	Thomas West
1872–83	James West
1884–97	August Wilhelm Kappel

1897–1913	Vacant
1913	W. H. T. Tams
1913–14	Edwin Ephraim Riseley
1914–16	Vacant
1916–51	W. S. Warton
1956–68	B. Wislawski
1969–70	Mrs S. Banister
1971	Mrs Gerda Semple
1972	Miss Lesley Sheppard
1972–75	Mrs Linda Davis
	Mrs Ann Whitehead
1975	Miss Helen Cohn Hollander
1978	Redwood Fryxell
1983–	Miss Linda Glavin

During 1884–86 Cecil Duncan was employed as an extra assistant in the Library.

During 1887–88 Alexander de Zandt (Robert) was employed as an extra assistant in the Library.

Alfred William Sheppard, FLS, voluntary worker in the Library from 1928–38, died on 9 October 1938.

List of Curators of Collections

1926–27	Benjamin Daydon Jackson
1951–80	Willie Horace Thomas Tams (Zoological Curator)
1951–59	Noel Yvri Sandwith (Botanical Curator)
1959–85	William Thomas Stearn (Botanical Curator)
1980–	Michael Geoffrey Fitton (Zoological Curator)
1985–	Norman Keith Boner Robson (Botanical Curator)

Index

Illustrations are cited within brackets at end of entries, e.g. (63, IX) referring to
Plate IX on p. 63